The Journals of
JAMES BOSWELL

The Journals of
JAMES BOSWELL
1762–1795

selected and introduced by

JOHN WAIN

Yale University Press
New Haven and London

Published with the assistance of the
Annie Burr Lewis Fund.

First published 1991
Copyright © Yale University 1991
Introduction and additional notes © John Wain 1991

Excerpts from the Private Papers of James Boswell published
originally by McGraw Hill and Heinemann, and to be
published in the future by Edinburgh University Press.

Printed in the United States of America by
BookCrafters, Inc., Chelsea, Michigan.

Library of Congress catalog card number: 92–60414
International Standard Book Number: 0–300–05652–4

A CIP catalogue record for this book
is held by the British Library

The paper in this book meets the guidelines for permanence
and durability of the Committee on Production Guidelines
for Book Longevity of the Council on Library Resources.

10 9 8 7 6 5 4 3 2 1

Contents

Introduction

There have been clear signs in the last few decades that James Boswell is at last coming into his own; that he does not belong merely to eighteenth-century Scotland, nor even to eighteenth-century London, of which he has given us such a colourful portrayal in the *Life of Johnson*. It is nearly half a century since Yale University began the task of publishing, volume by volume, the immense cache of personal writings – diaries, letters, memoranda, feverishly penned outpourings of remorse and contrition or sweet savourings of moments of triumph, notes on journeys, analyses of expenditure – that make up what we tersely lump together as 'Boswell's Journals'. During that half-century he has emerged, not merely as the devoted biographer of a great man, not merely as the half-ludicrous, half-lovable figure who flits through so many memoirs of the period, but as one of the most fascinating writers to emerge from that brilliant age. He wrote not for the world but for his own eye, and now and then for the eye of a trusted friend; but his writings have now, after two hundred years, reached the world, and the world, after an initial period of bewilderment, is at last willing to pay him the attention he deserves.

The best indication of when a subject has reached 'the world' is that it begins to attract the attention of journalists, who have many claims on their limited space and must be absolutely sure before they sit down at the typewriter that their chosen subject will hold the attention of the majority. Boswell has reached that first base. One of the most successful of present-day columnists, Mr Neal Ascherson, recently devoted an article to him under the headline, 'Let There be a Boswell Day – of Lust, Enquiry and Exultation' (the *Independent on Sunday*, 4 November 1990). There, he lays Boswell firmly before his readers as a 'hero of both his times and ours', who 'faced and described the agony of being a new man trapped in dying times'.

Part of Boswell's problem, as Mr Ascherson sees it, is that he is dismissed as 'a sort of glorified secretary' because for two hundred years he has been best remembered for his *Life of Johnson*; and though in deciding to write Johnson's life Boswell was acting entirely on his own initiative and was so far from being pressed into service that for a long time he hesitated to mention his plan in case Johnson forbade it, there is no shortage of people who feel that he needs to be rescued from his idol, that somehow or other Johnson must be blown apart before Boswell can crawl out from the ruins. Thus Mr Ascherson avers, in an arresting opening paragraph (and any journalist knows that the stuff you put up front will make the most lasting impact), 'The time has come to declare that Boswell and what he had to say are more interesting than Johnson and all his works.'

Strange, how many people feel obliged to go into a well-and-buckets act where Boswell and Johnson are concerned. If Johnson is profound, Boswell is a nonentity. If Boswell is interesting, then Johnson is a comic ogre. In fact anyone not in the grip of that particular compulsion can see that they were both interesting, both valuable. Not least because they were so contrasting: and in one point particularly. Johnson, who had bouts of melancholy and sometimes agonizing introspection, bared his soul only in the compressed and majestic words of a few prayers, composed as an essential part of his devotional life. He penned a few pages of facts about his life, under the heading of 'Annals', but these were not, and not intended to be, revealing of his inner mind. He was, on principle, no diarist. In this respect, as in so many others, Boswell completes the duet by offering precisely what Johnson does not attempt, and offering it in prodigal abundance. He is not merely a contrast to the reticent Johnson; he is the all-time, record-breaking contrast.

In his life, which spanned the years 1740 to 1795, all the compulsions, all the needs and wishes, it may be all the neuroses, that make people into diarists met at a pitch of energy so intense as to be daemonic. Starting at about sixteen, he kept a journal of his life both public and private, writing with equal fascination about those episodes that he would gladly have conducted in a blaze of world publicity (for he was a tremendous attention-seeker) and those he would have wished to keep hidden from all but a very select circle of trusted friends (for he was the kind of person who needs to have a bosom friend or two, ready to hear even the most shocking confessions without being shocked). The Journals answered both purposes. They memorialized his achievements and they listened to his sorrowful admissions and fascinated probings into the strange recesses of his own psychology. Born at a time when correct classical taste held sway in life and in art, when the most admired writers were the epic poets who sang of the destinies of nations, he lived into the age of the great poet who wrote a poem of epic proportions on the development of his own mind. He was fascinated by the individual imagination and how it came to be as it was; to that extent he was a Wordsworthian before Wordsworth, and the Journals are his *Prelude* as they are his *Ulysses*, his *Fleurs du Mal*, his *A la Recherche du Temps Perdu*, his *Catch-22*.

Certainly there was a neurotic compulsion at work. 'I should live no more than I can record,' he wrote in an often quoted sentence, 'as one should not have more corn growing than one can get in. There is a waste of good if it be not preserved.' Obviously all our experience makes some mark on our personality and is 'preserved' to that extent whether it is written down or not. But there would have been no sense in pointing this out to Boswell. No one is ever argued out of a mania. And a mania is what he had – fortunately for the rest of us. We need his Journals, all eight thousand sheets of them; for that was the staggering extent of the pile of manuscript he left behind at his death. True, he had quarried three books out of it during his lifetime: his *Journal of a Tour to Corsica* (1768); his *Journal of a Tour to the Hebrides with Dr Samuel Johnson* (1785); and the classic *Life of Johnson* itself, which devotes its early pages to a carefully researched but not compelling narrative of Johnson's youth and early middle life and then suddenly bursts into glorious vitality with the entry of Boswell himself into its pages in 1763 – the point, that is, where the Journals effectively take over.

No one describes Boswell's life better than Boswell, but a summary of the main events may well make the Journals, particularly in the stop-and-start form in which they have to be presented in a short selection, easier to find one's way about in. Such a summary now follows. He was the eldest son of a Scottish laird, which meant that he

knew from infancy that he would one day be laird himself, responsible
for the considerable family estate at Auchinleck (pronounced 'Affleck')
in Ayrshire. It was a distinguished line. On the terrible field of Flodden
in 1513, when the reckless gallantry of King James IV of Scotland led to
slaughter the flower of his knighthood against the dour army of Henry
VIII of England, every great family in Scotland lost a husband, a son
or a brother; and the Boswell who fell at his King's side had been
granted the estate of Auchinleck by the King's own hand. Recent
generations of Boswells had tended to be prosaic and reliable, a
background which threw into disconcerting relief the instability of
James's own character. His father, Alexander Boswell, was known
as Lord Auchinleck not because he was a peer of the realm but
because he was a judge in Scotland's two principal law courts, the
Court of Session and the High Court of Justiciary, the highest courts
in the land for civil and criminal cases respectively, and the title was
honorific. The Judge, a solid, industrious, scrupulous man, shook his
head over James's vagaries and escapades, his sudden changes of
course, his wild fads and fancies; how at eighteen he plunged into
a love affair with a married actress in Edinburgh (a city where the
theatre was then a forbidden amusement), how he chanced on some
convincing arguments for Roman Catholicism in the course of his
miscellaneous reading and, abandoning the religion of his nation, his
class and his family, bolted to London with the intention of becoming
a monk or a priest; how he then took it into his head that he must have
a commission in the Royal Foot Guards (having in the meantime fallen
in love with London and the fashionable life, which he imagined to be
the natural concomitants of a military career).

Finally, when he was twenty-two, he and his father made a bargain.
James was to study law with the intention of qualifying as an advocate
in Scotland, and meanwhile he was to be allowed £200 a year (many a
humble family lived on less) and allowed a period in London. Even the
notion of becoming an army officer was not formally forbidden; Lord
Auchinleck wisely confined himself to dropping hints in the right places
that his son was to be given no encouragement in this line, and in a few
months the itch wore off. James enjoyed a hectic spell of immersion in
London life, from November 1762 until August 1763, during which
his adventures – social, intellectual, sexual and psychological – were
faithfully committed to the pages of the Journal. It was during this brief

spell that he managed to fulfil an ambition by making the acquaintance of the great Samuel Johnson, an acquaintance which his impulsive, naive, irrepressible vitality and genuine admiration soon converted to real friendship. 'Give me your hand,' said Johnson on their fourth brief meeting, 'I have taken a liking to you.' And the liking, however flecked by occasional irritation, remained firm till Johnson's death twenty-one years later.

A striking proof of Johnson's affection for the young man over thirty years his junior is given by the fact that in August 1763 he accompanied Boswell all the way to Harwich to see him take ship to Holland, and remained on the quayside, 'rolling his majestic frame, in the usual manner', until the ship was out of sight. This voyage was the result of another bargain between Boswell and his uneasy father. Lord Auchinleck, and his father before him, had studied law in Holland, a tradition that had grown up during centuries of Anglo-Scottish hostility when Holland offered a short and easy sea-passage as against a long and expensive land journey through unwelcoming country (the English counties that lay nearest the border were particularly hostile to Scottish travellers) and a legal system, like Scotland's own, firmly based on Roman law. Besides, the Dutch were good Protestants and, for the most part, as straitlaced as a good Scots burgher could desire. To Holland, then, James Boswell should go; he was to study law at Utrecht, and afterwards as a reward was to be allowed a tour of the scatter of little kingdoms which in that epoch made up what is now Germany. He suffered through a year in Utrecht, enduring chastity (in his case always a depressant) and the discipline of regular study, enlivened only by a friendship with an interesting and bookish young woman (in the parlance of the eighteenth century, a 'bluestocking'), Belle de Zuylen, whom he addressed by her pen-name of Zélide. She irritated Boswell about as much as she attracted him, but he had serious ideas of proposing marriage to her, and was a long time getting her out of his system.

After Holland, the German tour proved delightful; he was made very welcome at the characterful little courts, except that of Frederick II of Prussia, who brushed aside his request for an audience. Then came a typically Boswellian act of madcap rebellion. Instead of dutifully directing his footsteps homeward, he moved to Switzerland, where he visited the great philosophers Rousseau and Voltaire – neither of whom could possibly have been objects of admiration to Lord Auchinleck any more than they were to Samuel Johnson – and, more defiantly still, went on to Italy, where he spent a year.

A very blissful year it was, mostly engaged in amatory adventures and in hobnobbing with John Wilkes, whose audacious political effrontery had for the time being made England too hot to hold him and who was regaining his strength in Naples. (The name of Wilkes would just about complete the trio of world-class villains, as seen by Lord Auchinleck and by Dr Johnson.) Even then he was not ready for home. There was an urgent matter to be attended to first. He had to visit Corsica.

It seems to be a necessity of the human mind to believe in the existence, in the contemporary world, of one ideal country, one place where the system of government really is just and where the people really are free and happy, or would be if they could be left undisturbed in their paradise of rationality and benevolence. In our century this spot has been filled by a long succession of states – Republican Spain, the USSR, Cuba, North Vietnam, Nicaragua. (Even China had a turn, particularly among French progressives in the 1960s.) Most of these claimants were hastily dropped when fuller information revealed what life was actually like for their inhabitants, but there was always another waiting to fill the vacuum, to serve as a focus for idealistic reveries or, for the rebellious, a stick with which to beat their own society. In the 1760s this pinnacle was occupied by Corsica, an island in permanent revolt against the cynical exploitative tyranny of the Genoese Republic, backed by an alliance with the French which had planted Corsica with French garrisons. The Corsican leader, Pasquale Paoli, was as much a name to be conjured with among the young and generous-minded as any of the transient idols of our own day – and with infinitely better title than most, for Paoli seems genuinely to have been an ideal patriot, a brave fighter for liberty, and a wise and learned man fit to preside over the birth of a new nation.

As soon as Boswell learnt of the brave stance of Corsica in the international arena, and the personal charisma of Paoli (and the message was carried by no less a person than Rousseau), nothing would do but that he must go to this wild, rocky island with its savagely beautiful mountain landscapes and its heroic, uncomplicated peasantry under their philosopher-king, see it all for himself, meet them, meet him, and of course write about it, both for the eye of the British public and for his own eye. His *Journal of a Tour to Corsica* came out in February 1768, not alone but in a volume also containing his more impersonal *Account of Corsica*. Johnson read both parts and said he preferred the more personal section of the book, which he praised highly.

Time has confirmed this. Historical accounts of this or that place are inevitably superseded by newer accounts, but Boswell's Corsican journal is literature and can never be repeated. He found, as travellers nearly always do, what he went expecting to find; but it seems to have been really like that, and the writing is in any case superb: rapid, vivacious, full of perfectly chosen detail. Some of the scenes are unforgettable. Boswell's first meeting with Paoli, when, his confidence deserting him just before the encounter, he came in wondering at his own temerity in thrusting himself into the great man's company with no clear justification, and was terrified by Paoli's silent scrutiny as 'for ten minutes we walked backwards and forwards through the room, hardly saying a word, while he looked at me, with a steadfast, keen and penetrating eye, as if he searched my very soul'. Boswell surrounded by eager, unceremonious soldiers and peasants, playing to them, amateurishly and at their request, on his German flute, traditional Scottish airs, 'Gilderoy', 'The Lass of Patie's Mill', 'Corn Rigs are Bonny'! They were 'charmed': and one likes him for adding, 'The pathetic simplicity and pastoral gaiety of the Scots music will always please those who have the genuine feelings of nature.'

In the end of course both the austere General and the doughty peasantry came to value Boswell for his good humour, his readiness to admire and be impressed, his ardour and impetuosity. All fire and enthusiasm for the noble Corsican cause, he had himself fitted out in a complete suit of the national costume as a demonstration of solidarity, wore it while he was on the island, and of course, being Boswell, found occasion enough to wear it when he got home. When in 1768 David Garrick organized the first annual celebration of Shakespeare's birthday at Stratford-on-Avon (a custom kept up ever since), Boswell arrived and took his place in the procession wearing his Corsican outfit and, as an aid to instant identification, bore in his hat a placard reading 'Corsica Boswell'. It was the familiar Boswellian mixture of motives – sincere and generous support for a cause, a streak of childish showing-off, and a shrewd wish to push the sales of his book.

Returning home via Paris, where to his grief he read in a newspaper that his mother had died, Boswell took a house in Edinburgh, qualified at last as an attorney, and settled down to the life of a Scottish lawyer and prospective landowner: or would have settled down if he could only have burnt out of himself his restless hankering after the glamour and excitement of London, the resplendent prizes to be won there, and the wonderful beings who walked its streets. The success in 1768 of his book on Corsica (its full title was *An Account of Corsica, The Journal of A Tour to that Island, and Memoirs of Pascal Paoli*) drove the 'fever of renown' still more deeply into his bloodstream, and a contented acceptance of Scottish life became for ever impossible for him.

As the prospective transmitter of a family name, however, the next step was obviously to get married, and Boswell began the search for a suitable bride. This led him into some unexpected and various adventures, and the list of prospective partners, each one eagerly pursued, rhapsodized over and then discarded (or in some cases doing the discarding), grew almost month by month until Boswell realized whom he really wished to spend his life with, marrying the lady in question for love rather than for any other consideration. They were married in November 1769, and for three years Boswell gave up the sexual adventurism that had become habitual with him since his year in Italy. After that sunny and tranquil Scottish honeymoon the lure of his old ways proved too strong, and he was never again a faithful husband, though a loving one. The marriage was fruitful; his wife suffered several miscarriages, but five children survived: Veronica, Euphemia, Alexander, James and Elizabeth, in descending order of age.

Lord Auchinleck died in 1782 and James Boswell at forty-one became Laird. He took his position very seriously, giving careful thought to his responsibilities to his tenants and to the estate itself; as late as 1791, only four years before his own death, he bought the neighbouring property of Knockroon, which had once been part of the Boswell estate and in his opinion belonged with it, though the purchase sank him deeply into debt.

Matters were complicated, as usual, by his inability to settle contentedly at home and be bounded by a Scottish horizon. Johnson, more than ever important as a father-figure since Lord Auchinleck's death, was repeatedly pestered for advice on whether Boswell, already a member of the Scottish bar, should apply also to be called to the English bar. By 'advice' Boswell of course meant approval, which Johnson in the end gave, reluctantly, and Boswell took this shaky step in 1786. In September of that year he brought his family to London; the move was bad for his wife, whose health was frail and who found the smoke and bustle did not suit her. Briefs came to hand with crippling slowness – only one in the first eight months – and the Boswells had to live on the Auchinleck rents and borrowed money.

Worse was to follow. Driven by a devouring hunger for power and importance, he began to pay court to a man of wealth and influence who, he thought, might help him into a seat in Parliament. His choice lighted on James Lowther, first Earl of Lonsdale, an unscrupulous power-broker, wielder of vast wealth and influence, a man evidently without any of the more kindly human instincts, who, after using him in some grubby political manoeuvres in Carlisle, contemptuously slammed the door in his face when he ventured to bring up the topic of a seat in Parliament as a reward for his obsequious services. (The final insult came when the two men were travelling in a coach, and almost resulted in a duel: see below, Chapter 7.)

Boswell's wife, her condition worsening, had returned to Auchinleck in 1788, and the following year, while Boswell was still frisking obediently at the side of Lonsdale, she died. He had heard of the worsening of her condition and was actually on the road home when she breathed her last. Her death shattered him, and in many ways he was never the same man again. The wretched subservience to Lonsdale collapsed in despair and wounded pride, and Boswell had hardly anything to show for the move to England, except, comically enough, his complacent satisfaction at having given his children an English education so that they had lost their Scottish accents. This paradoxical combination of a fierce pride in Scottish ancestry and a fixed belief that the accent and manners of England are a mark of superior status evidently existed then among the Scottish gentry. Perhaps it is not yet quite extinct.

Balked of success in the law and in politics, Boswell had one last string to his bow, his undoubted powers as a writer. Johnson had died in 1784; Boswell had not been at his death-bed or anywhere near it,

but his account in the *Life* of their last meeting shows movingly that
he saw the shadow of death over his hero. Scarcely was the breath out
of Johnson's body when the publisher Charles Dilly, a friend of both
men, wrote to urge Boswell to begin work on the biography which, as
was widely known, he had been planning for years, collecting material
at every opportunity.

Collecting a haystack of material is one thing; orchestrating it into
a narrative is another, and Boswell quailed at the enormous task. He
played for time by bringing out his *Journal of a Tour to the Hebrides with
Samuel Johnson, LL.D*, the record he had kept during Johnson's Scottish
journey of 1773, not forgetting to inform prospective readers that this
was 'the very Journal that Dr Johnson read'; for he had written it as
they went along, and shown it to Johnson in the evenings. Johnson had
given the work his blessing, but had discouraged Boswell from actually
publishing it immediately after their return, probably because it would
have competed with his own *Journey to the Western Islands of Scotland*,
which he began to write as soon as they got home and published in 1775.
There was, of course, no essential clash between the two books; they
are as different as their authors. Johnson went to the Hebrides to see
how an ancient way of life, based on clan loyalty, fishing, hunting and
primitive agriculture, with occasional bouts of inter-tribal warfare, was
managing to survive into a world that was becoming urban, commercial
and imperialist. He found that it was not in fact surviving. The united
military effort of the Highlanders in 1745, when they threw themselves
into the Jacobite Rising and tried to set a Stuart once more on the throne
of England, had been defeated; with their confidence in themselves
as a fighting force destroyed, and their manpower devoured year by
year by emigration, they were like wild animals whose habitat is being
taken over by intensive farming, and Johnson's book is a dignified and
sorrowful witness to the dying of a species. Boswell's, true to form, is
gossipy, rambling, anecdotal, crammed with detail, the same kind of
'Dutch painting' that he produced on a larger scale in the *Life*.

In the same way, the supreme merit of the *Life*, which Boswell finally
brought out in 1791, and a merit inseparable from its intimate and
accumulative character, is its power as a dialogue: a long, rambling,
inconclusive dialogue between Johnson (English; conservative; classical; judging everything by its truth to 'general nature'; a man of
the Renaissance) and Boswell (Scotch; fervidly ancestor-worshipping;

romantic, accepting the individual as the yardstick in judgements of value). Their dialogue begins straight away in that wonderful Punch-and-Judy scene in the bookseller's back parlour, where every time Boswell says anything at all, Johnson immediately knocks him on the floor; but it goes on throughout the book, swirling round the great setpieces like the tide through rocks. Johnson is a man of the old world, Boswell of the new. Johnson's mind drives towards impersonality; he looks into biography and history to discover general examples and general principles. Boswell is all for individuality; he is interested in quirks and oddities; he pokes into the recesses of people's characters, he likes to put unexpected questions even to the august Johnson.

> I know not how so whimsical a thought came into my mind, but I asked, 'If, Sir, you were confined in a castle, and a new-born child with you, what would you do?' JOHNSON. 'Why, Sir, I should not much like my company.' BOSWELL. 'But would you take the trouble of rearing it?' He seemed, as may well be supposed, unwilling to pursue the subject: but upon my persevering in my question, replied, 'Why, yes, Sir, I would. But I must have all conveniences. If I had no garden, I would make a shed on the roof, and take it there for fresh air. I should feed it, and wash it much, and with warm water to please it, not with cold water to give it pain.' BOSWELL. 'But, Sir, does not heat relax?' JOHNSON. 'Sir, you are not to imagine the water is to be very hot. I would not *coddle* the child. No, Sir, the hardy method of treating children does no good.' ... BOSWELL. 'Would you not have a pleasure in teaching it?' JOHNSON. 'No, I should *not* have a pleasure in teaching it.'

One can hear the mounting irritation; but the answers have been elicited.

Johnson, who had inherited a melancholy temperament from his father, was often afraid of going mad; he said that of all the burdens that oppressed the human spirit, one of the worst was the 'uncertain continuance of reason'. In public, and in his utterances on paper, he compensated for this fear by seeking always to appear not only sane but rock-like in his sturdy reasonableness, a kind of intellectual John Bull. Boswell went to the other extreme. He had every bit as much reason to fear insanity as Johnson; he, too, had inherited a difficult temperament from his father and the dread finger of madness had been laid on several members of his immediate family. His twin uncles,

James and John, were both unbalanced. James, after long periods of pathological indolence during which he mostly stayed in bed, went mad and had to be put in a straitjacket. John was never actually mad (clinically), but he was a well-known eccentric. He belonged to a Christian sect who believed in salvation by faith and not by works (the Glassites), and to demonstrate his belief that the redemption of a man's soul depended on what he believed and not at all on what he did, became a conspicuous frequenter of brothels. Even closer to James Boswell that shadow hovered. His brother John, three years his junior, became a mental patient shortly after reaching the age of nineteen, and from then on suffered fits of insanity, sometimes violent, for the rest of his life.

But Boswell's answer to this situation was not, like Johnson's, to turn his gaze away from it and resolutely cultivate sanity. He was a man of the incoming, not the outgoing, age. 'Romantic' is one of his favourite words. It is a word habitually avoided by Johnson. About as near as he comes to using it is when, describing a beautiful morning in the Hebrides, he writes, 'I sat down on a bank such as a writer of Romance would have been delighted to feign.' Boswell, by comparison, peppers his pages with the word, whether describing landscapes that stir his emotions or his own temperament ('my romantic soul!'). To be deeply stirred by his feelings was to him the beginning of wisdom: to Johnson it could be the shout that started an avalanche.

The great hinge of Boswell's life, when we stand back and look at it, is easy to see: it is the lifelong hesitation between Scotland and England, an identity crisis that lasted half a century. The rise of Scotland during the eighteenth century was meteoric: starting from a condition of what we would have to call Third World poverty, after the Act of Union in 1707 the country increased in prosperity so rapidly that the Scotland into which Boswell was born was hardly recognizable as that of his father's youth; and before his death at the end of the century it had risen higher still. The Union left the country with its own legal system, but swept away economic barriers, so that the Scots were at last free to use English world markets and trade routes. There was no longer any discrimination against Scottish trade and industry, as there was and continued to be against Irish. Scots energy did the rest. Edinburgh, as Boswell knew it, was a thriving city whose intellectual life was centred in a dynamic university – Adam Smith, later author of *The Wealth of Nations* and one of the fathers of modern economic theory, was a professor there, for example.

If Boswell had been content to live his life as a fairly big fish in this fairly big pond, he could have been what his father was – a respected, valuable, confident pillar of society. But, brilliant as Edinburgh was, he hankered for the greater brilliance of London – the London of Burke and Johnson, of Fox and Pitt, Reynolds, Garrick, Sheridan, the London of Drury Lane and Covent Garden. To London, accordingly, he went, as often as he could get south of the border. And, in London, what awaited him was failure. No, that is unfair and one-sided. What awaited him was almost total failure on one level, the level of practical achievement. He wanted to be a successful barrister in London and he was a failed barrister. He wanted to be a Westminster MP and never got anywhere near the House. In 1758 he made a bid to unseat and replace Henry Dundas, political manager of the Government's affairs in Scotland, and tried to rally support by publishing a pamphlet, *Letter to the People of Scotland*; nothing came of it. Still he did not give up. When in 1794, the last full year of his life, British forces helped the Corsicans to drive out the French garrisons, and the islanders, from Paoli downwards, were willing to form an alliance with Britain and become virtually a protectorate, Boswell stepped forward and offered himself as the ideal candidate for the position of commissioner or whatever the official British representative was to be called, pointing out that his qualifications had 'such weight as almost to preclude competition'. He was not appointed.

In short, he wanted office, importance, influence on great events, and never even sniffed them. All these things could have been his in their smaller, more domestic Scottish form. But he was a moth who yearned for the bright and destructive candle-flame. That, indeed, was the metaphor that Johnson used for him, one evening when they were sitting together; and, candid as ever, he puts on record the sage's exact words (*Life*, 5 August 1763). 'A moth having fluttered round the candle, and burnt itself, he laid hold of this little incident to admonish me; saying, with a sly look and in a solemn but quiet tone, "That creature was its own tormentor, and I believe its name was BOSWELL."'

So much for the down side. But turn the coin over, and we see Boswell's English adventure as a string of successes. These successes were on the personal level. He never wanted for friends, and his friends included some of the most fascinating people of that splendid age. He was welcomed, and the more welcomed as they got to know him, by brilliant men, and by beautiful and gifted women. And such a variety of them! His many-sidedness was a genuine part of his character; the different facets that flashed out when it was turned this way or that puzzled and intrigued him as much as they do us. He could be a boon companion to a rakehell like Wilkes, and also accepted as a true friend by men of austere character like Paoli and Johnson. It was not merely a matter of being a clever parrot, with nothing behind the phrases that came tumbling out. The qualities that these friends found in him were real qualities, certainly there. For the same reasons he could be a truly loving husband, passionately fond of his wife and broken by grief at her death, and an insatiably lecherous womanizer whenever he was out of her sight. He, even more than the statesman portrayed in Dryden's poem, was

> A man so various that he seemed to be
> Not one, but all mankind's epitome.

Needless to say, a temperament like this is sometimes disconcerting to its possessor. In his bleaker moods of introspection, when he confronted his own shortcomings and wondered what failings of his own had stood in the way of the worldly success he so much wanted, he could sometimes be appalled at the blankness of his own nature, how it was like an always renewed sheet of white paper ready to be written on by some decisive hand, and reverting to perfect emptiness when that hand had moved on: almost as if there were no essential self, no *Boswellus ipsissimus* under the perpetually willing receptiveness. As he put it in a late Journal entry, the experience of thirty years seemed to have left no trace on his character; the friendship of men like Johnson and Paoli, and his own undoubted achievements, had left him as unstable, as prey to depression and uneasiness, as in his callow youth. Had it all really happened to him, James Boswell? 'I was as a board on which fine figures had been painted, but which some corrosive application had reduced to its original nakedness' (7 July 1790).

Sad thoughts. But all the time there *was* a true self, an irreducible

Boswellian essence, and it consisted precisely in this openness to other personalities. He put up no guard; he held nothing back. This was the quality that enabled him to keep, for life, the friendship of a college companion like Temple, and to win the affection and support of a solid scholar like Malone. Jean-Jacques Rousseau and Voltaire both began by resenting his pushiness and ended by genuinely liking him. His wife truly loved him, in spite of the enormous amount she had to put up with from him, and he seems to have been on the best of terms with his children. As for Johnson, he never had cause to regret welcoming the young Scotsman into his life in the summer of 1763. Many years later, when he had not long to live, he remarked when the two of them were sitting alone in his study one morning, 'Boswell, I think I am easier with you than with almost anybody.'

As if Boswell's own life were not interesting and varied enough, the Journals, letters and private papers in which this life was described have themselves been the chief character in an extraordinary, sometimes almost incredible, chain of events. Boswell's manuscripts are not of course the only work of importance to be written in one century and read in another. But the circumstances of their long immurement and the successive stages of their coming to light make a strange and absorbing story. That story in anything like completeness would swamp this brief introduction. Many pages would be needed to give even a brief summary of the disputes, rival claims, complications pored over by generations of lawyers, that tossed their ownership this way and that, for the Boswell estate subsided for many years into a morass of litigation over property and inheritances, entails and codicils until, like most legal stories, it begins to sound like the Fourth Act of *The Merchant of Venice*. For our purposes it will be enough to say, baldly, that the material was yielded up from the shades in four distinct instalments which we may summarily designate as (1) Boulogne, (2) Malahide 1, (3) Fettercairn, (4) Malahide 2.

(1) *Boulogne*. It is impossible to read far in Boswell's Journals without coming to a mention of William Johnson Temple, a fellow student at Edinburgh University and a lifelong friend. Boswell and Temple saw each other when possible, but the distance separating them was formidable by eighteenth-century standards – Temple became a Church of England clergyman first in Devon and then in Cornwall –

and they were forced to keep in touch mostly by letter. The two men corresponded throughout life; Boswell's earliest surviving letter to Temple dates from his nineteenth year and the latest from very shortly before his death. He had no secrets from Temple, to whom his letters are artlessly confiding and self-revelatory to an unusual degree even by his standards. No one knows what Temple did with the letters – he only survived Boswell by a year – but over forty years later an Englishman named Major Stone made a purchase at a shop in Boulogne kept by a Madame Noël. She wrapped this purchase, whatever it was, in paper, and when Major Stone took off the paper he noticed that it was covered with manuscript and was signed 'James Boswell'. Intrigued, he asked Mme Noël where it came from; and she said she had had it from a hawker of waste paper who occasionally passed through Boulogne. Some of the paper had already gone; Major Stone bought what she had left, which turned out to be ninety-seven letters to Temple. They were issued in a well-publicized edition in 1856, and from the wealth of references they contained to a journal, the world became aware that such a journal had existed and might, in whole or in part, exist still.

(2) *Malahide 1*. Boswell's great-granddaughter married an Irish peer and moved to Malahide Castle, near Dublin. During her lifetime there was increasing talk that Auchinleck might be rented. Concerned for the safety of the contents, Lady Talbot (as she had become) caused much furniture, along with its contents, to be moved to Malahide. The Journals seemed to her interesting and valuable, but when in 1911 she and Lord Talbot approached a publisher, Sir John Murray, he unhesitatingly declined them. The Talbots had had the Journals typed out (what a job that must have been!) and in the typescript the more scandalous material was, doubtless on their instructions, left out. But, even as it stood, the typescript was too much for Sir John, and too much for an unnamed 'friend of great literary experience' whom he had consulted for an independent verdict:

> Our opinions agree in almost every detail and I am sorry to say that the prevailing impression left upon both of us is one of disappointment, I had almost said dismay, at finding how badly Boswell's character shows itself throughout. Macaulay, as you are no doubt aware, formed but a poor opinion of Boswell . . . but Macaulay had not seen these journals: had he done so he would have added that he was an incurable sot and libertine.

It was left to the next generation, in a less prudish age, to launch the Journals towards publication. An American book collector, Lieutenant-Colonel Ralph Isham, got wind of them and finally managed, with infinite patience and resourcefulness, to acquire them from the sixth Lord Talbot and his wife, the daughter-in-law of Boswell's great-granddaughter, she who had caused the manuscripts to be brought over from Auchinleck. Isham's troubles were, however, not yet over. Lord Talbot would only agree to the sale of the manuscripts on condition that anything was cut out that (a) might distress any living member of the Boswell family, (b) offend the descendants of any individual named in the Journals, (c) be seen as gratifying a taste purely prurient (or, in the words of his wife, attract 'that section of the public, at present so much in the majority, who will run after anything of a particularly nasty nature').

It was Lady Talbot who undertook the task of censoring the Journals, which, be it remembered, had already been bought and in large measure paid for by Isham. Her method was simple and practical. Of the typescript that had been prepared for the inspection of Sir John Murray in 1911, about half was still in existence. She began with this, and laying it page by page beside Boswell's manuscript, compared the two. Where the typescript contained an omission, she brought the manuscript into line by identifying the passage that had been omitted and deleting it, using black paint or carbon ink. For the missing part of the typescript, she had a fresh one prepared, and to this she applied similar methods of Bowdlerization. Her husband's father, the fifth Lord Talbot, had left notes that certain passages should not be published, and in general she suppressed these too.

As she completed her work batch by batch, she sent each instalment of the typescript to Isham, at the same time depositing the corresponding part of the manuscript in the bank, to stay there until Isham had handed over the full purchase price of £20,000.

When, in December 1927, Isham began to receive these instalments of typescript, he wrote to her in panic, 'I am seriously alarmed by the thought that the actual manuscript when I receive it may be as mutilated as the typescript.' His fears turned out to be true. Fortunately it proved possible, with infinite patience and the squandering of many weeks of valuable time, for Isham and his English editor, Geoffrey Scott, to examine the manuscripts in a strong light, sometimes reading them from the reverse side of the sheet, and recover most of the deleted passages. But the episode remains as a good example of the shocks and setbacks that were to be Isham's lot from this moment in 1927 to his death, broken in health, exhausted and impoverished, in 1955. Fortunately Isham, a colourful character with the temperament of a soldier of fortune (he was an American who had served as an officer in the British Army, which must have given him a broad base of varied experience at the outset), recovered from this first blow and went on with preparations for a trade edition of Malahide 1.

Unfortunately for him, though fortunately for the rest of us, Fate had another wallop in store.

(3) *Fettercairn*. In 1928 Claude Colleer Abbott, a lecturer at Aberdeen University, was investigating the life and work of James Beattie, an interesting minor poet of the late eighteenth and early nineteenth century (his poem 'The Minstrel' was an early influence on the work of Byron). Abbott knew that Sir William Forbes, Boswell's friend and counsellor, had written a life of Beattie, and he thought there might be useful material at Pitsligo, the country seat of the Forbes family. He went to Pitsligo, found nothing, but happened to make the acquaintance of a man named Alistair Tayler, who, in collaboration with his sister Henrietta, had edited a volume of Jacobite letters to Lord Pitsligo, 1745–6, at Fettercairn House. Fettercairn was the home, in Kincardineshire, of Baron Clinton of Maxstock and Saye. Tayler had seen at Fettercairn some material evidently relating to Beattie, and he also knew that Clinton was the great-great-grandson of Sir William Forbes. Accordingly, in the innocent quest for knowledge about James Beattie, Abbott went to Fettercairn. What met his astonished gaze there, when he began to rummage, was a haul of Boswell manuscript, obviously material that Boswell had sent to his friend Forbes. About half as much in bulk as the Isham purchase from Malahide, it rivalled it in importance, containing such gems as the London Journal of 1762–3, plus numerous letters to Boswell from celebrities such as Wilkes, even one from Johnson, and a long series from Temple.

(4) *Malahide 2*. The sixth Lord Talbot de Malahide and his youthful wife, Joyce, had lived tranquilly at Malahide Castle since the excitement of the late 1920s when collectors, headed by Isham, bombarded them with offers for the Boswell papers. That business had, it seemed reasonable to assume, been laid to rest by Isham's final bulk purchase.

It is true that in 1930 their calm was disturbed by Lady Talbot's discovery of a cardboard box full of yet more Boswell manuscripts. This was a box of whose existence she had been aware, but which she had never opened because she accepted without question that it could not possibly contain manuscripts. She thought it contained croquet balls, which indeed at one time it had, but they had evidently been removed and the space filled with a bundle of manuscripts wrapped in newspapers of 1905. Probably they had been among the material shipped over from Auchinleck to Malahide by the fifth Lady Talbot, who, finding them in a damp condition, used the croquet-ball box to store them in a cupboard next to a fireplace where they could dry out. Having put the box in this cupboard she had forgotten all about it and never mentioned it till her dying day, nor indeed then.

If Lady Talbot the sixth was surprised to find yet more papers, Isham was jolted. He had already spent as much as he could on the Boswell collection and wanted to keep it entire, which of course meant snapping up anything new. Lady Talbot sold him the contents of the croquet box for £4,000, which in spite of great difficulties (he had suffered in the stock-market crash of 1929–30) he just about managed to scrape up. Peace, for the time being, descended again. Not, however, for long. In 1936 the Fettercairn discoveries were duly made known, and still Isham survived and clung to his dream of uniting the material in a single collection which would ultimately find a home at Yale, his alma mater.

Then came the Second World War. Even in a non-combatant country, food had to be conserved. The Malahide Parish Council, in December 1939, requested of Lord Talbot that a loft in one of the farmyard buildings should be cleared as a grain store. He assented. The loft was tightly crammed with furniture that had not been moved for years. To take it out, a special exterior staircase had to be built, and the furniture was handed down piece by piece into the farmyard. In the corner furthest from the door, and therefore last to come down, were two large packing-cases. One was full of papers by, and relating to, James Boswell; the other concerned his elder son, Alexander. In the James Boswell case there was an astounding haul. There were, for instance, twenty-four important letters from Boswell to his friend Temple. Major Stone had bought most of these in the consignment of wrapping paper from Mme Noël's shop nearly a century earlier, but this batch, which related to Boswell's continental tour, had been borrowed by him to use as source material for an account of that tour which he never got round to writing, and he had died with them in his possession. Virtually the complete side of the Boswell–Temple correspondence was now recovered. And the loft also contained 160 letters from Temple to Boswell, about as many as Abbott had found at Fettercairn, thus rounding off the Temple side. There were, also, numerous letters from Boswell to his almost equally close friend John Johnston of Grange, important manuscripts of Samuel Johnson, which Boswell begged from his hero over a long span of years, drafts and outlines for the *Life*, a mass of correspondence with the Boswell children, and so on.

The story of how Isham ultimately managed to steer this new material into Yale, and as a crowning achievement to add the Fettercairn papers as well, has been told in two books, David Buchanan's *The Treasure of Auchinleck* (Heinemann, 1975) and F.A. Pottle's *Pride and Negligence* (McGraw-Hill, 1981). Each writes from a deep personal involvement in the story. Mr Buchanan is the son of Eric P. Buchanan, the Edinburgh solicitor who acted as Isham's British legal representative throughout the whole saga and, as a partner in the same law firm, was able to draw the threads of the story finally together. Professor Pottle (1897–1987) was of course the principal world authority on Boswell and what he has left us, devoting his life to the gathering and study of this material.

And finally, now that the work is done and this selection from Boswell's Journals is ready to go to the printer, taking its chance with the public as his own immortal masterpiece took its chance exactly two centuries ago, my own feeling is not so much a sense of achievement as the pleasure of issuing invitations to a feast that I know to be a splendid one. Of achievement I can of course claim very little. The essential work has been done, decade by decade, at Yale University by the team of scholars assembled under the guidance of Frederick Pottle, to sort out and gradually publish the mass of material that arrived at the University Library in 1946. Since then, two editions have been going forward in parallel: one for scholars, which aims to make available to them the illumination the Journals provide on every aspect of eighteenth-century life, whether literary, legal, political, social, whatever. This edition is not completed and it is hard to see, at any rate for a lay observer, how it ever can be completed. The edition for the general reader, on the other hand, which presents the text in an attractive and intelligible form, keeping footnotes and apparatus down to the essential minimum that a non-specialist public needs, and making the book-reading world in general free of the mad, touching, funny and endearing country of Boswell's mind and life, is at last (1990) complete in thirteen volumes, forty years after the world was startled and delighted by the appearance of the initial volume, *Boswell's London Journal*. That volume was edited by Pottle himself and he continued to guide and direct the enterprise until his death in 1987. The completed edition is his monument; his first successor was Professor Marshall Waingrow, who has since retired; the list will continue and grow. To scholars like these, and to the late Frank Brady, biographer of Boswell's later years as Pottle was of the earlier, and before them to C.B. Tinker who first edited Boswell's letters, and ineffaceably in the background, Ralph Isham and Geoffrey Scott, readers of this book – if they enjoy it, which they surely will – should feel grateful.

The material in those thirteen substantial volumes is itself a selection, so this modest-sized book is a selection of a selection. The overriding aim has been to select passages which, strung on a slender but I hope serviceable thread of terse interconnecting information of the 'now read on' variety, will read straight through as an entertaining and sometimes moving story of Boswell's life, told in his own words. He has been known for two hundred years as the world's most celebrated biographer, but I think there is another laurel waiting for him, as one of the great autobiographers, and I should like to bind it about his brow.

In selection, arrangement and commentary, this book has doubtless some faults, since no book of this kind ever had none. It would have many more had I not enjoyed, from beginning to end of the work, the skilful help and discerning advice of William Wain.

J.W.
Oxford, 1991

A Note on the Text

Needless to say I have done no primary editing, that is I have not gone behind the text as issued by the Yale editors to whose keeping it was entrusted. Since it has been their policy, in order not to scare away the twentieth-century reader with unfamiliar spelling and punctuation that might throw an unnecessary veil of quaintness over the whole, Boswell's text as we have it in their version is given in modern spelling and in accordance with modern conventions as to capitalization and so on. All this, gladly, I have followed, which means that there can be hardly a sentence that is printed here exactly as it was written down by Boswell. In addition, I have sometimes felt it necessary to cut some material from a day's Journal entry or a letter; this has happened especially where a heavy infrastructure of endnotes would have been needed to make the passage intelligible. Endnotes indeed have been kept light, though I hope adequate for the understanding of what is going on and among whom. Any reader who finds a name or a situation that seems unexplained is referred, first, to the Chronology which follows or to the Who's Who at the end of the book; what is not there must be sought in the appropriate volume of the Yale edition, where the footnotes, though naturally modest by comparison with the encyclopaedic footnotes of the Scholars' Edition, are authoritative and satisfying.

Chronology of Boswell's Life and Times

1740 James Boswell born, eldest son of Alexander and Euphemia, in Edinburgh. Frederick II (the Great) becomes King of Prussia.

1743 Britain defeats France at Dettingen in War of Austrian Succession.

1746–53 J.B. schooled in Edinburgh and later tutored at home.

1745 Jacobite rebellion led by Young Pretender, Prince Charles Edward; crushed at Culloden 1746.

1749 Alexander Boswell becomes Laird of Auchinleck on death of his father James.

1755 Paoli leads Corsican revolt against Genoa.

1759 J.B. begins year at University of Glasgow. Anglo-French conflict in North America: British capture Quebec. Voltaire's *Candide*; Johnson's *Rasselas*.

1760 J.B. runs off to London; almost converts to Roman Catholicism; returns to Scotland and studies law at Edinburgh until 1762. Affair with Peggy Doig and subsequent birth of illegitimate son Charles.

1760 George III crowned. MacPherson's Ossian epic.

1761 Bute's ministry; Rousseau's *Nouvelle Héloïse*.

1762–3 J.B. to London in hope of becoming Foot Guards officer; meets Johnson, Goldsmith, Wilkes et al.

1763 Peace of Paris ends Seven Years War. Wilkes imprisoned, later released, for attack on Government in No. 45 of the *North Briton*.

August 1763 J.B. leaves for Utrecht to study law. Friendship with Belle de Zuylen begins, Charles dies.

1764 Begins Grand Tour; visits German courts, meets Rousseau and Voltaire; time in Italy. Wilkes removed from Parliament: later flees to Italy. Foundation of The Club.

1765 J.B. in Corsica, meets Pasquale Paoli; home via Paris where learns of mother's death (1766); begins law career in Edinburgh. First criminal client, John Reid.

1766 Pitt forms ministry. Goldsmith's *Vicar of Wakefield.*

1766–9 J.B.'s Tour to Corsica published (1768); attends Garrick's first annual Shakespeare's birthday celebration in Stratford in Corsican costume. Courts Catherine Blair, Mary Anne Boyd. Affair with Mrs Dodds, birth of daughter Sally.

1767 Rousseau settles in England.

1768 Pitt resigns. Corsica under French control. Wilkes, elected to Parliament, rejected by House of Commons. Captain Cook's first trip to Antipodes.

1769 J.B. marries and settles in Edinburgh. Paoli in exile in London.

1770 Thomas Chatterton commits suicide.

1772–84 J.B.'s visits to London to see Johnson et al., plus tour of Highlands and Islands (1773), spells with Johnson at Ashbourne, Lichfield, Oxford. Children born: Veronica (1773), Euphemia (1774), Alexander (1775), James (1778), Elizabeth (1780).

1773 Boston Tea Party. Goldsmith's *She Stoops to Conquer.*

1774 Wilkes into Parliament as MP for Middlesex.

1775 War of American Independence begins. Trial of Margaret Caroline Rudd.

1776 American Declaration of Independence. Adam Smith's *Wealth of Nations.* Watt and Boulton's first commercial steam engine. Cook begins third (and last) voyage to southern hemisphere. David Hume dies.

1777–83 J.B. writes regularly in the London Magazine *as 'The Hypochondriack'.*

1778 Death of Pitt. Fanny Burney's *Evelina,* Sheridan's *School for Scandal.*

1779 Cook killed in Hawaii.

1780 Anti-Catholic Gordon riots in London. Johnson's *Lives of the Poets.*

1781 British surrender in America at Saratoga. Rousseau's *Confessions.*

1782 J.B. becomes Laird of Auchinleck on his father's death.

1783 Britain recognizes American independence – Treaty of Versailles.

1784 *Johnson dies. Boswell begins preparation of* Life.

1785 Journal of a Tour to the Hebrides *published.* *The Times* founded.

1786 *To the English bar. Moves family to London. Living on Auchinleck rents.* Frederick II dies. Mozart's *Marriage of Figaro.*

1788 *Association with Lord Lonsdale; becomes Recorder of Carlisle.*

1789 *Wife dies.* French Revolution, fall of Bastille. George Washington first US President. Blake's *Songs of Innocence.* First Eisteddfod held.

1790 *J.B. resigns as Recorder.* Burke's *Reflections on the French Revolution.*

1791 Life of Samuel Johnson, LL.D. *published. (Second edition 1793.)* Wilberforce moves to abolish slavery. French revolutionary calendar. Thomas Paine's *Rights of Man.*

1792 Revolutionary France declares war on Austria.

1793 War between Britain and France. Louis XVI executed; the Terror. Repression in Britain.

1794 Habeas Corpus suspended. British capture Corsica from France.

1795 *J.B. dies in London; buried at Auchinleck.*

Prologue:

Sketch of the Early Life of James Boswell, Written by Himself for Jean-Jacques Rousseau
5 December 1764

Boswell wrote the following account of his childhood, youth and early adult years for Rousseau in December 1764. In a sense it contains material that jumps ahead of our story, but as a well-written and entertaining summary of Boswell's life in the years before he began keeping a journal, we have included it here.

I present you, Sir, with a sketch of my life. To men of the world who delight in reading biographies, it would be nothing, for they would find in it few amusing adventures. But if I am not mistaken, it will be a treasure to M. Rousseau. You who love the study of mankind so much will find in it evidence to confirm you in your opinions. You will see in me an extraordinary example of the effects of a bad education. I have a very good memory for the things that interest me. I have a lively imagination. I can recall the whole development of my existence since I was able to think. I shall give you the principal ideas. I shall not conceal my weaknesses and follies. I shall not even conceal my crimes.

Illustrious philosopher! you shall see me completely, just as I am. You will judge me with indulgence. You will advise me. Perhaps you will find me worthy of your counsel.

I was born with a melancholy temperament. It is the temperament of our family. Several of my relations have suffered from it. Yet I do not regret that I am melancholy. It is the temperament of tender hearts, of noble souls. But such temperaments require a very careful education. There is danger either that they will fall into a debility which will completely destroy them, or that they will form a habit of viewing everything in such colours as to make their lives miserable.

I was brought up very tenderly. Consequently I began at an early age to be indisposed, and people pitied me as a very delicate child. My mother was extremely kind, but she was too anxious when I had some small ailment. If I did not feel well, I was treated with excessive attention. I was not made to go to school, which I detested. She gave me sweetmeats and all sorts of pretty things to amuse me. When my health was restored, my slavery would begin again. I knew it, and I preferred being weak and ill to being strong and healthy. What a perverted notion! Nature must receive a terrible shock before it submits to such a change. In a state of Nature, a child should feel miserable in illness and joyful in health. It is for that reason that he is encouraged to struggle with his illnesses. I encouraged them; and instead of jumping and running about, I lolled in an arm-chair. I was discontented and capricious. It is surprising that I did not often say that I was ill when I was actually well. But my worthy father had impressed upon me a respect for the truth which has always remained firm in my mind. Accordingly I never lied, but I hung my head down towards the floor until I got a headache, and then I complained that I was ill.

My mother was extremely pious. She inspired me with devotion. But unfortunately she taught me Calvinism. My catechism contained the gloomiest doctrines of that system. The eternity of punishment was the first great idea I ever formed. How it made me shudder! Since fire was a material substance, I had an idea of it. I thought but rarely about the bliss of heaven because I had no idea of it. I had heard that one passed one's time there in endless praise of God, and I imagined that that meant singing psalms as in church; and singing psalms did not appeal to me. I should not have wished to go to heaven if there had been any other way of not going to hell. I imagined that the saints passed the whole of eternity in the state of mind of people recently saved from a conflagration, who congratulate themselves on being in safety while they listen to the mournful shrieks of the damned.

My mother was of that sect which believes that to be saved, each individual must experience a strong conversion. She therefore entreated me often to yield to the operations of Divine Grace; and she put in my hands a little book in which I read of the conversions of very young children. I remember that one of these children was only three years old. The servants diverted me with an infinity of stories about robbers, murderers, witches, and ghosts, so that my imagination was continually in a state of terror. I became the most timid and contemptible of beings.

However, from the age of eight to the age of twelve I enjoyed reasonably good health. I had a governor who was not without sentiment and sensibility. He began to form my mind in a manner that delighted me. He set me to reading *The Spectator*; and it was then that I acquired my first notions of taste for the fine arts and of the pleasure there is in considering the variety of human nature. I read the Roman poets, and I felt a classic enthusiasm in the romantic shades of our family's seat in the country. My governor sometimes spoke to me of religion, but in a simple and pleasing way. He told me that if I behaved well during my life, I should be happy in the other world. There I should hear beautiful music. There I should acquire the sublime knowledge that God will grant to the righteous; and there I should meet all the great men of whom I had read, and all the dear friends I had known. At last my governor put me in love with heaven, and some hope entered into my religion.

My father, who is one of the ablest and worthiest men in the world, was very busy and could not take much immediate care of my education. He did as others do and trusted me to teachers. From five to eight I attended a school, where I was very unhappy. From eight to twelve I had my first governor, and during those four years I can say that I was happy except on Sundays, when I was made to remember the terrible Being whom those about me called God. The Scots Presbyterians are excessively rigid with regard to the observance of the Sabbath. I was taken to church, where I was obliged to hear three sermons in the same day, with a great many impromptu prayers and a great many sung psalms, all rendered in a stern and doleful manner. In the evening I was made to say my catechism and to repeat psalms translated into the vilest doggerel. I was obliged by my religion 'not to do my own work, speak my own words, nor think my own thoughts, on God's holy day'. I tried in sincerity of heart to conform to that command; especially not to think my own thoughts. A fine exercise for a child's mind!

When I was twelve years old, my governor was appointed minister of a parish, and I was given another governor, a very honest man but harsh and without knowledge of the human mind. He had gone through the usual course of school and college. He had learned his lessons well, and all he had learned he had made part of himself. He was a dogmatist who never doubted. He felt and acted according to system. One day when I said I had a friend whom I loved more than my brothers, he called me a blockhead and said, 'Do you not know how affection develops? First you love your parents, then your brothers, then you spread yourself abroad on the rest of the human race.' He made me read the ancient authors, but without getting any pleasure from them. He had no other idea than to make me perform a task. When I asked him questions about the poets, for instruction or amusement – and why should I not have looked for amusement? – he lost his temper and cried out with a schoolmaster's arrogance, 'Come, come, keep at work, keep at work, don't interrupt the lesson. Time is flying.' Consequently I got the habit of reading without any profit. It was enough to say that I had read such and such an author.

In my twelfth year I caught a very severe cold. I was given a great many medicines, and my naturally weak stomach became so upset that I could hardly digest anything. I confess that the fear of having to go back to what were called my studies made me hope I could stay ill. The greatest doctors in Scotland were called in. I was naughty enough to take measures to prevent their medicines from having any effect on me. I could somehow or other control the operations of my stomach, and I immediately threw up everything they made me take. I even endured blisters, congratulating myself on not having to *work*. The Faculty decided that I was suffering from an extraordinary nervous illness, and I confess I laughed heartily to myself at their consultations. I was weakened in body and mind, and my natural melancholy increased. I was sent to Moffat, the Spa of Scotland. I was permitted a great deal of amusement. I saw many lively people. I wished to be lively myself, and insensibly regained my health, after having imagined that I should certainly be ill all my life.

At thirteen I was sent to the University. There I had more freedom. The place rather pleased me, and during the three years that I was studying languages, I attained high distinction and my professors said I would be a very great man.

My youthful desires became strong. I was horrified because of the fear that I would sin and be damned. It came into my troubled mind that I ought to follow the example of Origen. But that madness passed. Unluckily a terrible hypochondria seized me at the age of sixteen. I studied logic and metaphysics. But I became Methodist. I went back to Moffat. There I met an old Pythagorean. I attached myself to him. I made an obstinate resolve never to eat any flesh, and I was resolved to suffer everything as a martyr to humanity. I looked upon the whole human race with horror. That passed, I know not how; I think by yielding to received opinions. For even now it does not seem clear to me.

At eighteen I became a Catholic. I struggled against paternal affection, ambition, interest. I overcame them and fled to London with the intention of hiding myself in some gloomy retreat to pass my life in sadness. My Lord — made me a deist. I gave myself up to pleasure without limit. I was in a delirium of joy. I wished to enter the Guards. My father took me back to Scotland. I spent two years there studying Civil Law. But my mind, once put in ferment, could never apply itself again to solid learning. I had no inclination whatever for the Civil Law. I learned it very superficially. My principles became more and more confused. I ended a complete sceptic. I held all things in contempt, and I had no idea except to get through the passing day agreeably. I had intrigues with married actresses. My fine feelings were absolutely effaced.

I was in love with the daughter of a man of the first distinction in Scotland. She married a gentleman of great wealth. She let me see that she loved me more than she did her husband. She made no difficulty of granting me all. She was a subtle philosopher. She said, 'I love my husband as a husband, and you as a lover, each in his own sphere. I perform for him all the duties of a good wife. With you I give myself up to delicious pleasures. We keep our secret. Nature has so made me that I shall never bear children. No one suffers because of our loves. My conscience does not reproach me, and I am sure that God cannot be offended by them.' Philosophy of that sort in the mouth of a charming woman seemed very attractive to me. But her father had heaped kindnesses on me. Her husband was one of the most amiable of men. He insisted that I make extended visits at his seat in the country. I was seized with the bitterest remorse. I was unhappy. I was almost in despair, and often wished to confess everything to Mr —, so as to induce him to deprive me of my wretched life. But that would have been madness of the most fatal sort. I opened my heart to Mrs —. Although she was affectionate and generous, she was set in her ideas.

She reproached me for my weakness. What could I do? I continued my criminal amour, and the pleasures I tasted formed a counterpoise to my remorse. Sometimes even in my very transports I imagined that heaven could not but smile on so great a happiness between two mortals.

At twenty-two my father allowed me to go to London. I was glad to escape from Mrs —'s vicinity. I made a resolve never to write to her, and for two years we have had no news of each other excepting merely that we were in health. At London I had an intrigue with a woman hackneyed in the ways of gallantry. For that I could not reproach myself. But I fell into a heartless commerce with girls who belonged to any man who had money. For that I do reproach myself. I made the acquaintance of a famous scholar who proved to me the truth of the Christian religion, though his variety of Christianity was a little severe.

My father was still anxious. He wished to make me an advocate in Scotland. Finally I consented, on condition that he would permit me to travel. I went to Utrecht. There I forced myself to study hard, but I profited little. I have never really learned how to apply myself. The blackest melancholy overwhelmed me. My gloomy ideas of religion returned, and sometimes I believed nothing at all. I thought with irresolute horror of taking my own life.

My Lord Marischal took me with him to Germany. His conversation gave me a change of ideas. His virtues brought warmth to my frozen soul. I confessed my melancholy to him. He has written to my father to allow me to travel in Italy. I expect at Neuchâtel to find my father's answer.

Sir, I have given you in haste an account of all the evil in my nature. I have told you of all the good. Tell me, is it possible for me yet to make myself a man? Tell me if I can be a worthy Scots laird. If I can – heavens, how much I fear the contrary! – if I can be virtuous in my relations with Mrs —. Perhaps she has changed too. O charitable philosopher, I beg you to help me. My mind is weak but my soul is strong. Kindle that soul, and the sacred fire shall never be extinguished.

'I Could Not Contain My Ardour':

Journal from the Time
of My Leaving Scotland
15 November 1762

James Boswell had spent time in London before, as a rebellious youth fleeing from his father's discipline in 1760. As this chapter opens he is going back with his father's permission (if not his actual blessing), ostensibly to gain a commission in the Foot Guards, but more to have a year enjoying London society.

Boswell's ambitions and dreams were something he always fully deliberated in his Journals, as were his wild swings of mood from reckless optimism to black despair: the 'hypochondria' or depression he suffered throughout his life already fully documented in this, perhaps his most vivid and entertaining journal. As the story unfolds his ambitions become clearer, both to his latter-day readers and to himself, and so do his public and private self-images – Boswell the social entity, the friend and protégé of the famous and the rich who fill these pages, the 'easy gentleman', the traveller, lover and young cosmopolite, is the same Boswell mortally afraid of highwaymen and venereal disease, crushed by his father's behind-the-scenes influence wielded to stop him getting his place in the Guards. When he was not dining with Lord and Lady Northumberland or cutting a figure in Covent Garden, we see him in his rooms making a meal of shop cheese, rolls and a glass of water, or selling his old clothes to raise money. He is the same Boswell deeply 'hyp'd', infected with self-doubt and morbid introspection, wondering if his move to London has not been a terrible mistake. There is, too, a third Boswell, through which the others are mediated: Boswell the compulsive journalizer, who records every action and many snippets of conversation participated in or merely overheard, and in whose faithfully written entries he himself is the always entertaining hero.

London in the mid-eighteenth century was a city of around 700,000 inhabitants, a tiny place by modern or even Victorian standards, but nevertheless the centre of an emerging political, commercial and financial empire.

It extended from Knightsbridge and Tyburn Lane in the west to Stepney in the east; beyond, green fields and country villages such as Barnet, Putney and Hammersmith. The aristocracy with which Boswell tried to mingle whenever he could was being challenged by a rising and self-confident middle class; they dined and socialized in chop- and coffee-houses, read the new novelists Fielding, Sterne and Richardson as well as innumerable newspapers, broadsheets and magazines such as the Gentleman's *or the infant* Spectator, *and were enthusiastic theatre-goers (see Boswell's friendship with Sheridan, Goldsmith and Garrick). Great Britain had recently emerged triumphant from the Seven Years War, with the 'Peace' (of Paris) leaving her with huge territorial spoils in North America and India as well as much-enhanced status in Continental Europe. At home, George III and his Scots Minister Lord Bute were railed at by the would-be MP John Wilkes – he appears throughout this book – in the famous No. 45 issue of the* North Briton. *He was later challenged to a duel, wounded, and forced to flee to Italy for a while (which is where Boswell first got to know him). The Jacobite Rebellion of 1745 had not been forgotten, especially in the Highlands, and this chapter contains several references to the Scots-English antipathy – not least the attitude of Johnson when he first met this young awestruck Scot James Boswell. Women participated to some extent in the social – if not the political – life of the country, perhaps less below the ideological surface than they were a century later, although they remained without power, the vote or any outlet other than music or the theatre for their voices. And beyond the better-off minority, the poor, of both sexes, are fleetingly to be seen in these journals, as maids, soldiers, beggars, servants and prostitutes, sharing the same streets if not the same dwellings as the rest. As Boswell shows us elsewhere in the book, emigration to America increased steadily during these years, more from the impoverished peasantry and agricultural workers (soon to be dispossessed by the so-called Enclosure Movements) than from the small class of industrial workers growing around the raw-materials industries and the new 'manufactories' springing up across the country.*

To such a city of extremes, then, James Boswell came as a young man not quite twenty-two, with his inbuilt sense of inferiority as a Scotsman, his subsistence-level allowance from Lord Auchinleck, and his intense curiosity and eagerness to get the most out of life. What follows contains as good an insight into that society as exists anywhere.

INTRODUCTION. The ancient philosopher certainly gave a wise counsel when he said, 'Know thyself.' For surely this knowledge is of all the most important. I might enlarge upon this. But grave and serious declamation is not what I intend at present. A man cannot know himself better than by attending to the feelings of his heart and to his external actions, from which he may with tolerable certainty judge 'what manner of person he is'. I have therefore determined to keep a daily journal in which I shall set down my various sentiments and my various conduct, which will be not only useful but very agreeable. It will give me a habit of application and improve me in expression; and knowing that I am to record my transactions will make me more careful to do well. Or if I should go wrong, it will assist me in resolutions of doing better. I shall here put down my thoughts on different subjects at different times, the whims that may seize me and the sallies of my luxuriant imagination. I shall mark the anecdotes and the stories that I hear, the instructive or amusing conversations that I am present at, and the various adventures that I may have.

I was observing to my friend Erskine that a plan of this kind was dangerous, as a man might in the openness of his heart say many things and discover many facts that might do him great harm if the journal should fall into the hands of my enemies. Against which there is no perfect security. 'Indeed,' said he, 'I hope there is no danger at all; for I fancy you will not set down your robberies on the highway, or the murders that you commit. As to other things there can be no harm.' I laughed heartily at my friend's observation, which was so far true. I shall be upon my guard to mention nothing that can do harm. Truth shall ever be observed, and these things (if there should be any such) that require the gloss of falsehood shall be passed by in silence. At the same time I may relate things under borrowed names with safety that would do much mischief if particularly known.

In this way I shall preserve many things that would otherwise be lost in oblivion. I shall find daily employment for myself, which will save me from indolence and help to keep off the spleen, and I shall lay up a store of entertainment for my after life. Very often we have more pleasure in reflecting on agreeable scenes that we have been in than we had from the scenes themselves. I shall regularly record the business or rather the pleasure of every day. I shall not study much correctness, lest the labour of it should make me lay it aside altogether. I hope it will be of use to my worthy friend Johnston, and that while he laments my personal absence, this journal may in some measure supply that defect and make him happy.

MONDAY 15 NOVEMBER. Elated with the thoughts of my journey to London, I got up. I called upon my friend Johnston, but found he was not come from the country, which vexed me a little, as I wished to bid him cordially adieu. However, I excused him to myself, and as Cairnie told me that people never took leave in France, I made the thing sit pretty easy. I had a long serious conversation with my father and mother. They were very kind to me. I felt parental affection was very strong towards me; and I felt a very warm filial regard for them. The scene of being a son setting out from home for the wide world and the idea of being my own master, pleased me much. I parted with my brother Davy, leaving him my best advices to be diligent at his business as a banker and to make rich and be happy.

At ten I got into my chaise, and away I went. As I passed the Cross, the cadies and the chairmen bowed and seemed to say, 'GOD prosper long our noble Boswell.' I rattled down the High Street in high elevation of spirits, bowed and smiled to acquaintances, and took up my partner at Boyd's Close. He was a Mr Stewart, eldest son to Ardsheal, who was forfeited in the year 1746.[1] He had made four voyages to the East Indies, and was now going out first mate. I made the chaise stop at the foot of the Canongate; asked pardon of Mr Stewart for a minute; walked to the Abbey of Holyroodhouse, went round the Piazzas, bowed thrice: once to the Palace itself, once to the crown of Scotland above the gate in front, and once to the venerable old Chapel. I next stood in the court before the Palace, and bowed thrice to Arthur Seat, that lofty romantic mountain on which I have so often strayed in my days of youth, indulged meditation and felt the raptures of a soul filled with ideas of the magnificence of GOD and his creation. Having thus gratified my agreeable whim and superstitious humour, I felt a warm glow of satisfaction. Indeed, I have a strong turn to what the cool part of mankind have named superstition. But this proceeds from my genius[2] for poetry, which ascribes many fanciful properties to everything. This I have great pleasure from; as I have now by experience and reflection gained the command of it so far that I can keep it within just bounds by the power of reason, without losing the agreeable feeling and play to the imagination which it bestows. I am surely much happier in this way than if I just considered Holyroodhouse as so much stone and lime which has been put together in a certain way, and Arthur Seat as so much earth and rock raised above the neighbouring plains.

We then pursued our journey. I found my companion a jolly honest plain fellow. I set out with a determined resolution against *shaving*, that is to say, playing upon people; and therefore I talked sensibly and roughly. We did very well till we passed Old Camus, when one of the wheels of our chaise was so much broke that it was of no use. The driver proposed that we should mount the horses and ride to Berwick. But this I would by no means agree to; and as my partner let me be the principal man and take the direction of our journey, I made the chaise be dragged on to Ayton, where we waited till the driver rode to Berwick and brought us a chaise. Never did I pass three hours more unhappily. We were set down in a cold ale-house in a little dirty village. We had a beefsteak ill-dressed and had nothing to drink but thick muddy beer. We were both out of humour so that we could not speak. We tried to sleep but in vain. We only got a drowsy headache. We were scorched by the fire on the one hand and shivering with frost on the other. At last our chaise came, and we got to Berwick about twelve at night. We had a slice of hard dry toast, a bowl of warm negus,3 and went comfortable to bed.

TUESDAY 16 NOVEMBER. We set off at six; breakfasted at Alnwick, where we had with us a Captain Elliot of the East Indies, and were hearty. Stewart and I began now to be acquainted and to talk about the Peace and voyages and ways of living. We had a safe day, and got at night to Durham.

WEDNESDAY 17 NOVEMBER. We had a very good day of it, and got at night to Doncaster.

THURSDAY 18 NOVEMBER. We chatted a good deal. Stewart told me that some blacks in India were attacking their boat in order to plunder it, and that he shot two with his own hand. In the afternoon between Stamford and Stilton there was a young unruly horse in the chaise which run away with the driver, and jumping to one side of the road, we were overturned. We got a pretty severe rap. Stewart's head and my arm were somewhat hurt. However, we got up and pursued our way. During our two last stages this night, which we travelled in the dark, I was a good deal afraid of robbers. A great many horrid ideas filled my mind. There is no passion so distressing as fear, which gives us great pain and makes us appear contemptible in our own eyes to the last degree. However, I affected resolution, and as each of us carried a loaded pistol in his hand, we were pretty secure. We got at night to Biggleswade.

FRIDAY 19 NOVEMBER. It was very cold. Stewart was as effeminate as I. I asked him how he, who shivered if a pane of glass was broke in a post-chaise, could bear the severe hardship of a sea life. He gave me to understand that necessity made anything be endured. Indeed this is very true. For when the mind knows that it cannot help itself by struggling, it quietly and patiently submits to whatever load is laid upon it. When we came upon Highgate hill and had a view of London, I was all life and joy. I repeated Cato's soliloquy on the immortality of the soul, and my soul bounded forth to a certain prospect of happy futurity. I sung all manner of songs, and began to make one about an amorous meeting with a pretty girl, the burthen of which was as follows:

> She gave me *this*, I gave her *that*;
> And tell me, had she not tit for tat?

I gave three huzzas, and we went briskly in.

I got from Digges⁴ a list of the best houses on the road, and also a direction to a good inn at London. I therefore made the boy drive me to Mr Hayward's, at the Black Lion, Water Lane, Fleet Street. The noise, the crowd, the glare of shops and signs agreeably confused me. I was rather more wildly struck than when I first came to London. My companion could not understand my feelings. He considered London just as a place where he was to receive orders from the East India Company. We now parted, with saying that we had agreed well and been happy, and that we should keep up the acquaintance. I then had a bit of dinner, got myself shaved and cleaned, and had my landlord, a civil jolly man, to take a glass of wine with me. I was all in a flutter at having at last got to the place which I was so madly fond of, and being restrained, had formed so many wild schemes to get back to. I had recourse to philosophy, and so rendered myself calm.

I immediately went to my friend Douglas's, surgeon in Pall Mall, a kind-hearted, plain, sensible man, where I was cordially received. His wife is a good-humoured woman, and is that sort of character which is often met with in England: very lively without much wit. Her fault is speaking too much, which often tires people. He was my great adviser as to everything; and in the mean time insisted that I should have a bed in his house till I got a lodging to my mind. I agreed to come there next day. I went to Covent Garden – *Every Man in His Humour*. Woodward played Bobadil finely. He entertained me much. It was fine after the fatigues of my journey to find myself snug in a theatre, my body warm and my mind elegantly amused. I went to my inn, had some negus, and went comfortably to bed.

SATURDAY 20 NOVEMBER. I got into a hackney-coach with my baggage and drove to Douglas's. We calculated my expenses, and I found that to live would require great economy. However, I was upon honour to do my best. I strolled about all the forenoon calling for different people, but found nobody in. I went and saw a collection of wild beasts. I felt myself bold, easy and happy. Only I had a kind of uneasiness from feeling no amazing difference between my existence now and at Edinburgh. I dined at Douglas's; sat in all the afternoon and wrote letters.

SUNDAY 21 NOVEMBER. I got up well and enjoyed my good situation. I had a handsome dining-room and bed-chamber, just in Pall Mall, the finest part of the town; I was in pursuit of my commission, which I was vastly fond of; and I had money enough to live like a gentleman.

I went to Mayfair Chapel and heard prayers and an excellent sermon from the Book of Job on the comforts of piety. I was in a fine frame. And I thought that GOD really designed us to be happy. I shall certainly be a religious old man. I was much so in youth. I have now and then flashes of devotion, and it will one day burn with a steady flame.

I waited on Mr George Lewis Scott, who was very kind and polite to me, and on the Laird of Macfarlane, with whom I was a good deal diverted. He was keenly interested in the reigning contests between Scots and English. He talked much against the Union. He said we were perfect underlings; that our riches were carried out of the country; that no town but Glasgow had any advantage of trade by it, and that many others were hurt by it.

I dined with Dr Pringle, where were Mr Murdoch, the publisher, or rather the editor, of Thomson; Mr Seymours, a travelling governor, and some more, all Scotch. I found the Doctor in the way of discouraging me, which as from my father's friend I took patiently and intended to get the better of. The conversation was on indifferent common topics: the Peace, Lord Bute, footmen and cookery.

I went to Douglas's and drank tea. I next went and called in Southampton Street, Strand, for Miss Sally Forrester, my first love, who lived at the Blue Periwig. I found that the people of the house were broke and dead, and could hear nothing of her. I also called for Miss Jeany Wells in Barrack Street, Soho, but found that she was fled, they knew not whither, and had been ruined with extravagance. Good heaven, thought I, what an amazing change in two years! I saw in the year 1760 these young ladies in all the glow of beauty and admiration; and now they are utterly erased or worse. I then called on Love, and saw him and Mrs Love and Billy. I eat a tart there. He showed me a pantomime, called *The Witches*, of his.

Since I came up, I have begun to acquire a composed genteel character very different from a rattling uncultivated one which for some time past I have been fond of. I have discovered that we may be in some degree whatever character we choose. Besides, practice forms a man to anything. I was now happy to find myself cool, easy and serene.

MONDAY 22 NOVEMBER. I strolled about all day looking for lodgings. At night I went to Drury Lane and saw Garrick play Scrub and the Farmer returned, and Love play Boniface, which brought the Canongate5 full in my head. I was exceedingly well entertained.

WEDNESDAY 24 NOVEMBER. I called on Dodsley,6 and found that although he had refused to take the hazard of publishing my *Cub*, that it had sold well, and that there was thirteen shillings of profit, which I made him pay me down. Never did I set so high a value on a sum. I was much in spirits. I still went about seeking lodgings, but could find none that would answer. At night I called on Pringle. He was sour. Indeed, he is a good deal so, although a sensible learned man, a good philosopher, and an excellent physician. By the cheerful ease of my address I made him smile and be very kind to me. I consulted him about all my plans. I began to find that £200 a year was very little. I left him before twelve. I began to tire much of Mrs Douglas, she spoke so much. And I was rather somewhat low-spirited.

THURSDAY 25 NOVEMBER. I had been in a bad situation during the night for I dreamt that Johnston did not care for me. That he came to see me set off on a long journey, and that he seemed dissipated and tired, and left me before I got away. I lay abed very gloomy. I thought London did me no good. I rather disliked it; and I thought of going back to Edinburgh immediately. In short, I was most miserable.

I got up and breakfasted. I got a card from Lord Eglinton asking me to the House of Lords. I accordingly went and heard the King make his speech. It was a very noble thing. I here beheld the King of Great Britain on his throne with the crown on his head addressing both the Lords and the Commons. His Majesty spoke better than any man I ever heard: with dignity, delicacy, and ease. I admired him. I wished much to be acquainted with him.

I went to Love's and drank tea. I had now been some time in town without female sport. I determined to have nothing to do with whores, as my health was of great consequence to me. I went to a girl with whom I had an intrigue at Edinburgh, but my affection cooling, I had left her. I knew she was come up. I waited on her and tried to obtain my former favours, but in vain. She would by no means listen. I was really unhappy for want of women. I thought it hard to be in such a place without them. I picked up a girl in the Strand; went into a court with intention to enjoy her in armour. But she had none. I toyed with her. She wondered at my size, and said if I ever took a girl's maidenhead, I would make her squeak. I gave her a shilling, and had command enough of myself to go without touching her. I afterwards trembled at the danger I had escaped. I resolved to wait cheerfully till I got some safe girl or was liked by some woman of fashion.

I went to Lord Eglinton's; John Ross Mackye was there. We had a little bit of supper, and I was easy. I have never yet mentioned General Douglas, whom I found to be a plain, civil man. I learnt that the Duke of Queensberry was not to be in town till Sunday, so that till then I could know nothing certain of my commission.

FRIDAY 26 NOVEMBER. I waited on Lord Adam Gordon, who was very polite. I liked to see a Colonel of the Guards in his elegant house. I was much difficulted about lodgings. A variety I am sure I saw, I dare say fifty. I was amused in this way. At last I fixed in Downing Street, Westminster.7 I took a lodging up two pair of stairs with the use of a handsome parlour all the forenoon, for which I agreed to pay forty guineas a year, but I took it for a fortnight first, by way of a trial. I also made bargain that I should dine with the family whenever I pleased, at a shilling a time. My landlord was Mr Terrie, chamber-keeper to the Office for Trade and Plantations. He was originally from the Shire of Moray. He had a wife but no children. The street was a genteel street, within a few steps of the Parade; near the House of Commons, and very healthful. I went to Mr Cochrane, my banker, and received £25, my allowance every six weeks.

I then dined with Lord Eglinton. Lord Elibank was there, a man of great genius, great knowledge, and much whim, and Sir James Macdonald, a remarkable young man of good parts and great application. So that he knows a great deal. Also Sir Simeon Stuart, much of a gentleman. We had much ingenious talk. But I am dull, and cannot recollect it. Before this I saw *The Witches*, a pantomime. I felt composed, serene, happy.

SATURDAY 27 NOVEMBER. I walked into the City and ordered a remaining parcel of my *Cub* to be sent to Donaldson. I then breakfasted at Child's Coffee-house, read the political papers, and had some chat with citizens. On Sunday I had called at the Inner Temple for my old friend Temple, but did not find him. This day I called again. He was out of town. I longed to see him.

I then went to Lord Eglinton's. Finding him very obliging, I was glad to take the benefit of it. He carried me to Covent Garden in a coach and bid me wait in the Bedford Coffee-house till he sent for me. In a few minutes the famous Mr Beard of Covent Garden Theatre came for me and carried me up a great many steps to a handsome room above the theatre, in which was met the Beefsteak Club, a society which has subsisted these thirty years. The room where it met was once burnt. The Gridiron (in Scotch, *brander*) was almost consumed, but a thin image of it remained entire. That they have fixed in the stucco in the roof. The president sits in a chair under a canopy, above which you have in golden letters, *Beef and Liberty*. We were entertained by the Club. Lord Sandwich was in the chair, a jolly, hearty, lively man. It was a very mixed society: Lord Eglinton, Mr Beard, Colonel West of the Guards, Mr Havard the actor, Mr Churchill the poet, Mr Wilkes the author of the *North Briton*, and many more. We had nothing to eat but beefsteaks, and had wine and punch in plenty and freedom. We had a number of songs.

Lord Eglinton and I talked a little privately. He imagined me much in the style that I was three years ago: raw, curious, volatile, credulous. He little knew the experience I had got and the notions and the composure that I had obtained by reflection. 'My Lord,' said I, 'I am now a little wiser.' 'Not so much as you think,' said he. 'For, as a boy who has just learned the alphabet when he begins to make out words thinks himself a great master of reading, so the little advance you have made in prudence appears very great, as it is so much before what you was formerly.' I owned that there was some justice in what he said. And I hoped that a little diffidence would help to keep me safe.

My Lord's character is very particular. He is a man of uncommon genius for everything: strong good sense, great quickness of apprehension and liveliness of fancy, with a great deal of humour. He was neglected in his education, so that his knowledge from books is superficial. Yet he has picked up an infinite variety of knowledge from conversation. He has at the same time a flightiness, a reverie and absence of mind, with a disposition to downright trifling. Pope's lines may be applied to him:

> With too much quickness ever to be taught;
> With too much thinking to have common thought.

He is very selfish and deceitful, yet he has much good nature and affection. He now declared to me that he liked me as well as ever. And I believe he spoke truth. For I have such an opinion of myself as to imagine that nobody can be more agreeable company to him. Yet I kept aloof in some measure, and, finding myself too fond of him, I pulled the reins hard.

We parted at seven. I went to my lodging in Downing Street and put up my things, then went and saw the King and Queen pass from the Opera, and then saw the Guards drawn up in the court of the Palace while the moon shone and showed their splendour. I was all gentle felicity, and thought on an Edinburgh Saturday passed in a variety of amusing scenes. I had now got a genteel violet-coloured frock suit. I went home, sat a while with my landlord and landlady. They made too much work about me. I went to bed.

SUNDAY 28 NOVEMBER. I breakfasted with Mr Douglas. I went to St James's Church and heard service and a good sermon on 'By what means shall a young man learn to order his ways', in which the advantages of early piety were well displayed. What a curious, inconsistent thing is the mind of man! In the midst of divine service I was laying plans for having women, and yet I had the most sincere feelings of religion. I imagine that my want of belief is the occasion of this, so that I can have all the feelings. I would try to make out a little consistency this way. I have a warm heart and a vivacious fancy. I am therefore given to love, and also to piety or gratitude to GOD, and to the most brilliant and showy method of public worship.

I then walked in the Park and went home to dinner, which was just a good joint of veal and a pudding. This they told me was their usual fare, which I approved of. I found my landlord rather too free. Therefore I carried myself with reserve and something of state.

At six I went to Mr Sheridan's. He had been at Court and was splendidly dressed. He met me at the door with a cordial warmth. I felt a little out, as his plan for me of the Temple was changed. He is a man of great genius and understands propriety of speech better than anybody. But he is rather too much of an enthusiast in favour of his darling study. He has read much and seen much and is very good company. I was introduced to Mrs Sheridan, a woman of very homely looks, but very sensible and very clever, as appears from her *Memoirs of Miss Sidney Bidulph*. I let myself appear by degrees, and I found that I was agreeable to her, which flattered me a good deal.

I asked for Mr Samuel Johnson. Sheridan said he now could not bear him, because he had taken a pension of three hundred a year from the Court, by the particular interest of Lord Bute, and yet he still railed against the royal family and the Scots minister. I said I imagined he put it upon this: that the pension was not a *favour* but a reward *due* to his merit, and therefore he would show still the same principles of opposition freely and openly. 'No, Sir,' said he. 'Johnson took it as a favour; waited on Lord Bute, said he could not find an English word to express what he felt, and was therefore obliged to have recourse to the French: "I am *pénétré* with his Majesty's goodness." This being the case, his business was to be silent; or, if called upon to give his opinion, to say, "Gentlemen, my sentiments are just the same that they were. But an obligation forbids me to say much."' It hurt me to find Sheridan abusing a man for whom I have heard him profess the greatest regard. He added, 'The bearish manners of Johnson were insupportable without the idea of his having a good heart. But since he has been made the object of royal favour, his character has been sifted and is bad.' I drank tea and coffee and was very well. I came home and went to bed.

TUESDAY 30 NOVEMBER. I dined with Mr Sheridan. He was quite enthusiastic about oratory. He said Garrick had no real feeling; that his talents for mimicry enabled him to put on the appearance of feeling, and that the nicety of his art might please the fancy and make us cry, 'That's fine.' But as it was art, it could never touch the heart. Mr Sheridan's distinction was just, but does not apply to Garrick, because he often has touched the heart and drawn tears from multitudes. After dinner, old Victor, many years joint-manager of the Dublin stage, poet laureate of Ireland and author of the *History of the Theatres*, came in. He is an honest, indolent, conversable man, and has a great many anecdotes. He told us that he was one day dining with Mr Booth, when Mrs Booth brought in a girl to sing some lively songs. She was much liked and taken into the theatre at twenty shillings a week, and who was this but Mrs Pritchard, who had risen so high in dramatic fame.

Sheridan said there were not three lines in a play spoke well on Drury Lane stage. Victor looked at me and shook his head. 'Without propriety of speech,' said Sheridan, 'all the powers of acting are nothing. It is just like time in dancing. And let a dancer play never so many tricks and feats of agility, he will not be applauded if he does not observe time.' This comparison is not just. Because the greatest part of an audience have ear enough to judge of time, but very, very few can judge of propriety of speech, as that is a thing never taught them; and therefore the ornaments of action must please them independent of that.

I was very easy, as he never mentioned my own plan, which I resolved by degrees to talk freely to him of. He asked me to come to his house in a family way whenever I had nothing to engage me elsewhere. I resolved to comply with his kind invitation. I found a good table, ease and hospitality, and useful and agreeable conversation there.

I thought my present lodgings too dear, and therefore looked about and found a place in Crown Street, Westminster, an obscure street but pretty lodgings at only £22 a year. Much did I ruminate with regard to lodgings. Sometimes I considered that a fine lodging denoted a man of great fashion, but then I thought that few people would see it and therefore the expense would be hid, whereas my business was to make as much show as I could with my small allowance. I thought that an elegant place to come home to was very agreeable and would inspire me with ideas of my own dignity; but then I thought it would be hard if I had not a proportionable show in other things, and that it was better to come gradually to a fine place than from a fine to a worse. I therefore resolved to take the Crown Street place, and told my present landlord that I intended to leave him. He told me that he was very sorry, and that he would allow me to make my own terms rather than quit his house; for he was in such circumstances that he was not obliged to let lodgings for bread, and that as I was extremely agreeable to the family, he begged I would stay, and he would let me have my three rooms for £30. I thanked him for his good opinion of me, but told him that economy at present was my object, although I was very happy in his house; and that I could not ask him to let me have three rooms in a genteel street as cheap as two in an obscure one. He paused a while and then told me that I should have them at the same price. He only begged that I would not mention it, as he certainly let them below value. I therefore struck a bargain and settled myself for a year.

I do think this a very strong proof of my being agreeable. For here was I, a perfect stranger to my landlord, who showed so great regard for me. I thought my seeking a lodging was like seeking a wife. Sometimes I aimed at one of two guineas a week, like a rich lady of quality. Sometimes at one guinea, like a knight's daughter; and at last fixed on £22 a year, like the daughter of a good gentleman of moderate fortune. Now when fixed, I felt very comfortable, having got rid of the inconstant roving disposition of a bachelor as to lodging. However, I hope my choice of a wife will be more elegant. I hope that shall not be in haste. When I strolled in high spirits through London, full of gay expectation, I considered how much happier I was than if I had been married last year to Miss Colquhoun or Miss Bruce, and been a poor regular animal tied down to one. I thanked Johnston for his kind advices.

THURSDAY 2 DECEMBER. I went to Leicester Street, where Lady Betty had a house taken. I pitied Macfarlane, who is very narrow, and had now house and footmen and coach and dress and entertainment of all kinds to pay. Captain Erskine said that he was past pity, for that he only knew the value of money in trifles; and he also said that to the length of five guineas the Laird might retain some degree of rationality, but when the sum exceeded that, he became perfectly delirious. What an absurd thing was it for this old clumsy dotard to marry a strong young woman of quality. It was certainly vanity, for which he has paid very heavily. Her marrying him was just to support herself and her sisters; and yet to a woman of delicacy, poverty is better than sacrificing her person to a greasy, rotten, nauseous carcass and a narrow vulgar soul. Surely she who does that cannot properly be called a woman of virtue. She certainly wants feeling who can submit to the loathed embraces of a monster. She appears to me unclean: as I said to Miss Dempster, like a dirty table-cloth. I am sure no man can have the gentle passion of love for so defiled a person as hers − O my stomach rises at it!

FRIDAY 3 DECEMBER. I began now to be much at home in my lodgings and to get into a regular method. I resolved to want a servant for my first year and in every respect to be frugal, that I might learn the value of money, see what I could afford to do with my allowance, and rather live within than exceed my income. I am really surprised at the coolness and moderation with which I am proceeding. GOD grant I may continue to do well, which will make me happy and all my friends satisfied. (I have all along been speaking in the perfect tense, as if I was writing the history of some distant period. I shall after this use the present often, as most proper. Indeed, I will not confine myself, but take whichever is most agreeable at the time.) I never had a fire in my bedroom, but one in my parlour in the morning and one in my dining-room in the evening. I had my own tea and sugar, and got in bread and butter and milk as I wanted it. In short I regulate everything in the most prudent way. At the end of the year I shall subjoin a succinct account of my expenses. Sure no minister of state could talk with more formality.

TUESDAY 7 DECEMBER. In the evening I went to Northumberland House, to the rout, which was indeed magnificent. Three large rooms and the gallery (a prodigious one) were full of the best company, between three and four hundred of them. The gallery is like one of the rooms in Holyroodhouse for size and richly adorned on the walls and ceiling with landscapes and gilding. The King and Lady Northumberland are exhibited in full-length portraits, in their robes. As I was standing in pleasing reverie in the gallery musing on the splendid scene around me and joining with that the ancient ideas of the family of Percy, my Lady came up to me with the greatest complacency[8] and kindness: 'Mr Boswell, I am very happy to see you. How do you do? I hope you are come to settle among us. I was very sorry that I was not at home when you called. I gave positive orders that you should be admitted whenever you called.' This put me into the finest humour. I thanked her sincerely. I chatted easily. She then carried me to my Lord, who was very glad to see me and very civil to me. This is indeed a noble family in every respect. They live in a most princely manner, perfectly suitable to their high rank. Yet they are easy and affable. They keep up the true figure of old English nobility.

I felt a little awkward this night, as I scarcely knew anybody in the room. I told my Lady so. She said that would go off by degrees. I could observe people looking at me with envy, as a man of some distinction and a favourite of my Lady's. Bravo! thought I. I am sure I deserve to be a favourite. It was curious to find of how little consequence each individual was in such a crowd. I could imagine how an officer in a great army may be killed without being observed. I came home quiet, laid by my clothes, and went coolly to bed. There's conduct for you.

WEDNESDAY 8 DECEMBER. I sat in writing till one. I then strolled through the streets. I was somewhat dull and thought myself a poor sort of a being. At night I went to Covent Garden and saw *Love in a Village*, a new comic opera, for the first night. I liked it much. I saw it from the gallery, but I was first in the pit. Just before the overture began to be played, two Highland officers came in. The mob in the upper gallery roared out, 'No Scots! No Scots! Out with them!', hissed and pelted them with apples. My heart warmed to my countrymen, my Scotch blood boiled with indignation. I jumped up on the benches, roared out, 'Damn you, you rascals!', hissed and was in the greatest rage. I am very sure at that time I should have been the most distinguished of heroes. I hated the English; I wished from my soul that the Union was broke and that we might give them another battle of Bannockburn. I went close to the officers and asked them of what regiment they were of. They told me Lord John Murray's, and that they were just come from the Havana. 'And this', said they, 'is the thanks that we get – to be hissed when we come home. If it was French, what could they do worse?' 'But', said one, 'if I had a *grup o yin or twa o the tamd rascals I sud let them ken what they're about.*' The rudeness of the English vulgar is terrible. This indeed is the liberty which they have: the liberty of bullying and being abusive with their blackguard tongues. They soon gave over. I then went to the gallery and was really well entertained with the opera.

THURSDAY 9 DECEMBER. I called on Erskine and related to him the history of the opera. I was in an immoderate flow of spirits and raged away. We then sauntered through the streets. He gave me a very sensible advice against repeating what people said, which may do much harm. I have an unlucky custom of doing so. I acknowledged my error and promised to be on my guard.

In the afternoon I drank tea at Macfarlane's. The ladies had now got everything in good order, and were pretty fond of London. I liked them better.

This was the great day of debate in the Houses of Parliament on the Peace. But I could not get in. However, I was curious to hear how things were carried on. I went to Dempster's at twelve to wait till he should come in. I stayed till three without him, and came home, cold and sleepy and wearied with waiting.

FRIDAY 10 DECEMBER. I went to Northumberland House in the forenoon. The porter told me there was nobody at home; but looking at me, 'Sir,' said he, 'is your name Boswell?' Upon my answering, 'Yes,' 'My Lady is at home, Sir,' said he. Upon which I was shown up to her Ladyship, with whom I sat about twenty minutes in the most easy, agreeable way. She told me that she had a private party every Friday for particular friends, and that she would always be glad to see me there when I had nothing else to do. I exulted, and thanked her, and said that I could not think how I deserved all this, but that I hoped we should be better acquainted, and that I should run about the house like a tame spaniel. An old gentleman then came in. I sat a little longer and then withdrew, full of joy at being reckoned a particular friend of the heir of the great Percy and a woman of the first consequence in London. She mentioned my commission, and kindly desired me not to be impatient, and I would get it. If the Duke does not do it for me, she will be my next resource. But it is better to have but one patron at a time and stick close to him.

At night I went back to Northumberland House, about seven. We had tea and chatted for a while till the company (about twenty picked people) gathered. They then sat down to the card-tables. But I told my Lady that I never played, which she found no fault with. A few did not play besides. However, I felt not so easy as those who did, and began to tire. I stayed there till eleven, and then came home.

SATURDAY 11 DECEMBER. I breakfasted with Macpherson, the

translator of *Fingal*, a man of great genius and an honest Scotch Highlander. It did my heart good to hear the spirit with which he talked. 'The
Highlanders', said he, 'are hospitable and love society. They are very
hardy, and can endure the inconveniences of life very well. Yet they
are very fond of London when they get to it, and indulge as much
in its pleasures as anybody. Let me', said he, 'have something in
perfection: either the noble rudeness of barbarous manners or the
highest relish of polished society. There is no medium. In a little
town you have the advantage of neither.' He told me that he was
very susceptible of tormenting love. But that London was the best
place in the world to cure it. 'In the country,' said he, 'we see a
beautiful woman; we conceive an idea that it would be heaven to
be in her arms. We think that impossible almost for us to attain.
We sigh. We are dejected. Whereas here we behold as fine women
as ever were created. Are we fond of one of them? For a guinea we
get the full enjoyment of her, and when that is over we find that it is
not so amazing a matter as we fancied. Indeed, after a moderate share
of the pleasures of London, a man has a much better chance to make
a rational unprejudiced marriage.' Macpherson said he had strong and
nice feelings, and therefore was easily made happy or miserable. 'But
then,' said he, 'nothing will make me either happy or the reverse above
a day. It is hard', said he, 'that we tire of everything.'

I then took Dempster with me to the City, and to Child's. He did not
enter into the spirit of it and went away soon. It is quite a place to my
mind; dusky, comfortable, and warm, with a society of citizens and physicians who talk politics very fully and are very sagacious and sometimes
jocular. 'What is the reason', said one, 'that a sole is not a good fish?'
'Why, it is a good fish,' said another, 'if you dress it with a plain butter
sauce. But you must have something so dev'lish high-seasoned. You
might as well have a sauce of fire and brimstone.' I shall hereafter for the
sake of neatness throw our conversation into my journal in the form of a
dialogue. So that every Saturday this my Journal shall be adorned with

A DIALOGUE AT CHILD'S

1 CITIZEN. Pray now, what do you really think of this Peace?
2 CITIZEN. That it is a damned bad one, to be sure!
PHYSICIAN. Damned bad one? Pray what would you be at? Have not

you had all that you wanted? Did you not begin the war to settle your boundaries in North America? And have not you got that done, as Mr Pitt the great champion of the Opposition acknowledged in the House, better than could have been expected? Have not you got a large tract of country ceded to you? Is not the line of division plain and straight?

BOSWELL. Suppose, Sir, I went out a-hunting with intention to bring home a hare to dinner, and catch three hares. Don't you think that I may also bring home the other two? Now, Sir, I grant you that we began the war with intention only to settle our boundaries in America and would have been satisfied with that and nothing more. But, Sir, we have had uncommon success. We have not only got what we intended, but we have also picked up some other little things, such as the Havana, Guadeloupe, &c. I should be glad to know why we are to part with them?

PHYSICIAN. Because the French will not make peace except we do so. And we cannot carry on the war another year.

1 CITIZEN. But we can.

PHYSICIAN. From whence have you the money? Who will furnish that?

1 CITIZEN. The City of London.

PHYSICIAN. Where will you get the men?

BOSWELL. I own to you that is a difficulty.

PHYSICIAN. Lord, Sir! We could not raise men for another campaign. Consider how the country has been drained. Ay, ay, it is easy for a merchant in London to sit by his warm fire and talk of our army abroad. They imagine we have got a hundred thousand stout soldiers ready to march up against the enemy. Little do they know what the severities they have suffered produce. Indeed we have a very thin army. And those that remain, what are they? Why, like Jack Falstaff's scarecrows. No, no, no more war! Let us not sink ourselves so many more millions in debt, and let our contractors, like Dundas, bring home a couple of hundred thousand pounds. We are now making a very good peace; let us be content.

MONDAY 13 DECEMBER. This forenoon Mr Sheridan was with me. I told him that I had great difficulty to get to London. 'And how could it be otherwise,' said he, 'when you pushed the plan most opposite to your father's inclinations?' This immediately led us to talk fully on his scheme of the Temple, which I told him my father disapproved of, as my going to London at all was the thing that he could not think of. I told him that I could not study law, and being of a profession where you do no good is to a man of spirit very disagreeable. That I was determined to be in London. That I wanted to be something; and that the Guards was the only scene of real life that I ever liked. I feel a surprising change to the better on myself since I came to London. I am an independent man. I think myself as good as anybody, and I act entirely on my own principles. Formerly I was directed by others. I took every man's advice, that I regarded; I was fond to have it. I asked it. I told all my story freely. But now I keep my own counsel, I follow the dictates of my own good sense, than which I can see no better monitor, and I proceed consistently and resolutely. I now spoke to Sheridan with a manly firmness and a conscious assurance that I was in the right. He said that application (by which he meant business) was necessary to keep a young man from being hurried down the stream. I swelled with satisfaction at the thoughts of showing him how well I should conduct myself as an officer of the Guards.

TUESDAY 14 DECEMBER. It is very curious to think that I have now been in London several weeks without ever enjoying the delightful sex, although I am surrounded with numbers of free-hearted ladies of all kinds: from the splendid Madam at fifty guineas a night, down to the civil nymph with white-thread stockings who tramps along the Strand and will resign her engaging person to your honour for a pint of wine and a shilling. Manifold are the reasons for this my present wonderful continence. I am upon a plan of economy, and therefore cannot be at the expense of first-rate dames. I have suffered severely from the loathsome distemper, and therefore shudder at the thoughts of running any risk of having it again. Besides, the surgeons' fees in this city come very high. But the greatest reason of all is that fortune, or rather benignant Venus, has smiled upon me and favoured me so far that I have had the most delicious intrigues with women of beauty, sentiment and spirit, perfectly suited to my romantic genius.

Indeed, in my mind, there cannot be higher felicity on earth enjoyed by man than the participation of genuine reciprocal amorous affection with an amiable woman. There he has a full indulgence of all the delicate feelings and pleasures both of body and mind, while at the same time in this enchanting union he exults with a consciousness that he is the superior person. The dignity of his sex is kept up. These paradisial scenes of gallantry have exalted my ideas and refined my taste, so that I really cannot think of stooping so far as to make a most intimate companion of a grovelling-minded, ill-bred, worthless creature, nor can my delicacy be pleased with the gross voluptuousness of the stews. I am therefore walking about with a healthful stout body and a cheerful mind, in search of a woman worthy of my love, and who thinks me worthy of hers, without any interested views, which is the only sure way to find out if a woman really loves a man. If I should be a single man for the whole winter, I will be satisfied. I have had as much elegant pleasure as I could have expected would come to my share in many years.

However, I hope to be more successful. In this view, I had now called several times for a handsome actress of Covent Garden Theatre, whom I was a little acquainted with, and whom I shall distinguish in this my journal by the name of LOUISA. This lady had been indisposed and saw no company, but today I was admitted. She was in a pleasing undress and looked very pretty. She received me with great politeness. We chatted on the common topics. We were not easy – there was a constraint upon us – we did not sit right on our chairs, and we were unwilling to look at one another. I talked to her on the advantage of having an agreeable acquaintance, and hoped I might see her now and then. She desired me to call in whenever I came that way, without ceremony. 'And pray,' said she, 'when shall I have the pleasure of your company at tea?' I fixed Thursday, and left her, very well satisfied with my first visit.

I then called on Mr Lee, who is a good, agreeable, honest man, and with whom I associate fine gay ideas of the Edinburgh Theatre in my boyish days, when I used to walk down the Canongate and think of players with a mixture of narrow-minded horror and lively-minded pleasure; and used to wonder at painted equipages and powdered ladies, and sing 'The bonny bush aboon Traquair', and admire Mrs Bland in her chair with tassels, and flambeaux before her.

I did not find Lee at home. I then went to Love's. They were just sitting down to a piece of roast beef. I said that was a dish which I never let pass, and so sat down and took a slice of it. I was vexed at myself for doing it, even at the time. Love abused Mr Digges grossly;

said he was a worse player than the lowest actor in Covent Garden. Their vulgarity and stupid malevolence (for Mrs Love also joined in the abuse) disgusted me much. I left them, determined scarcely to keep up an acquaintance with them, and in general to keep clear of the players, which indeed I do at present.

THURSDAY 16 DECEMBER. In the afternoon I went to Louisa's. A little black young fellow,9 her brother, came in. I could have wished him at the Bay of Honduras. However, I found him a good quiet obliging being who gave us no disturbance. She talked on a man's liking a woman's company, and of the injustice people treated them with in suspecting anything bad. This was a fine artful pretty speech. We talked of French manners, and how they studied to make one another happy. 'The English', said I, 'accuse them of being false, because they misunderstand them. When a Frenchman makes warm professions of regard, he does it only to please you for the time. It is words of course. There is no more of it. But the English, who are cold and phlegmatic in their address, take all these fine speeches in earnest, and are confounded to find them otherwise, and exclaim against the perfidious Gaul most unjustly. For when Frenchmen put a thing home seriously and vow fidelity, they have the strictest honour. O they are the people who enjoy time; so lively, pleasant and gay. You never hear of madness or self-murder among them. Heat of fancy evaporates in fine brisk clear vapour with them, but amongst the English often falls heavy upon the brain.'

We chatted pretty easily. We talked of love as a thing that could not be controlled by reason, as a fine passion. I could not clearly discern how she meant to behave to me. She told me that a gentleman had come to her and offered her £50, but that her brother knocked at the door and the man run out of the house without saying a word. I said I wished he had left his money. We joked much about the £50. I said I expected some night to be surprised with such an offer from some decent elderly gentlewoman. I made just a comic parody to her story. I sat till past eight. She said she hoped it would not be long before she had the pleasure of seeing me again.

This night I made no visible progress in my amour, but I in reality was doing a great deal. I was getting well acquainted with her. I was appearing an agreeable companion to her; I was informing her by my looks of my passion for her.

FRIDAY 17 DECEMBER. I engaged in this amour just with a view of convenient pleasure but the god of pleasing anguish now seriously seized my breast. I felt the fine delirium of love. I waited on Louisa at one, found her alone, told her that her goodness in hoping to see me *soon* had brought me back: that it appeared long to me since I saw her. I was a little bashful. However, I took a good heart and talked with ease and dignity. 'I hope, Madam, you are at present a single woman.' 'Yes, sir.' 'And your affections are not engaged?' 'They are not, Sir.' 'But this is leading me into a strange confession. I assure you, Madam, my affections are engaged.' 'Are they, Sir?' 'Yes, Madam, they are engaged to you.' (She looked soft and beautiful.) 'I hope we shall be better acquainted and like one another better.' 'Come, Sir, let us talk no more of that now.' 'No, Madam, I will not. It is like giving the book in the preface.' 'Just so, Sir, telling in the preface what should be in the middle of the book.' (I think such conversations are best written in the dialogue way.) 'Madam, I was very happy to find you. From the first time that I saw you, I admired you.' 'O, Sir.' 'I did, indeed. What I like beyond everything is an agreeable female companion, where I can be at home and have tea and genteel conversation. I was quite happy to be here.' 'Sir, you are welcome here as often as you please. Every evening, if you please.' 'Madam, I am infinitely obliged to you.'

[*Boswell is at Sheridan's.*] We talked of Johnson. He told me a story of him. 'I was dining', said Johnson, 'with the Mayor of Windsor, who gave me a very hearty dinner; but, not satisfied with feeding my body, he would also feed my understanding. So, after he had spoke a great deal of clumsy nonsense, he told me that at the last Sessions he had transported three people to the Plantations. I was so provoked with the fellow's dullness and impertinence that I exclaimed, "I wish to GOD, Sir, I was the fourth."' Nothing could more strongly express his dissatisfaction.

Mrs Sheridan told me that he was very sober, but would sit up the whole night. He left them once at two in the morning and begged to be excused for going away so soon, as he had another visit to make. I like to mark every anecdote of men of so much genius and literature.

I found out Sheridan's great cause of quarrel with him was that when Johnson heard of his getting a pension, 'What!' said he, 'has *he* got a pension? Then it is time for me to give up mine.' 'Now,' said he, 'here was the greatest ingratitude. For it was I and Wedderburn that first set the thing a-going.' This I believe was true.

SATURDAY 18 DECEMBER.

DIALOGUE AT CHILD'S

1 CITIZEN. Pray, Doctor, what became of that patient of yours? Was not her skull fractured?

PHYSICIAN. Yes. To pieces. However, I got her cured.

1 CITIZEN. Good Lord.

Enter 2 CITIZEN *hastily.* I saw just now the Duke of Kingston pass this door, dressed more like a footman than a nobleman.

1 CITIZEN. Why, do you ever see a nobleman, dressed like himself, *walking?*

2 CITIZEN. He had just on a plain frock. If I had not seen the half of his star, I should not have known that it was him.[10] But maybe you'll say a half-star is sometimes better than a whole moon. Eh? ha! ha! ha!

There was a hearty loud laugh.

I then went to Louisa's. I was really in love. I felt a warmth at my heart which glowed in my face. I attempted to be like Digges, and considered the similarity of our genius and pleasures. I acquired confidence by considering my present character in this light: a young fellow of spirit and fashion, heir to a good fortune, enjoying the pleasures of London, and now making his addresses in order to have an intrigue with that delicious subject of gallantry, an actress.

I talked on love very freely. 'Madam,' said I, 'I can never think of having a connection with women that I don't love.' 'That, Sir,' said she, 'is only having a satisfaction in common with the brutes. But when there is a union of minds, that is indeed estimable. But don't think, Sir, that I am a Platonist. I am not indeed.' (This hint gave me courage.) 'To be sure, Madam, when there is such a connection as you mention, it is the finest thing in the world. I beg you may just show me civility according as you find me deserve it.' 'Such a connection, Sir, requires time to establish it.' (I thought it honest and proper to let her know that she must not depend on me for giving her much money.) 'Madam,' said I, 'don't think too highly of me. Nor give me the respect which men of great fortune get by custom. I am here upon a very moderate allowance. I am upon honour to make it serve me, and I am obliged to live with great economy.' She received this very well.

SUNDAY 19 DECEMBER. I can come home in an evening, put on my old clothes, nightcap and slippers, and sit as contented as a cobbler writing my journal or letters to my friends. While I can thus entertain myself, I must be happy in solitude. Indeed there is a great difference between solitude in the country, where you cannot help it, and in London, where you can in a moment be in the hurry and splendour of life.

MONDAY 20 DECEMBER. I went to Louisa's after breakfast. 'Indeed,' said I, 'it was hard upon me to leave you so soon yesterday. I am quite happy in your company.' 'Sir,' said she, 'you are very obliging. But', said she, 'I am in bad humour this morning. There was a person who professed the greatest friendship for me; I now applied for their assistance, but was shifted. It was such a trifle that I am sure they could have granted it. So I have been railing against my fellow creatures.' 'Nay, dear Madam, don't abuse them all on account of an individual. But pray what was this favour? Might I know?' (She blushed.) 'Why, Sir, there is a person has sent to me for a trifling debt. I sent back word that it was not convenient for me to let them have it just now, but in six weeks I should pay it.'

I was a little confounded and embarrassed here. I dreaded bringing myself into a scrape. I did not know what she might call a trifling sum. I half-resolved to say no more. However, I thought that she might now be trying my generosity and regard for her, and truly this was the real test. I thought I would see if it was in my power to assist her.

'Pray, Madam, what was the sum?' 'Only two guineas, Sir.' Amazed and pleased, I pulled out my purse. 'Madam,' said I, 'if I can do you any service, you may command me. Two guineas is at present all that I have, but a trifle more. There they are for you. I told you that I had very little, but yet I hope to live. Let us just be honest with one another. Tell me when you are in any little distress, and I will tell you what I can do.' She took the guineas. 'Sir, I am infinitely obliged to you. As soon as it is in my power, I shall return them. Indeed I could not have expected this from you.' Her gratitude warmed my heart. 'Madam! though I have little, yet as far as ten guineas, you may apply to me. I would live upon nothing to serve one that I regarded.'

I did not well know what to think of this scene. Sometimes I thought it artifice, and that I was taken in. And then again, I viewed it just as a circumstance that might very easily happen. Her mentioning returning the money looked well. My naming the sum of ten guineas was rash; however, I considered that it cost me as much to be cured of what I contracted from a whore, and that ten guineas was but a moderate expense for women during the winter.

I had all along treated her with a distant politeness. On Saturday I just kissed her hand. She now sung to me. I got up in raptures and kissed her with great warmth. She received this very genteelly. I had a delicacy in presuming too far, lest it should look like demanding goods for my money. I resumed the subject of love and gallantry. She said, 'I pay no regard to the opinion in the world so far as contradicts my own sentiments.' 'No, Madam, we are not to mind the arbitrary rules imposed by the multitude.' 'Yet, Sir, there is a decency to be kept with the public. And I must do so, whose bread depends upon them.' 'Certainly, Madam. But when may I wait upon you? Tomorrow evening?' 'Sir, I am obliged to be all day with a lady who is not well.' 'Then next day, Madam.' 'What? to drink a dish of tea, Sir?' 'No, no, not to drink a dish of tea.' (Here I looked sheepish.) 'What time may I wait upon you?' 'Whenever you please, Sir.' I kissed her again, and went away highly pleased with the thoughts of the affair being settled.

I dined at Macfarlane's. We were very hearty. I indulged in it much. Erskine and I walked down the Haymarket together, throwing out sallies and laughing loud. 'Erskine,' said I, 'don't I make your existence pass more cleverly than anybody?' 'Yes, you do.' 'Don't I make you say more good things?' 'Yes. You extract more out of me, you are more chemical to me, than anybody.' We drank tea at Dempster's.

I went and sat a while with Captain Webster. He told me that the fatigues of a German campaign are almost incredible. That he was fourteen nights running without being under cover, and often had scarcely any victuals. He said he never once repented his being a soldier, although he cursed the sad fatigues. 'Men', said he, 'are in that way rendered desperate; and I have wished for an action, either to get out of the world altogether or to get a little rest after it.' We talked on a variety of old stories. He is a lively young fellow, and has humour. We were very merry. He returned me many thanks for my company and said it revived him.

TUESDAY 21 DECEMBER. I had resolved not to dine with my landlord, nor to see them much this week, in order to recover my proper dignity and distance. Another very good reason now glared me strong in the face. By my letting Louisa have two guineas, I had only thirteen shillings left; and my term of payment, as I have £25 every six weeks, was not till the 7 of January. I therefore could not afford a shilling, nor near so much, for dinner. So that I was put to my shifts, as I would not be indebted for dinner nor go and ask my allowance before it was due. I sat in till between four and five. I then went to Holborn, to a cheesemonger's, and bought a piece of 3 lb 10 oz, which cost me 14¹/₂d. I eat part of it in the shop, with a halfpenny roll, two of which I had bought at a baker's. I then carried home my provision, and eat some more cheese with the other roll, and a halfpennyworth of apples by way of relish, and took a drink of water. I recollected that I had left a guinea of security at Noble's circulating library. I went and told him that he should put confidence in me, so got it back. This was a most welcome guest to my pocket and communicated spirit to my heart. But, alas, of short duration was this state of opulence. I was reminded by Miss Terrie of a pair of lace ruffles that I had bespoke, which came to 16s. 'Very well,' said I, and paid them. There was the genteel determined spirit. I comforted myself by thinking that I suffered in the service of my Mistress; and I was romantically amused to think that I was now obliged to my wits, and living on the profit of my works, having got just 13s by my *Cub*.

WEDNESDAY 22 DECEMBER. I stood and chatted a while with the sentries before Buckingham House. One of them, an old fellow, said he was in all the last war. 'At the battle of Dettingen,' said he, 'I saw our cannon make a lane through the French army as broad as that' (pointing to the Mall), 'which was filled up in as short time as I'm telling you it.' They asked me for a pint of beer, which I gave them. I talked on the sad mischief of war and on the frequency of poverty. 'Why, Sir,' said he, 'GOD made all right at first when he made mankind.' ('I believe', said the other, 'he made but few of them.') 'But, Sir, if GOD was to make the world today, it would be crooked again tomorrow. But the time will come when we shall all be rich enough. To be sure, salvation is promised to those that die in the field.' I have great pleasure in conversing with the lower part of mankind, who have very curious ideas.

This forenoon I went to Louisa's in full expectation of consummate bliss. I was in a strange flutter of feeling. I was ravished at the prospect of joy, and yet I had such an anxiety upon me that I was afraid that my powers would be enervated. I almost wished to be free of this assignation. I entered her apartment in a sort of confusion. She was elegantly dressed in the morning fashion, and looked delightfully well. I felt the tormenting anxiety of serious love. I sat down and I talked with the distance of a new acquaintance and not with the ease and ardour of a lover, or rather a gallant. I talked of her lodgings being neat, opened the door of her bedchamber, looked into it. Then sat down by her in a most melancholy plight. I would have given a good deal to be out of the room.

I then sat near her and began to talk softly, but finding myself quite dejected with love, I really cried out and told her that I was miserable; and as I was stupid, would go away. I rose, but saluting her with warmth, my powers were excited, I felt myself vigorous. I sat down again. I beseeched her, 'You know, Madam, you said you was not a Platonist. I beg it of you to be so kind. You said you are above the finesse of your sex.' (Be sure always to make a woman better than her sex.) 'I adore you.' 'Nay, dear Sir' (I pressing her to me and kissing her now and then), 'pray be quiet. Such a thing requires time to consider of.' 'Madam, I own this would be necessary for any man but me. But you must take my character from myself. I am very good-tempered, very honest and have little money. I should have some reward for my particular honesty.' 'But, Sir, give me time to recollect myself.' 'Well then, Madam, when shall I see you?' 'On Friday, Sir.' 'A thousand thanks.' I left her and came home and took my bread and cheese with great contentment.

I sat this evening a while with Webster. He entertained me and raised my spirits with military conversation. Yet he sunk them a little; as he brought into my mind some dreary Tolbooth Kirk ideas, than which nothing has given me more gloomy feelings. I shall never forget the dismal hours of apprehension that I have endured in my youth from narrow notions of religion while my tender mind was lacerated with infernal horror. I am surprised how I have got rid of these notions so entirely. Thank GOD, my mind is now clear and elevated. I am serene and happy. I can look up to my Creator with adoration and hope.

THURSDAY 23 DECEMBER. I eat my cold repast today heartily. I have great spirits. I see how little a man can live upon. I find that Fortune cannot get the better of me. I never can come lower than to live on bread and cheese.

FRIDAY 24 DECEMBER. I waited on Louisa. Says she, 'I have been very unhappy since you was here. I have been thinking of what I said to you. I find that such a connection would make me miserable.' 'I hope, Madam, I am not disagreeable to you.' 'No, Sir, you are not. If it was the first duke in England I spoke to, I should just say the same thing.' 'But pray, Madam, what is your objection?' 'Really, Sir, I have many disagreeable apprehensions. It may be known. Circumstances might be very troublesome. I beg it of you, Sir, consider of it. Your own good sense will agree with me. Instead of visiting me as you do now, you would find a discontented, unhappy creature.' I was quite confused. I did not know what to say. At last I agreed to think of it and see her on Sunday. I came home and dined in dejection. Yet I mustered up vivacity, and away I went in full dress to Northumberland House. There was spirit, to lay out a couple of shillings and be a man of fashion in my situation. There was true economy.

SATURDAY 25 DECEMBER. The night before I did not rest well. I was really violently in love with Louisa. I thought she did not care for me. I thought that if I did not gain her affections, I would appear despicable to myself. This day I was in a better frame, being Christmas day, which has always inspired me with most agreeable feelings. I went to St Paul's Church and in that magnificent temple fervently adored the GOD of goodness and mercy, and heard a sermon by the Bishop of Oxford on the publishing of glad tidings of great joy. I then went to Child's, where little was passing. However, here goes the form of a

DIALOGUE AT CHILD'S

1 CITIZEN. Why, here is the bill of mortality. Is it right, Doctor?
PHYSICIAN. Why, I don't know.

1 CITIZEN. I'm sure it is not. Sixteen only died of cholics! I dare say you have killed as many yourself.

2 CITIZEN. Ay, and hanged but three! O Lord, ha! ha! ha!

I then sat a while at Coutts's, and then at Macfarlane's, and then went to Davies's. Johnson was gone to Oxford. I was introduced to

Mr Dodsley, a good, jolly, decent, conversable man, and Mr Goldsmith, a curious, odd, pedantic fellow with some genius. It was quite a literary dinner. I had seen no warm victuals for four days, and therefore played a very bold knife and fork. It is inconceivable how hearty I eat and how comfortable I felt myself after it. We talked entirely in the way of Geniuses.

We talked of poetry. Said Goldsmith, 'The miscellaneous poetry of this age is nothing like that of the last; it is very poor. Why there, now, Mr Dodsley, is your *Collection*.' DODSLEY. 'I think that equal to those made by Dryden and Pope.' GOLDSMITH. 'To consider them, Sir, as villages, yours may be as good; but let us compare house with house, you can produce me no edifices equal to the *Ode on St Cecilia's Day*, *Absalom and Achitophel*, or *The Rape of the Lock*.' DODSLEY. 'We have poems in a different way. There is nothing of the kind in the last age superior to *The Spleen*.' BOSWELL. 'And what do you think of Gray's odes? Are not they noble?' GOLDSMITH. 'Ah, the rumbling thunder! I remember a friend of mine was very fond of Gray. "Yes," said I, "he is very fine indeed; as thus –

> Mark the white and mark the red,
> Mark the blue and mark the green;
> Mark the colours ere they fade,
> Darting thro' the welkin sheen."

"O, yes," said he, "great, great!" "True, Sir," said I, "but I have made the lines this moment."' BOSWELL. 'Well, I admire Gray prodigiously. I have read his odes till I was almost mad.' GOLDSMITH. 'They are terribly obscure. We must be historians and learned men before we can understand them.' DAVIES. 'And why not? He is not writing to porters or carmen. He is writing to men of knowledge.' GOLDSMITH. 'Have you seen *Love in a Village*?' BOSWELL. 'I have. I think it a good, pleasing thing.' GOLDSMITH. 'I am afraid we will have no good plays now. The taste of the audience is spoiled by the pantomime of Shakespeare. The wonderful changes and shiftings.' DAVIES. 'Nay, but you will allow that Shakespeare has great merit?' GOLDSMITH. 'No, I know Shakespeare very well.' (Here I said nothing, but thought him a most impudent puppy.) BOSWELL. 'What do you think of Johnson?' GOLDSMITH. 'He has exceeding great merit. His *Rambler* is a noble work.' BOSWELL. 'His *Idler* too is very pretty. It is a lighter performance; and he has thrown off the classical fetters very much.' DAVIES. 'He is a most entertaining companion. And how can it be otherwise, when he has so much imagination, has read so much and digested it so well?'

We had many more topics which I don't remember. I was very well. I then went to Macfarlane's. We were very merry. Erskine and I had some bread and wine and talked for near two hours. He told me that he was kept as a blackguard when he was a boy, then went to sea, and then came into the Army. And that he wondered how he had been turned out a tolerable being.

SUNDAY 26 DECEMBER. I went to Whitehall Chapel and heard service. I took a whim to go through all the churches and chapels in London, taking one each Sunday.

At one I went to Louisa's. I told her my passion in the warmest terms. I told her that my happiness absolutely depended upon her. She said it was running the greatest risk. 'Then,' said I, 'Madam, you will show the greatest generosity to a most sincere lover.' She said that we should take time to consider of it, and that then we could better determine how to act. We agreed that the time should be a week, and that if I remained of the same opinion, she would then make me blessed. There is no telling how easy it made my mind to be convinced that she did not despise me, but on the contrary had a tender heart and wished to make me easy and happy.

I this day received a letter from the Duke of Queensberry, in answer to one that I had wrote him, telling me that a commission in the Guards was a fruitless pursuit, and advising me to take to a civil rather than a military life. I was quite stupefied and enraged at this. I imagined my father was at the bottom of it. I had multitudes of wild schemes. I thought of enlisting for five years as a soldier in India, of being a private man either in the Horse or Footguards, &c. At last good sense prevailed, and I resolved to be cheerful and to wait and to ask it of Lady Northumberland. At night I sat at Macfarlane's pretty well.

1763

SATURDAY 1 JANUARY. I received for a suit of old clothes 11s, which came to me in good time. I went to Louisa at one. 'Madam, I have been thinking seriously.' 'Well, Sir, I hope you are of my way of thinking.' 'I hope, Madam, you are of mine. I have considered this matter most seriously. The week is now elapsed, and I hope you will not be so cruel as to keep me in misery.' (I then began to take some liberties.) 'Nay, Sir – now – but do consider—' 'Ah, Madam!' 'Nay, but you are an encroaching creature!' (Upon this I advanced to the greatest freedom by a sweet elevation of the charming petticoat.) 'Good heaven, Sir!' 'Madam, I cannot help it. I adore you. Do you like me?' (She answered me with a warm kiss, and pressing me to her bosom, sighed, 'O Mr Boswell!') 'But, my dear Madam! Permit me, I beseech you.' 'Lord, Sir, the people may come in.' 'How then can I be happy? What time? Do tell me.' 'Why, Sir, on Sunday afternoon my landlady, of whom I am most afraid, goes to church, so you may come here a little after three.' 'Madam, I thank you a thousand times.' 'Now, Sir, I have but one favour to ask of you. Whenever you cease to regard me, pray don't use me ill, nor treat me coldly. But inform me by a letter or any other way that it is over.' 'Pray, Madam, don't talk of such a thing. Indeed, we cannot answer for our affections. But you may depend on my behaving with civility and politeness.'

SUNDAY 2 JANUARY. I had George Home at breakfast with me. He is a good honest fellow and applies well to his business as a merchant. He had seen me all giddiness at his father's, and was astonished to find me settled on so prudent a plan. As I have made it a rule to dine every Sunday at home, and have got my landlady to give us regularly on that day a piece of good roast beef with a warm apple-pie, I was a little difficulted today, as our time of dining is three o'clock, just my hour of assignation. However, I got dinner to be at two, and at three I hastened to my charmer.

Here a little speculation on the human mind may well come in. For here was I, a young man full of vigour and vivacity, the favourite lover of a handsome actress and going to enjoy the full possession of my warmest wishes. And yet melancholy threw a cloud over my mind. I could relish nothing. I felt dispirited and languid. I approached Louisa with a kind of an uneasy tremor. I sat down. I toyed with her. Yet I was not inspired by Venus. I felt rather a delicate sensation of love than a violent amorous inclination for her. I was very miserable. I thought myself feeble as a gallant, although I had experienced the reverse many a time. Louisa knew not my powers. She might imagine me impotent. I sweated almost with anxiety, which made me worse. She behaved extremely well; did not seem to remember the occasion of our meeting at all. I told her I was very dull. Said she, 'People cannot always command their spirits.' The time of church was almost elapsed when I began to feel that I was still a man. I fanned the flame by pressing her alabaster breasts and kissing her delicious lips. I then barred the door of her dining-room, led her all fluttering into her bedchamber, and was just making a triumphal entry when we heard her landlady coming up. 'O Fortune, why did it happen thus?' would have been the exclamation of a Roman bard. We were stopped most suddenly and cruelly from the fruition of each other. She ran out and stopped the landlady from coming up. Then returned to me in the dining-room. We fell into each other's arms, sighing and panting, 'O dear, how hard this is.' 'O Madam, see what you can contrive for me.' 'Lord, Sir, I am so frightened.'

Her brother then came in. I recollected that I had been at no place of worship today. I begged pardon for a little and went to Covent Garden Church, where there is evening service between five and six. I heard a few prayers and then returned and drank tea. She entertained us with her adventures when travelling through the country. Some of them were excellent. I told her she might make a novel. She said if I would put them together that she would give me material. I went home at seven. I was unhappy at being prevented from the completion of my wishes, and yet I thought that I had saved my credit for prowess, that I might through anxiety have not acted a vigorous part; and that we might contrive a meeting where I could love with ease and freedom.

MONDAY 3 JANUARY. I begged Louisa to invent some method by which we might meet in security. I insisted that she should go and pass the night with me somewhere. She begged time to think of it.

TUESDAY 4 JANUARY. Louisa told me that she would go with me to pass the night when she was sure that she would not be wanted at the playhouse next day; and she mentioned Saturday as most convenient, being followed by Sunday, on which nothing is done. 'But, Sir,' said she, 'may not this be attended with expense? I hope you'll excuse me.' There was something so kind and so delicate in this hint that it charmed me. 'No, Madam, it cannot be a great expense, and I can save on other articles to have money for this.'

I recollected that when I was in London two years ago I had left a guinea with Mr Meighan, a Roman Catholic bookseller in Drury Lane, of which I had some change to receive. I went to him and got 5s and 6d, which gave me no small consolation. Elated with this new acquisition of pecuniary property, I instantly resolved to eat, drink and be merry. I therefore hied me to a beer-house; called for some bread and cheese and a pint of porter.

Close by the fire sat an old man whose countenance was furrowed with distress. He said his name was Michael Cholmondeley, that he was a day-labourer but out of work, that he had laid out a penny for some beer, and had picked up a bit of bread in the street which he was eating with it. I immediately ordered such a portion of victuals and drink for him as I took for myself. He then told me he was a sad dog in his youth, run off from his friends to London, wrought here some time, and at last, wanting money, he had sold himself for a slave to the Plantations for seven years. 'Upon my word,' said I, 'you are a most extraordinary genius. How much did you get?' CHOLMONDELEY. 'Twenty pounds.' BOSWELL. 'And pray, what sort of a life had you there?' CHOLMONDELEY. 'O, Sir, a very good life. We had plenty of meat and drink, and wrought but five hours a day.' He said he then came back, and afterwards made voyages in lighters both to France and Spain. Poor creature! He had got falls and was sorely bruised, and often, even in severe weather, has been obliged to lie in the streets. I paid for his meal and gave him a penny. Why such a wretched being subsists is to me a strange thing. But I am a weak creature. I submit to GOD's will, I hope to know the reason of it some time.

I then bethought me of a place to which Louisa and I might safely go. I went to my good friend Hayward's at the Black Lion, told him that I had married, and that I and my wife, who was to be in town on Saturday, would sleep in his house till I got a lodging for her. The King of Prussia says in one of his poems that gallantry comprises every vice. That of lying it certainly does, without which intrigue can never be carried on. But as the proverb says, in love and war all is fair. I who am a lover and hope to be a soldier think so. In this instance we could not be admitted to any decent house except as man and wife. Indeed, we are so if union of hearts be the principal requisite. We are so, at least for a time. How cleverly this can be done here. In Scotland it is impossible. We should be married with a vengeance. I went home and dined. I thought my slender diet weakened me. I resolved to live hearty and be stout. This afternoon I became very low-spirited. I sat in close. I hated all things. I almost hated London. O miserable absurdity! I could see nothing in a good light. I just submitted and hoped to get the better of this.

WEDNESDAY 5 JANUARY. I was agreeably surprised at breakfast with the arrival of my brother John in good health and spirits, although he had been for three months lately in a most terrible way. I walked with him in the Park. He talked sensibly and well.

WEDNESDAY 12 JANUARY. Louisa and I agreed that at eight at night she would meet me in the Piazzas of Covent Garden. I was quite elevated, and felt myself able and undaunted to engage in the wars of the Paphian Queen.

At the appointed hour of eight I went to the Piazzas, where I sauntered up and down for a while in a sort of trembling suspense, I knew not why. At last my charming companion appeared, and I immediately conducted her to a hackney-coach which I had ready waiting, pulled up the blinds, and away we drove to the destined scene of delight. We contrived to seem as if we had come off a journey, and carried in a bundle our night-clothes, handkerchiefs, and other little things. We also had with us some almond biscuits, or as they call them in London, macaroons, which looked like provision on the road. On our arrival at Hayward's we were shown into the parlour, in the same manner that any decent couple would be. I here thought proper to conceal my own name (which the people of the house had never heard), and assumed the name of Mr Digges. We were shown up to the very room where he slept. I said my cousin, as I called him, was very well. That Ceres and Bacchus might in moderation lend their assistance to Venus, I ordered a genteel supper and some wine.

We supped cheerfully and agreeably and drank a few glasses, and then the maid came and put the sheets, well aired, upon the bed. I now contemplated my fair prize. Louisa is just twenty-four, of a tall rather than short figure, finely made in person, with a handsome face and an enchanting languish in her eyes. She dresses with taste. She has sense, good humour and vivacity, and looks quite a woman in genteel life. As I mused on this elevating subject, I could not help being somehow pleasingly confounded to think that so fine a woman was at this moment in my possession, that without any motives of interest she had come with me to an inn, agreed to be my intimate companion, as to be my bedfellow all night, and to permit me the full enjoyment of her person.

When the servant left the room, I embraced her warmly and begged that she would not now delay my felicity. She declined to undress before me, and begged I would retire and send her one of the maids. I did so, gravely desiring the girl to go up to Mrs Digges. I then took a candle in my hand and walked out to the yard. The night was very dark and very cold. I experienced for some minutes the rigours of the season, and called into my mind many terrible ideas of hardships, that I might make a transition from such dreary thoughts to the most gay and delicious feelings. I then caused make a bowl of negus, very rich of the fruit, which I caused be set in the room as a reviving cordial.

I came softly into the room, and in a sweet delirium slipped into bed and was immediately clasped in her snowy arms and pressed to her milk-white bosom. Good heavens, what a loose did we give to amorous dalliance! The friendly curtain of darkness concealed our blushes. In a moment I felt myself animated with the strongest powers of love, and, from my dearest creature's kindness, had a most luscious feast. Proud of my godlike vigour, I soon resumed the noble game. I was in full glow of health. Sobriety had preserved me from effeminacy and weakness, and my bounding blood beat quick and high alarms. A more voluptuous night I never enjoyed. Five times was I fairly lost in supreme rapture. Louisa was madly fond of me; she declared I was a prodigy, and asked me if this was not extraordinary for human nature. I said twice as much might be, but this was not, although in my own mind I was somewhat proud of my performance. She said it was what there was no just reason to be proud of. But I told her I could not help it. She said it was what we had in common with the beasts. I said no. For we had it highly improved by the pleasures of sentiment. I asked her what she thought enough. She gently chid me for asking such questions, but said two times. I mentioned the Sunday's assignation, when I was in such bad spirits, told her in what agony of mind I was, and asked her if she would not have despised me for my imbecility. She declared she would not, as it was what people had not in their own power.

She often insisted that we should compose ourselves to sleep before I would consent to it. At last I sunk to rest in her arms and she in mine. I found the negus, which had a fine flavour, very refreshing to me. Louisa had an exquisite mixture of delicacy and wantonness that made me enjoy her with more relish. Indeed I could not help roving in fancy to the embraces of some other ladies which my lively imagination strongly pictured. I don't know if that was altogether fair. However, Louisa had all the advantage. She said she was quite fatigued and could neither stir leg nor arm. She begged I would not despise her, and hoped my love would not be altogether transient. I have painted this night as well as I could. The description is faint; but I surely may be styled a Man of Pleasure.

THURSDAY 13 JANUARY. We awaked from sweet repose after the luscious fatigues of the night. I got up between nine and ten and walked out till Louisa should rise. I patrolled up and down Fleet Street, thinking on London, the seat of Parliament and the seat of pleasure, and seeming to myself as one of the wits in King Charles the Second's time. I then came in and we had an agreeable breakfast, after which we left Hayward's, who said he was sorry he had not more of our company, and calling a hackney-coach, drove to Soho Square, where Louisa had some visits to pay. So we parted. Thus was this conquest completed to my highest satisfaction. I can with pleasure trace the progress of this intrigue to its completion. I am now at ease on that head, having my fair one fixed as my own. As Captain Plume says, the best security for a woman's mind is her body. I really conducted this affair with a manliness and prudence that pleased me very much. The whole expense was just eighteen shillings.

I called at Louisa's and seemed to be surprised that she was abroad. I then went and called at Drury Lane Playhouse for Mr Garrick.

SATURDAY 15 JANUARY. I breakfasted with Dempster in exceeding lively spirits. I then hied me to the City, blithe and gay. As I passed Water Lane, I superstitiously took off my hat and bowed to the Black Lion.

DIALOGUE AT CHILD'S

PHYSICIAN. Do, Sir, stand a little to one side that we may see the fire.

1 CITIZEN. Sir! I think I make atonement for my error by leaving it.

PHYSICIAN. Have not you observed a certain gentleman with a broad backside who frequents this coffee-house, have not you seen him clap his backside to the fire, so as to cover it from us and almost to burn his own clothes, if not called to?

2 CITIZEN. Why the devil is he called to? Why not let him burn his clothes?

PHYSICIAN. That would be uncharitable.

SUNDAY 16 JANUARY. I went to Louisa and was permitted the rites of love with great complacency; yet I felt my passion for Louisa much gone. I felt a degree of coldness for her and I observed an affectation about her which disgusted me. I had a strong proof of my own inconstancy of disposition, and I considered that any woman who married me must be miserable. Here I argued wrong. For as a licentious love is merely the child of passion, it has no sure ground to hope for a long continuance, as passion may be extinguished with the most sudden and trifling breath of wind; but rational esteem founded on just motives must in all probability endure, especially when the opinion of the world and many other considerations contribute to strengthen and preserve it. Louisa and I began this day to read French. Our book was a little light piece of French gallantry entitled *Journal Amoureux*. She pronounced best and I translated best. Between us we did very well.

MONDAY 17 JANUARY. Louisa and I continued our study of French, which was useful as it gave us some employment and prevented us from tiring on account of conversation becoming insipid from a sameness that must necessarily happen when only two people are much together. I this day again had full fruition of her charms. I still, though, found that the warm enthusiasm of love was over. Yet I continued to mention my fears of her having some other favourite. I first said that I would watch her carefully, and would come at different times and by surprise if possible, that I might find out the truth. But I recovered myself and said I was sure I had no reason, so would not anxiously enquire. 'Indeed, Sir,' said she, 'it is better not. For it is a maxim with me, where there is no confidence, there is no breach of trust.'

I dined at Lady Betty's. Erskine was not there. We were very happy and in a better style than I ever knew us in. We were in a composed and sensible and at the same time a lively style. We talked of happiness, as we then owned that we were much so. I said that of making money was certainly great, as it lasted for ever, and as you had always something to show. I lamented that the happiness of the mind was so very transient, and that you had nothing left. For that a man may have a great quantity of happiness today, and tomorrow it is all gone, and what a man had avails him nothing. 'True,' said Lady Betty, 'but you must consider, though you are thus a bankrupt, yet you may quickly again be worth ten thousand pound.'

We then fell upon political topics, and all agreed in our love of the Royal Family of Stuart and regret at their being driven from Britain. I maintained that their encroachments were not of so bad consequence as their being expelled the throne. In short, the substance of our conversation was that the family of Stuart, although unfortunate, did nothing worthy of being driven from the throne. That their little encroachments were but trifles in comparison of what Oliver Cromwell did, who overturned the whole Constitution and threw all into anarchy; and that in a future period King William, who came over the defender of our liberties, became a most domineering monarch and stretched his prerogative farther than any Stuart ever did. That by the Revolution[11] we got a shabby family to reign over us, and that the German War, a consequence of having a German sovereign, was the most destructive thing this nation ever saw. That by the many changes and popular confusions the minds of the people were confused and thrown loose from ties of loyalty, so that public spirit and national principle were in a great measure destroyed. This was a bold and rash way of talking; but it had justice, and it pleased me.

TUESDAY 18 JANUARY. I this day began to feel an unaccountable alarm of unexpected evil: a little heat in the members of my body sacred to Cupid, very like a symptom of that distemper with which Venus, when cross, takes it into her head to plague her votaries. But then I had run no risks. I had been with no woman but Louisa; and sure she could not have such a thing. Away then with such idle fears, such groundless, uneasy apprehensions! When I came to Louisa's, I felt myself stout and well, and most courageously did I plunge into the fount of love, and had vast pleasure as I enjoyed her as an actress who had played many a fine lady's part. She was remarkably fond of me today, and sighing said, 'What will become of me if I lose you now?'

I dined at Lady Betty's. I said I sometimes contracted my plan. Says Erskine, 'You should contract nothing but debt.' To which Macfarlane added, 'And marriage.' We were very merry. They declared their hearty joy at this scheme of dining every day chancing to become part of my plan.

At five I left them for an hour and went to Sheridan's. In order to explain my errand there, I must give a narration of several sentences. Mrs Sheridan some weeks ago asked me to write a prologue to her new comedy. She said there were very few good poets in this age; and she said that if they had been in good terms with Johnson, she would have asked him. Her applying to me after this no doubt flattered me a good deal. She said there were few who had sense and temper enough to allow a fair criticism on their verses, as they were too much attached to their favourite productions. But I told her she need be under no apprehension of making me angry, for that I was perfectly easy in that respect. Indeed, my ease proceeds not from the good sense it might be imputed to, but from a carelessness of fame and a happy indifference, from a thorough conviction of the vanity of all things. As I had written no verses for some months, the task appeared very formidable. However, I wrote one which she said had good lines but was too general. I therefore wrote another, which she said was near the mark, and with a little polishing would do. The thing now pleased me exceedingly. I thought it fine to have my lines spoken by Mr Garrick and resounding through Drury Lane. I mentioned it to the Kellies and the Dempsters, and walked about elated, but would not let them hear it. To get a definite answer about this prologue was now my errand to Sheridan's. I must observe that from the first Sheridan himself never seemed hearty in the thing. I bid Mrs Sheridan not show it him, as he was a severe critic. After sitting a little, he said, 'Why, Sir, you don't ask about your prologue?' 'Indeed,' said I, 'I am too indifferent.'

SHERIDAN. Well, but prepare your utmost philosophy.

BOSWELL. How so?

SHERIDAN. It is weighed in the balances and found light.

BOSWELL. What, is not good?

SHERIDAN. Indeed, I think it is very bad.

BOSWELL. Pray, Mrs Sheridan, what is the meaning of this?

MRS SHERIDAN. Mr Sheridan, Sir, does not like it, and he has insisted upon me to write one which he thinks will do.

'Oho!' thought I, 'is this it?' I then desired to hear the faults of mine. Sheridan pointed them out with an insolent bitterness and a clumsy ridicule that hurt me much, and when I answered them, bore down my words with a boisterous vociferation. It is incredible with what seeming good humour I behaved. I declared that I must either be a man of the finest temper or the nicest art. He then read Mrs Sheridan's, which was much duller, as I thought.

We disputed about poems. Sheridan said that a man should not be a poet except he was very excellent; for that to be a *mediocris poeta* was but a poor thing. I said I differed from him. For the greatest part of those who read poetry have a mediocre taste; consequently one may please a great many. Besides, to write poems is very agreeable, and one has always people enough to call them good; so that a man of a tolerable genius rather gains than loses.

I returned to Lady Betty's at six really a good deal mortified, and in that sort of humour that made me consider writing as a dangerous thing and wish that I had never wrote and think I would not write again. I really have still a great degree of imbecility of mind; I am easily persuaded by what other people say, and cannot have a firm enough judgement. I told them my lamentable story.

Now did I ponder most seriously with myself how to behave to Sheridan. I was certainly used ungenteelly. Yet to take notice of it was low, and made him triumph in having been able to vex me. So is human nature constituted that I now had an aversion at Sheridan. I saw his bad taste, his insolence, his falsehood, his malevolence in the strongest light. I was sorry that I had been so much with him, and I resolved to take an opportunity of breaking off acquaintance and then lashing him for a presumptuous dunce, like as my friend Erskine and other people do in great abundance. But then I thought I was entertained in his company, so had better keep in with him. I just resolved that I would be upon a sort of indifferent footing. Be diverted with him, and not care a straw how he thought of me.

WEDNESDAY 19 JANUARY. This was a day eagerly expected by Dempster, Erskine and I, as it was fixed as the period of our gratifying a whim proposed by me: which was that on the first day of the new tragedy called *Elvira*'s being acted, we three should walk from the one end of London to the other, dine at Dolly's, and be in the theatre at night; and as the play would probably be bad, and as Mr David Malloch, the author, who has changed his name to David Mallet, Esq., was an arrant puppy, we determined to exert ourselves in damning it. I this morning felt stronger symptoms of the sad distemper, yet I was unwilling to imagine such a thing. However, the severe exercise of today, joined with hearty eating and drinking, I was sure would confirm or remove my suspicions.

We walked up to Hyde Park Corner, from whence we set out at ten. Our spirits were high with the notion of the adventure, and the variety that we met with as we went along is amazing. As the *Spectator* observes, one end of London is like a different country from the other in look and in manners. We eat an excellent breakfast at the Somerset Coffee-house. We turned down Gracechurch Street and went upon the top of London Bridge, from whence we viewed with a pleasing horror the rude and terrible appearance of the river, partly froze up, partly covered with enormous shoals of floating ice which often crashed against each other. Dempster said of this excursion from the road that our Epic Poem would be somewhat dull if it were not enlivened by such episodes. As we went along, I felt the symptoms increase, which was very confounding and very distressing to me. I thought the best thing I could do was not to keep it secret, which would be difficult and troublesome, but fairly to own it to Dempster and Erskine and ask their advice and sympathy. They really sympathized, and yet they could not help smiling a little at my catching a tartar so very unexpectedly, when I imagined myself quite safe, and had been vaunting most heroically of my felicity in having the possession of a fine woman, to whom I ascribed so many endearing qualities.

We met a coach loaded with passengers both within and without. Said I, 'I defy all the philosophers in the world to tell me why this is.' 'Because', said Erskine, 'the people wanted a quick carriage from one place to another.' So very easily are the most of the speculations which I often perplex myself with refuted. And yet if some such clever answerer is not at hand, I may puzzle and confound my brain for a good time upon many occasions. To be sure this instance is too ludicrous. But surely I and many more speculative men have been thrown into deep and serious thought about matters very little more serious. Yet the mind will take its own way, do what we will. So that we may be rendered uneasy by such cloudy reveries when we have no intention to be in such a humour. The best relief in such a case is mirth and gentle amusement.

We had a room to ourselves, and a jolly profusion of smoking juicy beefsteaks. I eat like a very Turk, or rather indeed like a very John Bull, whose supreme joy is good beef. We had some port, and drank damnation to the play and eternal remorse to the author. We then went to the Bedford Coffee-house and had coffee and tea; and just as the doors opened at four o'clock, we sallied into the house, planted ourselves in the middle of the pit, and with oaken cudgels in our hands and shrill-sounding catcalls in our pockets, sat ready prepared, with a generous resentment in our breasts against dullness and impudence, to be the swift ministers of vengeance. About five the house began to be pretty well filled. As is usual on first nights, some of us called to the music to play *Roast Beef.* But they did not comply with our request and we were not numerous enough to turn that request into a command, which in a London theatre is quite a different sort of public speech. This was but a bad omen for our party. It resembled a party's being worsted in the choice of praeses[12] and clerk, at an election in a Scotch county.

However, we kept a good spirit, and hoped the best. The prologue was politically stupid. We hissed it and had several to join us. That we might not be known, we went by borrowed names. Dempster was Clarke; Erskine, Smith; and I, Johnston. We did what we could during the first act, but found that the audience had lost their original fire and spirit and were disposed to let it pass. Our project was therefore disconcerted, our impetuosity damped. As we knew it would be needless to oppose that furious many-headed monster, the multitude, as it has been very well painted, we were obliged to lay aside our laudable undertaking in the cause of genius and the cause of modesty.

After the play we went to Lady Betty's, and as they were not disposed to eat and we were very hungry after our fatigues, we were set down in the parlour by ourselves to an excellent warm supper. We were in high glee, and after supper threw out so many excellent sallies of humour and wit and satire on Malloch and his play that we determined to have a joint sixpenny cut,[13] and fixed next day for throwing our sallies into order. The evening was passed most cheerfully. When I got home, though, then came sorrow. Too, too plain was Signor Gonorrhoea. Yet I could scarce believe it, and determined to go to friend Douglas next day.

THURSDAY 20 JANUARY. I rose very disconsolate, having rested very ill by the poisonous infection raging in my veins and anxiety and vexation boiling in my breast. I could scarcely credit my own senses. What! thought I, can this beautiful, this sensible, and this agreeable woman be so sadly defiled? Can corruption lodge beneath so fair a form? Can she who professed delicacy of sentiment and sincere regard for me, use me so very basely and so very cruelly? No, it is impossible. I have just got a gleet by irritating the parts too much with excessive venery. And yet these damned twinges, that scalding heat, and that deep-tinged loathsome matter are the strongest proofs of an infection. But she certainly must think that I would soon discover her falsehood. But perhaps she was ignorant of her being ill. A pretty conjecture indeed! No, she could not be ignorant. Yes, yes, she intended to make the most of me. And now I recollect that the day we went to Hayward's, she showed me a bill of thirty shillings about which she was in some uneasiness, and no doubt expected that I would pay it. But I was too cautious, and she had not effrontery enough to try my generosity in direct terms so soon after my letting her have two guineas. And am I then taken in? Am I, who have had safe and elegant intrigues with fine women, become the dupe of a strumpet? Am I now to be laid up for many weeks to suffer extreme pain and full confinement, and to be debarred all the comforts and pleasures of life? And then must I have my poor pocket drained by the unavoidable expense of it? And shall I no more (for a long time at least) take my walk, healthful and spirited, round the Park before breakfast, view the brilliant Guards on the Parade, and enjoy all my pleasing amusements? And then am I prevented from making love to Lady Mirabel, or any other woman of fashion? O dear, O dear! What a cursed thing this is! What a miserable creature am I!

In this woeful manner did I melancholy ruminate. I thought of applying to a quack who would cure me quickly and cheaply. But then the horrors of being imperfectly cured and having the distemper thrown into my blood terrified me exceedingly. I therefore pursued my resolution of last night to go to my friend Douglas, whom I knew to be skilful and careful; and although it should cost me more, yet to get sound health was a matter of great importance, and I might save upon other articles. I accordingly went and breakfasted with him.

After breakfast Mrs Douglas withdrew, and I opened my sad case to Douglas, who upon examining the parts, declared I had got an evident infection and that the woman who gave it me could not but know of it. I joked with my friend about the expense, asked him if he would take a draught on my arrears, and bid him visit me seldom that I might have the less to pay. To these jokes he seemed to give little heed, but talked seriously in the way of his business. And here let me make a just and true observation, which is that the same man as a friend and as a surgeon exhibits two very opposite characters. Douglas as a friend is most kind, most anxious for my interest, made me live ten days in his house, and suggested every plan of economy. But Douglas as a surgeon will be as ready to keep me long under his hands, and as desirous to lay hold of my money, as any man. In short, his views alter quite. I have to do not with him but his profession.

I then went to Louisa. With excellent address did I carry on this interview, as the following scene, I trust, will make appear.

LOUISA. My dear Sir! I hope you are well today.

BOSWELL. Excessively well, I thank you. I hope I find you so.

LOUISA. No, really, Sir. I am distressed with a thousand things. (Cunning jade, her circumstances!) I really don't know what to do.

BOSWELL. Do you know that I have been very unhappy since I saw you?

LOUISA. How so, Sir?

BOSWELL. Why, I am afraid that you don't love me so well, nor have not such a regard for me, as I thought you had.

LOUISA. Nay, dear Sir! (Seeming unconcerned.)

BOSWELL. Pray, Madam, have I no reason?

LOUISA. No, indeed, Sir, you have not.

BOSWELL. Have I no reason, Madam? Pray think.

LOUISA. Sir!

BOSWELL. Pray, Madam, in what state of health have you been in for some time?

LOUISA. Sir, you amaze me.

BOSWELL. I have but too strong, too plain reason to doubt of your regard. I have for some days observed the symptoms of disease, but was unwilling to believe you so very ungenerous. But now, Madam, I am thoroughly convinced.

LOUISA. Sir, you have terrified me. I protest I know nothing of the matter.

BOSWELL. Madam, I have had no connection with any woman but you these two months. I was with my surgeon this morning, who declared I had got a strong infection, and that she from whom I had it could not be ignorant of it. Madam, such a thing in this case is worse than from a woman of the town, as from her you may expect it. You have used me very ill. I did not deserve it. You know you said where there was no confidence, there was no breach of trust. But surely I placed some confidence in you. I am sorry that I was mistaken.

LOUISA. Sir, I will confess to you that about three years ago I was very bad. But for these fifteen months I have been quite well. I appeal to GOD Almighty that I am speaking true; and for these six months I have had to do with no man but yourself.

BOSWELL. But by G–D, Madam, I have been with none but you, and here am I very bad.

LOUISA. Well, Sir, by the same solemn oath I protest that I was ignorant of it.

BOSWELL. Madam, I wish much to believe you. But I own I cannot upon this occasion believe a miracle.

LOUISA. Sir, I cannot say more to you. But you will leave me in the greatest misery. I shall lose your esteem. I shall be hurt in the opinion of everybody, and in my circumstances.

BOSWELL (to himself). What the devil does the confounded jilt mean by being hurt in her circumstances? This is the grossest cunning. But I won't take notice of that at all. – Madam, as to the opinion of everybody, you need not be afraid. I was going to joke and say that I never boast of a lady's *favours*. But I give you my word of honour that you shall not be discovered.

LOUISA. Sir, this is being more generous than I could expect.

BOSWELL. I hope, Madam, you will own that since I have been with you I have always behaved like a man of honour.

LOUISA. You have indeed, Sir.

BOSWELL (rising). Madam, your most obedient servant.

During all this conversation I really behaved with a manly composure and polite dignity that could not fail to inspire an awe, and she was pale as ashes and trembled and faltered. Thrice did she insist on my staying a little longer, as it was probably the last time that I should be with her. She could say nothing to the purpose. And I sat silent. As I was going, said she, 'I hope, Sir, you will give me leave to enquire after your health.' 'Madam,' said I, archly, 'I fancy it will be needless for some weeks.' She again renewed her request. But unwilling to be plagued any more with her, I put her off by saying I might perhaps go to the country, and left her. I was really confounded at her behaviour. There is scarcely a possibility that she could be innocent of the crime of horrid imposition. And yet her positive asseverations really stunned me. She is in all probability a most consummate dissembling whore.

Thus ended my intrigue with the fair Louisa, which I flattered myself so much with, and from which I expected at least a winter's safe copulation. It is indeed very hard. I cannot say, like young fellows who get themselves clapped in a bawdy-house, that I will take better care again. For I really did take care. However, since I am fairly trapped, let me make the best of it. I have not got it from imprudence. It is merely the chance of war.

I then called at Drury Lane for Mr Garrick. He was vastly good to me. 'Sir,' said he, 'you will be a very great man. And when you are so, remember the year 1763. I want to contribute my part towards saving you. And pray, will you fix a day when I shall have the pleasure of treating you with tea?' I fixed next day. 'Then, Sir,' said he, 'the cups shall dance and the saucers skip.'

What he meant by my being a great man I can understand. For really, to speak seriously, I think there is a blossom about me of something more distinguished than the generality of mankind. But I am much afraid that this blossom will never swell into fruit, but will be nipped and destroyed by many a blighting heat and chilling frost. Indeed, I sometimes indulge noble reveries of having a regiment, of getting into Parliament, making a figure, and becoming a man of consequence in the state. But these are checked by dispiriting reflections on my melancholy temper and imbecility of mind. Yet I may probably become sounder and stronger as I grow up. Heaven knows. I am resigned. I trust to Providence. I was quite in raptures with Garrick's kindness – the man whom from a boy I used to adore and look upon as a heathen god – to find him paying me so much respect! How amiable is he in comparison of Sheridan!

SATURDAY 22 JANUARY. Calmly and considerately did I sit down in my arm-chair this morning and endeavour to call up all the philosophy that I could. A distemper of this kind is more dreadful to me than most people. I am of a warm constitution: a complexion, as physicians say, exceedingly amorous, and therefore suck in the poison more deeply. I have had two visitations of this calamity. The first lasted ten weeks. The second four months. How severe a reflection is it! And, O, how severe a prospect! Yet let me take courage. Perhaps this is not a very bad infection, and as I shall be scrupulously careful of myself, I may get rid of it in a short time. Then, as Smith[14] used to observe, a time of indisposition is not altogether a time of misery. There is a softness of disposition and an absence of care which attend upon its indolent confinement. Then, I have often lamented my ignorance of English history. Now I may make up that want. I may read all Hume's six volumes. I may also be amused with novels and books of a slighter nature.

I gave orders to say at the door that I was gone to the country, except to a few friends. Dempster, Erskine and my brother were with me today. Though bad, my spirits did not flag. Yet to be kept from comfortable Child's is somewhat hard. However, I will be patient.

SUNDAY 23 JANUARY. I was very dull this day. I considered the Guards as a most improper scene of life for me. I thought it would yield me no pleasure, for my constitution would be gone, and I would not be able to enjoy life. I thought London a bad place for me. I imagined I had lost all relish of it. Nay, so very strange is wayward, diseased fancy that it will make us wish for the things most disagreeable to us merely to procure a change of objects, being sick and tired of those it presently has. I thought I would go immediately down to Edinburgh, and would be an advocate in the Parliament House, and so lead a comfortable life. I was vexed to find all my gay plans vanished, and I had a struggle between hope and despair.

THURSDAY 3 FEBRUARY. I thought the treacherous Louisa deserved to suffer for her depravity. I therefore wrote her the following letter:

Madam: – My surgeon will soon have a demand upon me of five guineas for curing the disease which you have given me. I must therefore remind you of the little sum which you had of me some time ago. You cannot have forgot upon what footing I let you have it. I neither *paid* it for prostitution nor *gave* it in charity. It was fairly borrowed, and you promised to return it. I give you notice that I expect to have it before Saturday sennight.

I have been very bad, but I scorn to upbraid you. I think it below me. If you are not rendered callous by a long course of disguised wickedness, I should think the consideration of your deceit and baseness, your corruption both of body and mind, would be a very severe punishment. Call not that a misfortune which is the consequence of your own unworthiness. I desire no mean evasions. I want no letters. Send the money sealed up. I have nothing more to say to you.

JAMES BOSWELL

This, I thought, might be a pretty bitter potion to her. Yet I thought to mention the money was not so genteel. However, if I get it (which is not probable), it will be of real service to me; and to such a creature as her a pecuniary punishment will give most pain. Am not I too vindictive? It appears so; but upon better consideration I am only sacrificing at the shrine of Justice; and sure I have chosen a victim that deserves it.

THURSDAY 10 FEBRUARY. This forenoon a maid from Louisa left a packet for me. It was most carefully sealed up, 'by the hands of attention', but was not addressed to me. I opened it up and found my two guineas returned, without a single word written. I felt a strange kind of mixed confusion. My tender heart relented. I thought I had acted too harshly to her. I imagined she might – perhaps – have been ignorant of her situation. I was so foolish as to think of returning her the money and writing her a letter of atonement. I have too much of what Shakespeare calls 'the milk of human kindness'. I mentioned the thing to Dempster. He said it was just a piece of deep artifice in her. I resolved to think no more on the matter, and was glad that I had come off two guineas better than I expected.

THURSDAY 24 FEBRUARY. Dr McQuhae had sent me a letter enclosed in mine to Mr Alexander Macdonald, surgeon to the *Lord Mansfield* Indiaman. This young fellow has been long intimate with McQuhae, who has often given him an excellent character; and as he is besides a Highlandman from the Isle of Skye, I thought I would like to see him. I accordingly sent to him and begged he might come here. He came this morning to breakfast. He was going out to India on his first voyage. In a few minutes he and I were as easy and chatty as could be. The Highlanders have all a vivacity and a frankness that is very agreeable. I was in fine spirits, and I thought of many agreeable ideas. I found him warmly attached to the family of Stuart; and he said the Scotch Jacobites had yet great hopes of a restoration, in which they were confirmed by a dream which he had. He told me it and he promised to write it out for me. It was really very fanciful and strongly allegorical. He repeated it to me with the greatest enthusiasm. It was very entertaining to see the superstitious warmth of an old Highland seer mixed with the spirited liveliness of a neat clever young fellow. He had a picture of Mary Queen of Scots set in a ring, which he wore with much affection. I really took a liking to the lad. He passed the forenoon with me, and he promised to call again before he sailed. It gave me pleasure to see him animated with the prospect of making a fortune and then returning to Scotland.

This afternoon I was very high-spirited and full of ambition. I wanted much to be a man of consequence, and I considered that I could only be that in my own country, where my family and connections would procure it. I also considered that the law was my plain road to preferment. That if I would go to the Scotch bar I would soon be well employed, and as this confinement has made me see that I can sit in and labour very well, I thought I might be able very well to do business. By this means I would make money which would enable me to jaunt about wherever I pleased in the vacations. I would have an opportunity of being of much real use, of being of service to my friends by having weight in the country, and would make my father exceedingly happy. I considered that the law seemed to be pointed out by fate for me. That the family of Auchinleck had been raised by it. That I would soon be made Advocate Depute on the circuits and in all probability be made a Baron of Exchequer, and by this means have respect and yet an easy life – *otium cum dignitate*. I considered that my notions of an advocate were false. That I connected with that character low breeding and Presbyterian stiffness, whereas many of them were very genteel people. That I might have the wit and humour of Sir David Dalrymple, the jollity of Duncan Forbes, the whim of Baron Dalrymple, the show of Baron Maule, and the elegant taste of Baron Grant. I thought I might write books like Lord Kames and be a buck like Mr James Erskine. That I might keep a handsome machine. Have a good agreeable wife and fine children and keep an excellent house. That I might show all the dull, vulgar, plodding young lawyers how easily superior parts can outstrip them. That I might keep them at a distance, have my own few select friends, and that Johnston and I might enjoy life comfortably together. I thought I might go to the Church of England Chapel, like Pitfour;[15] and, in short, might live in the most agreeable manner.

I viewed this plan in every favourable light and became exceedingly fond of it. As I am most impetuous in whatever I take a fancy for, I was beginning to determine that I would write to my father and propose the thing to him, on condition that he made me a handsome settlement; that is to say, continued my £200 a year and agreed that I should have lodgings of my own and be quite an independent man.

But then such a step taken precipitantly would not be the thing. I therefore thought I had better get his permission to go abroad for a year or two to Holland, where we have some Dutch relations, to France and to Italy; after which I would be better satisfied and more settled. So great was my impatience to be a man of consequence that I thought this would keep me too long from the Session House. So very violent an inclination could not last, as will appear hereafter.

FRIDAY 25 FEBRUARY. I continued in exceeding high spirits. Variety of fine cheering ideas glanced athwart my blest imagination, ideas which gave me exquisite sensations at the time but which are so very nice that they elude endeavours to paint them. A man of similar feelings with me may conceive them. The law scheme appeared in another light. I considered it as bringing me back to a situation that I had long a rooted aversion to. That my father might agree to let me be upon the footing of independence, but when he had me under his eye, he would not be able to keep to it. I considered that I would at once embark myself for all my life in a labyrinth of care, and that my mind would be harassed with vexation. That the notion of being of consequence was not much, for that just now I knew from experience that just by strength of imagination I could strut about and think myself as great as any man. That the Guards was a situation of life that had always appeared most enchanting to me, as I could in that way enjoy all the elegant pleasures of the gay world, and by living in the Metropolis and having plenty of time, could pursue what studies and follow what whims I pleased, get a variety of acquaintances of all kinds, get a number of romantic adventures, and thus have my satisfaction of life. That if a man who is born to a fortune cannot make himself easier and freer than those who are not, he gains nothing. That if I should suddenly relinquish my favourite schemes, I should deservedly be considered as a man of no stability but inconstant and wavering with every breath. I considered that at present I was not a fair judge of a question of so much importance; that by a long course of confinement and medicine my animal spirits were necessarily tamed and my relish for pleasure and amusement and whim evaporated. That the mere satisfaction of ease after a situation of pain and the happy prospect of a recovery of health had elevated me too much and made me imagine nothing too difficult for me to compass. That indeed I had laboured hard, but it had been in writing my journal, letters and essays, which were all

works chiefly of the imagination. But that I would find it very irksome
to sit for hours hearing a heavy agent explain a heavy cause, and then to
be obliged to remember and repeat distinctly the dull story, probably of
some very trivial affair. I considered that when I should again go about
and mix in the hurry and bustle of life and have my spirits agitated
with a variety of brilliant scenes, this dull legal scheme would appear
in its usual colours.

Such were my reasonings upon both sides of this question, which
are, in my own opinion, very ingenious. It is strange to consider that
the same man who could waver so much could produce them. I was
somewhat uneasy at the consideration of my indetermined state of
mind, which argues a degree of imbecility. I wished much for some
of my sincerely affectionate friends to whom I might unbosom myself,
and whose kind counsel might relieve and direct me. I had much ado to
keep myself from mentioning the thing to people who must laugh at me
and had not my interest deeply at heart. However, I resolved to keep my
own counsel, and I was sure it was a thing that nobody would suspect.
I was anxious a little about my commission, and thought I should be
disappointed in it and become peevish and turn a sort of misanthrope.
But I summoned up more cheerful ideas and imagined that my noble
Countess was pushing for me. At any rate, I determined to give it a
year's run; and after that time I would be fully able to judge what to
think of great people and what plan of life I should pursue.

SUNDAY 27 FEBRUARY. I had now kept the house five complete weeks.
My disorder was now over. Nothing but a gleet remained, which gave
me no pain and which could be removed in three days. But I chose
to give it a little longer time, that I might get clear of every the least
tincture of infection. I thought, since I had been so much in earnest
hitherto to have a complete cure, I would undoubtedly complete it.
Douglas gave it as his opinion that I should confine myself no longer.
There was now no danger; and he thought a little air, exercise and
amusement would be of great use both to my health and spirits. This
day the sun shone prettily, yet I doubted as to going abroad. However,
a battalion of the Guards from Germany were this day to march into
town; and when I heard the beat of their drums, I could not restrain
my ardour, and thought this the happiest occasion for me to emerge
from obscurity and confinement, to light and to life.

MONDAY 28 FEBRUARY. I walked about half an hour in the Park very sweetly. The languor attendant on a man enfeebled with sickness has something in't not disagreeable to me. Then the taking care of one's self is amusing. At night I received the following letter from David Hume, Esq.

> You must know, Mr James Boswell, or James Boswell, Esq., that I am very much out of humour with you and your two companions or co-partners. How the devil came it into your heads, or rather your noddles (for if there had been a head among you, the thing had not happened; nor are you to imagine that a parcel of volatile spirits enclosed in a skull, make a head) – I repeat it, how the devil came it into your noddles to publish in a book to all the world what you pretend I told you in private conversation? I say *pretend I told you*; for as I have utterly forgot the whole matter, I am resolved utterly to deny it. Are you not sensible that by this *étourderie*, to give it the lightest name, you were capable of making a quarrel between me and that irascible little man with whom I live in very good terms? Do you not feel from your own experience that among us gentlemen of the quill there is nothing of which we are so jealous (not even our wives, if we have any) as the honour of our productions? And that the least touch of blame on that head puts us into the most violent fury and combustion? I reply nothing to your letter till you give me some satisfaction for this offence, but only assure you that I am not, Sir, your most obedient and most humble servant,
>
> DAVID HUME
>
> Edinburgh, 24 February 1763

This letter was occasioned by a paragraph in our strictures on Mr Malloch's *Elvira* which ran thus: 'We heard it once asserted by David Hume, Esq., that Mr Malloch was destitute of the Pathetic.' This was actually true. He said so to Captain Erskine and me just before I left Scotland. The conversation is to be found at large in the Journal of my Harvest Jaunt, 1762. Indeed, to repeat a private conversation and that in so very public a manner was rather using Mr Hume ungenteelly. But we were all alive for sharp criticism, and thought this so fine a hit that it is no wonder we did not advert to the impropriety we were guilty of. Mr Hume seems by his letter to have been seriously offended, although he has been so good-natured as to lighten his reproof by blending it with an agreeable pleasantry. I agreed to write him an answer.

Erskine told me that he was in Becket's shop this forenoon, where was Mr Murphy, the dramatic writer, who told an anecdote of the Reverend Dr Brown, author of *An Estimate of the Manners and Principles of the Times*. Sir Hanbury Williams lived some weeks at a house in the country where Brown had lodged, and where he discovered there was a pretty girl whom the Doctor was fond of and had even attempted to offend with. 'Well,' said Erskine, 'I think since he railed against the effeminacy of the age, he was right to show that he himself had some vigour left.'

TUESDAY 1 MARCH. I was made acquainted with the quarrels and commotions of my landlord's family. He is a fellow of a high Scotch spirit, very passionate and very easily persuaded. His sister who stayed in the house with us and other two who are in London are wicked malicious beings, and have always endeavoured to make a difference between him and his wife, who is a mild, agreeable creature as can be, but whom they hate. Poor Molly the maid, having been born at Norwich (which is the town her mistress came from), was for that reason an object of their hatred; and they have provoked Mr Terrie against her so much that she is to leave us next month. This led me to the knowledge of all the broils. For poor Mrs Terrie with the tear in her eye related to me all the mischiefs occasioned by the malevolence of the sisters, by whose instigation Mr Terrie formerly behaved so harshly to her that she parted from him and went and lived as a kind of better servant with a lady in Ireland for near a twelvemonth. But told me how her husband was just as glad to get her back again. She has now turned the other sister out of the house, which I rejoice at. She proved to be an abominable, cunning, revengeful little wretch. There is really in Scotland a species of low insidious wicked women worse than any creatures in the world. Terrie is a sad harsh dog, but not a bad fellow in the main. However, I shall always have a worse opinion of him, and have less acquaintance with him, though I shall make him very serviceable to me, as usual.

At night I wrote to David Hume as follows:

My dear Sir, – The heavy charge which you have given us demands a reply of proportionate weight of mettle. We are equally surprised and afflicted at your imagining that we meant you when we mentioned David Hume, Esq. To be sure, Sir, you are *the* David Hume, Esq., but you are not the sole one. He whose authority we have made bold to quote is a bookseller at Glasgow, who from his employment must be supposed to be well known in the world of letters. He is a man of very good understanding and more genius than most of his brethren, but his contempt for Mr Malloch's abilities as a tragic poet almost exceed belief. He will not so much as allow his works to stand in his shop, and he constantly affirms that he is destitute of the Pathetic.

Now, Sir, we shall suppose that we really meant you; and in that case we are ready to make oath either before Sir John Fielding or Mr Saunders Welch that we heard you utter that very expression. As to the consequences of this affair: we are very sorry that you live in good terms with Mr Malloch, and if we can make a quarrel between you, it will give us infinite pleasure. We shall glory in being the instruments of dissolving so heterogeneous an alliance; of separating the mild from the *irascible*, and the divine from the *bestial*.

We know very well how sore every author is when sharply touched in his works. We are pleased with giving acute pain to Mr Malloch. We have vast satisfaction in making him smart by the rod of criticism, as much as many a tender bum has smarted by his barbarous birch when he was janitor of the High School at Edinburgh.

As to the giving you satisfaction for the offence, you may receive full gratification by reading the Reviews on our performance. You will there find us held forth both as fools and as knaves; and if you will give us any other abusive appellations, we shall most submissively acquiesce. I hope this affair is now perfectly settled. I insist upon your writing to me in your usual humane style, and I assure you most sincerely that *I am*, my dear Sir, your most obedient humble servant,

BOSWELL & CO.

This letter I think a very good one; it is well expressed and has a proper mixture of compliment and spirit and jocularity. Erskine and Dempster were much pleased with it.

TUESDAY 3 MAY. I walked up to the Tower in order to see Mr Wilkes come out. But he was gone.[16] I then thought I should see prisoners of one kind or other, so went to Newgate. I stepped into a sort of court before the cells. They are surely most dismal places. There are three rows of 'em, four in a row, all above each other. They have double iron windows, and within these, strong iron rails; and in these dark mansions are the unhappy criminals confined. I did not go in, but stood in the court, where were a number of strange blackguard beings with sad countenances, most of them being friends and acquaintances of those under sentence of death. Mr Rice the broker was confined in another part of the house. In the cells were Paul Lewis for robbery and

Hannah Diego for theft. I saw them pass by to chapel. The woman was a big unconcerned being. Paul, who had been in the sea-service and was called Captain, was a genteel, spirited young fellow. He was just a Macheath.[17] He was dressed in a white coat and blue silk vest and silver, with his hair neatly queued and a silver-laced hat, smartly cocked. An acquaintance asked him how he was. He said, 'Very well'; quite resigned. Poor fellow! I really took a great concern for him, and wished to relieve him. He walked firmly and with a good air, with his chains rattling upon him, to the chapel.

Erskine and I dined at the renowned Donaldson's, where we were heartily entertained. All this afternoon I felt myself still more melancholy, Newgate being upon my mind like a black cloud. Poor Lewis was always coming across me. I felt myself dreary at night, and made my barber try to read me asleep with Hume's *History*, of which he made very sad work. I lay in sad concern.

WEDNESDAY 4 MAY. My curiosity to see the melancholy spectacle of the executions was so strong that I could not resist it, although I was sensible that I would suffer much from it. In my younger years I had read in the *Lives of the Convicts* so much about Tyburn that I had a sort of horrid eagerness to be there. I also wished to see the last behaviour of Paul Lewis, the handsome fellow whom I had seen the day before. Accordingly I took Captain Temple with me, and he and I got upon a scaffold very near the fatal tree, so that we could clearly see all the dismal scene. There was a most prodigious crowd of spectators. I was most terribly shocked, and thrown into a very deep melancholy.

I went home and changed my clothes. But gloomy terrors came upon me so much as night approached that I durst not stay by myself; so I went and had a bed (or rather half a one) from honest Erskine, which he most kindly gave me.

FRIDAY 6 MAY. I awaked as usual heavy, confused and splenetic. Every morning this is the case with me. Dempster prescribed to me to cut two or three brisk capers round the room, which I did, and found attended with most agreeable effects. It expelled the phlegm from my heart, gave my blood a free circulation, and my spirits a brisk flow; so that I was all at once made happy. I must remember this and practise it. Though indeed when one is in low spirits he generally is so indolent and careless that rather than take a little trouble he will just sink under the load.

This morning the famous Wilkes was discharged from his confinement and followed to his house in Great George Street by an immense
mob who saluted him with loud huzzas while he stood bowing from
his window.

THURSDAY 12 MAY. I went to Drury Lane and saw Mr Garrick play
King Lear. So very high is his reputation, even after playing so long,
that the pit was full in ten minutes after four, although the play did
not begin till half an hour after six. I kept myself at a distance from all
acquaintances, and got into a proper frame. Mr Garrick gave me the
most perfect satisfaction. I was fully moved, and I shed abundance of
tears. The farce was *Polly Honeycomb*, at which I laughed a good deal.
It gave me great consolation after my late fit of melancholy to find
that I was again capable of receiving such high enjoyment.

FRIDAY 13 MAY. I breakfasted with Mr Garrick. I was proud at being
admitted to the society of so great an actor. O'Brien the player was
there, a lively little fellow, but priggish. Mr Garrick was pleased to
hear that Donaldson had set up a shop for cheap books, and he walked
out with me to the shop, where I introduced Donaldson to him. The
prodigious Vendor of Literature was very proud of this. It was really
curious to see Mr Garrick in Donaldson's shop, and the two talking
away busily. Mr Garrick and I then walked to Lincoln's Inn, where
he went to call for Colman. He said he would undoubtedly go to
Scotland some one summer and play a night for each of the charities
at Edinburgh. I told him that he would be adored as something above
humanity.

SUNDAY 15 MAY. I was in an excellent calm and serious mood. I
attended divine service in Ludgate Church with patience and satisfaction, and was much edified. I then dined at honest Cochrane's,
after which he and I and two other gentlemen went to Dr Fordyce's
meeting in Monkwell Street and heard Dr Blair preach. I thought
this would have done me good. But I found the reverse. Blair's New
Kirk delivery and the Dissenters roaring out the Psalms sitting on
their backsides, together with the extempore prayers, and in short the
whole vulgar idea of the Presbyterian worship, made me very gloomy.
I therefore hastened from this place to St Paul's, where I heard the
conclusion of service, and had my mind set right again.

I should have mentioned that I breakfasted this morning with the
illustrious Donaldson. In the evening I went to Temple's; he brought

me acquainted with a Mr Claxton, a very good sort of a young man, though reserved at first. Mr Nicholls was there too. Our conversation was sensible and lively. I wish I could spend my time always in such company.

MONDAY 16 MAY. Temple and his brother breakfasted with me. I went to Love's to try to recover some of the money which he owes me. But, alas, a single guinea was all I could get. He was just going to dinner, so I stayed and eat a bit, though I was angry at myself afterwards. I drank tea at Davies's in Russell Street, and about seven came in the great Mr Samuel Johnson, whom I have so long wished to see. Mr Davies introduced me to him. As I knew his mortal antipathy at the Scotch, I cried to Davies, 'Don't tell where I come from.' However, he said, 'From Scotland.' 'Mr Johnson,' said I, 'indeed I come from Scotland, but I cannot help it.' 'Sir,' replied he, 'that, I find, is what a very great many of your countrymen cannot help.' Mr Johnson is a man of a most dreadful appearance. He is a very big man, is troubled with sore eyes, the palsy and the king's evil. He is very slovenly in his dress and speaks with a most uncouth voice. Yet his great knowledge and strength of expression command vast respect and render him very excellent company. He has great humour and is a worthy man. But his dogmatical roughness of manners is disagreeable. I shall mark what I remember of his conversation.

He said that people might be taken in once in imagining that an author is greater than other people in private life. 'Uncommon parts require uncommon opportunities for their exertion.

'In barbarous society superiority of parts is of real consequence. Great strength or wisdom is of value to an individual. But in more polished times you have people to do everything for money. And then there are a number of other superiorities, such as those of birth and fortune and rank, that dissipate men's attention and leave superiority of parts no extraordinary share of respect. And this is wisely ordered by Providence, to preserve a mediocrity.

'Lord Kames's *Elements* is a pretty essay and deserves to be held in some estimation, though it is chimerical.

'Wilkes is safe in the eye of the law. But he is an abusive scoundrel; and instead of sending my Lord Chief Justice to him, I would send a parcel of footmen and have him well ducked.

'The notion of liberty amuses the people of England and helps to keep off the *taedium vitae*. When a butcher says that he is in distress for his country, he has no uneasy feeling.

'Sheridan will not succeed at Bath, for ridicule has gone down before him, and I doubt Derrick is his enemy.'

I was sorry to leave him there at ten, when I had engaged to be at Dr Pringle's, with whom I had a serious conversation much to my mind.

I stayed this night at Lord Eglinton's.

TUESDAY 17 MAY. I sauntered up and down all this forenoon, and dined with Lord Eglinton, where was Sir James, who said he wondered how I could complain of being miserable who had always such a flow of spirits. Melancholy cannot be clearly proved to others, so it is better to be silent about it. I should have been at Lady Northumberland's rout tonight, but my barber fell sick; so I sallied to the streets, and just at the bottom of our own, I picked up a fresh, agreeable young girl called Alice Gibbs. We went down a lane to a snug place, and I took out my armour, but she begged that I might not put it on, as the sport was much pleasanter without it, and as she was quite safe. I was so rash as to trust her, and had a very agreeable congress.

WEDNESDAY 18 MAY. Much concern was I in from the apprehension of being again reduced to misery, and in so silly a way too. My benevolence indeed suggested to me to put confidence in the poor girl; but then said cool reason, 'What abandoned, deceitful wretches are these girls, and even supposing her honest, how could she know with any certainty that she was well?' Temple was much vexed and dreaded the worst.

I dined with him at Clifton's, and at five Erskine and I walked out to Dempster's, where we passed a very pleasant segment of a four-and-twenty. Erskine has now got into a way of going to taverns with one Fitzgerald and other riotous gentlemen, which I don't like.

THURSDAY 19 MAY. Mr James Coutts told me that he and his brother and Mr Cochrane were to dine with a Mr Trotter, upholsterer, a particular friend, and that he never went thither without carrying somebody along with him; so he insisted that I should go. I accordingly went, and was introduced to Mr Trotter, who is originally from Scotland, but has been here so long that he is become quite an Englishman. He is a bachelor, an honest, hearty, good-humoured fellow. The company were all Scottish except an American lady, wife to Mr Elliot, a son of Lord Minto's; Mr Stewart, formerly the noted Provost of Edinburgh; and some more of these kind of old half-English gentry. We had a good dinner and plenty of wine. I resolved to be merry while I could, and soon see whether the foul fiend of the genitals had again prevailed. We were plain and hearty and comfortable; much better than the people of high fashion. There was a Miss Rutherford there, a Scotch girl who had been long in America. She and I chatted very neatly.

We stayed and drank tea and coffee; and at seven, being in high glee, I called upon Miss Watts, whom I found by herself, neatly dressed and looking very well. I was free and easy with her, and begged that she would drink a glass of wine with me at the Shakespeare, which she complied with. I told her my name was Macdonald, and that I was a Scotch Highlander. She said she liked them much, as they had always spirit and generosity. We were shown into a handsome room and had a bottle of choice sherry. We sat near two hours and became very cheerful and agreeable to each other. I told her with a polite freedom, 'Madam, I tell you honestly I have no money to give you, but if you allow me favours without it, I shall be much obliged to you.' She smiled and said she would. Her maid then brought her a message that a particular friend from the country was waiting for her; so that I was obliged to give her up this night, as I determined to give her no money. She left me pleased, and said she hoped to have the pleasure of my company at tea when it was convenient. This I faithfully promised and took as a good sign of her willingness to establish a friendly communication with me.

I then sallied forth to the Piazzas in rich flow of animal spirits and burning with fierce desire. I met two very pretty little girls who asked me to take them with me. 'My dear girls,' said I, 'I am a poor fellow. I can give you no money. But if you choose to have a glass of wine and my company and let us be gay and obliging to each other without money, I am your man.' They agreed with great good humour. So back to the Shakespeare I went. 'Waiter,' said I, 'I have got here a couple of human beings; I don't know how they'll do.' 'I'll look, your Honour,' cried he, and with inimitable effrontery stared them in the face and then cried, 'They'll do very well.' 'What,' said I, 'are they good fellow creatures? Bring them up, then.' We were shown into a good room and had a bottle of sherry before us in a minute. I surveyed my seraglio and found them both good subjects for amorous play. I toyed with them and drank about and sung *Youth's the Season* and thought myself Captain Macheath; and then I solaced my existence with them, one after the other, according to their seniority. I was quite *raised*, as the phrase is: thought I was in a London tavern, the Shakespeare's Head, enjoying high debauchery after my sober winter. I parted with my ladies politely and came home in a glow of spirits.

FRIDAY 20 MAY. My blood still thrilled with pleasure. I breakfasted with Macpherson, who read me some of the Highland poems in the original. I then went to Lord Eglinton's, who was highly entertained with my last night's exploits, and insisted that I should dine with him, after having walked in Hyde Park with Macpherson, who was railing against the human species, and in vast discontent.

MONDAY 23 MAY. I dined with Dempster, having engaged to meet Dr Blair and Macpherson at his house. The Sublime Savage (as I call Macpherson) was very outrageous today, throwing out wild sallies against all established opinions. We were very merry. He and I and Blair walked into town together. I brought on the subject of reserve and dignity of behaviour. Macpherson cursed at it, and Blair said he did not like it. It was unnatural, and did not show the weakness of humanity. In my opinion, however, it is a noble quality. It is sure to beget respect and to keep impertinence at a distance. No doubt (as Blair affirmed) one must give up a good deal of social mirth. But this I think should not be too much indulged, except among particular friends. Blair and I went and sat a while by ourselves in Prince's Street Coffee-house and had a serious conversation.

TUESDAY 24 MAY. [*At the home of Bonnell Thornton, essayist.*] In a little, Mr Wilkes came in, to whom I was introduced, as I also was to Mr Churchill. Wilkes is a lively, facetious man, Churchill a rough, blunt fellow, very clever. Lloyd too was there, so that I was just got into the middle of the London Geniuses. They were high-spirited and boisterous, but were very civil to me, and Wilkes said he would be glad to see me in George Street.

From this chorus, which was rather too outrageous and profane, I went and waited upon Mr Samuel Johnson, who received me very courteously. He has chambers in the Inner Temple, where he lives in literary state, very solemn and very slovenly. He had some people with him, and when they left him, I rose too. But he cried, 'No, don't go away.' 'Sir,' said I, 'I am afraid that I intrude upon you. It is benevolent to allow me to sit and hear you.' He was pleased with this compliment, which I sincerely paid him, and he said he was obliged to any man who visited him. I was proud to sit in such company.

He said that mankind had a great aversion at intellectual employment. But even supposing knowledge easily attained, most people were equally content to be ignorant.

'Moral good depends on the motive from which we act. If I fling half a crown at a beggar with intention to break his head, and he picks it up and buys victuals with it, the physical effect is good; but with respect to me, the action is very wrong. In the same way, religious services, if not performed with an intention to please GOD, avail us nothing. As our Saviour saith of people who perform them from other motives, "Verily they have their reward."

'The Christian religion has very strong evidences. No doubt it appears in some degree strange to reason. But in history we have many undoubted facts against which *a priori* in the way of ratiocination we have more arguments than we have for them; but then testimony has great weight, and casts the balance. I would recommend Grotius, Dr Pearse on Miracles, and Dr Clarke.'

I listened to this great oracle with much satisfaction; and as I feel myself uneasy by reason of scepticism, I had great comfort in hearing so able an advocate for Revelation; and I resolved to read the books he mentioned. He pressed me to stay a second time, which I did. He said he went out at four in the afternoon and did not come home, for most part, till two in the morning. I asked him if he did not think it wrong to live so and not make use of his talents. He said it was a bad habit.

He said Garrick was the first man in the world for sprightly conversation.

I begged that he would favour me with his company at my lodgings some evening. He promised he would. I then left him, and he shook me cordially by the hand. Upon my word, I am very fortunate. I shall cultivate this acquaintance.

WEDNESDAY 25 MAY. Temple and his brother and I dined in their chambers, where we had dinner brought, thinking it a more genteel and agreeable way than in a chop-house. But we found it inconvenient, and so resolved to continue constant to Clifton's. I gave Bob a ticket to the play, and my worthy friend and I talked seriously. He advised me to force myself to be reserved and grave in a greater degree, otherwise I would just be Jamie Boswell, without any respect. And he said he imagined that my journal did me harm, as it made me hunt about for adventures to adorn it with, whereas I should endeavour to be calm and studious and regular in my conduct, in order to attain by habit a proper consistency of conduct. No doubt consistency of conduct is of the utmost importance. But I cannot find fault with this my journal, which is far from wishing for extravagant adventures, and is as willing to receive my silent and serious meditations as my loud and boisterous rodomontades. Indeed, I do think the keeping of a journal a very excellent scheme if judiciously executed. To be sure, it may take up too much time from more serious concerns. But I shall endeavour to keep it with as much conciseness as possible.

SATURDAY 25 JUNE. At nine in the evening Mr Johnson and I went to the Mitre Tavern in Fleet Street. He was vastly obliging to favour me with his company. I was quite proud to think on whom I was with.

He said Colly Cibber[18] was by no means a blockhead; but by arrogating to himself too much, he was in danger of losing what he really had. He said his friends gave out that he intended his Birthday Odes should be bad, but that was not the case. 'For a few years before he died, he showed me', said Johnson, 'one of them with the greatest care, and I made some corrections. Sir, he had them many months by him. Indeed Cibber's familiar style was better than that which Whitehead has taken. That grand nonsense is terrible. Whitehead is but a little man, to write verses inscribed to players.'

I shall mark Johnson's conversation without any order or without marking my questions; only now and then, I shall take up the form of dialogue.

'Sir, I do not think Mr Gray a superior sort of poet. He has not a bold imagination, nor much command of words. The obscurity in which he has involved himself will not make us think him sublime. His *Elegy in a Churchyard* has a happy selection of images, but I don't like his great things. His ode which begins

> Ruin seize thee, ruthless King.
> Perdition on thy banners wait!

has been celebrated for its abrupt breaking off and plunging into the subject all at once. But such arts as these have no merit but in being original. The first time is the only time that we admire them; and that abruptness is nothing new. We have had it often before. Nay, we have it in the song of Johnny Armstrong:

> There is never a man in the North Country
> To compare with Johnny Armstrong.

There, now, you plunge into the subject. You have no previous narration.'

I then told my history to Mr Johnson, which he listened to with attention. I told him how I was a very strict Christian, and was turned from that to infidelity. But that now I had got back to a very agreeable way of thinking. That I believed the Christian religion; though I might not be clear in many particulars. He was much pleased with my ingenuous open way, and he cried, 'Give me your hand. I have taken a liking to you.' He then confirmed me in my belief, by showing the force of testimony, and how little we could know of final causes; so that the objections of why was it so? or why was it not so? can avail little; and that for his part he thought all Christians, whether Papists or Protestants, agreed in the essential articles, and that their differences were trivial, or were rather political than religious.

He talked of belief in ghosts; and he said that he made a distinction between what a man might find out by the strength of his imagination, and what could not possibly be found out so. 'Thus, suppose I should think that I saw a form and heard a voice cry, "Johnson! you are a very wicked fellow, and unless you repent you will certainly be punished." This is a thought which is so deeply impressed upon my mind that I might imagine I saw and heard so and so; and therefore I would not credit this, at least would not insist on your believing it. But if a form appeared, and a voice told me such a man is dead at such a place and such an hour; if this proves true upon enquiry, I should certainly think I had supernatural intelligence given me.' He said that he himself was once a talker against religion; for he did not think against it, but had an absence of thought.

I told him all my story. 'Sir,' said he, 'your father has been wanting to make the man of you at twenty which you will be at thirty. Sir, let me tell you that to be a Scotch landlord, where you have a number of families dependent upon and attached to you, is perhaps as high a situation as humanity can arrive at. A merchant upon 'Change with a hundred thousand pounds is nothing. The Duke of Bedford with all his immense fortune is but a little man in reality. He has no tenants who consider themselves as under his patriarchal care.

'Sir, a father and a son should part at a certain time of life. I never believed what my father said. I always thought that he spoke *ex officio*, as a priest does.

'Sir, I am a friend to subordination. It is most conducive to the happiness of society. There is a reciprocal pleasure in governing and being governed.

'Sir, I think your breaking off idle connections by going abroad is a matter of importance. I would go where there are courts and learned men.'

I then complained to him how little I knew, and mentioned study. 'Sir,' said he, 'don't talk of study just now. I will put you upon a plan. It will require some time to talk of that.' I put out my hand. 'Will you really take a charge of me? It is very good in you, Mr Johnson, to allow me to sit with you thus. Had I but thought some years ago that I should pass an evening with the Author of *The Rambler*!' These expressions were all from the heart, and he perceived that they were; and he was very complacent and said, 'Sir, I am glad we have met. I hope we shall pass many evenings and mornings too together.'

SUNDAY 26 JUNE. I should have mentioned that Mr Johnson said he thought I had a lucky escape from the Guards (*of* the Guards I mean), as I was past those puerilities. I breakfasted with Douglas and dined with my landlord, which brought back the ideas of the beginning of winter. I then walked out to Islington and went to Canonbury House, a curious old monastic building, now let out in lodgings, where Dr Goldsmith stays. I drank tea with him, and found him very chatty. He lamented however that the praise due to literary merit is already occupied by the first writers, who will keep it and get the better even of the superior merit which the moderns may possess. He said David Hume was one of those, who, seeing the first place occupied on the right side, rather than take a second, wants to have a first in what is wrong. I supped with Lord Eglinton.

TUESDAY 5 JULY. At night Temple and his brother sat with me at my lodgings over some negus, and as they were in a frolicsome humour, and were tickling me, and jumping about, we made a good deal of noise. Mr Terrie, my landlord, whose character I have formerly delineated pretty strongly in this my journal, now showed himself in full force of low rudeness and passionate ill manners. He took it into his head that we had the maid with us, and came and rapped furiously at the parlour door, calling my name. I went out and asked him what he meant. He bawled out that he would be in, and would turn us every one out. He then called the watch, desired him at his peril to bring more of his brethren, and said he charged us with a riot, and would send us to the roundhouse. However, when the watch returned, he began to dread the consequence of false imprisonment, and desisted. But he still behaved very impertinently. Unluckily, I had taken the parlour only for the mornings, and my being there at night was a matter of courtesy; for if it had been my own lodging, I could have got him severely soused. I luckily kept my temper and behaved with the greatest calmness. I determined, however, to quit his house, as Temple was of the same opinion.

WEDNESDAY 6 JULY. Those who would endeavour to extirpate evil from the world know little of human nature. As well might punch be palatable without souring as existence agreeable without care. I got up this morning before seven, finely agitated, and away I went to Mr Cochrane, my merchant, with whom I breakfasted; and after telling my story, got him to advance me my next allowance, and carried him with me to the Plantation Office, where we found Terrie, with whom I talked over the affair. The dog denied he was drunk, and continued as obstinate as ever. When he had told Mr Cochrane his story, Mr Cochrane said, 'I was afraid, Sir, that my friend had perhaps been in the wrong, but from your own account of the matter, I find that you have behaved very rudely; and, Sir, no gentleman can put up with such usage.' I then demanded how much I owed him. He said, with a hard-faced impudence, 'We go by English laws.' 'I wish, Sir,' said I, 'that you had English manners.' He looked at me with a Northland sulkiness. As he would not then say how much was due, I left him.

By the advice of Mr Coutts, I went to Sir John Fielding's, that great seat of Westminster justice. A more curious scene I never beheld: it brought fresh into my mind the ideas of London roguery and wickedness which I conceived in my younger days by reading

The Lives of the Convicts, and other such books. There were whores and chairmen and greasy blackguards of all denominations assembled together. The blind Justice had his court in a back hall. His clerk, who officiates as a sort of chamber counsel, hears all the causes, and gives his opinion. As I had no formal complaint to make, he did not carry me in to the Justice, but told me that as my landlord had used me rudely, although I had taken my lodging by the year, I was only obliged to pay him for the time that I had lived in his house.

A great difficulty still remained. I had engaged Mr Johnson and some more company to sup at my lodgings, and as my having the parlour of an evening was a favour from my landlord, I would by no means think of it. I went to Mr Johnson and told him my distress. He laughed and bid me consider how little a distress it would appear a twelvemonth hence. He said that if my landlord insisted that the bargain should stand and the lodgings be mine for a year, that I could certainly use them as I pleased. 'So, Sir,' said he, 'you may quarter two Life Guard[19] men upon him; or you may get the greatest scoundrel you can find and send into his house; or you may say that you want to make some experiments in natural philosophy and may burn a large quantity of asafoetida in his house.' Such ludicrous fertility can this great man throw out!

What amazing universality of genius has Mr Johnson, who has written *The English Dictionary*, a work of infinite labour and knowledge; *The Rambler*, which contains a rich store of morality and knowledge of human life, embellished with great imagination; *Rasselas*, where we find a humane preceptor delighting the fancy and mending the heart; *The Life of Savage*, which is distinguished for perspicuity of narration, and abounds with excellent reflection; *The Translations of the Third and Tenth Satires of Juvenal*, and *The Prologue spoken at Mr Garrick's Opening Drury-Lane Theatre*, which display strong poetical genius, strength of sentiment, keenness of satire, vivaciousness of wit and humour, and manly power of versification. His conversation, too, is as great as his writing. He throws out all his powers with force of expression; and he mixes inimitable strokes of vivacity with solid good sense and knowledge, so that he is highly instructive and highly entertaining.

I made myself easy as to my company by letting them know that they were consider the Mitre Tavern as my lodgings for that night. Accordingly, I ordered supper there, and I had as my guests Mr Samuel

Johnson, Dr Goldsmith, Mr Ogilvie, Mr Davies, bookseller, and Mr Eccles, an Irish gentleman of fortune, a good ingenious sort of man. I was well dressed and in excellent spirits, neither muddy nor flashy. I sat with much secret pride, thinking of my having such a company with me. I behaved with ease and propriety, and did not attempt at all to show away; but gently assisted conversation by those little arts which serve to make people throw out their sentiments with ease and freedom.

Ogilvie was rapt in admiration of the Stupendous Johnson. Goldsmith was in his usual style, too eager to be bright, and held a keen dispute with Johnson against that maxim in the British Constitution, 'The King can do no wrong'; affirming that what was morally false could not be politically true. And as the King might command and cause the doing of what was wrong, he certainly could do wrong. Johnson showed that in our Constitution the King is the head, and that there is no power by which he can be tried; and therefore it is that redress is always to be had against oppression by punishing the immediate agents. 'The King cannot force a judge to condemn a man wrongfully; therefore it is the judge that we pursue. Political institutions are formed upon the consideration of what will most frequently tend to the good of the whole, although now and then exceptions may occur. Thus it is better in general that a nation should have a supreme legislative power, although it may at times be abused. But, then, there is this consideration: that if the abuse be enormous, Nature will rise up, and claiming her original rights, overturn a corrupted political system.'

In recollecting Mr Johnson's conversation, I labour under much difficulty. It requires more parts than I am master of even to retain that strength of sentiment and perspicuity of expression for which he is remarkable. I shall just do my best and relate as much as I can.

He said that great parts were not requisite for a historian, as in that kind of composition all the greatest powers of the human mind are quiescent. 'He has facts ready to his hand, so he has no exercise of invention. Imagination is not required in any high degree; only about as much as is used in the lower parts of poetry. Some penetration, accuracy and colouring will fit a man for such a task, who can give the application which is necessary.'

He said Bayle's *Dictionary* was a very useful work to consult for those who love the biographical part of literature; which he said he loved most.

We talked of Scotland. Ogilvie, who is a rank Scot, defended his native land with all the powers that he could muster up. I was diverted to see how great a man a London wit is in comparison of one of your country swans who sing ever so *bonnily*. Ogilvie said there was very rich country round Edinburgh. 'No, no,' said Goldsmith, with a sneering laugh; 'it is not rich country.' Ogilvie then said that Scotland had a great many noble wild prospects. 'Sir,' said Johnson, 'I believe you have a great many noble wild prospects. Norway too has some noble wild prospects; and Lapland is remarkable for prodigious noble wild prospects. But, Sir, I believe the noblest prospect that a Scotsman ever sees is the road which leads him to England!'

We gave a roar of applause to this most excellent sally of strong humour. At the same time, I could not help thinking that Mr Johnson showed a want of taste in laughing at the wild grandeur of nature, which to a mind undebauched by art conveys the most pleasing awful, sublime ideas. Have not I experienced the full force of this when gazing at thee, O Arthur Seat, thou venerable mountain! whether in the severity of winter thy brow has been covered with snow or wrapped in mist; or in the gentle mildness of summer the evening sun has shone upon thy verdant sides diversified with rugged moss-clad rocks and rendered religious by the ancient Chapel of St Anthony. Beloved hill, the admiration of my youth! Thy noble image shall ever fill my mind! Let me travel over the whole earth, I shall still remember thee; and when I return to my native country, while I live I will visit thee with affection and reverence!

Mr Johnson was exceeding good company all this evening. We parted at one. I was very happy. I am now reaping the fruits of my economy during the winter; and I have got rid of the narrowness and love of money which my frugality made me contract. I am afraid I have a disposition to be a miser. But I will combat this by my benevolence, which I have much of. I find I can cure narrowness by practising free liberality. I have certainly had more enjoyment of my money this evening than if I had spent it in one of your splendid Court-end taverns[20] among a parcel of people that I did not care a farthing for, and could receive no benefit from. This evening I have had much pleasure. That is being truly rich. And riches are only a good because men have a pleasure in spending them, or in hoarding them up. I have received this night both instruction and pleasure.

THURSDAY 7 JULY. Yesterday afternoon, before I went to the Mitre, I went to my lodgings in Downing Street, got Chetwynd, who has been a sort of prime minister to me, and packed up all my things. Then called up Mrs Terrie and discharged what little debts I owed her. Poor woman! she seemed much affected and hoped I would not mention Mr Terrie's behaviour. I told her that I should always speak well of her, but that I would most certainly represent her husband as a very rude unmannerly fellow, in whose house no gentleman could be safe to stay. And I advised her to make him give over letting lodgings, as he was very unfit for it. So curious a composition is the mind of man that I felt a degree of sorrow at leaving the room in which I had passed the winter, where I had been confined five weeks, and where this my journal and all my other little lucubrations have been written.

THURSDAY 14 JULY. I told Mr Johnson what a strange mortal Macpherson was, or affected to be; and how he railed at all established systems. 'So would he tumble in a hog-sty,' said Johnson, 'as long as you look at him and cry to him to come out. But let him alone, never mind him, and he'll soon give it over.'

Mr Johnson and I had formerly drank the health of Sir David Dalrymple, whom he gave as his toast. I this night read part of a letter from Sir David, since my informing him of it, in which he bid me assure him of the veneration which he entertained for the author of *The Rambler* and of *Rasselas*. He paid Mr Johnson some very pretty compliments, which pleased him much.

Mr Johnson considered reading what you have an inclination for as eating what you have an appetite for. But then I consider that a stomach which has fasted very long will have no desire for any kind of food. The longer it wants food, it will be the worse; and therefore we must not wait till an appetite returns, but immediately throw in some wholesome sustenance. The stomach may then recover its tone, and its natural taste may spring up and grow vigorous, and then let it be indulged. So it is with the mind, when by a long course of dissipation it is quite relaxed. We must recover it gradually, and then we can better judge what course of study to pursue. This must now be my endeavour. And when I go to Utrecht, I hope to make proficiency in useful literature.

When we went into the Mitre tonight, Mr Johnson said, 'We will not drink two bottles of port.' When one was drank, he called for another pint; and when we had got to the bottom of that, and I was distributing it equally, 'Come,' said he, 'you need not measure it so exactly.' 'Sir,' said I, 'it is done.' 'Well, Sir,' said he, 'are you satisfied? or would you choose another?' 'Would you, Sir?' said I. 'Yes,' said he, 'I think I would. I think two bottles would seem to be the quantity for us.' Accordingly we made them out.

I take pleasure in recording every little circumstance about so great a man as Mr Johnson. This little specimen of social pleasantry will serve me to tell as an agreeable story to literary people. He took me cordially by the hand and said, 'My dear Boswell! I do love you very much.' – I *will* be vain, there's enough.

FRIDAY 15 JULY. A bottle of thick English port is a very heavy and a very inflammatory dose. I felt it last time that I drank it for several days, and this morning it was boiling in my veins. Dempster came and saw me, and said I had better be palsied at eighteen than not keep company with such a man as Johnson. I sailed with Dempster up to the Navy Office, and then sailed back to his house in Manchester Buildings (for he has now got a house in town). It was a prodigious bad day. We got into a covered boat. But it was very horrid, as it rained and thundered all the time that we were going up the river. I dined with Dempster and his sister. We talked lively enough. But conversation without a subject and constantly mixed up with ludicrous witticisms appears very trifling after being with Mr Johnson.

SATURDAY 16 JULY. I carried Bob Temple with me to breakfast at Dempster's and introduced him to Dempster and his sister, where he was very well received. Since my being honoured with the friendship of Mr Johnson, I have more seriously considered the duties of morality and religion and the dignity of human nature. I have considered that promiscuous concubinage is certainly wrong. It is contributing one's share towards bringing confusion and misery into society; and it is a transgression of the laws of the Almighty Creator, who has ordained marriage for the mutual comfort of the sexes and the procreation and right educating of children. Sure it is that if all the men and women in Britain were merely to consult animal gratification, society would be a most shocking scene. Nay, it would soon cease altogether. Notwithstanding of these reflections, I have stooped to mean profligacy even yesterday. However, I am now resolved to guard against it.

At my last meeting with Mr Johnson, he said that when he came first to London and was upon his shifts, he was told by a very clever man who understood perfectly the common affairs of life that £30 a year was enough to make a man live without being contemptible; that is to say, you might be always clean. He allowed £10 for clothes and linen. He said you might live in a garret at eighteen-pence a week, as few people would enquire where you lodge; and if they do, it is easy to say, 'Sir, I am to be found at such a place.' For spending threepence in a coffee-house, you may be for hours in very good company. You may dine for sixpence, you may breakfast on bread and milk, and you may want supper.

He advised me to keep a journal of my life, fair and undisguised. He said it would be a very good exercise, and would yield me infinite satisfaction when the ideas were faded from my remembrance. I told him that I had done so ever since I left Scotland. He said he was very happy that I pursued so good a plan. And now, O my journal! art thou not highly dignified? Shalt thou not flourish tenfold? No former solicitations or censures could tempt me to lay thee aside; and now is there any argument which can outweigh the sanction of Mr Samuel Johnson? He said indeed that I should keep it private, and that I might surely have a friend who would burn it in case of my death. For my own part, I have at present such an affection for this my journal that it shocks me to think of burning it. I rather encourage the idea of having it carefully laid up among the archives of Auchinleck. However, I cannot judge fairly of it now. Some years hence I may. I told Mr Johnson that I put down all sorts of little incidents in it. 'Sir,' said he, 'there is nothing too little for so little a creature as man. It is by studying little things that we attain the great knowledge of having as little misery and as much happiness as possible.'

TUESDAY 2 AUGUST. In the afternoon [Johnson] carried me to drink tea with Miss Williams, who has a snug lodging in Bolt Court, Fleet Street. I found her a facetious, agreeable woman, though stone-blind. I was cheerful, and well received. He then carried me to what he called his walk, which is a paved long court overshadowed by some trees in a neighbouring garden. There he advised me when fixed in a place abroad to read with a keenness after knowledge, and to read every day an hour at Greek. And when I was moving about, to read diligently the great book of mankind. We supped at the Turk's Head. I was somewhat melancholy, but it went off. Mr Johnson filled my mind with so many noble and just sentiments that the Demon of Despondency was driven away.

WEDNESDAY 3 AUGUST. I should have mentioned that on Monday night, coming up the Strand, I was tapped on the shoulder by a fine fresh lass. I went home with her. She was an officer's daughter, and born at Gibraltar. I could not resist indulging myself with the enjoyment of her. Surely, in such a situation, when the woman is already abandoned, the crime must be alleviated, though in strict morality, illicit love is always wrong.

I last night sat up again, but I shall do so no more, for I was very stupid today and had a kind of feverish headache. At night Mr Johnson and I supped at the Turk's Head. He talked much for restoring the Convocation of the Church of England to its full powers, and said that religion was much assisted and impressed on the mind by external pomp. My want of sleep sat heavy upon me, and made me like to nod, even in Mr Johnson's company. Such must be the case while we are united with flesh and blood.

THURSDAY 4 AUGUST. This is now my last day in London before I set out upon my travels, and makes a very important period in my journal. Let me recollect my life since this journal began. Has it not passed like a dream? Yes, but I have been attaining a knowledge of the world. I came to town to go into the Guards. How different is my scheme now! I am now upon a less pleasurable but a more rational and lasting plan. Let me pursue it with steadiness and I may be a man of dignity. My mind is strangely agitated. I am happy to think of going upon my travels and seeing the diversity of foreign parts; and yet my feeble mind shrinks somewhat at the idea of leaving Britain in so very short a time from the moment in which I now make this remark. How strange must I feel myself in foreign parts. My mind too is gloomy and dejected at the thoughts of leaving London, where I am so comfortably situated and where I have enjoyed most happiness. However, I shall be the happier for being abroad, as long as I live. Let me be manly. Let me commit myself to the care of my merciful Creator.

THE END OF MY JOURNAL BEFORE MY TRAVELS

'A Crowd of Great Thoughts':

Holland, Rousseau, Voltaire

Boswell's stay in Holland, studying law at Utrecht and visiting Rotterdam, Amsterdam and The Hague, was on the whole a productive but not a very happy one. His first letters, to Temple and Johnston, show him 'hyp'd' (infected with depression, what he called hyphochondria) to a terrible extent, although it later greatly receded. He studied hard if intermittently, and by the end of the year could write to Temple that 'all is clear around me. Upon a retrospective view of that time which I have passed with so much anxiety and so much horror, it looks like a dream.' He had kept in sparing touch with Samuel Johnson, and in closer contact with his school and college friends; letters from his friends contained scandalized reports on the latest exploits of Wilkes and his associate the poet Charles Churchill. We reprint, also, Boswell's answer to a letter from Johnston bearing sad news about his illegitimate son Charles, the result of an encounter with a servant, Peggy Doig, early in 1762.

Boswell's amorous life in Holland was chiefly remarkable for his close friendship with a view to marriage – with the young bel esprit Belle de Zuylen (see p. 395). For several years after Boswell left Holland, they kept up a remarkable flow of correspondence which is fully reprinted in Boswell in Holland in the Yale series (1952). We cannot do it justice here, and Boswell's romantic adventures in Holland are represented by an interlude, in dialogue, with the young widow Madame Geelvinck, whom he was hotly pursuing at the time. At the end of his Dutch stay we reprint his 'Inviolable Plan', a typically Boswellian statement of intent in which he remonstrates with, upbraids and exhorts himself, all the time addressing himself in the second person.

Boswell's real triumph in this section, however, lies in the visits to Rousseau and Voltaire after undertaking a tour of the German courts. His

*relationship with Rousseau in particular was immensely important to him:
his natural charm and amiability won over the philosopher's initial suspicion
(a pattern that Boswell had established with Johnson and was to repeat with
others in the future, such as Paoli). Boswell's record of their conversation is
fascinating and unique, and they led to another important stage in his life,
the visit to Corsica. The call on Rousseau was followed by a shorter one
on Voltaire, of which unfortunately only rough notes – his memoranda –
survive, containing some dialogue between the two in dramatic form. They
are augmented by the letter to Temple describing the meeting, and another
letter, to Voltaire's niece, asking for permission to stay one night under her
uncle's roof.*

*This section, then, begins with Boswell's preparation in London for his
journey to Holland in August 1763, and ends at Ferney, in France, at the
very end of 1764, saying farewell to Voltaire.*

MONDAY 1 AUGUST 1763 [*London*]. Resolve now study in earnest. Consider you're not to be so much a student as a traveller. Be a liberal student. Learn to be reserved. Keep your melancholy to yourself, and you'll easily conceal your joy. Prepare like Father. Mark this and keep in pocket. You are not to consider yourself alone. You have a worthy father whose happiness depends on your behaving so as at least to give no offence, and there is a prudent way to save appearances. Be reserved and calm, and sustain a consistent character. It will please you when high, and when low it will be a sure comfort, though all things seem trifling; and when high again, 'twill delight. So when you return to Auchinleck, you'll have dignity.

TUESDAY 2 AUGUST. Bring up journal. Be with Johnson at two and dress at three. Give out linens, and pack up, and be placid, and get into grave humour for journey, and write out instructions, &c.

[UNDATED MEMORANDUM] Set out for Harwich like Father, grave and comfortable. Be alert all along, yet composed. Speak little, make no intimates. Be in earnest to improve. It is not you alone concerned, but your worthy father. Be reserved in grief, you'll be so in joy. Go abroad with a manly resolution to improve, and correspond with Johnson. Be grateful to him. See to attain a fixed and consistent character, to have dignity. Never despair. Remember Johnson's precepts on experience of mankind. Consider there *is* truth. Consider that when you come home with a settled composure you will enjoy life much, without exhausting spirits and setting yourself up as a buffoon or a jolly dog. Study to be like Lord Chesterfield, manly. You're your own master quite.

Boswell to Johnston

Utrecht, 23 September 1763

My dear Johnston, – I find myself at a loss how to begin this letter. As it is my first to you from a foreign country, I should perhaps break off[1] with a pompous exordium; but a pompous exordium will not offer me its services. Perhaps, too, I should begin with an apology for not writing sooner; but this I imagine you will own is hardly necessary after you have read this page. I am now fairly begun, and shall say no more on the subject. I shall give you my history since I set out from London as well as I can. I tell you beforehand that it is strange and affecting; so do not be suddenly shocked.

I set out upon my travels with a kind of gloom upon my mind. My enthusiastic love of London made me leave it with a heavy heart. It might not have been the case had I been setting out on an immediate tour through the gay regions of Italy and France. But to comply with my father's inclinations I had agreed to pass my first winter at Utrecht, a Dutch university town of which I had received the most disagreeable prepossessions. Mr Samuel Johnson honoured me with his company to Harwich, where he saw me embark and set sail from Britain. I was sick and filled with a crowd of different ideas. But we had a good passage, and landed on Sunday the 7 of August, at twelve at noon. I shall not be tedious with particulars, but give you the great lines of my story. I went to Rotterdam, where I met with Mr Archibald Stewart (Sir Michael's youngest son), who is settled a merchant there. I was not much acquainted with him. But he insisted that I should stay in his house, where I met with every civility. Novelties entertained me for a day or two, and then I went to Leyden and passed some days. I began to turn low-spirited, and set out for Utrecht. I travelled between Leyden and Utrecht nine hours in a sluggish *trek schuit* without any companion, so that I brooded over my own dismal imaginations. I arrived at Utrecht on a Saturday evening. I went to the Nouveau Château d'Anvers. I was shown up to a high bedroom with old furniture, where I had to sit and be fed by myself. At every hour the bells of the great tower played a dreary psalm tune. A deep melancholy seized upon me. I groaned with the idea of living all winter in so shocking a place. I thought myself old and wretched and forlorn. I was worse and worse next day. All the horrid ideas that you can imagine, recurred upon me. I was quite unemployed and had not a soul to speak to but the clerk of the English meeting, who could do me no good. I sunk quite into despair. I thought that at length the time was come that I should grow mad. I actually believed myself so. I went out to the streets, and even in public could not refrain from groaning and weeping bitterly. I said always, 'Poor Boswell! is it come to this? Miserable wretch that I am! what shall I do?' – O my friend, pause here a little and figure to yourself what I endured. I took general speculative views of things; all seemed full of darkness and woe. Tortured in this manner, I determined to leave Utrecht, and next day returned to Rotterdam in a condition that I shudder to recollect.

Boswell to Temple

Rotterdam, 16 August 1763

My dearest Temple, – Expect not in this letter to hear of anything but the misery of your poor friend. I have been melancholy to the most shocking and most tormenting degree. You know the weakness and gloominess of my mind, and you dreaded that this would be the case. I have been at Leyden; from thence I went to Utrecht, which I found to be a most dismal place. I was there entirely by myself and had nobody to speak to. I lived in an inn. I sunk altogether. My mind was filled with the blackest ideas, and all my powers of reason forsook me. Would you believe it? I ran frantic up and down the streets, crying out, bursting into tears, and groaning from my innermost heart. O good GOD! what have I endured! O my friend, how much was I to be pitied! What could I do? I had no inclination for anything. All things appeared good for nothing, all dreary. I thought I should never recover, and that now the time was come when I should really go mad. I could not wait on Count Nassau. I sent him Sir David Dalrymple's letter, said I was obliged to go to Rotterdam upon business of importance, and did not know if I should return.

I set out yesterday at twelve o'clock and came here at night to the house of Mr Archibald Stewart, the gentleman whom Nicholls spoke of. He is a very fine fellow. Though volatile, he has good sense and generosity. I told him my miserable situation and begged his assistance as the most unfortunate of mortals. He was very kind, took me to his house, talked with me, endeavoured to amuse me, and contrived schemes for me to follow.

I am distracted with a thousand ideas. The pain which this affair will give my worthy father shocks me in the most severe degree. And yet, alas! what can I do? But perhaps I should have endured the utmost torment rather than have left Utrecht. But how can a man endure anything when his mind is quite ruined? My mind is just as if it were in a mortification. O Temple! all my resolutions of attaining a consistent character are blown to the winds. All my hopes of being a man of respect are gone. I would give a thousand worlds to have only mere ease. I look back on the days I passed in the Temple with you as on days of the highest satisfaction. And yet, my friend, I cannot but remember that even then we passed many a weary hour. But was not that owing to ourselves? Was it not because we were idle and allowed time to lie heavy on our hands? Alas, what can I do? I cannot read. My mind is destroyed by dissipation. But is not dissipation better than melancholy? Oh, surely, anything is better than this. My dear friend, I am sensible that my wretchedness cannot be conceived by one whose mind is sound. I am terrified that my father will impute all this to mere idleness and love of pleasure. I am not yet determined what to do. Sometimes I think I should no more yield to this than to any other passion. But, indeed, it forces me to yield. It weighs me down. It crushes my spirit. I am filled with shame on account of my weakness. Shall I not be utterly exposed? Shall I not be utterly contemptible?

Boswell to Johnston, Continued

Consider, my friend, what a noble discovery I have made, that melancholy can be got the better of. I don't say entirely. But by vigorously opposing it, I have a conscious satisfaction even in my dark hours; and when I have the 'sunshine of the soul', then I am doubly blest. My dear Johnston! this is a strange letter. I had not room to be full enough. But from what I have said you may by the assistance of your fancy have matter of thought for some time. Pray let my victory have a proper effect upon you. I shall think this late shock a fortunate affair if it help us both to a method of preserving constant satisfaction of soul. I shall write more to you on the subject. I continue my journal, and much entertainment will it afford. I shall transmit it to Temple; and when I return, we shall read it together. O my dear Johnston! felicitate your poor friend restored to comfort! This last affair appears now almost incredible. Luckily I did not write all the time to my father. I hope now to be in no danger.

Pray take care of Charles. Temple will send you a bill for some money soon. Write immediately, before you leave Grange for old Edina. I ever am, my dear Johnston, affectionately yours,

JAMES BOSWELL

Received 26 November, Dempster to Boswell

Manchester Buildings [London], 19 November 1763 Dear Boswell, – The enclosed letter you will perceive by the date was intended for you long ago. I wrote it in Scotland, transmitted it to Fordyce at London, who was by that time on his way to Edinburgh. There I received it from him again, brought it up with myself, and in the hurry of Parliamentary affairs, have carried it a week in my pocket. All this to prove you may be long of hearing from Dempster without being forgotten or neglected by him.

I just came to town time enough to witness the prosecution against Wilkes. The King insisted on his ministers bringing him to punishment, which I am informed they were in some doubts about the possibility of. However his Majesty has found the House of Commons more zealous and unanimous than any of his ministers expected.

The whole House condemned the *North Briton*, No. 45, and three hundred of the members voted it all the hard names which Lord North, Norborne Berkeley, Chace Price or Bamber Gascoyne could bestow upon it. In the course of the debate, Martin of the Treasury said the author of that paper in which his character was traduced and in which he had received a stab in the dark was a coward and a scoundrel. Next morning Wilkes sent him that *North Briton* with his name at bottom.

Martin then challenged Wilkes. They met in Hyde Park, both parties behaved gallantly, and at the second shot Wilkes received a wound in his lower belly, of which, though not in danger, he is at present very ill. Proceedings have been stopped against Wilkes till his recovery.

You must know that Wilkes was just about publishing twelve or thirteen copies (printing, indeed, more properly) of a most extraordinary work entitled *An Essay on Woman*, a parody on *The Essay on Man*, to which he had likewise added, to complete the burlesque, Warburton's notes. The work was inscribed to Fanny Murray, and consisted chiefly of a parallel between that courtesan and the Blessed Virgin, much in favour of the former. Instead of *The Universal Prayer* was subjoined a parody of *Veni Creator*. In point of obscenity and blasphemy, nothing can surpass this work. The Bishop of Gloucester (Warburton) complained of a violation of his character and of a breach of privilege. The House of Lords have addressed his Majesty to have the author prosecuted according to law. Poor devil, how thick misfortunes fall upon him! How lucky your *jeu d'esprit*[2] and Erskine's never was published. It is, you find, a serious affair to laugh at a bishop; and so it should, else their white wigs, lawn-sleeves, sycophantish dispositions, and hypocritical lives would render them eternal subjects of ridicule and contempt.

Adieu, you immense rascal. May you and all your posterity be damned; may the United Provinces be again reclaimed by the Zuider Zee; and if by chance you should escape the deluge, may you be doomed to study law in the next town in the world that resembles Utrecht. Yours very affectionately.

Temple to Boswell

We are all in a combustion here. Mr Wilkes has been wounded in a duel by Mr Martin of the Treasury. It was occasioned by some reflections in the *North Briton* and some words that passed in the House of Commons. Mr Wilkes is better. No. 45 is voted a false, scandalous and seditious libel, and is to be burnt by the hands of the hangman. It is expected Mr Wilkes will be expelled the House tomorrow. The House of Lords are then to send him to Newgate for a profane pamphlet which, however, he never published but they say printing in the eye of the law is publishing, and it seems the Ministry have discovered by low bribery that he had printed thirteen copies for his own use. It is imagined he will leave England and disappoint their revenge. The pamphlet was written by the late Mr Potter, and is entitled *An Essay on Woman*. The notes are Mr Wilkes's, but he supposes them the Bishop of Gloucester's. The frontispiece is a Priapus with this inscription: Σωτὴρ Κόσμου.3 The Lords proceed against him for a breach of privilege in using the name of one of their house. But perhaps this is no news to you.

Do not draw a bill upon me for the guineas, but tell me to whom I must pay it, and I shall do so as soon as ever I can. This is not grammar, but it does not signify. I shall return to Cambridge about the end of next month. Pray write to me soon, and believe me, my dear Boswell, your most affectionate friend,

WILLIAM JOHNSON TEMPLE

Does Mr Johnson write to you? Churchill is to be examined today by the House of Lords about Wilkes's pamphlet. He ran off the other day with a beautiful young lady of fifteen, but is already returned. When the afflicted father asked him when he would send back his daughter, he answered perhaps he would *have done with her* in about ten days. Such a monster!

Nicholls has changed his plan and is to take orders.

WEDNESDAY 30 NOVEMBER

> Men must not still in politics give law;
> No, Kate Macaulay4 too her pen must draw,
> That odious *thing*, a monarch, to revile,
> And drawl of freedom till ev'n Johnson smile.
> Like a Dutch *vrouw* all shapeless, pale and fat,
> That hugs and slabbers her ungainly brat,
> Our Cath'rine sits sublime o'er steaming tea
> And takes her dear Republic on her knee;
> Sings it all songs that ever yet were sung,
> And licks it fondly with her length of tongue.

Received 14 December, Samuel Johnson to Boswell

London, 8 December 1763

Dear Sir, – You are not to think yourself forgotten or criminally neglected that you have had yet no letter from me. I love to see my friends, to hear from them, to talk to them, and to talk of them; but it is not without a considerable effort of resolution that I prevail upon myself to write. Whether I shall easily arrive at an exact punctuality of correspondence, I cannot tell. I shall at present expect that you will receive this in return for two which I have had from you. The first, indeed, gave me an account so hopeless of the state of your mind that it hardly admitted or deserved an answer; by the second I was much better pleased.

You know a gentleman, who, when first he set his foot in the gay world, as he prepared himself to whirl in the vortex of pleasure, imagined a total indifference and universal negligence to be the most agreeable concomitants of youth and the strongest indication of an airy temper and a quick apprehension. Vacant to every object and sensible of every impulse, he thought that all appearance of diligence would deduct something from the reputation of genius; and hoped that he should appear to attain, amidst all the ease of carelessness and all the tumult of diversion, that knowledge and those accomplishments which mortals of the common fabric obtain only by mute abstraction and solitary drudgery. He tried this scheme of life a while, was made weary of it by his sense and his virtue; he then wished to return to his studies; and finding long habits of idleness and pleasure harder to be cured than he expected, still willing to retain his claim to some extraordinary prerogatives, resolved the common consequences of irregularity into an unalterable decree of destiny, and concluded that Nature had originally formed him incapable of rational employment.

Let all such fancies, illusive and destructive, be banished henceforward from your thoughts for ever. Resolve, and keep your resolution; choose, and pursue your choice. This, my dear Boswell, is advice which perhaps has been often given you, and given you without effect. But this advice, if you will not take from others, you must take from your own reflections.

Let me have a long letter from you as soon as you can. I hope you continue your journal. I am, dear Sir, your most affectionate servant,

Sam. Johnson

Boswell to Johnston

Utrecht, 9 April 1764

My dear Friend, – On the 8 of March I received your last letter, which contained the melancholy news of my poor boy's death. It has affected me more than you could have imagined. I had cherished a fond idea. I had warmed my heart with parental affection. I had formed many agreeable plans for the young Charles. All is now wrapped in darkness. All is gone. My dear Sir! let me repeat my sincere sentiments of friendship. Let me again assure you that you are ever dear to me. Your care of my child while he lived was always tender. It showed your attachment to his father. I much approve of your having given him a decent interment and of the company that you selected. Cairnie is a worthy fellow.5 I have been very much obliged to him. I retain a very grateful sense of his kindness, and wish much for an opportunity of being of use to him. I have not written to him since I came abroad. I did not choose to put him to the expense of postage. Pray assure him fully of my sentiments towards him. Let me know what his schemes are, and find out if my writing to him is expected.

My jaunt during the Christmas vacation produced some alteration on my mind. When I returned to Utrecht, I had not the same internal firmness that I had carried from it.

I fell desperately in love with a young, beautiful, amiable and rich widow. . . .

From Boswell's Journals

BOSWELL. At what age, &c, did you first truly fall in love?

MME GEELVINCK. Really! That is certainly being frank.

BOSWELL. Oh, how happy I am! And since you became a widow, have you been in love?

MME GEELVINCK. No. Really!

BOSWELL. But, Madame, I am very much in love. I adore you. Will you make a distinction between Madame Geelvinck and my friend, and give me your advice?

MME GEELVINCK. Yes. But I am truly sorry. I advise you to cure your passion.

BOSWELL. But, Madame, how?

MME GEELVINCK. You have been in love before?

BOSWELL. Yes, I have been in love before, but those passions had no foundation. I always had the help of reason to cure them. But I believe I have never really been in love before now.

MME GEELVINCK. Oh, fancy that!

BOSWELL. But, Madame, is it impossible for you to fall in love?

MME GEELVINCK. I shall never do so.

BOSWELL. There is more good than bad in love.

MME GEELVINCK. I am happy as things stand. I am free. I can go from one city to another. One ought not to give up a certainty.

BOSWELL. But, Madame, have you no thought of a pleasure you have not yet tasted? Only think how you could begin a new life.

MME GEELVINCK. Really, I am sorry that you are like this; it will make you unhappy. I will be your friend.

BOSWELL. Will you be my friend always, for the whole of your life?

MME GEELVINCK. Yes.

BOSWELL. But did you not know that I was in love with you?

MME GEELVINCK. No, really. I thought it was with Mademoiselle de Zuylen; and I said nothing about it.

BOSWELL. Oh, my dear Madame, what heavenly pleasure I have at this moment in looking at you. I am speaking as you told me to – as though I were alone. I can trust in you; you will not expose me?

MME GEELVINCK. No, I assure you on my conscience.

BOSWELL. You believe that I am in love? I swear it to you by all the hope I have of happiness in this existence or the other. You believe that I am sincere?

MME GEELVINCK. If you are not, you are horrible.

BOSWELL. You believe me, then?

MME GEELVINCK. Yes, I believe you when you say it.

BOSWELL. But I ought not to despair. One must have a little indulgence. Oh, if you please, say only that perhaps—

MME GEELVINCK. That would be to behave like a coquette.

BOSWELL. But say that perhaps—, something like that. – But what do you think on the subject of religion?

MME GEELVINCK. Have you not the same religion in Scotland as we?

BOSWELL. Yes, but I have found women here who thought themselves wiser than other people, women who did not believe it.

MME GEELVINCK. At any rate, those who have the hope of another world lose nothing. Those who do not believe it must be in a bad way.

BOSWELL. But do you believe that GOD has given a revelation of his will?

MME GEELVINCK. Yes.

BOSWELL. Oh, I am glad of it. Yes, Madame, you have in the Christian faith a system conformable to the perfections of GOD, confirmed by proofs which are sufficient to comfort us.

MME GEELVINCK. Yes, and there are mysteries; but although I do not understand mathematical problems, am I to deny the truth of mathematics?

BOSWELL. Madame, can you believe that only six months ago I was completely heedless, and gave great concern to the most excellent of fathers? I changed completely. Have I not made progress?

MME GEELVINCK [*changing the subject*]. I would sacrifice myself for my son.

BOSWELL. That is a delicate sentiment. I could not love you so much as I do if I did not love your child.

MME GEELVINCK. If I should marry again, my husband could not love my son like his own, and perhaps I should not love my other children so much.

BOSWELL. But if you should find a man of whom you can be certain that he loves you sincerely, and that through duty and affection he would do everything for your son – is it not possible to find such a man?

MME GEELVINCK. It is possible.

BOSWELL. Think, Madame, you will lose half your life. You will leave the world without having tasted of love. – Will you have the generosity to write me only one or two lines from The Hague? That will convince me that you are sincerely my friend.

MME GEELVINCK. Yes, provided that you do not answer.

BOSWELL. You are afraid that I would say something so tender as to touch your pity. But I have permission to write if I am reasonable?

MME GEELVINCK. Yes.

BOSWELL. Tell me, everybody is looking at me with envy: is it right to be vain?

MME GEELVINCK. Um.

BOSWELL. Do you know my address?

MME GEELVINCK. Yes, *chez* Bart.

BOSWELL. I am happy now, but when I am alone, I shall think of a thousand things I ought to have said. How happy I am to have had an opportunity to confess all this to you. It is, I suppose, necessary for it to remain unknown?

MME GEELVINCK. Yes, do not tell it to anyone.

BOSWELL. It gives me some relief to have confessed it instead of letting it lie in gloomy silence. What must I say to people who ask me questions?

MME GEELVINCK. Oh, you have wit enough to parry such questions.

BOSWELL. But after you have come back from The Hague, if I cannot forget my passion, what will you do? But I must not ask. Say only, 'We shall see.' Are you fickle?

MME GEELVINCK. No, I do not have that kind of disposition.

BOSWELL. As for me, I am very fickle, so much so that I am never sure of myself; and I assure you, if you were in love with me, I should advise you not to be.

MME GEELVINCK. That is most extraordinary.

BOSWELL. It is a pity you are so rich, although I am very fond of money.

MME GEELVINCK. Shame!

BOSWELL. But listen. I am not greedy, yet, after religion, my chief aim is to uphold a respectable and ancient family of which I am the representative, and so –

MME GEELVINCK. I leave my heart with you.

Boswell to Johnston, Continued

This passion tore and hurt my mind. I was seized with a severe cold. My nerves were relaxed, my blood was thickened. Low spirits approached. I heard of Charles's death. It shocked me. It filled me with gloomy reflections on the uncertainty of life, and that every post might bring me accounts of the departure of those whom I most regarded. I saw all things as so precarious and vain that I had no relish of them, no views to fill my mind, no motives to incite me to action. I groaned under those dismal truths which nothing but a lucky oblivion prevents from weighing down the most vivacious souls. Black melancholy again took dominion over me. All my old dreary and fretful feelings recurred. I was much worse on this account, that after my first severe fit on coming to Utrecht, I really believed that I had conquered spleen for ever, and that I should never again be overcome by it. I lived in this persuasion for four months. I had my dull hours. But I considered myself as a soldier. I endured such hardships; but I kept my post.

You may conceive what I felt on the sad conviction that my hopes were fanciful. Oh, how I was galled! Oh, how did I despise myself! I must mention one circumstance which is very hard. When I am attacked by melancholy, I seldom enjoy the comforts of religion. A future state seems so clouded, and my attempts towards devotion are so unsuitable, that I often withdraw my mind from divine subjects lest I should communicate to the most sublime and cheering doctrines my own imbecility and sadness. In short, for some weeks past I have suffered much.

I shall be here till July or August. My route after that is not yet fixed. You shall hear it particularly. Come, my friend, let us both determine to be manly; let us 'resist the devil and he will flee far from us'. Here is my plan. I am to travel. I am to return to Scotland, put on the gown, remain advocate or get into Parliament, and at last be comfortably settled in a good office. I hope also to do good at Auchinleck. The great point is to be always employed, as my worthy father says. Upon this principle he has always been happy. Long may he be so.

I have now proper ideas of religion. That is the most important article indeed. I am determined to act my part with vigour, and I doubt not to have a reward. My mind will go always stronger by discipline. Even this last attack has not been unrepelled by me. I really believe that these grievous complaints should not be vented; they should be considered as absurd chimeras, whose reality should not be allowed in words. One thing I am sure of, that if a man can believe himself well, he will be really so. The dignity of human nature is a noble preservative of the soul. Let us consider ourselves as immortal beings, who though now in a state inferior to our faculties, may one day hope to exult in the regions of light and glory. My dear Johnston, let us retain this splendid sentiment. Let us take all opportunities of elevating our minds by devotion, and let us indulge the expectation of meeting in heaven. But, at the same time, let us do our best in the state where GOD has placed us. Let us imitate the amiable Pitfour. Who is a better member of society? Yet who is a greater saint?

Write to me very fully. I will disdain to own that the melancholy fiend can get the better of me. I even hesitated if I should inform *you* of this last conflict. But to my friend I will own every weakness. My great loss[6] is an inconstancy of mind. I never view things in the same light for a month together. Are you so? This letter carries its own apology. Write soon and give me full advices, and put my future life in Britain in agreeable colours. I have need of your assistance. May GOD bless you, my dear friend, prays yours ever,

JAMES BOSWELL

Boswell to Temple

Utrecht, 17 April 1764

My dearest Temple, – You must not grudge a shilling extraordinary this post. Were I now in London, you should be put to much more expense. I would hurry you away to Drury Lane or to Covent Garden, to Ranelagh or to the tavern. Perhaps a chariot might be ordered to the Temple Gate, and we might drive with gay velocity to Richmond or to Windsor. You see my foreign airs. Nothing will serve me but a chariot. It is so long since I have seen a post-chaise that I have almost forgot there is such a machine.

Could I but see my worthy friend at this moment! Could I but behold the wonder and pleasure which spreads over his countenance! But sea and land conspire to separate us. It is impossible for me to talk to you. I therefore sit down to write. My letter of last night, which is enclosed in this, is the sedate production of a man just recovered from a severe fit of melancholy. The letter which you are now reading is the spontaneous effusion of a man fully restored to life and to joy, whose blood is bounding through his veins, and whose spirits are at the highest pitch of elevation. Good heaven! what is Boswell? Last night he was himself. Today he is more than himself.

Now the cloud is removed. All is clear around me. Upon a retrospective view of that time which I have passed with so much anxiety and so much horror, it looks like a dream. What had I to fear? What cause of terror existed then which does not equally exist at present? Yet let me remember this truth: I am subject to melancholy, and of the operations of melancholy, reason can give no account. Ah! Temple! is it not morally certain that I shall ere long be as much depressed as ever?

Shall I not again groan beneath a weight of woe? Shall I not despise this very letter which conveys to you the accounts of my exceeding elevation? Perhaps not. Perhaps I shall never again be melancholy. This is possible; much more so than those chimeras which I have shuddered to think of. Formerly I have had vivacious days. But I had no solid cause to hope for their continuance. My mind had no stable principles. I was the mere slave of caprice. Now I can calmly revolve my plan of conduct. I can 'know myself a Man'!

I wrote to my father an account of my late dreary state of mind. Worthy man! I hope to give him satisfaction. He is perhaps too anxiously devoted to utility. He tells me that he thinks little time should be spent in travelling; and that he would have me make a tour through some of the German courts, or through Flanders and part of France, and return to Scotland against winter. You will agree with me in thinking this scheme greatly too confined. I laid my account with travelling for at least a couple of years after leaving this. I must however compound matters. I shall insist upon being abroad another winter, and so may pursue the following plan.

I shall set out from Utrecht about the middle of June. I shall make the tour of The Netherlands, from thence proceed to Germany, where I shall visit the Courts of Brunswick and Lüneburg, and about the end of August arrive at Berlin. I shall pass a month there. In the end of September I shall go to the Court of Baden-Durlach, from thence through Switzerland to Geneva. I shall visit Rousseau and Voltaire, and about the middle of November shall cross the Alps and get fairly into Italy. I shall there pass a delicious winter, and in April shall pass the Pyrenees and get into Spain, remain there a couple of months, and at last come to Paris. Upon this plan, I cannot expect to be in Britain before the autumn of 1765. Pray give me your opinion of it. I think it is an excellent plan. Perhaps I allow myself too little time for it. However, I may perhaps prevail with my father to allow me more time. When a son is at a distance, he can have great influence upon an affectionate parent. I would by no means be extravagant; I would only travel genteelly.

Miss Stewart is now Lady Maxwell. So much for that scheme, which I consulted you upon some months ago. There are two ladies here, a young, handsome, amiable widow with £4,000 a year, and Mademoiselle de Zuylen, who has only a fortune of £20,000. She is a charming creature. But she is a *savante* and a *bel esprit*, and has published some things. She is much my superior. One does not like that. One does not like a widow, neither. You won't allow me to yoke myself here? You *will* have me married to an Englishwoman?

I have written now my most intimate thoughts. Tomorrow I go to The Hague for a week. GOD bless you. – Write soon. I ever remain, your most affectionate friend,

JAMES BOSWELL

Inviolable Plan
To be read over frequently

Written by James Boswell in October 1763 at Utrecht.

You have got an excellent heart and bright parts. You are born to a respectable station in life. You are bound to do the duties of a *Laird* of Auchinleck. For some years past you have been idle, dissipated, absurd and unhappy. Let those years be thought of no more. You are now determined to form yourself into a man. Formerly all your resolutions were overturned by a fit of the spleen. You believed that you had a real distemper. On your first coming to Utrecht you yielded to that idea. You endured severe torment. You was pitiful and wretched. You was in danger of utter ruin. This severe shock has proved of the highest advantage. Your friend Temple showed you that idleness was your sole disease. The Rambler showed you that vacuity, gloom and fretfulness were the causes of your woe, and that you was only afflicted as others are. He furnished you with principles of philosophy and piety to support the soul at all times. You returned to Utrecht determined. You studied with diligence. You grew quite well. This is a certain fact. You must never forget it. Nor attempt to plead a real incurable distemper; for you cured it, when it was at its very worst, merely by following a proper plan with diligence and activity. This is a great era in your life; for from this time you fairly set out upon solid principles to be a man.

Your worthy father has the greatest affection for you and has suffered much from your follies. You are now resolved to make reparation by a rational and prudent conduct. Your dear mother is anxious to see you do well. All your friends and relations expect that you will be an honour to them and will be useful to them as a lawyer, and make them happy as an agreeable private gentleman.

You have been long without a fixed plan and have felt the misery of being unsettled. You are now come abroad at a distance from company with whom you lived as a frivolous and as a ludicrous fellow. You are to attain habits of study, so that you may have constant entertainment by yourself, nor be at the mercy of every company; and to attain propriety of conduct, that you may be respected. You are not to set yourself to work to become stiff and unnatural. You must avoid affectation. You must act as you ought to do in the general tenor of life, and that will establish your character. Lesser things will form of course.

Remember that idleness renders you quite unhappy. That then your imagination broods over dreary ideas of its own forming, and you become contemptible and wretched. Let this be no more. Let your mind be filled with nobler principles. Remember religion and morality. Remember the dignity of human nature. Remember everything may be endured.

Have a sense of piety ever on your mind, and be ever mindful that this is subject to no change, but will last you as long as life and support you at death. Elevate your soul by prayer and by contemplation without mystical enthusiasm. Preserve a just, clear and agreeable idea of the divine Christian religion. It is very clearly proved. You cannot expect demonstration. There is virtue in faith; in giving a candid assent upon examination. Keep quite clear of gloomy notions which have nothing to do with the mild and elegant religion of Jesus as it is beautifully displayed in the New Testament. Have this faith always firm. Be steady to the Church of England, whose noble worship has always raised your mind to exalted devotion and meditation on the joys of heaven. Be firm to religion, and at all times show your displeasure to profanity, like a decent gentleman. But don't enter into disputes in riotous and ludicrous companies where sacred things cannot be properly weighed.

Without a real plan, life is insipid and uneasy. You have an admirable plan before you. You are to return to Scotland, be one of the Faculty of Advocates, have constant occupation, and a prospect of being in Parliament, or having a gown. You can live quite independent and go to London every year; and you can pass some months at Auchinleck, doing good to your tenants and living hospitably with your neighbours, beautifying your estate, rearing a family, and piously preparing for immortal felicity. To have all these advantages, firmness is necessary. Have constant command of yourself. Restrain ludicrous talents and, by habit, talk always on some useful subject, or enliven conversation with moderate cheerfulness. Keep to study ever to improve. Have your own plan and don't be put out of it. Your friends Temple and Johnston will assist you to do well. Never talk of yourself, nor repeat what you hear in a company. Be firm, and persist like a philosopher.

Now remember what you have resolved. Keep firm to your plan. Life has much uneasiness; that is certain. Always remember that, and it will never surprise you. Remember also life has much happiness. *To bear* is the noble power of man. This gives true dignity. Trifles are more frequently the causes of our disturbance than great matters. Be prepared therefore for uneasy trifles. You have indulged antipathies to places and persons. That is the sign of a weak and diseased mind. A hysteric lady or a sickly peevish boy may be so swayed. But let not antipathies move a man. It is not sensibility. You can cure it and at all times do so.

Resolve to make constant experiments, and be more and more confirmed in your theory. A man has much the command of his ideas. Check little uneasy ones. Encourage little pleasing ones. He who has baseless antipathies is foolishly deprived of much pleasure. Your great loss is too much wildness of fancy and ludicrous imagination. These are fine if regulated and given out in moderation, as Mr Addison has done and as Sir David Dalrymple does. The pleasure of laughing is great. But the pleasure of being a respected gentleman is greater.

You have a character to support. You have to keep up the family of Auchinleck. To do this, your mind must be settled and filled with knowledge, and with good plain ideas of common sense and the practice of mankind, although you may be a Church of England man and indulge any other favourite principles; only never talk at random. Every man should be the best judge how to regulate his own conduct; there are many minutiae particular to every character. For some time be excessively careful against rattling, though cheerful to listen to others. What may be innocent to others is a fault to you till you attain more command of yourself. Temperance is very necessary for you, so never indulge your appetites without restraint. Be assured that restraint is always safe and always gives strength to virtue. Exercise must never be neglected, for without that you cannot have health, and health contributes much to render you fit for every duty. Never indulge the sarcastical Scotch humour. Be not jocular and free, and then you will not be hurt by the jocularity and freedom of others. If you are polite, you will seldom meet with uneasy rubs in conversation.

Τίμα σεαυτόν: reverence thyself. But at the same time be afraid for thyself. Ever keep in mind your firm resolutions. If you should at times forget them, don't be cast down. Return with redoubled vigour to the field of propriety. Upon the whole you will be an excellent character. You will have all advantages from the approbation of the World, in your rational plan, which may be enlarged as you see occasion. But yield not to whims, nor ever be rash.

At the end of that year, after a tour of the German Courts, Boswell surfaces at Neuchâtel, on his way to see Rousseau.

SATURDAY 1 DECEMBER. Betimes I set out in a good coach and in agreeable indolence drove to Neuchâtel. I sent to Colonel Chaillet a letter which my Lord Marischal had given me to him. He asked me to sup with him. But I had already eaten heartily of excellent trout.

SUNDAY 2 DECEMBER. I waited on Colonel Chaillet, whom I found to be a sensible, hearty, brave old fellow. I dined at my inn, the Treize Cantons, with my landlord, Meuron. I was a little hipped. At four Madame Chaillet carried me to a company where we played cards.

MONDAY 3 DECEMBER. I let Jacob go for a week to see his relations, which made him very happy. One great object which I have ever had in view since I left Britain has been to obtain the acquaintance, and if possible the regard, of Rousseau. I was informed that he lived in a wild valley, five leagues from Neuchâtel. I set out early this morning, mounted on a little horse, with a *Reysesac7* which held some shirts. I was joined by Abraham François, a merchant here. My horse was lazy; he lent me a spur and a whip, and on we jogged very cordially. He taught me a French song, 'Sous le nom de l'amitié, Phillis, je vous adore', to a minuet tune. I amused myself with him, and this amusement formed an excellent contrast to the great object which occupied my mind.

We had a fine, hard road amidst mountains covered with snow. We stopped at Brot, the half-way inn. Monsieur Sandoz, the landlord, had a handsome daughter, very lively and very talkative, or rather chatty, to give the young lady a lighter word. She told us, 'Monsieur Rousseau often comes and stays here several days with his housekeeper, Mademoiselle Le Vasseur. He is a very amiable man. He has a fine face. But he doesn't like to have people come and stare at him as if he were a man with two heads. Heavens! the curiosity of people is incredible. Many, many people come to see him; and often he will not receive them. He is ill, and doesn't wish to be disturbed. Over there is a pass where I have gone with him and Mademoiselle Le Vasseur. We have dined there. He will walk in such wild places for an entire day. Gentlemen who have come here have asked me a thousand questions: "And his housekeeper, is she young? Is she pretty?"' All this chat of Mademoiselle helped to frighten me.

There was here a stone-cutter who had wrought for Voltaire. The most stupid of human beings will remember some anecdote or other of a great man whom he has had occasion to see. This stone-cutter told me, 'Sir, there used to be a horse that pulled a cart at Ferney, and Monsieur Voltaire always said, "Poor horse! you are thin, you are like me."' Any trifle of such a genius has a value.

Abraham François and I drank a glass of good wine and pursued our journey. We passed one place exactly like Killiecrankie and another where a group of broken rocks seemed every moment ready to tumble down upon us. It will most certainly tumble ere long. Monsieur Rousseau lives in the village of Môtiers. A league on this side of it, Abraham parted from me, after I had returned him his whip and his spur. I advanced with a kind of pleasing trepidation. I wished that I might not see Rousseau till the moment that I had permission to wait upon him. I perceived a white house with green window-boards. He mentions such a one in *Emile*. I imagined it might perhaps be his, and turned away my eyes from it. I rode calmly down the street, and put up at the Maison de Village. This inn is kept by Madame Grandpierre, a widow, and her two daughters, fat, motherly maidens. The eldest received me. I told her, 'I have let my servant go and see his friends and relations, so I am alone. You must take good care of me.' Said she, 'We shall do our best.'

I asked for Monsieur Rousseau. I found he kept himself very quiet here, as my landlady had little or nothing to chatter concerning him. I had heard all that could be said as to his being difficult of access. My Lord Marischal had given me a card with compliments to him, which I was sure would procure me admission. Colonel Chaillet had given me a letter to the Châtelain, Monsieur Martinet, the Principal Justice of the place, who could introduce me without difficulty. But my romantic genius, which will never be extinguished, made me eager to put my own merit to the severest trial. I had therefore prepared a letter to Monsieur Rousseau, in which I informed him that an ancient Scots gentleman of twenty-four was come hither with the hopes of seeing him. I assured him that I deserved his regard, that I was ready to stand the test of his penetration. Towards the end of my letter I showed him that I had a heart and a soul. I have here given no idea of my letter. It can neither be abridged nor transposed, for it is really a masterpiece. I shall ever preserve it as a proof that my soul can be sublime. I dressed and dined and sent my letter *chez* Monsieur Rousseau, ordering the maid to leave it and say she'd return for the answer, so that I might give him time to consider a little, lest perhaps he might be ill and suddenly refuse to see me. I was filled with anxiety. Is not this romantic madness? Was I not sure of admittance by my recommendations? Could I not see him as any other gentleman would do? No: I am above the vulgar crowd. I would have my merit fairly tried by this great judge of human nature. I must have things in my own way. If my bold attempt succeeds, the recollection of it will be grand as long as I live. But perhaps I may appear to him so vain, or so extraordinary, that he may be shocked by such a character and may not admit me. I shall then be in a pretty situation, for I shall be ashamed to present my recommendations. But why all this doubt and uneasiness? It is the effect of my melancholy timidity. What! can the author of *Eloisa* be offended at the enthusiasm of an ingenuous mind? But if he does admit me, I shall have a very difficult character to support; for I have written to him with unusual elevation, and given him an idea of me which I shall hardly come up to.

Boswell to Rousseau

Val de Travers, 3 December 1764
Sir: – I am a Scots gentleman of ancient family. Now you know my rank. I am twenty-four years old. Now you know my age. Sixteen months ago I left Great Britain a completely insular being, knowing hardly a word of French. I have been in Holland and in Germany,

but not yet in France. You will therefore excuse my handling of the language. I am travelling with a genuine desire to improve myself. I have come here in the hope of seeing you.

I have heard, Sir, that you are very difficult, that you have refused the visits of several people of the first distinction. For that, Sir, I respect you the more. If you admitted all those who from vanity wished to be able to say, 'I have seen him,' your house would not longer be the retreat of exquisite genius or elevated piety, and I should not be striving so eagerly to be received into it.

I present myself, Sir, as a man of singular merit, as a man with a feeling heart, a lively but melancholy spirit. Ah, if all that I have suffered does not give me singular merit in the eyes of Monsieur Rousseau, why was I made as I am? Why did he write as he has written?

Do you ask if I have recommendations? Surely you do not need them? In the commerce of the world a recommendation is necessary in order to protect people who lack penetration from impostors. But you, Sir, who have made such deep study of human nature, can you be deceived in a character? I think of you thus: excepting for the incomprehensible essence of the soul, you have a perfect knowledge of all the principles of body and mind, of their movements, their sentiments; in short, of everything they can do, of everything they can acquire which truly affects man as man. And yet, Sir, I dare present myself before you. I dare to put myself to the test. In cities and in courts, where there are numerous companies, one can disguise one's self, one can sometimes dazzle the eyes of the greatest philosophers. But for my part, I put myself to the severest test. It is in the silence and the solitude of your sacred retreat that you shall judge of me, and think you in such circumstances I shall be able to dissimulate?

Your writings, Sir, have melted my heart, have elevated my soul, have fired my imagination. Believe me, you will be glad to have seen me. You know what Scots pride is. Sir, I am coming to see you in order to make myself more worthy of a nation that has produced a Fletcher of Saltoun and a Lord Marischal. Forgive me, Sir, I feel myself moved. I cannot restrain myself. O dear Saint-Preux![8] Enlightened Mentor! Eloquent and amiable Rousseau! I have a presentiment that a truly noble friendship will be born today.

I learn with deep regret, Sir, that you are often indisposed. Perhaps you are so at present. But I beg you not to let that prevent you from receiving me. You will find in me a simplicity that will put you to no trouble, a cordiality that may help you forget your pains.

I have much to tell you. Though I am only a young man, I have experienced a variety of existence that will amaze you. I find myself in serious and delicate circumstances concerning which I eagerly hope to have the counsel of the author of the *Nouvelle Héloïse*. If you are the charitable man I believe you to be, you cannot hesitate to grant it to me. Open your door, then, Sir, to a man who dares to tell you that he deserves to enter it. Place your confidence in a stranger who is different. You will not regret it. But I beg you, be alone. In spite of all my enthusiasm, after having written to you in this fashion, I know not if I would not prefer never to see you than to see you for the first time in company. I await your reply with impatience.

BOSWELL

MONDAY 3 DECEMBER [*continued*]. To prepare myself for the great interview, I walked out alone. I strolled pensive by the side of the River Reuse in a beautiful wild valley surrounded by immense mountains, some covered with frowning rocks, others with clustering pines, and others with glittering snow. The fresh, healthful air and the romantic prospect around me gave me a vigorous and solemn tone. I recalled all my former ideas of J. J. Rousseau, the admiration with which he is regarded over all Europe, his *Héloïse*, his *Emile*: in short, a crowd of great thoughts. This half hour was one of the most remarkable that I ever passed.

I returned to my inn, and the maid delivered to me a card with the following answer from Monsieur Rousseau: 'I am ill, in pain, really in no state to receive visits. Yet I cannot deprive myself of Mr Boswell's, provided that out of consideration for the state of my health, he is willing to make it short.'

My sensibility dreaded the word 'short'. But I took courage, and went immediately. I found at the street door Mademoiselle Le Vasseur waiting for me. She was a little, lively, neat French girl and did not increase my fear. She conducted me up a darkish stair, then opened a door. I expected, 'Now I shall see him' – but it was not so. I entered a room which serves for vestibule and for kitchen. My fancy formed many, many a portrait of the wild philosopher. At length his door opened and I beheld him, a genteel black man in the dress of an Armenian. I entered saying, 'Many, many thanks.' After the first looks and bows were over, he said, 'Will you be seated? Or would you rather take a turn with me in the room?' I chose the last, and happy I was to escape being formally placed upon a chair. I asked him how he was. 'Very ill. But I have given up doctors.' 'Yes, yes; you have no love for them.' As it is impossible for me to relate exactly our conversation, I shall not endeavour at order, but give sentences as I recollect them.

BOSWELL. 'The thought of your books, Sir, is a great source of pleasure to you?' ROUSSEAU. 'I am fond of them; but when I think of my books, so many misfortunes which they have brought upon me are revived in my memory that really I cannot answer you. And yet my books have saved my life.' He spoke of the Parlement of Paris: 'If any company could be covered with disgrace, that would be. I could plunge them into deep disgrace simply by printing their edict against me on one side, and the law of nations and equity on the side opposite. But I have reasons against doing so at present.' BOSWELL. 'We shall have it one day, perhaps?' ROUSSEAU. 'Perhaps.'

I was dressed in a coat and waistcoat, scarlet with gold lace, buck-skin breeches and boots. Above all I wore a greatcoat of green camlet lined with fox-skin fur, with the collar and cuffs of the same fur. I held under my arm a hat with a solid gold lace, at least with the air of being solid. I had it last winter at The Hague. I had a free air and spoke well, and when Monsieur Rousseau said what touched me more than ordinary, I seized his hand, I thumped him on the shoulder. I was without restraint. When I found that I really pleased him, I said, 'Are you aware, Sir, that I am recommended to you by a man you hold in high regard?'

ROUSSEAU. 'Ah! My Lord Marischal?' BOSWELL. 'Yes, Sir; my Lord furnished me with a note to introduce me to you.' ROUSSEAU. 'And you were unwilling to take advantage of it?' BOSWELL. 'Nay, Sir; I wished to have a proof of my own merits.' ROUSSEAU. 'Sir, there would have been no kind of merit in gaining access to me by a note of Lord Marischal's. Whatever he sends will always find a welcome from me. He is my protector, my father; I would venture to say, my friend.' One circumstance embarrassed me a little: I had forgotten to bring with me from Neuchâtel my Lord's billet. But a generous consciousness of innocence and honesty gives a freedom which cannot be counterfeited.

I told Monsieur Rousseau, 'To speak truly, I have forgotten to bring his letter with me; but you accept my word for it?'

ROUSSEAU. 'Why, certainly. Numbers of people have shown themselves ready to serve me in their own fashion; my Lord Marischal has served me in mine. He is the only man on earth to whom I owe an obligation.' He went on, 'When I speak of kings, I do not include the King of Prussia. He is a king quite alone and apart. That force of his! Sir, there's the great matter, to have force – revenge, even. You can always find stuff to make something out of. But when force is lacking, when everything is small and split up, there's no hope. The French, for example, are a contemptible nation.' BOSWELL. 'But the Spaniards, Sir?' ROUSSEAU. 'Yes, you will find great souls in Spain.' BOSWELL. 'And in the mountains of Scotland. But since our cursed Union, ah—' ROUSSEAU. 'You undid yourselves.' BOSWELL. 'Truly, yes. But I must tell you a great satisfaction given me by my Lord. He calls you Jean Jacques out of affection. One day he said to me, "Jean Jacques is the most grateful man in the world. He wanted to write my brother's life; but I begged him rather to write the life of Mr Fletcher of Saltoun, and he promised me he would do so."' ROUSSEAU. 'Yes, Sir; I will write it with the greatest care and pleasure. I shall offend the English, I know. But that is no matter. Will you furnish me with some anecdotes on the characters of those who made your Treaty of Union, and details that cannot be found in the historians?' BOSWELL. 'Yes, Sir; but with the warmth of an ancient Scot.' ROUSSEAU. 'By all means.'

He spoke of ecclesiastics. 'When one of these gentlemen provides a new explanation of something incomprehensible, leaving it as incomprehensible as before, everyone cries, "Here's a great man." But, Sir, they will tell you that no single point of theology may be neglected, that every stone in God's building, the mystic Jerusalem, must be considered as sacred. "But they have added stones to it. – Here, take off this; take off that! Now you see, the building is admirably complete, and you have no need to stand there to hold it up." "But *we* want to be necessary!" Ah!—

'Sir, you don't see before you the bear you have heard tell of. Sir, I have no liking for the world. I live here in a world of fantasies, and I cannot tolerate the world as it is.' BOSWELL. 'But when you come across fantastical men, are they not to your liking?' ROUSSEAU. 'Why, Sir, they have not the same fantasies as myself. – Sir, your country is formed for liberty. I like your habits. You and I feel at liberty to stroll here together without talking. That is more than two Frenchmen can do. Mankind disgusts me. And my housekeeper tells me that I am in far better humour on the days when I have been alone than on those when I have been in company.' BOSWELL. 'There has been a great deal written against you, Sir.' ROUSSEAU. 'They have not understood me. As for Monsieur Vernet at Geneva, he is an Arch-Jesuit, that is all I can say of him.'

BOSWELL. 'Tell me, Sir, do you not find that I answer to the description I gave you of myself?' ROUSSEAU. 'Sir, it is too early for me to judge. But all appearances are in your favour.' BOSWELL. 'I fear I have stayed too long. I shall take the honour of returning tomorrow.' ROUSSEAU. 'Oh, as to that, I can't tell.' BOSWELL. 'Sir, I shall stay quietly here in the village. If you are able to see me, I shall be enchanted; if not, I shall make no complaint.' ROUSSEAU. 'My Lord Marischal has a perfect understanding of man's feelings, in solitude no less than in society. I am overwhelmed with visits from idle people.' BOSWELL. 'And how do they spend their time?' ROUSSEAU. 'In paying compliments. Also I get a prodigious quantity of letters. And the writer of each of them believes that he is the only one.' BOSWELL. 'You must be greatly surprised, Sir, that a man who has not the honour of your acquaintance should take the liberty of writing to you?' ROUSSEAU. 'No. I am not at all surprised. For I got a letter like it yesterday, and one the day before yesterday, and others many times before that.' BOSWELL. 'Sir, your very humble servant. – What, you are coming further?' ROUSSEAU. 'I am not coming with you. I am going for a walk in the passage. Goodbye.'

I had great satisfaction after finding that I could support the character which I had given of myself, after finding that I should most certainly be regarded by the illustrious Rousseau. I had a strange kind of feeling after having at last seen the author of whom I had thought so much. I sat down immediately and wrote to Dempster. I sat up too late.

Boswell to Dempster

Val de Travers, 3 December 1764

My dear Dempster, – Where am I now, think you? In the village which contains Rousseau. I arrived here this day at noon from Neuchâtel, in

order to wait upon the Wild Philosopher. I had heard all that could
be said of his being difficult of access, but was not a bit discouraged.
I wrote him a letter which I was sure would recommend me, for I told
him my character and claimed his regard as what I had a title to. I
wrote with manly confidence, and told him I was not afraid to stand
the test of his penetration.

Dempster, I have been with him. I have been most politely received.
Would you see easy elegance, see the author of *Héloïse*. I must not
pretend to give you in a hasty letter an idea of our conversation. Let
me only assure you of one fact. The Corsicans have actually applied
to Monsieur Rousseau to give them a set of laws. He has answered,
'It exceeds my power but not zeal.' He is like to break his heart at
this French invasion. Oh, Dempster, how much pain did it give me
to see Rousseau distressed; and yet an hour and a half run on ere I
could think of quitting him. We have made an agreement. I shall stay
quietly in this village for some days, and he will see me as much as
his health permits. I am here in a beautiful wild valley surrounded by
immense mountains. I am supremely happy. I write this partly from a
pardonable vanity, partly from a desire to give you pleasure. Adieu,
Dempster. A good Parliament.

BOSWELL

TUESDAY 4 DECEMBER. At five I went to Monsieur Rousseau, whom I
found more gay than he had been yesterday. We joked on Mademoiselle
Le Vasseur for keeping him under lock and key. She, to defend herself,
said he had another door to get out at. Said he, 'Ah, Mademoiselle,
you can keep nothing to yourself.'

He gave me the character of the Abbé de Saint-Pierre, 'a man
who did good, simply because he chose to do good: a man without
enthusiasm. One might say that he was passionately reasonable. He
would come to a discussion armed with notes, and he used to say, "I
shall be sneered at for this," "I shall get a hissing for that." It was
all one to him. He carried his principles into the merest trifles. For
example, he used to wear his watch suspended from a button on his
coat, because that was more convenient. As he was precluded from
marriage, he kept mistresses, and made no secret of it. He had a
number of sons. He would allow them to adopt none but the most
strictly useful professions; for example, he would not allow any son

of his to be a wig-maker. "For", said he, "so long as Nature continues to supply us with hair, the profession of wig-making must always be full of uncertainty." He was completely indifferent to the opinion of men, saying that they were merely overgrown children. After paying a long visit to a certain lady, he said to her, "Madam, I perceive I am wearisome to you, but that is a matter of no moment to me. You amuse me." One of Louis XIV's creatures had him turned out of the Academy for a speech he had made there. Yet he perpetually visited this man. "For", said he, "he acted in his own interests, and I bear him no grudge for that. He amuses me. He has no grounds for being offended with me. I have grounds for offence against him, but I am not offended." In short, he continued to call on this Academician, until the latter put a stop to it because he found it disagreeable to see a man whom he had injured. He had plenty of good sense, but a faulty style: long-winded and diffuse, yet always proving his point. He was a favourite with women; he would go his own way independently, and he won respect. If you become a Member of Parliament, you must resemble the Abbé de Saint-Pierre. You must stick to your principles.' BOSWELL. 'But, then, one must be very well instructed.' ROUSSEAU. 'Ah, sure enough. You must have a well-furnished head.' BOSWELL. 'But, Sir, a Member of Parliament who behaves as a strictly honest man is regarded as a crazy fool.' ROUSSEAU. 'Well then, you must be a crazy fool of a Member; and believe me, such a man will be respected – that is, if he holds consistently by his principles. A man who changes round on every occasion is another affair.'

He talked of his *Plan for Perpetual Peace, taken from the Abbé de Saint-Pierre*. I frankly owned that I had not read it. 'No?' said he – then took one down from his bookcase and gave it me. I asked him smilingly if he would not put his name upon it. He laughed heartily at me. I talked to him of the German album and how I had been forced to take one; but that except what was written by the person who gave it me, there was nothing in it. Said he, 'Then your album is *album*.'9 There was a sally for you. A precious pearl; a pun made by Rousseau. He said, 'I have seen the Scottish Highlanders in France. I love the Scots; not because my Lord Marischal is one of them but because he praises them. *You* are irksome to me. It's my nature. I cannot help it.' BOSWELL. 'Do not stand on ceremony with me.' ROUSSEAU. 'Go away.'

Mademoiselle always accompanies me to the door. She said, 'I have been twenty-two years with Monsieur Rousseau; I would not give up my place to be Queen of France. I try to profit by the good advice he gives me. If he should die, I shall have to go into a convent.' She is a very good girl, and deserves to be esteemed for her constancy to a man so valuable. His simplicity is beautiful. He consulted Mademoiselle and her mother on the merits of his *Héloïse* and his *Emile*.

I supped with the Châtelain. He said, 'We two are alone, so as to be free to talk of my Lord Marischal and nothing else.' We were hearty.

WEDNESDAY 5 DECEMBER. When I waited upon Monsieur Rousseau this morning, he said, 'My dear Sir, I am sorry not to be able to talk with you as I would wish.' I took care to waive such excuses, and immediately set conversation a-going. I told him how I had turned Roman Catholic and had intended to hide myself in a convent in France. He said, 'What folly! I too was a Catholic in my youth. I changed, and then I changed back again. I returned to Geneva and was readmitted to the Protestant faith. I went again among Catholics, and used to say to them, "I am no longer one of you"; and I got on with them excellently.' I stopped him in the middle of the room and I said to him, 'But tell me sincerely, are you a Christian?' I looked at him with a searching eye. His countenance was no less animated. Each stood steady and watched the other's looks. He struck his breast, and replied, 'Yes. I pique myself upon being one.' BOSWELL. 'Sir, the soul can be sustained by nothing save the Gospel.' ROUSSEAU. 'I feel that. I am unaffected by all the objections. I am weak; there may be things beyond my reach; or perhaps the man who recorded them made a mistake. I say, God the Father, God the Son, God the Holy Ghost.'

BOSWELL. 'But tell me, do you suffer from melancholy?' ROUSSEAU. 'I was born placid. I have no natural disposition to melancholy. My misfortunes have infected me with it.' BOSWELL. 'I, for my part, suffer from it severely. And how can I be happy, I, who have done so much evil?' ROUSSEAU. 'Begin your life anew. God is good, for he is just. Do good. You will cancel all the debt of evil. Say to yourself in the morning, "Come now, I am going to *pay off* so much evil." Six well-spent years will pay off all the evil you have committed.' BOSWELL. 'But what do you think of cloisters, penances and remedies of that sort?' ROUSSEAU. 'Mummeries, all of them, invented by men. Do not be guided by men's judgements, or you will find yourself tossed to and fro perpetually. Do not base your life on the judgements of others; first, because they are as likely to be mistaken as you are, and further, because you cannot know that they are telling you their true thoughts; they may be impelled by motives of interest or convention to talk to you in a way not corresponding to what they really think.' BOSWELL. 'Will you, Sir, assume direction of me?' ROUSSEAU. 'I cannot. I can be responsible only for myself.' BOSWELL. 'But I shall come back.' ROUSSEAU. 'I don't promise to see you. I am in pain. I need a chamber-pot every minute.' BOSWELL. 'Yes, you will see me.' ROUSSEAU. 'Be off; and a good journey to you.'

About six I set out.[10]

Memorandum of Topics to Discuss with Rousseau

Suicide. Hypochondria. A real malady: family madness. Self-destruction: your arguments, not answered. – Was poet, praised in journals. – Suppose not slave to appetites, more than in marriage, but will have Swiss girl, amiable, &c. Quite adventure. [I would name my natural sons] Marischal Boswell, Rousseau Boswell. Anxious to see if children sound ere marry. Hurt nobody. If clear against this, can abstain, can live as Templar in Malta. Would have no deceit, all clear. – Scots familiarity and sarcasm: used to repress it by reserve and silence, but this rendered hypochondriac. May I not be gay, and fight the first man who is rude with me? Coward from youth; how could it be otherwise? Now firm. His sentiment of duels. – Court of London? No. Envoy? No. Parliament or home, and lawyer. Old estate, good principle. Propagate family great thing of all. Shall I suffer gloom as [expiation of] evil? And you, O great philosopher, will you befriend me? Am I not worthy? Tell me. You have no interest, no *ménagement*. If I am, take care of me. I tell you that the idea of being bound even by the finest thread to the most enlightened of philosophers, the noblest of souls, will always uphold me, all my life. Come, then, let us make a compact: 'I will meet you in heaven.' Say that, and it will suffice for my entire life.

FRIDAY 14 DECEMBER. At eight I got on horseback and had for my guide a smith called Dupuis. I said, 'Since when (*depuis quand*) have you had that name?' I passed the Mountain Lapidosa, which is monstrously steep and in a great measure covered with snow. I was going to Rousseau, which consideration levelled the roughest mountains. I arrived at Môtiers before noon. I alighted at Rousseau's door. Up and I went and found Mademoiselle Le Vasseur, who told me, 'He is very ill.' 'But can I see him for a moment?' 'I will find out. Step in, Sir.' I found him sitting in great pain.

ROUSSEAU. 'I am overcome with ailments, disappointments and sorrow. I am using a probe. – Every one thinks it my duty to attend to him.' BOSWELL. 'That is most natural; and are you not pleased to find you can be of so much help to others?' ROUSSEAU. 'Why—'

I had left with him when I was last here what I called a 'Sketch of My Life', in which I gave him the important incidents of my history and my melancholy apprehensions, and begged his advice and friendship. It was an interesting piece. He said, 'I have read your Memoir. You have been gulled. You ought never to see a priest.' BOSWELL. 'But can I yet hope to make something of myself?' ROUSSEAU. 'Yes. Your great difficulty is that you think it so difficult a matter. Come back in the afternoon. But put your watch on the table.' BOSWELL. 'For how long?' ROUSSEAU. 'A quarter of an hour, and no longer.' BOSWELL. 'Twenty minutes.' ROUSSEAU. 'Be off with you! – Ha! Ha!' Notwithstanding the pain he was in, he was touched with my singular sally and laughed most really. He had a gay look immediately.

I dined in my old room with the two boarders. After dinner I walked out. There had fallen much rain, and the *vallon* was all overflowed. Nature looked somewhat different from the time that I was first here. I was sorry that such a scene was subject to any change.

At four I went to Monsieur Rousseau. 'I have but a moment allowed me; I must use it well. – Is it possible to live amongst other men, and to retain singularity?' ROUSSEAU. 'Yes, I have done it.' BOSWELL. 'But to remain on good terms with them?' ROUSSEAU. 'Oh, if you want to be a wolf, you must howl. – I attach very little importance to books.' BOSWELL. 'Even to your own books?' ROUSSEAU. 'Oh, they are just rigmarole.' BOSWELL. 'Now you are howling.' ROUSSEAU. 'When I put my trust in books, I was tossed about as you are – though it is rather by talking that you have been tossed. I had nothing stable here' (striking his head) 'before I began to meditate.' BOSWELL. 'But you would not have meditated to such good purpose if you had not read.' ROUSSEAU. 'No. I should have meditated to better purpose if

I had begun sooner.' BOSWELL. 'But I, for example, would never have had the agreeable ideas I possess of the Christian religion, had I not read "The Savoyard's Creed". – Yet, to tell the truth, I can find no certain system. Morals appear to me an uncertain thing. For instance, I should like to have thirty women. Could I not satisfy that desire?' ROUSSEAU. 'No!' BOSWELL. 'Why?' ROUSSEAU. 'Ha! Ha! If Mademoiselle were not here, I would give you a most ample reason why.' BOSWELL. 'But consider: if I am rich, I can take a number of girls; I get them with child; propagation is thus increased. I give them dowries, and I marry them off to good peasants who are very happy to have them. Thus they become wives at the same age as would have been the case if they had remained virgins, and I, on my side, have had the benefit of enjoying a great variety of women.' ROUSSEAU. 'Oh, you will be landed in jealousies, betrayals and treachery.' BOSWELL. 'But cannot I follow the Oriental usage?' ROUSSEAU. 'In the Orient the women are kept shut up, and that means keeping slaves. And, mark you, their women do nothing but harm, whereas ours do much good, for they do a great deal of work.' BOSWELL. 'Still, I should like to follow the example of the old Patriarchs, worthy men whose memory I hold in respect.' ROUSSEAU. 'But are you not a citizen? You must not pick and choose one law here and another law there; you must take the laws of your own society. Do your duty as a citizen, and if you hold fast, you will win respect. I should not talk about it, but I would do it. – And as for your lady,[11] when you go back to Scotland you will say, "Madam, such conduct is against my conscience, and there shall be no more of it." She will applaud you; if not, she is to be despised.' BOSWELL. 'Suppose her passion is still lively, and she threatens to tell her husband what has happened unless I agree to continue our intrigue?' ROUSSEAU. 'In the first place, she will not tell him. In the second, you have no right to do evil for the sake of good.' BOSWELL. 'True. None the less, I can imagine some very embarrassing situations. And pray tell me how I can expiate the evil I have done?' ROUSSEAU. 'Oh, Sir, there is no expiation for evil except good.'

A beautiful thought this. Nevertheless, I maintained my doctrine of satisfaction by punishment. Yes, I must ever think that immutable justice requires atonement to be made for transgressions, and this atonement is to be made by suffering. This is the universal idea of all nations, and seems to be a leading principle of Christianity. I gave myself full scope; for since I left England I have not had anybody to whom I could lay open entirely my mind till I found Monsieur Rousseau.

I asked him, 'When I get to France and Italy, may I not indulge in the gallantries usual to those countries, where the husbands do not resent your making love to their wives? Nay, should I not be happier as the citizen of such a nation?' ROUSSEAU. 'They are corpses. Do you want to be a corpse?' He was right. BOSWELL. 'But tell me, has a virtuous man any true advantages, is he really better off than a man given up to sensuality?' ROUSSEAU. 'We cannot doubt that we are spiritual beings; and when the soul escapes from this prison, from this flesh, the virtuous man will find things to his liking. He will enjoy the contemplation of happy souls, nobly employed. He will say, "I have already lived a life like that." Whereas those who experience nothing but the vile passions which have their origin in the body will be dissatisfied by the spectacle of pleasures which they have no means of enjoying.'

BOSWELL. 'Upon my word, I am at a loss how to act in this world; I cannot determine whether or not I should adopt some profession.' ROUSSEAU. 'One must have a great plan.' BOSWELL. 'What about those studies on which so much stress is laid? Such as history, for instance?' ROUSSEAU. 'They are just amusements.' BOSWELL. 'My father desires me to be called to the Scottish bar; I am certainly doing right in satisfying my father; I have no such certainty if I follow my light inclinations. I must therefore give my mind to the study of the laws of Scotland.' ROUSSEAU. 'To be sure; they are your tools. If you mean to be a carpenter, you must have a plane.' BOSWELL. 'I do not get on well with my father. I am not at my ease with him.' ROUSSEAU. 'To be at ease you need to share some amusement.' BOSWELL. 'We look after the planting together.' ROUSSEAU. 'That's too serious a business. You should have some amusement that puts you more on an equal footing: shooting, for example. A shot is missed and a joke is made of it, without any infringement of respect. You enjoy a freedom which you take for granted. – Once you are involved in a profession, you must keep on with it even though another, and apparently better, should present itself. If you keep changing, you can achieve nothing.'

(I should have observed that when I pushed the conversation on women, Mademoiselle went out, and Monsieur Rousseau said, 'See now, you are driving Mademoiselle out of the room.' She was now returned.) He stopped, and looked at me in a singular manner. 'Are you greedy?' BOSWELL. 'Yes.' ROUSSEAU. 'I am sorry to hear it.' BOSWELL. 'Ha! Ha! I was joking, for in your books you write in favour of greed. I know what you are about to say, and it is just what I was hoping to hear. I wanted to get you to invite me to dinner. I had a great desire to share a meal with you.' ROUSSEAU. 'Well, if you are not greedy, will you dine here tomorrow? But I give you fair warning, you will find yourself badly off.' BOSWELL. 'No, I shall not be badly off; I am above all such considerations.' ROUSSEAU. 'Come then at noon; it will give us time to talk.' BOSWELL. 'All my thanks.' ROUSSEAU. 'Good evening.'

Mademoiselle carried me to the house of a poor woman with a great many children whom Monsieur Rousseau aids with his charity. I contributed my part. I was not pleased to hear Mademoiselle repeat to the poor woman just the common consolatory sayings. She should have said something singular.

Memorandum of Topics to Discuss with Rousseau

From time to time a letter to rekindle me. – I am a fine fellow; really, I am so. – Not own *ridicules*? – Yet tell, and assure me as to women. Be honest, and I'll be firm. – As to prayer, what shall I do? – How do with my neighbours? – *Emile*, is it now practicable? Could he live in the world? – Young man with Savoyard, you or not? – Voltaire rogue. – Journal seven hundred pages. – Must I force study? I appear *instruit*. – Zélide's character; pronounce at once, what is she? – Worthy father, may I travel even though [he disapproves]? – Mahomet, what? Is there expiation or not by Christ? May I not just hold my peace in Scotland, not to offend tenants? – Is it worth the trouble, an individual, all for me? I am but one.

SATURDAY 15 DECEMBER. At seven in the morning I got on horseback and rode about a league to St Sulpice, where I saw the source of the Reuse, the river which runs through the Val de Travers. It is a prodigious romantic place. I could not determine whether the water gushes in an immediate spring from the rock, or only issues out here, having pierced the mountain, upon which is a lake. The water comes forth with great violence. All around here I saw mountains and rocks as at Hartfell in Annandale. Some of the rocks were in great courses like huge stone walls, along which grew the towering pines which we call pitch firs, and which are much handsomer than the firs of Scotland.

I was full of fine spirits. Gods! Am I now then really the friend of Rousseau? What a rich assemblage of ideas! I relish my felicity truly in such a scene as this. Shall I not truly relish it at Auchinleck? I was quite gay, my fancy was youthful, and vented its gladness in sportive sallies. I supposed myself in the rude world. I supposed a parcel of young fellows saying, 'Come, Boswell, you'll dine with us today?' 'No, gentlemen, excuse me; I'm engaged. I dine today with Rousseau.' My tone, my air, my native pride when I pronounced this! Temple! You would have given half a guinea to see me at that moment.

I returned to my inn, where I found the Court of Justice of the *vallon* assembled. I entered and was amused to hear a Justice of Peace and honest farmers and a country minister all talking French.

I then went to Monsieur Rousseau. 'I hope your health is better today.' ROUSSEAU. 'Oh, don't speak of it.' He seemed unusually gay. Before dinner we are all so, if not made to wait too long. A keen appetite gives a vivacity to the whole frame.

I said, 'You say nothing in regard to a child's duties towards his parents. You tell us nothing of your *Emile*'s father.' ROUSSEAU. 'Oh, he hadn't any. He didn't exist.' It is, however, a real pity that Monsieur Rousseau has not treated of the duties between parents and children. It is an important and a delicate subject and deserves to be illustrated by a sage of so clear a judgement and so elegant a soul.

He praised the *Spectator*. He said, 'One comes across allegories in it. I have no taste for allegories, though your nation shows a great liking for them.'

I gave him very fully the character of Mr Johnson. He said with force, 'I should like that man. I should respect him. I would not disturb his principles if I could. I should like to see him, but from a distance, for fear he might maul me.' I told him how averse Mr Johnson was to write, and how he had his levée. 'Ah,' said he, 'I understand. He is a man who enjoys holding forth.' I told him Mr Johnson's *bon mot* upon the innovators: that truth is a cow which will yield them no more milk, and so they are gone to milk the bull. He said, 'He would detest me. He would say, "Here is a corrupter: a man who comes here to milk the bull."'

I had diverted myself by pretending to help Mademoiselle Le

Vasseur to make the soup. We dined in the kitchen, which was neat and cheerful. There was something singularly agreeable in this scene. Here was Rousseau in all his simplicity, with his Armenian dress, which I have surely mentioned before now. His long coat and nightcap made him look easy and well.

Our dinner was as follows: 1. A dish of excellent soup. 2. A *bouilli* of beef and veal. 3. Cabbage, turnip and carrot. 4. Cold pork. 5. Pickled trout, which he jestingly called tongue. 6. Some little dish which I forget. The dessert consisted of stoned pears and of chestnuts. We had red and white wines. It was a simple, good repast. We were quite at our ease. I sometimes forgot myself and became ceremonious. 'May I help you to some of this dish?' ROUSSEAU. 'No, Sir. I can help myself to it.' Or, 'May I help myself to some more of that?' ROUSSEAU. 'Is your arm long enough? A man does the honours of his house from a motive of vanity. He does not want it forgotten who is the master. I should like every one to be his own master, and no one to play the part of host. Let each one ask for what he wants; if it is there to give, let him be given it; otherwise, he must be satisfied without. Here you see true hospitality.' BOSWELL. 'In England, it is quite another matter. They do not want to be at ease; they are stiff and silent, in order to win respect.' ROUSSEAU. 'In France, you find no such gloom among people of distinction. There is even an affectation of the utmost liberty, as though they would have you understand, "We stand in no fear of losing our dignity." That is a more refined form of self-esteem.'

BOSWELL. 'Well, and do you not share that yourself?' ROUSSEAU. 'Yes, I confess that I like to be respected; but only in matters of importance.' BOSWELL. 'You are so simple. I expected to find you quite different from this: the Great Rousseau. But you do not see yourself in the same light as others do. I expected to find you enthroned and talking with a grave authority.' ROUSSEAU. 'Uttering oracles? Ha! Ha! Ha!' BOSWELL. 'Yes, and that I should be much in awe of you. And really your simplicity might lay you open to criticism; it might be said, "Monsieur Rousseau does not make himself sufficiently respected." In Scotland, I assure you, a very different tone must be taken to escape from the shocking familiarity which is prevalent in that country. Upon my word, I cannot put up with it. Should I not be justified in forestalling it by fighting a duel with the first man who should treat me so, and thus live at peace for the rest of my life?' ROUSSEAU. 'No. That is not allowable.

It is not right to stake one's life on such follies. Life is given us for objects of importance. Pay no heed to what such men say. They will get tired of talking to a man who does not answer them.' BOSWELL. 'If you were in Scotland, they would begin at the very start by calling you Rousseau; they would say, "Jean Jacques, how goes it?" with the utmost familiarity.' ROUSSEAU. 'That is perhaps a good thing.' BOSWELL. 'But they would say, "Poh! Jean Jacques, why do you allow yourself all these fantasies? You're a pretty man to put forward such claims. Come, come, settle down in society like other people." And they would say it to you with a sourness which I am quite unable to imitate for you.' ROUSSEAU. 'Ah, that's bad.'

There he felt the thistle, when it was applied to himself on the tender part. It was just as if I had said, 'Hoot, Johnnie Rousseau man, what for hae ye sae mony figmagairies?'¹² Ye're a bonny man indeed to mauk siccan a wark; set ye up. Canna ye just live like ither fowk?' It was the best idea could be given in the polite French language of the rude Scots sarcastical vivacity.

BOSWELL. 'I have leanings towards despotism, let me tell you. On our estate, I am like an ancient laird, and I insist on respect from the tenants.' ROUSSEAU. 'But when you see an old man with white hair, do you, as a young man, have no feelings at all? Have you no respect for age?' BOSWELL. 'Yes. I have even on many occasions been very affable. I have talked quite freely with the tenants.' ROUSSEAU. 'Yes, you forgot yourself, and became a man.' BOSWELL. 'But I was sorry for it afterwards. I used to think, "I have lowered myself."' ROUSSEAU. 'Ha! Ha! Ha!'

BOSWELL. 'Yesterday I thought of asking a favour of you, to give me credentials as your ambassador to the Corsicans. Will you make me his Excellency? Are you in need of an ambassador? I offer you my services: Mr Boswell, Ambassador Extraordinary of Monsieur Rousseau to the Isle of Corsica.' ROUSSEAU. 'Perhaps you would rather be King of Corsica?' BOSWELL. 'On my word! Ha! Ha! Not I. It exceeds my powers' (with a low bow). 'All the same, I can now say, "I have refused a crown."'

ROUSSEAU. 'Do you like cats?' BOSWELL. 'No.' ROUSSEAU. 'I was sure of that. It is my test of character. There you have the despotic instinct of men. They do not like cats because the cat is free and will never consent to become a slave. He will do nothing to your order, as the other animals do.' BOSWELL. 'Nor a hen, either.' ROUSSEAU. 'A hen would obey your orders if you could make her understand them. But a cat will understand you perfectly and not obey them.' BOSWELL. 'But a cat is ungrateful and treacherous.' ROUSSEAU. 'No. That's all untrue. A cat is an animal that can be very much attached to you; he will do anything you please out of friendship. I have a cat here. He has been brought up with my dog; they play together. The cat will give the dog a blow with his tail, and the dog will offer him his paw.' (He described the playing of his dog and cat with exquisite eloquence, as a fine painter draws a small piece.) He put some victuals on a trencher, and made his dog dance round it. He sung to him a lively air with a sweet voice and great taste. 'You see the ballet. It is not a gala performance, but a pretty one all the same.' I think the dog's name was Sultan. He stroked him and fed him, and with an arch air said, 'He is not much *respected*, but he gets well looked after.'

BOSWELL. 'Suppose you were to walk in upon a drinking-party of young folk, who should treat you with ridicule, would you be above minding it?' ROUSSEAU. 'It would put me out of countenance. I am shy by nature. I have often, for example, been overcome by the raillery of women. A party such as you describe would be disagreeable to me. I should leave it.' I was comforted to find that my sensibility is not despicable weakness.

BOSWELL. 'The Anglican Church is my choice.' ROUSSEAU. 'Yes. It is no doubt an excellent religion, but it is not the Gospel, which is all simplicity. It is another kind of religion.' BOSWELL. 'The Gospel, at the outset, was simple but rigorous too, as when Paul says it is better not to marry than to marry.' ROUSSEAU. 'Paul? But that is not the Gospel.' BOSWELL. 'Then you have no liking for Paul?' ROUSSEAU. 'I respect him, but I think he is partly responsible for muddling your head. He would have been an Anglican clergyman.'

BOSWELL. 'Mr Johnson is a Jacobite, but he has a pension of £300 sterling from the King.' ROUSSEAU. 'He ought not to have accepted a pension.' BOSWELL. 'He says that he does not drink the health of King James with the wine given him by King George.' ROUSSEAU. 'But you should not employ the substance given you by this wine in attacking King George.'

Mademoiselle said, 'Shall you, Sir, see Monsieur de Voltaire?' BOSWELL. 'Most certainly.' (To Rousseau.) 'Monsieur de Voltaire has no liking for you. That is natural enough.' ROUSSEAU. 'Yes. One does not like those whom one has greatly injured. His talk is most enjoyable; it is even better than his books.' BOSWELL. 'Have you looked at the *Philosophical Dictionary?*' ROUSSEAU. 'Yes.' BOSWELL. 'And what of it?' ROUSSEAU. 'I don't like it. I am not intolerant, but he deserves—' (I forget his expression here.) 'It is very well to argue against men's opinions; but to show contempt, and to say, "You are idiots to believe this," is to be personally offensive. – Now go away.' BOSWELL. 'Not yet. I will leave at three o'clock. I have still five and twenty minutes.' ROUSSEAU. 'But I can't give you five and twenty minutes.' BOSWELL. 'I will give you even more than that.' ROUSSEAU. 'What! of my own time? All the kings on earth cannot give me my own time.' BOSWELL. 'But if I had stayed till tomorrow I should have had five and twenty minutes, and next day another five and twenty. I am not taking those minutes. I am making you a present of them.' ROUSSEAU. 'Oh! You are not stealing my money, you are giving it to me.' He then repeated part of a French satire ending with 'And whatever they leave you, they count as a gift.' BOSWELL. 'Pray speak for me, Mademoiselle.' (To Rousseau.) 'I have an excellent friend here.' ROUSSEAU. 'Nay, but this is a league.' BOSWELL. 'No league at all.' Mademoiselle said, 'Gentlemen, I will tell you the moment the clock strikes.' ROUSSEAU. 'Come; I need to take the air after eating.'

We walked out to a gallery pendant upon his wall. BOSWELL. 'In the old days I was a great mimic. I could imitate everyone I saw. But I have left it off.' ROUSSEAU. 'It is a dangerous talent, for it compels one to seize upon all that is small in a character.' BOSWELL. 'True. But I assure you there was a nobleness about my art, I carried mimicry to such a point of perfection. I was a kind of virtuoso. When I espied any singular character I would say, "It must be added to my collection."' He laughed with all his nerves: 'You are an odd character.' BOSWELL. 'I am a physiognomist, believe me. I have studied that art very attentively, I assure you, and I can rely on my conclusions.' He seemed to agree to this. ROUSSEAU. 'Yet I think the features of the face vary between one nation and another, as do accent and tone of voice; and these signify different feelings among different peoples.' This observation struck me as new and most ingenious. BOSWELL. 'But in time one learns to understand them.'

ROUSSEAU. 'The roads are bad. You will be late.' BOSWELL. 'I take the bad parts on foot; the last league of the way is good. – Do you think that I shall make a good barrister before a court of justice?' ROUSSEAU. 'Yes. But I regret that you have the talents necessary for defending a bad case.'

BOSWELL. 'Have you any commands for Italy?' ROUSSEAU. 'I will send a letter to Geneva for you to carry to Parma.' BOSWELL. 'Can I send you anything back?' ROUSSEAU. 'A few pretty tunes from the opera.' BOSWELL. 'By all means. Oh, I have had so much to say, that I have neglected to beg you to play me a tune.' ROUSSEAU. 'It's too late.'

MADEMOISELLE. 'Sir, your man is calling for you to start.' Monsieur Rousseau embraced me. He was quite the tender Saint-Preux. He kissed me several times, and held me in his arms with elegant cordiality. Oh, I shall never forget that I have been thus. ROUSSEAU. 'Goodbye. You are a fine fellow.' BOSWELL. 'You have shown me great goodness. But I deserved it.' ROUSSEAU. 'Yes. You are malicious; but 'tis a pleasant malice, a malice I don't dislike. Write and tell me how you are.' BOSWELL. 'And you will write to me?' ROUSSEAU. 'I know not how to reach you.' BOSWELL. 'Yes, you shall write to me in Scotland.' ROUSSEAU. 'Certainly; and even at Paris.' BOSWELL. 'Bravo! If I live twenty years, you will write to me for twenty years?' ROUSSEAU. 'Yes.' BOSWELL. 'Goodbye. If you live for seven years, I shall return to Switzerland from Scotland to see you.' ROUSSEAU. 'Do so. We shall be old acquaintances.' BOSWELL. 'One word more. Can I feel sure that I am held to you by a thread, even if of the finest? By a hair?' (Seizing a hair of my head.) ROUSSEAU. 'Yes. Remember always that there are points at which our souls are bound.' BOSWELL. 'It is enough. I, with my melancholy, I, who often look on myself as a despicable being, as a good-for-nothing creature who should make his exit from life – I shall be upheld for ever by the thought that I am bound to Monsieur Rousseau. Goodbye. Bravo! I shall live to the end of my days.' ROUSSEAU. 'That is undoubtedly a thing one must do. Goodbye.'

Mademoiselle accompanied me to the outer door. Before dinner she told me, 'Monsieur Rousseau has a high regard for you. The first time you came, I said to him, "That gentleman has an honest face. I am sure you will like him." ' I said, 'Mademoiselle is a good judge.' 'Yes,' said she, 'I have seen strangers enough in the twenty-two years that I have been with Monsieur Rousseau, and I assure you that I have sent many of them packing because I did not fancy their way of talking.' I said, 'You have promised to let me have news of you from time to time.' 'Yes, Sir.' 'And tell me what I can send you from Geneva. Make no ceremony.' 'Well, if you will, a garnet necklace.'

We shook hands cordially, and away I went to my inn. My eldest landlady looked at me and said, 'Sir, I think you are crying.' This I retain as a true elogium of my humanity. I replied, 'No. Yet I am unhappy to leave Monsieur Rousseau. I will see you again in seven years.' I got a-horseback and rode by the house of Monsieur Rousseau. Mademoiselle waited for me at the door, and cried, '*Bon voyage*; write to us.' Good creature. I rode gravely to Yverdon contemplating how this day will appear to my mind some years hence.

Boswell to Temple

Château de Ferney, 28 December 1764
My dear Temple, – Think not that I insult you when you read the full tale of my supreme felicity. After thanking you for your two letters of the month of October, I must pour forth the exultation of a heart swelling with joy. Call me bombast. Call me what you please. Thus will I talk. No other style can give the most distant expression of the feelings of Boswell. If I appear ridiculous, it is because our language is deficient.

I completed my tour through the German courts. At all of them I found state and politeness. At Baden-Durlach I found worth, learning and philosophy united in the Reigning Margrave. He is a prince whose character deserves to be known over Europe. He is the best sovereign, the best father, the most amiable man. He has travelled a great deal. He has been in England and he speaks the language in amazing perfection. During the time that I stayed at his court, I had many, many conversations with him. He showed me the greatest distinction. The inspector of his cabinet, his library-keeper and the officers of his court had orders to do everything in their power to render my stay agreeable. Madame la Margrave, who paints in perfection and has a general taste for the fine arts, treated me in the most gracious manner. The Margrave told me how happy he was to have me with him. I asked him if I could do anything that might show my gratitude. He replied, 'I shall write to you sometimes. I shall be very happy to receive your letters.' He was in earnest. I have already been honoured with a letter from His Most Serene Highness. I have promised to return and pass some weeks at his court. He is not far from France.

I have been with Rousseau. He lives in the village of Môtiers-Travers in a beautiful valley surrounded with immense mountains. I went thither from Neuchâtel. I determined to put my real merit to the severest test by presenting myself without any recommendation before the wild illustrious philosopher. I wrote him a letter in which I told him all my worth, and claimed his regard as what I had a title to. 'Open your door, then, Sir, to a man who dares to tell you that he deserves to enter it.' Such was my bold and manly style. He received me, although he was very ill.

And whence do I now write to you, my friend? From the château of Monsieur de Voltaire. I had a letter for him from a Swiss colonel at The Hague. I came hither Monday and was presented to him. He received me with dignity and that air of a man who has been much in the world which a Frenchman acquires in perfection. I saw him for about half an hour before dinner. He was not in spirits. Yet he gave me some brilliant sallies. He did not dine with us, and I was obliged to post away immediately after dinner, because the gates of Geneva shut before five and Ferney is a good hour from town. I was by no means satisfied to have been so little time with the monarch of French literature. A happy scheme sprung up in my adventurous mind. Madame Denis, the niece of Monsieur de Voltaire, had been extremely good to me. She is fond of our language. I wrote her a letter in English begging her interest to obtain for me the privilege of lodging a night under the roof of Monsieur de Voltaire, who, in opposition to our sun, rises in the evening. I was in the finest humour and my letter was full of wit. I told her, 'I am a hardy and a vigorous Scot. You may mount me to the highest and coldest garret. I shall not even refuse to sleep upon two chairs in the bedchamber of your maid. I saw her pass through the room where we sat before dinner.' I sent my letter on Tuesday by an express. It was shown to Monsieur de Voltaire, who with his own hand wrote this answer in the character of Madam Denis: 'You will do us much honour and pleasure. We have few beds. But you will (*shall*) not sleep on two chairs. My uncle, though very sick, hath guessed at your merit. I know it better; for I have seen you longer.' Temple, I am your most obedient. How do you find yourself? Have you got such a thing as an old friend in this world? Is he to be valued or is he not?

I returned yesterday to this enchanted castle. The magician appeared a very little before dinner. But in the evening he came into the drawing-room in great spirits. I placed myself by him. I touched the keys in unison with his imagination. I wish you had heard the music. He was all brilliance. He gave me continued flashes of wit. I got him to speak English, which he does in a degree that made me now and then start up and cry, 'Upon my soul this is astonishing!' When he talked our language he was animated with the soul of a Briton. He had bold flights. He had humour. He had an extravagance; he had a forcible oddity of style that the most comical of our *dramatis personae* could not have exceeded. He swore bloodily, as was the fashion when he was in England. He hummed a ballad; he repeated nonsense. Then he talked of our Constitution with a noble enthusiasm. I was proud to hear this from the mouth of an illustrious Frenchman. At last we came upon religion. Then did he rage. The company went to supper. Monsieur de Voltaire and I remained in the drawing-room with a great Bible before us; and if ever two mortal men disputed with vehemence, we did. Yes, upon that occasion he was one individual and I another. For a certain portion of time there was a fair opposition between Voltaire and Boswell. The daring bursts of his ridicule confounded my understanding. He stood like an orator of ancient Rome. Tully was never more agitated than he was. He went too far. His aged frame trembled beneath him. He cried, 'Oh, I am very sick; my head turns round,' and he let himself gently fall upon an easy chair. He recovered. I resumed our conversation, but changed the tone. I talked to him serious and earnest. I demanded of him an honest confession of his real sentiments. He gave it me with candour and with a mild eloquence which touched my heart. I did not believe him capable of thinking in the manner that he declared to me was 'from the bottom of his heart'. He expressed his veneration – his love – of the Supreme Being, and his entire resignation to the will of Him who is All-wise. He expressed his desire to resemble the Author of Goodness by being good himself. His sentiments go no farther. He does not inflame his mind with grand hopes of the immortality of the soul. He says it may be, but he knows nothing of it. And his mind is in perfect tranquillity. I was moved; I was sorry. I doubted his sincerity. I called to him with emotion, 'Are you sincere? are you really sincere?' He answered, 'Before God, I am.' Then with the fire of him whose tragedies have so often shone on the theatre of Paris, he said, 'I suffer much. But I suffer with patience and resignation; not as a Christian – but as a man.'

Temple, was not this an interesting scene? Would a journey from Scotland to Ferney have been too much to obtain such a remarkable interview? I have given you the great lines. The whole conversation of the evening is fully recorded, and I look upon it as an invaluable treasure. One day the public shall have it. It is a present highly worthy of their attention. I told Monsieur de Voltaire that I had written eight quarto pages of what he had said. He smiled and seemed pleased. Our important scene must not appear till after his death. But I have a great mind to send over to London a little sketch of my reception at Ferney, of the splendid manner in which Monsieur de Voltaire lives, and of the brilliant conversation of this celebrated author at the age of seventy-two.¹³ The sketch would be a letter, addressed to you, full of gaiety and full of friendship. I would send it to one of the best public papers or magazines. But this is probably a flight of my over-heated mind. I shall not send the sketch unless you approve of my doing so.

Thursday 27 December. Notes on Voltaire's English Conversation

VOLTAIRE. 'Shakespeare often two good lines, never six. A madman, by G–d, a buffoon at Bartholomew Fair. No play of his own, all old stories.' Chess. 'I shall lose, by G–d, by all the saints in Paradise. Ah, here I am riding on a black ram, like a whore as I am. – Falstaff from the Spaniards.' BOSWELL. 'I'll tell you why we admire Shakespeare.' VOLTAIRE. 'Because you have no taste.' BOSWELL. 'But, Sir—' VOLTAIRE. 'Et penitus toto divisos orbe Britannos¹⁴ – all Europe is against you. So you are wrong.' BOSWELL. 'But this is because we have the most grand imagination.' VOLTAIRE. 'The most wild. – Pope drives a chaise with a couple of neat trim nags but Dryden a coach and six, with postilions and all.' Repeated well some passages of Dryden. BOSWELL. 'What is memory? Where lodge all our ideas?' VOLTAIRE. 'As Thomson says, where sleep the winds when it is calm? Thomson was a great painter. Milton, many beauties and many faults, as there is nothing perfect in this damned world. His imitators are unintelligible. But when he writes well, he is quite clear.' BOSWELL. 'What think you of our comedy?' VOLTAIRE. 'A great deal of wit, a great deal of plot, and a great deal of bawdy-houses.' BOSWELL. 'What think you of *Fingal?*' VOLTAIRE. 'Why, it is like a psalm of David. But there are noble passages in it. There are in both. The Homer of Scotland.'

BOSWELL. 'You speak good English.' VOLTAIRE. 'Oho! I have scraps of Latin for the vicar. – Addison is a great genius. His character shines in his writings. – Dr Clarke was a metaphysical clock. A proud priest. He thought he had all by demonstration; and he who thinks so is a madman.' BOSWELL. 'Johnson is a most orthodox man, but very learned; has much genius and much worth.' VOLTAIRE. 'He is then a dog. A superstitious dog. No worthy man was ever superstitious.' BOSWELL. 'He said the King of Prussia wrote like your footboy, &c.' VOLTAIRE. 'He is a sensible man. – Will you go and see the Pretender at Rome?'15 BOSWELL. 'No. It is high treason.' VOLTAIRE. 'I promise you I shall not tell your king of you. I shall not betray you. You would see a bigot: a poor being.' BOSWELL. 'His son is worse. He is drunk every day. He kicks women, and he ought to be kicked.' VOLTAIRE. 'Homer was the only man who took it into his head to write twelve thousand verses upon two or three battles. – It is diverting to hear them say *Old England.*' BOSWELL. 'Sir, "Old England", "Old Scotland", and "Old France" have experienced a quite different effect from that.'

Thursday 27 December. Notes on Voltaire's Conversation, original partly in French

VOLTAIRE. 'You have the better government. If it gets bad, heave it into the ocean; that's why you have the ocean all about you. You are the slaves of laws. The French are slaves of men. In France every man is either an anvil or a hammer; he is a beater or must be beaten.' BOSWELL. 'Yet it is a light, a genteel hammer.' VOLTAIRE. 'Yes, a pocket hammer. We are too mean for our governors to cut off our heads. We are on the earth; they trample us.'

Saturday 29 December. Notes on Voltaire's English Conversation

BOSWELL. 'When I came to see you, I thought to see a very great, but a very bad, man.' VOLTAIRE. 'You are very sincere.' BOSWELL. 'Yes, but the same sincerity makes me own that I find the contrary. Only, your *Dictionnaire philosophique* troubles me. For instance, *Ame*, the Soul—' VOLTAIRE. 'That is a good article.' BOSWELL. 'No. Excuse me. Is it – immortality – not a pleasing imagination? Is it not more noble?' VOLTAIRE. 'Yes. You have a noble desire to be King of Europe. You say, "I wish it, and I ask your protection in continuing to wish it." But it is not probable.' BOSWELL. 'No, but all cannot be the one, and may be the other. Like Cato, we all say "It must be so," till we possess immortality itself.' VOLTAIRE. 'But before we say that this soul will exist, let us know what it is. I know not the cause. I cannot judge. I cannot be a juryman. Cicero says, *potius optandum quam probandum*.[16] We are ignorant beings. We are the puppets of Providence. I am a poor Punch.' BOSWELL. 'Would you have no public worship?' VOLTAIRE. 'Yes, with all my heart. Let us meet four times a year in a grand temple with music, and thank God for all his gifts. There is one sun. There is one God. Let us have one religion. Then all mankind will be brethren.' BOSWELL. 'May I write in English, and you'll answer?' VOLTAIRE. 'Yes. Farewell.'

Boswell to Temple, Continued

Before I left Britain, I was idle, dissipated, ridiculous and regardless of reputation. Often was I unworthy to be the friend of Mr Temple. Now I am a very different man. I have got a character which I am proud of. Speak, thou who hast known me from my earliest years! Couldst thou have imagined eight years ago that thy companion in the studies of Antiquity, who was debased by an unhappy education in the smoke of Edinburgh, couldst thou have imagined him to turn out the man that he now is? We are now, my friend, united in the strictest manner. Let us do nothing of any consequence without the consent of each other.

And must I then marry a Dutchwoman? Is it already marked in the rolls of heaven? Must the proud Boswell yield to a tender inclination? Must he in the strength and vigour of his youth resign his liberty for life to one woman? Rather (say you) shall not my friend embrace the happiness which fortune presents to him? Will not his pride be gratified by the attachment of a lady who has refused many advantageous offers? Must he not marry to continue his ancient family? and where shall he find a more amiable wife? Is he not a man of a most singular character? and would not an ordinary woman be insupportable to him? Should he not thank the Powers Above for having shown him Zélide, a young lady free from all the faults of her sex, with genius, with good humour, with elegant accomplishments? But, my dear Temple, she is not by half so rich as I thought. She has only £400 a year. Besides, I am not pleased with her conduct. We had agreed to correspond, and she directed me to send my letters to the care of her bookseller. I wrote to her from Berlin a long letter. She did not answer it. I was apprehensive that I had talked too severely of her faults, and wrote her from Anhalt-Dessau begging pardon for my too great freedom. Still I remain unanswered. Her father is a very worthy man. He and I correspond, and we write to each other of his daughter in a strange, mysterious manner. I have trusted him upon honour with a letter to her. So I shall be sure that she receives it, and shall see how she behaves. After all, when I consider my unhappy constitution, I think I should not marry, at least for some time; and when I do, should choose a healthy, cheerful woman of rank and fortune. I am now well, because I am agitated by a variety of new scenes. But when I shall return to the uniformity of Scotland, I dread much a relapse into the gloomy distemper. I must endeavour by some scheme of ambition, by elegant study and by rural occupations to preserve my mind. Yet I own that both of us are sadly undetermined. However, I hope the best.

My worthy father has consented that I shall go to Italy. O my friend, what a rich prospect spreads before me! My letter is already so long that I shall restrain my enthusiastic sallies. Imagine my joy. On Tuesday morning I set out for Turin. I shall pass the rigorous Alps with the resolution of Hannibal. I shall be four months in Italy and then return through France. I expect to pass some time at Paris.

Temple, I am again as loyal as ever. I abhor a despotic tyrant. But I revere a limited monarch. Shall I be a British courtier? Am I worthy of the confidence of my king? May George the Third choose that the most honest and most amiable of his subjects should stand continually in his royal presence? I will if he says, 'You shall be independent.' Temple, this is a noble letter. Fare you well, my ever dear friend.

JAMES BOSWELL

3

'A Gentleman of Fortune
upon His Travels':

Italy, Corsica, France

Lucca, 3 October 1765

If it were possible, illustrious philosopher! to write to you without that
respect which hinders the imagination by introducing a degree of fear,
I should flatter myself that I could entertain you with an account of
my tour of Italy. I shall do my best; and if I am not successful you
will know what to ascribe my failure to.

*The letter to Rousseau, quoted above, which Boswell wrote shortly before
leaving Tuscany en route for Corsica, is an eloquent summary of his nine
months in Italy. The style of the letter shows Boswell's buoyant mood at
the time: floating on the one hand between a completed sojourn in Italy,
with incredible romantic entanglements, cultural wonders and the blossoming
friendship with John Wilkes, and on the other looking forward to a visit (not
one often undertaken by young men on their Grand Tours) to the Corsican
freedom fighters and their famous and heroic leader Pasquale Paoli. Boswell's
amorous escapades in Italy fill his journals: after propositioning ageing
countesses and visiting brothels in Turin, at Naples he 'ran after girls
without restraint'; in Rome he was brought to a halt by 'an unpleasant
occurrence which all libertines have to reckon with'. But in Venice he was
back in his reckless ways: 'My mind was stirred by the brilliant stories I
had heard of Venetian courtesans,' as he and his travelling companion Lord
Mountstuart (son of Lord Bute) both pursued the same woman. In Siena a
farce was played out which is well worth following in its entirety in* The
Grand Tour: Italy, Corsica and France, *the fourth in the Yale series. For
sheer sexual gluttony and tangled romantic comedy, Boswell's journal of his
stay in Italy must be second to none.*

*His Corsican adventure was of a very different order. This section's
juxtaposition of libertinism (to rather dignify Boswell's escapades) with the*

study of tranquil and high-minded nobility, tends to anticipate the later chapter in which Boswell, after a valuable and abstemious interlude with Johnson in Lichfield and at Dr Taylor's house at Ashbourne, during which he recorded much conversation that later went almost undiluted into the Life, *comes roaring back to London to indulge himself in debauchery and drink. The Corsican Tour contained the characteristic Boswellian elements: the genuine desire for new experience and adventure, the wish to puff himself up in the eyes of the world, the avid and intrusive curiosity with which he sought out Paoli, and the literary ambition, the way he later turned his private journal into an early literary work which still anticipates many of the strengths of the more mature Boswell.*

The Corsican rebels had for some years been fighting a fairly success- ful guerrilla war against the island's Genoese overlords without actually capturing any of the heavily defended garrison towns on the coast. The country was never again as independent as when Boswell made his visit, except perhaps for a brief spell in the 1790s before she was subdued and annexed by France. By 1769 Paoli was in exile in London (see p. 213) and the island was overrun by French soldiers on behalf of the Genoese. Johnson later scoffed at Boswell's romantic notions ('Sir, empty your head of Corsica') but we can fairly say that his generosity of spirit and his love of liberty was genuine and commendable (he later supported the anti-Government side in the American War of Independence, much to Johnson's anger). His Journal of a Tour to Corsica, etc., *published in 1768 (see Introduction, p. xiii) won him the title of 'Corsica Boswell' and it still seems worth the acclaim it won him at the time. We reprint a few extracts here, mostly the ones concerning Paoli, from that printed text.*

The scene then shifts to Paris three months later, with Boswell on the last leg of his journey home, mixing with John Wilkes and unaware of the sad news about to fall upon him: a chance sighting of his mother's obituary in the St James's Chronicle. *On his long, slow journey back to Edinburgh he offers to take Rousseau's mistress, Thérèse Le Vasseur, across the Channel to await Rousseau's arrival in Britain. The chronicle of the seemingly inevitable affair between the two, a victim of Lady Talbot's cuts (p. xxiii), has been reduced to one sentence. Finally reaching London, Boswell has an emotional meeting with Johnson and reunions with Goldsmith and other friends. As a codicil, we follow Professor Pottle in quoting from one of his anonymous letters of self-advertisement with which he bombarded the*

London Chronicle *while on his way home. It is from that extract that the title of this chapter comes.*

Boswell to Rousseau, Continued

You were indeed right to congratulate me when my father gave me permission to travel in Italy. Nine months in this delicious country have done more for me than all the sage lessons which books, or men formed by books, could have taught me. It was my imagination that needed correction, and nothing but travel could have produced this effect.

I carried over the Alps ideas of the most rigorous morality. I thought of myself as a penitent who must expiate the sins which he had confessed to you in your sacred retreat; I felt like a hero of austerity in a dissolute age. But the ladies of Turin were very beautiful, and I thought that I might allow myself *one* intrigue in Italy, in order to increase my knowledge of the world and give me a contempt for shameless women. So I made myself into a gallant; but I was too modest a gallant to succeed with ladies who scorned the detours of delicacy, and who thought anyone a peasant or an imbecile who did not head straight for the main chance. Moreover, I had a heart. I was seized by passion, I could not hide it; and that was not reconcilable with the decorum which had to be maintained in public. In short, I had no success at all with the ladies of Piedmont. A French officer who was my instructor in gallantry, mortified by finding me *so young*, consoled me by procuring willing girls.

MONDAY 7 JANUARY. I arrived in the evening at Turin, which made me think of Lord Eglinton, who passed some time here and advised me to do the same. I put up at the Bonne Femme, a most magnificent *auberge*. I went dirty to the opera. The superb theatre struck me much, and the boxes full of ladies and gallants talking to each other, quite Italy. So fatigued was I that I fell asleep. When I got home and tumbled into a fine bed, it was most luxurious.

TUESDAY 8 JANUARY. I got up very fretful, but drove off the fiend. I got my coach and *valet de louage* and went to M. Torraz, my banker, a good, brisk, civil fellow. I received a letter from my dear mother, which gave me great comfort, for I had not heard from her since I left England and had formed to myself dreary ideas of her being dead, or sick, or offended with me, which it had been thought prudent to conceal from me. I had also an exceedingly good letter from my brother David, in which he very sensibly and genteelly reproved me for yielding so much to the attacks of melancholy.

I sent a letter of recommendation from Colonel Chaillet to the Comtesse de St Gilles. She received me at four o'clock. She was past fifty and had long been *hackneyed in the ways of men*, but, being strong, was still well enough. She talked of Duke Hamilton, who had been a great gallant of hers. She had animal spirits and talked incessantly. She carried me out in her coach to take the air. I was already then quite in the Italian mode. We returned to her house, where was a stupid *conversazione*, all men. After this we all went to a public ball at the Théâtre de Carignan. It was very handsome and gay. I danced a minuet with the Spanish Ambassadress. There was here many fine women. The counts and other pretty gentlemen told me whenever I admired a lady, 'Sir, you can have her. It would not be difficult.' I thought at first they were joking and waggishly amusing themselves with a stranger. But I at last discovered that they were really in earnest and that the manners here were so openly debauched that adultery was carried on without the least disguise. I asked them, 'But why then do you marry?' 'Oh, it's the custom; it perpetuates families.' I met here a Capitaine Billon to whom I had a letter from M. de Froment. He was a blunt Frenchman, very obliging. I also met here young Gray, son to my Lord, a good, brisk little fellow.

WEDNESDAY 9 JANUARY. There was at present no minister here from our Court. But M. Dutens, who acted in his place, carried me to wait on the Comte de Viry, the Prime Minister. The Court was in mourning, so I could not be presented till I had a black coat. I trifled away the morning.

I went at five to Mme de St Gilles', where I tired to death. Her husband was an old shrewd fellow, who had killed his man in Poland. The room was full of young rakes, mighty stupid, and old worn-out miscreants in whom impotence and stupidity were united. I attended her to the opera, as one of her cicisbays.[1] She had two of us. One held her gloves or her muff, and another her fan. After being heartily wearied in her box, I went down to the parterre, from whence I saw, in a high box, Mr Wilkes. To see a man whom I have so often thought of since I left England filled me with romantic agitation. I considered he might have been dead as well as Churchill, and methought I viewed him in the Elysian fields. When I got home I sent him another note.

THURSDAY 10 JANUARY. I tried to write this morning, but could do nothing. I drove about in the environs. At three I called on M. Bartoli, the King's antiquary, whom M. Schmidt at Karlsruhe had advised me to see. I was courteously received. I found him confusedly learned and lively. He improved the more I talked with him. I gave him anecdotes of Voltaire and Rousseau. He did not approve of the writings of either of the two, for he was a man attached to the Catholic religion. I told him that Rousseau said, 'I live in a world of chimeras.' He replied, 'Then let him keep his books there, and not be sending them out into the real world.' He offered me his services while I remained at Turin.

I then went to Mme St Gilles'. The whim seized me of having an intrigue with an Italian countess, and, as I had resolved to stay very little time here, I thought an oldish lady most proper, as I should have an easy attack. I began throwing out hints at the opera. I sat vis-à-vis to her and pressed her legs with mine, which she took very graciously. I began to lose command of myself. I became quite imprudent. I said, 'Surely there will be another world, if only for getting the King of Prussia flogged'; against whom I raged while the Imperial Minister sat by us. Billon carried me to the box of the Countess Burgaretta, and introduced me to her. She was a most beautiful woman. Billon told me I might have her. My mind was now quite in fermentation. I was a sceptic, but my devotion and love of decency remained. My desire to know the world made me resolve to intrigue a little while in Italy, where the women are so debauched that they are hardly to be considered as moral agents, but as inferior beings. I shall just mark little sketches of my attempts in that way. This night (the third of our acquaintance) I made plain addresses to Mme St Gilles, who refused me like one who wished to have me. But thinking me more simple than I really was, feared to trust me. I was too easy about the matter to take any pains.

FRIDAY 11 JANUARY. I had now my black clothes. My *valet de louage* told me my hair must be dressed 'in a horse-tail'. I was in droll bad humour and abused the fellow, saying, 'Then you must get me shod too. Have you a good blacksmith at Turin? Send for him.' However, I did comply with the courtly mode. I waited on Dutens, who was about publishing a complete edition of the works of Leibnitz with notes and I know not what more. *Opus magnum et ponderosum.* Will men still be plodding in this manner? Let them alone. It is as good as playing at cards. I was presented to the King of Sardinia, who, after all his Italian wars, was just a little quiet man. He only asked me whence? and whither? I looked at him as a kind of heir to the British Crown. There was a numerous Court, mostly military. I went to mass in the King's chapel, which he attends regularly every day.

This morning I was quite in love with Mme Burgaretta. Billon certainly officiated for me as a genteel pimp. To show how corruption may prevail without shame, thus in gross flattery did I write to him this morning:

> My dear Sir, – If you are a man worthy of respect, an obliging man whom one must love; in short, if you have any noble virtue in your soul, arrange for me to see Mme B— today. You told me yesterday that it will be possible for me to enjoy the favours of that goddess in a very little time. Oh, how adorable she is! I beg of you to be at the coffee-house after the Court. I shall have the honour of finding you there.

Was not this real rascality to prostitute the praises of merit in such a manner? But when a man gives himself up to gross gallantry he must lose much of his delicacy of principle. Billon told me with great simplicity, 'It's a low game.' I shall only talk in general of my Turin deviations. I had Billon to dine with me, after which Bartoli and I went and saw a church. I was madly in love with Mme B—. I called on her thrice this afternoon, but did not find admittance.

At four Dutens presented me at the French Ambassador's to his Excellency's lady. I had the honour to hand her to her coach. About the middle of the stair we were met by a marquise, who of course was to turn back. But the great question was, who should be led first to her coach? *Madame la marquise! Madame l'ambassadrice!* I was simple enough to be tossed from the one to the other, as I did just what I was bid; while the rogue Dutens enjoyed my perplexity and probably studied from it something to insert among his notes on Leibnitz on determining motives. At last her Excellency of France took the *pas*.

I was deeply hipped, and knew not what to make of myself. I went and lounged some time at Mme St Gilles'; then I returned to the drawing-room of the French Ambassadress, where I was presented to M. Chauvelin himself. I was quite loaded with gloom and stood at the back of the chairs of those who were playing, to whom I hardly gave any attention but was fixed in proud and sullen silence. This was a most sad evening.

SATURDAY 12 JANUARY. At night I sat a long time in the box of Mme B., of whom I was now violently enamoured. I made my declarations, and was amazed to find such a proposal received with the most pleasing politeness. She however told me, 'It is impossible. I have a lover' (showing him), 'and I do not wish to deceive him.' Her lover was the Neapolitan Minister, Comte Pignatelli, in whose box she sat. He was a genteel, amiable man. He went away, and then I pursued my purpose. Never did I see such dissimulation, for she talked aloud that I should think no more of my passion, and the *piémontais* around us heard this and said without the least delicacy, 'A traveller expects to accomplish in ten days as much as another will do in a year.' I was quite gone. She then said to me, 'Whisper in my ear,' and told me, 'We must make arrangements,' assuring me that she had talked severely to persuade people that there was nothing between us. She bid me call upon her next day at three. This was advancing with rapidity. I saw she was no very wise personage, so flattered her finely. 'Ah, Madame, I understand you well. This country is not worthy of you. That is true' (like a mere fool). 'You are not loved here as you ought to be.' Billon came and repeated gross bawdy. This was disgusting. When I got home I was so full of my next day's bliss that I sat up all night.

SUNDAY 13 JANUARY. By want of sleep and agitation of mind, I was quite feverish. At seven I received a letter from Mme — telling me that people talked of us, and forbidding me to come to her or to think more of the 'plus malheureuse de femmes'. This tore my very heart. I wrote to her like a madman, conjuring her to pity me. Billon came and went out with me in my coach. He told me I had lost her merely by being an *imprudent* and discovering my attachment to all the world. I had wrought myself up to a passion which I was not master of. I saw he looked upon me as a very simple young man; for amongst the thoroughbred libertines of Turin to have sentiment is to be a child. I changed my lodgings. She wrote to me again. I wrote to her an answer more mad than my former one. I was quite gone. At night I saw her at the opera. We were reserved. But I told her my misery. She said, 'C'est impossible.' I was distracted. I forgot to mention that I have paid her one visit.

Boswell to the Countess Burgaretta

[Turin] Sunday [13 January 1765]
I have no words, Madame, to tell you how your letter has pierced my heart. I have been so agitated by that passion you have inspired in me that I have not slept half an hour all night. The thought never left me of the happiness which was to be mine today at '*a quarter past three*'. And now comes your cruel letter, forbidding me to come today to your house.

Madame, I am wholly yours. You may dispose of me as it shall please you, but consider that a worthy man's happiness should be a matter of consequence to a woman such as I have the honour to conceive you to be. Your conduct has roused hopes which it will cost me the bitterest regret to abandon. O Madame, you are generous! Think, I entreat you, of your unhappy lover who is tortured by his passion for you and dares to ask your pity as his due.

Madame, with your brilliance, with your knowledge of the world, you can find means to console this lacerated heart. Grant me, I entreat you, an assignation this evening at any hour when you can be alone. Reflect. Let your humanity speak. I am unwilling to see you in company: I cannot do so without confusion and torment. Dear Madame, adieu. Answer me unless you wish to kill me.

MONDAY 14 JANUARY. Night before last I plainly proposed matters to Mme St Gilles. 'I am young, strong, vigorous. I offer my services as a duty, and I think that the Comtesse de St Gilles will do very well to accept them.' 'But I am not that kind of woman.' 'Very well, Madame, I shall believe you.' I thought to take her *en passant*. But she was cunning and saw my passion for Mme B—, so would not hazard with me.

This morning I waited on Mr Needham, who read me a defence of the Trinity which was most ingenious and really silenced me. I said,

'Sir, this defence is very good; but pray what did you do before you thought of it?' He replied that he submitted to it as a mystery. He said the Catholic religion was proved as a general system, like the Newtonian philosophy, and, although we may be perplexed with partial difficulties, they are not to shake our general belief. He said the world would very soon be divided into Catholics and Deists. He threw my ideas into the orthodox channel. But still I recalled Rousseau's liberal views of the benevolent Divinity, and so was more free. Needham said that a man whose melancholy hurt his rational powers could hardly be accountable for his moral conduct. He consoled me.

After dinner I called on Norton and Heath, two English gentlemen. I did not know what to say to them. I liked the opera much tonight, and my passion was already gone. Honest Billon said, 'If you want to make love, I can find you a girl.' I agreed to this by way of cooling my raging disposition to fall in love. At night Mme St Gilles seemed piqued that I pursued her no longer, and, suspecting that I was enchained by Mme B——, she said, 'Really, you are a little mad. You get notions, and your head turns. I'll tell you: I think you have studied a great deal. You ought to go back to your books. You should not follow the profession of gallant or you will be terribly taken in. Be careful of your health and of your purse. For you don't know the world.' Although my former love-adventures are proof enough that it is not impossible for me to succeed with the ladies, yet this abominable woman spoke very true upon the whole. I have too much warmth ever to have the cunning necessary for a general commerce with the corrupted human race.

TUESDAY 15 JANUARY. I went to Billon's, who had a very pretty girl for me with whom I amused myself. I then went to another ball at the Théâtre de Carignan. I tired much. Billon had promised to have a girl to sleep with me all night at his lodgings. I went there at eleven but did not find her. I was vexed and angry.

WEDNESDAY 16 JANUARY. Billon and another French officer dined with me. We were well. I then called on Needham, who explained his philosophical opinion of transubstantiation, by which I was convinced that it was not absurd. He and I then went and waited on the French Ambassadress. After which I went to Mme St Gilles', where I was quite disgusted. I went home very dull. What a strange day have I had of it!

THURSDAY 17 JANUARY. All the forenoon I wrote. After dinner I took

Bartoli to air in my coach. We went and saw the Bernardines' library. I was gloomy but patient. At night I was again at a ball. I was calm, pensive and virtuous. Sabbati, Secretary to the French Ambassador, talked a good deal with me, and said, 'You are a man from another century.' I had eyed a singular lady some time. She was very debauched. But I took a fancy to her. Sabbati presented me to her. I said, 'Mme S—, this is the fifth evening that I have tried to make your acquaintance.' She seemed gay and pleased.

FRIDAY 18 JANUARY. I passed the morning at home, but was so sadly dissipated that I could do no good. While I was at dinner, an Augustine monk came and asked charity. He said he had been twenty-seven years *religiosus et semper contentus*.[2]

I then went to Billon's, where I had a pretty girl. I was disgusted with low pleasure. Billon talked of women in the most indelicate manner. I then went to Mme Burgaretta's, where I found two more swains. She grumbled and complained of a headache; and she dressed before us, changing even her shirt. We indeed saw no harm; but this scene entirely cured my passion for her. Her *femme de chambre* was very clever, and, when the Countess was dressed, carried away her morning clothes in a little barrel. At the opera I sat in the box of Mme S—, who was soft and gentle, and seemed to like my compliments. I was at Mme St Gilles' in good spirits, and went home pretty much content.

SATURDAY 19 JANUARY. Here have I stayed a week longer than I intended, partly from love, partly to see a grand opera which is to be performed tomorrow. After dinner I sat some time with Needham, who told me he was in orders as a Catholic priest and had always lived with conscientious strictness. He said he had many severe struggles to preserve his chastity, but had done so, and was now quite serene and happy. He had also been distressed with a lowness of spirits which impedes devotion. Thomas à Kempis complains of a *siccitas animi*.[3] I was amazed to find a man who had such parts and had seen so much of the world, and yet so strict as worthy Needham. I talked of the eternity of hell's torments, which he defended as the continual shade which must be in the universe, which wicked beings ought justly to form. He said too that the pains would be in proportion to the offences, and that perhaps to exist with a certain degree of pain was better than to be annihilated.

At the opera I sat in Mme S—' box, and fairly told her my love, saying that I could not leave Turin, being entirely captivated by her. She seemed propitious. Mme St Gilles, deservedly balked of my services, was not a little angry. She was impudent enough to tell about that I had made a bold attack upon her. I did not like to hear this joke.

MONDAY 21 JANUARY. Never was mind so formed as that of him who now recordeth his own transactions. I was now in a fever of love for an abandoned being whom multitudes had often treated like a very woman of the town. I hesitated if I should not pass the winter here and gravely write to my father that really a melancholy man like myself so seldom found anything to attach him that he might be indulged in snatching a transient pleasure, and thus would I inform him that an Italian Countess made me remain at Turin. Was there ever such madness? O Rousseau, how am I fallen since I was with thee! I wrote a long letter to Mme S—, entreating her pity *and all that*. Her answer was that if she had known my letter was of such a nature, she would not have opened it. She had told me plainly her mind at the opera. Pedro, my stupid *valet de place*, brought me this shocking word-of-mouth message. I saw that amongst profligate wretches a man of sentiment could only expose himself.

After dinner I went to Needham, and was consoled with learned and solid conversation. We went to the opera together, and sat in the middle of the parterre, from whence I never stirred but was quite independent. I enjoyed fully the entertainment. Needham talked of the religious orders, particularly of the Trappe, and explained them in so philosophical a manner that I had much solemn satisfaction.

After the opera Norton and Heath insisted I should go home with them and sup. I went, like a simpleton. They carried me into a low room of their inn, where they romped with two girls and gave me a most pitiful supper. This, now, was true English. I had now and then looked from the parterre to Mme S—, but did not go to her box. I determined to set out next morning for Milan.

Boswell to the Countess Skarnavis

[Turin] Auberge d'Angleterre, 21 January 1765

Permit me, Madame, to write to you, for it is thus that I can best express to you the nature of my feelings towards you. I shall express them very briefly, without timidity and without restraint.

You are already aware that I feel for you the strongest of passions. I glory in it, and make no complaint of all I suffer. I shall not again repeat my ardent professions. You have no doubts on that head; if you have, it is from an excess of suspicion. I have heard many tales of you. I believe none. I am determined to believe none. No, Madame, I adore you, and nothing could avail to weaken that adoration.

Yesterday evening I told you I was consoling myself with hopes of your goodness. Your answer, both tender and cruel, was, 'It is far better to go away.' You gave me the most cautious advice. But you refrained from telling me it would be impossible to win your favour. I implore you, Madame, to reflect seriously, and to use no evasions with a romantic lover who deserves quite other consideration than one gives to the kind who may be had any day. Madame, I venture to affirm that never have your charms been more worthily felt than by me. If you accord me the supreme happiness, you will be showing yourself generous to an excellent man who would be attached by gratitude to you for the rest of his life. You are in perfect safety with me. You can rely on my honour in every respect. Our characters, Madame, are alike. Yes, I am sure of it. We have the liveliest ideas, which we express only by our glances. We have a modesty which nothing can destroy. Assuredly we are not novices in love. Nevertheless, with exquisite delicacy you prevent my touching your hand; and I, if I hear mention of Mme Skarnavis, find myself blushing. Ah! when we abandon ourselves to pleasures under the veil of darkness, what transports, what ecstasy will be ours! Pardon me, Madame, I am greatly agitated. I place myself under your protection: dispose of me as you see fit. If you tell me, 'Sir, think no more of that happiness; 'tis impossible,' – if you say that, I shall hear you with distress, I shall tear myself away from Turin, I shall leave on the instant.

But if I am not disagreeable to you, if your generous heart prompts you to say, 'Stay: I am one who can value a true passion at its worth,' you cannot conceive, Madame, how keenly I shall be touched. O Love! baneful and delicious madness, I feel you, and am your slave.

I well know, Madame, that I ought to remain long here to earn the great boon which I entreat. But just now I am not my own master. For the rest of my stay, I shall be entirely yours. I shall mix no more with the world. For all save you I shall have left Turin. I have tried to explain myself, Madame; it is for you to reflect and decide. It is a singular case. Have a care. Dear and amiable Countess, let your humanity speak. Let us see if you can rise superior to low prejudices and tell your true thoughts.

It shall be between ourselves. Oh, you have nothing to fear!

Reflect – and in a few hours' time give me your reply. I shall send to get it. You have told me what you would do in my case; I well know what I should do in yours. Have a care, Madame, there is here something important at stake. I tremble, but I have hopes. Heaven bless you.

TUESDAY 22 JANUARY. Needham and Gray breakfasted with me. I was quite easy and genteel. I sent to Mme S— and begged she would return me my letter. She bid the valet say that she had thrown it in the fire. Here was the extreme of mortification for me. I was quite sunk. Worthy Needham bid me continue to lay up knowledge, and took an affectionate leave of me, hoping we should meet again.

I set out at eleven. As I went out at one of the ports, I saw a crowd running to the execution of a thief. I jumped out of my chaise and went close to the gallows. The criminal stood on a ladder, and a priest held a crucifix before his face. He was tossed over, and hung with his face uncovered, which was hideous. I stood fixed in attention to this spectacle, thinking that the feelings of horror might destroy those of chagrin. But so thoroughly was my mind possessed by the feverish agitation that I did not feel in the smallest degree from the execution. The hangman put his feet on the criminal's head and neck and had him strangled in a minute. I then went into a church and kneeled with great devotion before an altar splendidly lighted up. Here then I felt three successive scenes: raging love – gloomy horror – grand devotion. The horror indeed I only *should* have felt. I jogged on slowly with my *vetturino*, and had a grievous inn at night.

Boswell to Rousseau, Continued

Thus, Sir, did I carry out the good resolutions I had made at Môtiers. I wrote on a piece of paper, 'O Rousseau! How am I fallen since I left you!' Yet my principles remained firm. I considered that I had

done wrong. I summoned my inclinations back to virtue, and at Parma
M. Deleyre strengthened me in my resolutions. I was charmed by the
fine mind and the finer soul of that amiable Frenchman; and the sincere
evidence which he gave of his attachment to me brought me back again
to the opinion that I was something above the crowd of mankind. You
told me when I was about to leave you, 'Sir, all you lack is a knowledge
of your own worth.' Believe me, illustrious philosopher! there is a great
deal in that remark. I know my worth sometimes, and I think and act
nobly. But then melancholy attacks me, I despise myself, and it seems
to me a waste of time to try to improve so petty a thing.

I was well enough on my trip from Turin to Rome. I interrupted it
often to stop in places where there was something to see. I was very
curious, and because I moved from one scene to another, melancholy
never had time to weigh me down greatly. I was struck with everything.
I had the agreeable sensation that derives from a half-knowledge of
things – to many minds perhaps as great a pleasure as knowing them
thoroughly.

I had recommendations to the Dominican fathers, and under their
protection I covered the whole of Italy. I visited many monasteries,
including those of the strictest orders. I shall never forget an hour that
I spent in conversation with the Prior and other reverend fathers of a
Carthusian convent near Bologna. I encouraged in myself a sceptical
but reverent superstition, which by a mysterious – an inexplicable –
mixture of feelings calmed my uneasy mind.

I entered Rome with full classical enthusiasm, but when I arrived
at my inn and found myself surrounded by the landlord, by *valets de
place*, by scoundrels, my fantastic sensibility was wounded, and at first
I was in a bad humour. I had an odd thought which now makes me
laugh heartily. As I was walking along the streets of Rome, which are
very little different from those of any other city, I said to myself, 'Was
the Epistle of St Paul to the Romans written to the inhabitants of this
city? And did I use to be so terrified by it?' At once the Epistle of St Paul
seemed to me to be just an ancient writing by some ecclesiastical zealot.
The word of GOD was no longer in it. Great chemist of human nature!
you see how a mind can be changed. Ah, we must analyse with the
most delicate nicety.

Within a few days I set out for Naples, where I was richly entertained
with the variety of interesting things to be seen there, especially in the

environs. I found the famous Mr Wilkes in his exile, and despite his sharp attacks on the Scots, we got along very well together. All theories of human nature are confounded by the resilient spirit of that singular factionary, who has experienced all the vicissitudes of pleasure and politics without ever having suffered a moment of uneasiness. He is a man who has thought much without being gloomy, a man who has done much evil without being a scoundrel. His lively and energetic sallies on moral questions gave to my spirit a not unpleasant agitation, and enlarged the scope of my views by convincing me that God could create a soul completely serene and gay notwithstanding the alarming reflection that we all must die. Wilkes pretended to be angry with you for having referred to him in so uncompromising a style in a note to one of your *Letters from the Mountain*. He even said boldly that he would write a public letter to you on this subject, which would be entitled, *A Letter from the Other Man of the Mountain*.

I went little into company at Naples, and remember solely that the Neapolitan ladies resembled country chamber-maids. I was there during Lent when there are no public entertainments. During my stay at Naples I was truly libertine. I ran after girls without restraint. My blood was inflamed by the burning climate, and my passions were violent. I indulged them; my mind had almost nothing to do with it. I found some very pretty girls. I escaped all danger. I have nothing to say about this period; I merely describe it for you as it occurred.

WEDNESDAY 6 MARCH [Naples]. Yesterday visits of English and Wilkes. WILKES. 'I wish I could write in any language as well as you.' BOSWELL. 'Such complaisance is not in character.' WILKES. 'Yes. I always tell truth – for which I'm here.' BOSWELL. 'Had you told such flattering truths to Government, you had not been here.' WILKES. 'I make it a rule to abuse him who is against me or any of my friends point-blank. If I find two or three faults, he's good for nothing.' BOSWELL. 'But Johnson, a respectable character in the world of literature.' WILKES. 'Oh I abuse Johnson as an impudent pretender to literature, which I don't think, but 'tis all one. So is my plan. At school and college I never read; always among women at Leyden. My father gave me as much money as I pleased. Three or four whores; drunk every night. Sore head morning, then read. I'm capable to sit thirty hours over a table to study. Plan for *North Briton*: grave revolutionary paper seasoned each time with a character from the Court list.'

WEDNESDAY 13 MARCH. Yesterday morning at home, and wrote a little. Wilkes came, gay, and excused himself for tomorrow, and asked *you*. You agreed, as he's an *extraordinary*. He said he did not mind if his friends don't like his wife, as 'tis not for them he has her, but for self. WILKES. 'After Lord Talbot's duel,4 Mother talked grave: "Rush into presence of Maker." "I've been always in it." "And into eternity." "Where have I been all this time?" – Never think on futurity, as not data enough.' This day Vesuvius.

THURSDAY 14 MARCH. Yesterday morning in chaise to Portici. Then on foot to Vesuvius. Monstrous mounting. Smoke; saw hardly anything. Dined Wilkes, gay. WILKES. 'Never a moment in my life low-spirited.' BOSWELL. 'What shall I do to get life over?' WILKES. 'While there's all ancient and modern learning and all arts and sciences, enough for life if three thousand years.' BOSWELL. 'Fate and free will?' WILKES. 'Let 'em alone.' BOSWELL. 'Why keep company with me?' WILKES. 'You're an original genius. But they'll spoil you in Paris; lop luxuriances from you. Talked to Baxter of soul; two quarto volumes and never since.'

FRIDAY 15 MARCH. Yesterday early, fine morn. Wilkes at door. Asses, Wilkes so mounted, excellent. Men to help; sad fatigue; oft rested. WILKES. 'I'm always happy. I thank God for good health, good spirits and the love of books. I'll live here retired, not go down to Naples; 'tis hell. "He descended into hell" shall not be said of me. *Imitatio Christi* there; I'll not be a Thomas à Kempis. Quin said of Francis: "Damn the fellow; he's but a curate in Norfolk and he has all the vices of a cardinal." When I was colonel of militia, wrote epitaphs on all my officers. Some were engraved at Winchester. Gardener died: "Here lies —, gardener, &c. *Hunc etiam flebant lauri*," &c. Minister angry at Virgil's being in churchyard, a heathen poet. But I said he prophesied of Christ and made all easy.' BOSWELL. 'If we were to die here, how they'd write of us!' WILKES. 'If I died and you lived, by the L—d a Middlesex jury would bring you in guilty of my murder.5 A man who has not money to gratify passions does right to govern them. He who can indulge, better. Thank heaven for having given me the love of women. To many she gives not the noble passion of lust.'

SUNDAY 17 MARCH. Yesterday hipped, but drove about and saw several churches. Called Colonel Edmondstone. Talked of Scots families and

love of younger brothers to elder. One of his kept account of all his
father had given him, with a firm resolution to restore it to the family.
Noble, great affection; great spirit. Had Wilkes to dine. WILKES. 'After
Rambler, liked Johnson more, but not abuse by halves. – Churchill
kissed Flexney's wife,[6] and he did it cheaper for him.' Read some
Zélide to him. WILKES. 'You've been topped. Go home by Holland
and roger her. You might be in her.' BOSWELL. 'A Presbyterian kirk
makes me tremble.' WILKES. 'That's the strength of your imagination.
Dr Hayes, when hipped, said cross things; Armstrong only held his
tongue. Lord Eglinton a good-humoured, laughing fellow, but never
suspected him of parts. Nature would not have given him that lank
yellow hair. An advantage to be in this fine climate; after thirty, though
your mind strong, your body may be easily hurt. By the Lord, a fever
makes you a Johnnie Home, and what will you do then?' Then opera
singer, &c.

Boswell to Wilkes

[Naples] Saturday [16 March 1765]
If you dine at home tomorrow, I hope you'll let me come to 'your
genial board', &c, as Armstrong says. I would *carpe diem* as much as I
can while you and I are near each other. I go for certain on Wednesday.
Pray don't grudge a little paper and ink and wax upon an *old* Scotsman
who loves you as much as any Englishman whatever.

MONDAY 18 MARCH. Yesterday dined Wilkes. Then *chanteuse*; ventured.
Swore no more here. Wilkes talked of wife; Tierney, surprised: 'Have
you a wife?' WILKES. 'Yes, Sir; very much at your service.'

Boswell to Rousseau, Continued

I returned to Rome for Holy Week. I grew calm. The solemn services
of the Roman Catholic Church made a serious impression on me. I
began to be a little melancholy and I recalled with religious regret
how I had once been, like you, in the bosom of the faithful. But your
Savoyard doctrines came to my aid and made me see a church even

more catholic than that which I revered: the entire Universe, all souls being emanations of the Eternal Being. On Easter I was in St Peter's, and in that superb temple I saw noble and mystical adorations offered to the Supreme Being. I was penetrated with devotion. I was sure that the revelation given by Jesus was true; and when I saw the Christian High Priest with venerable magnificence elevate before the Eternal Justice a Sacrifice for the sins of the whole world, I fell to my knees among the throng of my fellow men who remained fixed in respectful silence; I struck my breast, and with all the ardour of which my soul was capable I prostrated myself at the feet of my Father 'who is in Heaven', convinced that, by varied ways of which we know nothing clearly, he would one day lead all his creatures to happiness. Let cold beings sneer; I was never more nobly happy than on that day.

The study of antiquities, of pictures, of architecture and of the other arts which are found in such great perfection at Rome occupied me in a wise and elegant manner. You must know that I have a great taste for *virtù*. It entertains me agreeably during many hours when without it my mind would be a prey to ennui. I shall say no more on that head, because I do not know whether you like *virtù* or not. Moreover, you have a more sublime taste, and it is more sensible to acquaint you with traits of character from which you can derive some philosophical reflections useful to him who has supplied them, and perhaps to others.

I must admit that in the midst of my Roman studies I indulged in sensual relaxations. I sallied forth of an evening like an imperious lion, and I had a little French painter, a young academician, always vain, always alert, always gay, who served as my jackal. I remembered the rakish deeds of Horace and other amorous Roman poets, and I thought that one might well allow one's self a little indulgence in a city where there are prostitutes licensed by the Cardinal Vicar. Thus does an ill-regulated mind assemble scattered ideas and compose from them a principle for action. I was, however, brought to a halt by an unpleasant occurrence which all libertines have to reckon with. When we walked in your room, disputing about the commerce of the sexes, you said to me with a smile, 'Watch out for Italian girls – for several reasons.' I discovered at Rome that your advice was very sound.

In all the vicissitudes that I experienced, and which you are well qualified to imagine from what you have just read, I always preserved a certain external decency of character. But I suffered cruelly from hypochondria, whose pains are unimaginable to those who have not felt them. It is a certain truth, Sir, that I am afflicted by a malady which can make me see all things as either insipid or sad, which can take away all desire for enjoyment, which can make me lose taste even for virtue; and what is the darkest and the most inexplicable of all, it is a malady which can so destroy my spirit that I scarcely even wish to be cured. The variations of this malady are infinite. I write to you now when I am completely healthy, clear, happy. I am sure that to find myself existing after death will not be a more powerful sensation than that which I have in feeling myself the man I now am, after the state of prostration and despair in which I have been plunged. Can you believe that there are moments in my life when M. Rousseau appears to me a poor wretch who had tried to distinguish himself a little among his unfortunate fellows, and who will soon be lost like them in the darkness of the [grave]? In such moments it is impossible to enjoy those feelings of admiration for your genius and your character which give me such great pleasure when I am well. But what can be done about it? My judgement tries in vain to free me from the grasp of a troubled imagination. It is hard to suffer so much. Kindly philosopher! keep me in your thoughts. I sustain myself by a firm trust in GOD.

Until Holy Week, I had seen little of my countrymen in Italy. I was looked upon as an odd creature who studied a great deal and was very proud. I was presented to the Pope. I went to *conversazioni* in the palaces of Roman nobles, where there was a great deal of formality and also a certain air of pleasing richness and grandeur. At Rome everything is external. They have scarcely any real society. A prince makes a point of having his dinner sent in for half a crown, and does not know the number of his carriages or of his servants. The parties are also formal, being generally given their tone by two or three cardinals. I went to the levée of Cardinal Orsini, the present Protector of France. I had been highly recommended to him, but he did not once invite me to dine with him. I had opportunity there to see the gross flattery, the obvious scheming, the discontents and the universal ambition of ecclesiastical politicians.

I do not know that I did well in avoiding my compatriots so completely. I had good reason – to devote myself entirely to learning the language, studying the genius and absorbing the thought of the

Italian people. But in doing this I almost isolated myself. I formed
exaggerated ideas of myself, and when I fell in with Englishmen was
raw and irritable, and by too great a sensitivity I was inferior in social
life to mediocre young men who were accustomed to live in general
society.

I could not think of placing myself so soon on the footing of a
philosopher who wishes to retire from the world. I had to accustom
myself to being with my equals. I had to think of establishing some
political connection.

I found all these advantages happily combined. I formed a close
connection with Lord Mountstuart, eldest son of the worthy Lord
Bute, intimate friend of our King. My Lord Mountstuart is a young
nobleman who merits his being of the blood of the ancient kings of
Scotland.

My Lord Mountstuart insisted that I accompany him on the remain-
der of his tour of Italy, and I consented. He was already accompanied
by a Scottish colonel, a very worthy man, and by M. Mallet, sometime
professor from Geneva, who had been given a good pension in return
for giving my Lord lessons in history. It would have been impossible to
conceive of a more prudent or more agreeable project than ours. My
Lord and I counted on profiting together from M. Mallet's instructions.
The Colonel was the discreet governor, and I had the honour to be
regarded by my Lord as a friend who would be very useful to him, since
I should prevent him from being tempted by bad company to renew his
dissipations. But matters did not go well. I found myself in my Lord's
suite, and when I heard him hold forth on the pleasures of grandeur I
began to wish for employment at Court. I thought of his great interest.
Insensibly I tried to please him and was afraid of offending him. He
soon noticed it, and could not keep from profiting a little from it. I
realized it too. I was highly shocked by it. What! Boswell, *the man of
singular merit*! The friend of Rousseau! Is Boswell so far overcome by
vile interest as to depend on the moods of a young Lord? I recollected
myself. I made my Lord realize that I was as proud as ever. I did it
too emphatically. We began to dispute about our characters, and each
stated bluntly all the other's defects and all his own merits. You can
imagine that between two young men, both of whom have a good deal
of temperamental warmth, such a dispute, so conducted, could not but
occasion many disagreeable moments. Finally our spirits subsided, and

we were sometimes on a basis of puerile familiarity, and sometimes in the vilest humour possible, even to the point of not speaking to each other. I always had a great advantage, for I was four years older than my Lord, and was possessed of a little philosophy. The Colonel and Mallet suffered from the fatigues of the trip, and were vexed to see the differences between my Lord and me. The worthy Colonel rallied us roughly through mere clumsiness. Mallet, from whom we had taken hardly any lessons since we left Rome, became irritated with me because I never ceased attacking his opinions and discovering his tricks; and to tell you the truth, there were never four men who travelled so ill together. It was indeed ridiculous, and my Lord and I in our hours of good humour were sometimes ready to burst with laughing.

We went to Venice. For the first week I was charmed by the novelty and beauty of so singular a city, but I soon wearied of travelling continually by water, shut up in those lugubrious gondolas. Almost all the nobility was at Padua, where we had seen them for several days in passing through. There were buildings and paintings to see at Venice.

From Florence I went to Siena, where I passed a portion of my existence in perfect felicity. The nobility there form a society of the most amiable sort. They have a simplicity, an openness, a gaiety which you cannot imagine without having been there. They have no society manners, none of that affected air which to the philosopher betrays artificial beings. You, Sir, as delicate as you are, could live in the society of Siena. Since there is no Court there and the nobles think only of living within their moderate incomes, you never see in Siena those gentlemen with great interest who spoil every company in a city where it is thought that something may be gained by paying court. The Sienese are independent, equal and content to be so, and when a great prince comes among them he is politely received, but they do not put themselves out for him.

I had excellent apartments at Siena. I ate well. The wine of the district was very good, and on holidays I regaled myself with delicious Montepulciano. The air is fresh, and the weather is always fine. My health was very quickly restored. An Abbé of talent and obliging disposition dined with me every day, and accommodated himself perfectly to the little variations of my temperament. He helped me as teacher in Italian. Every morning for two hours I read the divine Ariosto, and you can imagine the effect which that produced on my romantic soul. I also wrote in Italian with equal regularity, and as I used no other language in conversation, I made rapid progress. The Sienese dialect is the most agreeable in all of Italy. For me it was a continual melody. I had lively sensations of pleasure when I heard people merely discussing the good weather. A 'professor' of music, who had very fine taste, came to me every afternoon, and we sang and played fine airs on the flute. Little by little I shall come to know something of music. I can already amuse myself with it tolerably. I lack application, but that will come. I have not forgotten you in a land where I have heard six different operas. I am sorry not to have some of your music with me. I remember only 'Quand on sait aimer et plaire' and a little air with which you amused a lady of Neuchâtel:

Nous habitons une maison,
Où les biens pleuvent à foison.

Ariosto, music and pleasant company occupied my days at Siena. The circumstances were most precious to my imagination. I was in a provincial city in the heart of beautiful Tuscany; a city completely at peace where not a single soldier was to be seen, not even a pensioner. I was the only foreigner there. I was as though in the most remote of countries, the most hidden of retreats. My mind was healthy, easy and joyful. Neither past nor future entered my thoughts. I thanked God for my present existence. It is an extraordinary mind which can do so.

But, Sir, I must tell you of more interesting things. Your Scot was very attentive to the ladies at Siena. I found that people lived there in a completely natural fashion, making love as their inclinations suggested. It was the custom of the society in which I lived. I yielded to custom. I allowed myself to become all sensation and immediate feeling. I did not wish to extend my mind to encompass a series of prudent considerations. I did not wish to be more profound than the others. To enjoy was the thing. Intoxicated by that sweet delirium, I gave myself up, without self-reproach and in complete serenity, to the charms of irregular love.

I paid court to a lady who had lived much in Florence, and whose noble manners incited my vanity; and through vanity I so heated my imagination with a desire to obtain that lady that I thought myself madly in love with her. As a matter of fact, I *did* suffer from her severity. She saw me frequently, showed a genteel esteem for me, called me her friend, wrote me tender letters, but assured me that she had really loved my Lord Mountstuart, and that he would be her last lover. I wrote her the most curious of letters on that subject. It was a delicate question whether to try the constancy of a friend's mistress, but as my Lord had given me permission to adore a goddess whom he scarcely gave a thought to any more, and as I was quite sure that Signora — had considerable inclination to be persuaded to change her mind, I continued to press her with great eagerness.

I was wicked enough to wait at the same time on a very amiable little woman to whom I made declarations of the most sincere passion, as can be easily done when one feels only a slight inclination. I fancied that she had no heart, and as I believed everything fair in the war of gallantry, I lied to her certainly no fewer than a hundred times a day. Behold me, then, very busy indeed, with two affairs going at the same time. It required an unparalleled dexterity, and I had it. Then nothing was difficult for me. I drifted pleasantly between my two loves, and my *valet de place*, a lout who could neither read nor write, was despatched with his face turned towards the east to carry a letter for Signora A. in his right-hand pocket and a letter for Signora B. in his left.

In a fortnight Signora B., who was the most trusting of persons, and with whom I had used the full force of my reasoning powers to prove that in me she would have the most faithful of lovers, but that my sufferings were so excruciating that, if she did not soon assure me of her affection, I feared so much the sad effects of a strong passion on a melancholy mind that I was determined to set out at once – and what a pity it would be to miss in this short life so fine an occasion for mutual happiness. This amiable person, whose heart was already touched, listened to me kindly and granted me all, saying, 'Ebbene, mi fido a voi com' a un galantuomo.'[7] My conscience reproached me. It happened that Signora A. revealed her character to me. I saw that she conducted intrigues strictly according to the rules, without being touched by love. I abandoned my design upon her. I attached myself completely to my dear little mistress, through a principle of true gratitude.

I studied her character. I found many good qualities in her. I even found charms in her which the dissipation of my spirit had caused me to overlook previously; and with extraordinary joy I found myself truly in love with her. I opened my heart to her, made a full confession of the deceit I had practised on her, while assuring her that she had gained my love. I enjoyed with her the exquisite pleasure of Italian gallantry, whose enchantments I had heard so much of; and I swear to you that experiencing them measured up to my ideas. She was struck with what I had told her. She reproached me tenderly for my treachery. But from that time on she had complete confidence in me. I was utterly happy and I risked nothing.

The times, Sir, are much changed in Italy. No longer does one have to fear the stiletto of a jealous husband. But as the dispositions of a people always persist under one form or another, and as the lively wit of the loose-living Romans is displayed in sonnets, in songs and in ecclesiastical intrigues, so Italian jealousy survives feebly in the hearts of *cavalieri serventi*, of whom every lady has one or two. A *cavaliere servente* is a being whom I regard as illustrating the last stage of human degradation. A lover without love, a soldier without pay, a being who is more a drudge than is a *valet de chambre*, who does continual duty, and enjoys only appearances! Since Signora B. had to keep some of these gentlemen in her train, we had to manage them, and we were sometimes a little embarrassed how to do it.

I loved her more and more. She had a natural *allegria* which never changed and which so alleviated my sombre humour that it buoyed me up until I was quite free of melancholy. I found her a woman made for a life of virtue. When I explained to her the sweet and durable bonds of the conjugal union, she was enchanted and regretted infinitely that she could not experience them, insisting strongly on the advantage which a virtuous mother of a family must enjoy in old age. But said she, 'They took me out of the convent and married me at sixteen, when I did not have the slightest idea what marriage meant. Ero totalmente senza malizia. Quando ero messa in letto col mio marito, trovava roba intorno di me, e pensava ch'era una bestia.'[8] The naïveté with which she made that remark and the laughable word *roba* diverted me infinitely. 'I am married', she continued, 'to a man considerably older than myself; a man whom I not only cannot love but whom I cannot even respect, for to tell the truth he has no liveliness of mind at all, and he is very coarse.'

Hear me, illustrious philosopher! I dare ask you to tell me honestly without prejudice whether that woman was really married, whether she had made a true contract, whether she was obliged to remain faithful to a man to whom her parents had bound her, whether it was her duty to sacrifice her finest inclinations to the hard circumstances in which she found herself. I could not answer her arguments, but in my moments of virtue and piety I warmly repeated to her the common sentiments against adultery. She was very fond of your works. I read to her with a grave and serious air the beautiful and affecting words of Julie9 on that terrible vice. I was so moved by them that she could not but feel something. But an onrush of passion overcame me. I embraced her with a kind of frenzy and repeated our criminal ecstasies. She said, 'Voi siete precisamente quel Rousseau. Tale quale. Parlate moltissimo della virtù, e però fate il male.'10 I was stirred by a pride of sentiment. She confessed to me all the love affairs in which she had engaged. She told me the names of her lovers, one of whom was always at our *conversazioni*. I wished him dead many and many a time. My extreme jealousy was tormented even by what no longer existed.

My Signora was sorry that I felt so. She assured me that I was the first for whom she had felt a true passion, because it was the first time that love had made her uneasy. The same thing, indeed, has happened to women of intrigue many times. I wished to believe her. But I could not endure the thought that she had been the mistress of others. Ah, I groaned from the heart. Signora B. made a rather subtle observation on that. She told me that a man is wrong to boast that he possesses the affections of a girl, because the poor ignorant being knows no better, never having had opportunity to know the merits of lovers. But when a woman has had a little experience and knows men, then her attachment is truly flattering. I believed that also. But do not call me a dupe. Do not say that I fell into very good hands. Have no suspicions of the sincerity of my charming Signora. No, Sir, although not from the richest of families, she was completely generous, completely disinterested. Although she could not doubt that I would lay everything at her feet that she might demand from me, she never made me play,11 never told me that she wanted the least thing; and, take my word for it, such a character is very rare among the ladies of

Italy, especially those of Tuscany where they make a regular business
of English 'milords', as they call all us British gentlemen in general.
She was a careful manager and advised me how to bargain so as not
to be taken in, so as to spend my money wisely. I felt as though I were
really married, so well did she play the part of an excellent wife. Never
was vice so sanctified by virtue. She made me go to mass with her, and
I dare say that while we were there we were as pious as if our conduct
had been completely innocent.

Thus my life slipped away in a delicious dream, while my principles
of systematic morality were melted down by the fire of a heated
imagination. But time was fleeing. My father was in momentary
expectation of news of my arrival in France, and before going there
I had secretly resolved to make a tour of Corsica. How was I to decide?
My inclination, and, according to the principles of true gallantry, my
duty – for vice, when it is social, has its principles also – demanded
that I remain with a woman who had made me happy and to whom
I owed so much. I thought also that a being who has had so sad an
existence as mine would do badly not to profit as much as possible
from happiness which he had finally found – if he did not drink
from the stream of pleasure as long as Heaven caused it to flow.
I was utterly happy. Everything seemed agreeable to me. Even GOD
took on for me the most agreeable aspect, as he will appear to us when
at the end our souls will be all purified and exalted into the divine
perfection. O dear St Preux! Yes, my soul is bound to yours. I have
loved like you, I am pious like you. If we have committed crimes, we
have also expiated them.

I resolved to leave Siena, and I told Signora — a week beforehand.
I was firm though sad. Her good sense was such that she admitted my
reasons for leaving were irrefutable. But she could not but complain
of her lot, which had made her taste real happiness only to feel its loss.
When we enjoyed those delicious murmurs which your divine delicacy
prefers to the moment of ecstasy itself, she said, 'Ah, io piangerò questi
momenti.'[12] Her sighs pierced my heart.

O love, passionate fever of the soul, meteor of joy whose essence
it is to be brief, how dearly we buy your transports! I tried to console
us both for the sadness of parting by depicting the beautiful prospect
of an eternal friendship. But the Signora insisted absolutely that she
must see me again.

FRIDAY 11 OCTOBER. After a few hours of sleep, was called at six by Signor Giuliano and another Corsican, who beat at my door. Was confused a little, but recollecting grand expedition, blood recovered bold circulation. Wrote Rousseau and Dempster; left also letters for Mme de Spaen and my dear Italian lady at Siena. At eight the little boat carried me to the bark, and we set sail. The good people had waited all night for me when the wind was so good that we should have been in Corsica ere morning. This day there was little wind. I was sick a very short while and threw up a little, but felt firm nerves in comparison of myself on the passage to Holland. A Corsican played a sort of guitar or lute, and I played my flute, and so did Jacob. The bark belonged to a Corsican of Pino. He carried wine to Leghorn. He spoke English. To save himself, he had the Tuscan flag (the Emperor's), and a Leghorn shipmaster, Ignazio Gentili. I lay down in the cabin bed, but was eat up by mosquitoes and other vermin. I eat cold tongue and bread and some of the crew's rice. There were ten aboard: two poor Corsican merchants, six Corsican sailors, the master and a boy from Leghorn. I tried to read a little the disputes of Corsica, but could give no attention. Thought hardly any, and was content to be so. Jacob was firm and felt no sickness but wished to have a long voyage, and at night was delighted to see nothing but the sky and the sea. They laid a mattress on the provision chest, and hung a sail on the side of the bark and on four chairs, and under this tent you slept. At the Ave Maria they all kneeled, and with great fervency said their evening orisons to the Queen of Heaven. It affected you a good deal.

Boswell to Rousseau

Leghorn, 11 October 1765

I have received your letter, illustrious philosopher. I see that you do not forget me. Some time ago I started to write a very long letter to you entirely about myself. At present, I account myself, my petty pleasures and petty anxieties, as nothing. In half an hour I embark for Corsica. I am going directly to the territories of Paoli. The worthy Count Rivarola has given me recommendations in plenty. I am all vigour, all nobility. If I perish on this expedition, think of your Spanish Scot with affection, and we shall meet in the paradise of imaginative souls.

If I return safely, you will have a valuable account. I cannot write. I shall be able to speak. Death is nothing to me.

From an Account of Corsica, and Memoirs of Pascal Paoli, by James Boswell

FRIDAY 18 OCTOBER 1765 (*Corte, Corsica*). I chose to stop a while at Corte to repose myself after my fatigues, and to see everything about the capital of Corsica.

I went up to the Castle of Corte. The Commandant very civilly showed me every part of it. As I wished to see all things in Corsica, I desired to see even the unhappy criminals. There were then three in the Castle: a man for the murder of his wife, a married lady who had hired one of her servants to strangle a woman of whom she was jealous, and the servant who had actually perpetrated this barbarous action. They were brought out from their cells that I might talk with them. The murderer of his wife had a stupid, hardened appearance, and told me he did it at the instigation of the devil. The servant was a poor despicable wretch. He had at first accused his mistress but was afterwards prevailed with to deny his accusation, upon which he was put to the torture by having lighted matches held between his fingers. This made him return to what he had formerly said, so as to be a strong evidence against his mistress. His hands were so miserably scorched that he was a piteous object. I asked him why he had committed such a crime; he said, 'Because I was without understanding.' The lady seemed of a bold and resolute spirit. She spoke to me with great firmness and denied her guilt, saying with a contemptuous smile as she pointed to her servant, 'They can force that creature to say what they please.'

The hangman of Corsica was a great curiosity. Being held in the utmost detestation, he durst not live like another inhabitant of the island. He was obliged to take refuge in the Castle, and there he was kept in a little corner turret, where he had just room for a miserable bed and a little bit of fire to dress such victuals for himself as were sufficient to keep him alive; for nobody would have any intercourse with him, but all turned their backs upon him. I went up and looked at him. And a more dirty, rueful spectacle I never beheld. He seemed sensible of his situation and held down his head like an abhorred outcast.

It was a long time before they could get a hangman in Corsica, so that the punishment of the gallows was hardly known, all their criminals being shot. At last this creature whom I saw, who is a Sicilian, came with a message to Paoli. The General, who has a wonderful talent for physiognomy, on seeing the man said immediately to some of the people about him, 'Behold our hangman.' He gave orders to ask the man if he would accept of the office, and his answer was, 'My grandfather was a hangman, my father was a hangman. I have been a hangman myself and am willing to continue so.' He was therefore immediately put into office, and the ignominious death dispensed by his hands hath had more effect than twenty executions by firearms.

It is remarkable that no Corsican would upon any account consent to be a hangman. Not the greatest criminals, who might have had their lives upon that condition. Even the wretch who for a paltry hire had strangled a woman would rather submit to death than do the same action as the executioner of the law.

When I had seen everything about Corte, I prepared for my journey over the mountains, that I might be with Paoli.

When I at last came within sight of Sollacarò, where Paoli was, I could not help being under considerable anxiety. My ideas of him had been greatly heightened by the conversations I had held with all sorts of people in the island, they having represented him to me as something above humanity. I had the strongest desire to see so exalted a character, but I feared that I should be unable to give a proper account why I had presumed to trouble him with a visit, and that I should sink to nothing before him. I almost wished yet to go back without seeing him. These workings of sensibility employed my mind till I rode through the village and came up to the house where he was lodged.

Leaving my servant with my guides, I passed through the guards and was met by some of the General's people, who conducted me into an antechamber where were several gentlemen-in-waiting. Signor Boccheciampe had notified my arrival, and I was shown into Paoli's room. I found him alone, and was struck with his appearance. He is tall, strong and well made; of a fair complexion, a sensible, free and open countenance, and a manly and noble carriage. He was then in his fortieth year. He was dressed in green and gold. He used to wear the common Corsican habit, but on the arrival of the French he thought a little external elegance might be of use to make the government appear in a more respectable light.

He asked me what were my commands for him. I presented him a letter from Count Rivarola, and when he had read it I showed him my letter from Rousseau. He was polite but very reserved. I had stood in the presence of many a prince, but I never had such a trial as in the presence of Paoli. I have already said that he is a great physiognomist. In consequence of his being in continual danger from treachery and assassination, he has formed a habit of studiously observing every new face. For ten minutes we walked backwards and forwards through the room hardly saying a word, while he looked at me with a steadfast, keen and penetrating eye, as if he searched my very soul.

This interview was for a while very severe upon me. I was much relieved when his reserve wore off and he began to speak more. I then ventured to address him with this compliment to the Corsicans: 'Sir, I am upon my travels, and have lately visited Rome. I am come from seeing the ruins of one brave and free people; I now see the rise of another.'

He received my compliment very graciously, but observed that the Corsicans had no chance of being like the Romans, a great conquering nation who should extend its empire over half the globe. Their situation, and the modern political systems, rendered this impossible. 'But', said he, 'Corsica may be a very happy country.'

He expressed a high admiration of M. Rousseau, whom Signor Buttafoco had invited to Corsica to aid the nation in forming its laws. It seems M. de Voltaire had reported, in his rallying manner, that the invitation was merely a trick which he had put upon Rousseau. Paoli told me that when he understood this, he himself wrote to Rousseau enforcing the invitation. Of this affair I shall give a full account in an after part of my Journal.

Some of the nobles who attended him came into the room, and in a little we were told that dinner was served up. The General did me the honour to place me next him. He had a table of fifteen or sixteen covers, having always a good many of the principal men of the island with him. He had an Italian cook who had been long in France, but he chose to have a few plain substantial dishes, avoiding every kind of luxury and drinking no foreign wine.

I felt myself under some constraint in such a circle of heroes. The General talked a great deal on history and on literature. I soon perceived that he was a fine classical scholar, that his mind was enriched with a variety of knowledge, and that his conversation at meals was instructive and entertaining. Before dinner he had spoken French. He now spoke Italian, in which he is very eloquent.

We retired to another room to drink coffee. My timidity wore off. I no longer anxiously thought of myself; my whole attention was employed in listening to the illustrious commander of a nation.

He recommended me to the care of the Abbé Rostini, who had lived many years in France. Signor Colonna, the lord of the manor here, being from home, his house was assigned for me to live in. I was left by myself till near supper time, when I returned to the General, whose conversation improved upon me as did the society of those about him, with whom I gradually formed an acquaintance.

Every day I felt myself happier. Particular marks of attention were shown me as a subject of Great Britain, the report of which went over to Italy and confirmed the conjectures that I was really an envoy. In the morning I had my chocolate served up upon a silver salver adorned with the arms of Corsica. I dined and supped constantly with the General. I was visited by all the nobility, and whenever I chose to make a little tour I was attended by a party of guards. I begged of the General not to treat me with so much ceremony, but he insisted upon it.

One day when I rode out, I was mounted on Paoli's own horse with rich furniture of crimson velvet, with broad gold lace, and had my guards marching along with me. I allowed myself to indulge a momentary pride in this parade, as I was curious to experience what could really be the pleasure of state and distinction with which mankind are so strangely intoxicated. When I returned to the Continent after all this greatness, I used to joke with my acquaintance and tell them that I could not bear to live with them, for they did not treat me with a proper respect.

My time passed here in the most agreeable manner. I enjoyed a sort of luxury of noble sentiment. Paoli became more affable with me. I made myself known to him. I forgot the great distance between us, and had every day some hours of private conversation with him.

From my first setting out on this tour, I wrote down every night what I had observed during the day, throwing together a great deal that I might afterwards make a selection at leisure.

Of these particulars, the most valuable to my readers, as well as to myself, must surely be the memoirs and remarkable sayings of Paoli, which I am proud to record.

Talking of the Corsican war, 'Sir,' said he, 'if the event prove happy, we shall be called great defenders of liberty. If the event shall prove unhappy, we shall be called unfortunate rebels.'

The French objected to him that the Corsican nation had no regular troops. 'We would not have them,' said Paoli. 'We should then have the bravery of this and the other regiment. At present every single man is as a regiment himself. Should the Corsicans be formed into regular troops, we should lose that personal bravery which has produced such actions among us as in another country would have rendered famous even a marshal.'

I asked him how he could possibly have a soul so superior to interest. 'It is not superior,' said he; 'my interest is to gain a name. I know well that he who does good to his country will gain that, and I expect it. Yet could I render this people happy, I would be content to be forgotten. I have an unspeakable pride. The approbation of my own heart is enough.'

He said he would have great pleasure in seeing the world and enjoying the society of the learned and the accomplished in every country. I asked him how with these dispositions he could bear to be confined to an island yet in a rude uncivilized state, and instead of participating Attic evenings, 'noctes coenaeque Deum', be in a continual course of care and of danger. He replied in one line of Virgil: 'Vincet amor patriae laudumque immensa cupido.'[13] This, uttered with the fine open Italian pronunciation, and the graceful dignity of his manner, was very noble. I wished to have a statue of him taken at that moment.

I asked him if he understood English. He immediately began and spoke it, which he did tolerably well. When at Naples, he had known several Irish gentlemen who were officers in that service. Having a great facility in acquiring languages, he learnt English from them. But as he had been now ten years without ever speaking it, he spoke very slow. One could see that he was possessed of the words, but for want of what I may call mechanical practice he had a difficulty in expressing himself.

I was diverted with his English library. It consisted of some broken volumes of the *Spectator* and *Tatler*, Pope's *Essay on Man*, *Gulliver's Travels*, a *History of France* in old English, and Barclay's *Apology for the Quakers*. I promised to send him some English books.

He convinced me how well he understood our language, for I took the liberty to show him a memorial which I had drawn up on the advantages to Great Britain from an alliance with Corsica, and he translated this memorial into Italian with the greatest facility. He has since given me more proofs of his knowledge of our tongue by his answers to the letters which I have had the honour to write to him in English, and in particular by a very judicious and ingenious criticism on some of Swift's works.

He was well acquainted with the history of Britain. He had read many of the Parliamentary debates, and had even seen a number of the *North Briton*. He showed a considerable knowledge of this country, and often introduced anecdotes and drew comparisons and allusions from Britain.

He said his great object was to form the Corsicans in such a manner that they might have a firm constitution, and might be able to subsist without him. 'Our state', said he, 'is young, and still requires the leading strings. I am desirous that the Corsicans should be taught to walk of themselves. Therefore when they come to me to ask whom they should choose for their Padre del Commune or other magistrate, I tell them, "You know better than I do the able and honest men among your neighbours. Consider the consequence of your choice, not only to yourselves in particular but to the island in general." In this manner I accustom them to feel their own importance as members of the state.'

After representing the severe and melancholy state of oppression under which Corsica had so long groaned, he said, 'We are now to our country like the prophet Elisha stretched over the dead child of the Shunammite, eye to eye, nose to nose, mouth to mouth. It begins to recover warmth and to revive. I hope it shall yet regain full health and vigour.'

I said that things would make a rapid progress, and that we should soon see all the arts and sciences flourish in Corsica. 'Patience, Sir,' said he. 'If you saw a man who had fought a hard battle, who was much wounded, who was beaten to the ground, and who with difficulty could lift himself up, it would not be reasonable to ask him to get his hair well dressed and to put on embroidered clothes. Corsica has fought a hard battle, has been much wounded, has been beaten to the ground, and with difficulty can lift herself up. The arts and sciences are like dress and ornament. You cannot expect them from us for some time. But come back twenty or thirty years hence, and we'll show you arts and sciences, and concerts and assemblies, and fine ladies, and we'll make you fall in love among us, Sir.'

He smiled a good deal when I told him that I was much surprised to find him so amiable, accomplished and polite; for although I knew I was to see a great man, I expected to find a rude character, an Attila King of the Goths, or a Luitprand King of the Lombards.

I observed that although he had often a placid smile upon his countenance, he hardly ever laughed. Whether loud laughter in general society be a sign of weakness or rusticity I cannot say; but I have remarked that real great men, and men of finished behaviour, seldom fall into it.

The variety, and I may say versatility, of the mind of this great man is amazing. One day when I came to pay my respects to him before dinner, I found him in much agitation, with a circle of his nobles around him and a Corsican standing before him like a criminal before his judge. Paoli immediately turned to me. 'I am glad you are come, Sir. You Protestants talk much against our doctrine of transubstantiation. Behold here the miracle of transubstantiation, a Corsican transubstantiated into a Genoese. That unworthy man who now stands before me is a Corsican, who has been long a lieutenant under the Genoese in Capo Corso. Andrew Doria and all their greatest heroes could not be more violent for the Republic than he has been, and all against his country.' Then turning to the man, 'Sir,' said he, 'Corsica makes it a rule to pardon the most unworthy of her children when they surrender themselves, even when they are forced to do so as is your case. You have now escaped. But take care. I shall have a strict eye upon you, and if ever you make the least attempt to return to your traitorous practices, you know I can be avenged of you.' He spoke this with the fierceness of a lion, and from the awful darkness of his brow one could see that his thoughts of vengeance were terrible.

Yet when it was over he all at once resumed his usual appearance, called out 'Come along,' went to dinner, and was as cheerful and gay as if nothing had happened.

He reasoned one day in the midst of his nobles whether the commander of a nation should be married or not. 'If he is married,' said he, 'there is a risk that he may be distracted by private affairs and swayed too much by a concern for his family. If he is unmarried, there is a risk that, not having the tender attachments of a wife and children, he may sacrifice all to his own ambition.' When I said he ought to marry and have a son to succeed him; 'Sir,' said he, 'what security can I have that my son will think and act as I do? What sort of a son had Cicero, and what had Marcus Aurelius?'

He said to me one day when we were alone, 'I never will marry, I have not the conjugal virtues. Nothing would tempt me to marry but a woman who should bring me an immense dowry with which I might assist my country.'

But he spoke much in praise of marriage, as an institution which the experience of ages had found to be the best calculated for the happiness of individuals and for the good of society. Had he been a private gentleman, he probably would have married, and I am sure would have made as good a husband and father as he does a supreme magistrate and a general. But his arduous and critical situation would not allow him to enjoy domestic felicity. He is wedded to his country, and the Corsicans are his children.

He often talked to me of marriage, told me licentious pleasures were delusive and transient, that I should never be truly happy till I was married, and that he hoped to have a letter from me soon after my return home, acquainting him that I had followed his advice and was convinced from experience that he was in the right. With such an engaging condescension did this great man behave to me. If I could but paint his manner, all my readers would be charmed with him.

He has a mind fitted for philosophical speculations as well as for affairs of state. One evening at supper he entertained us for some time with some curious reveries and conjectures as to the nature of the intelligence of beasts, with regard to which he observed human knowledge was as yet very imperfect. He in particular seemed fond of enquiring into the language of the brute creation. He observed that beasts fully communicate their ideas to each other, and that some of them, such as dogs, can form several articulate sounds. In different ages there have been people who pretended to understand the language of birds and beasts. 'Perhaps,' said Paoli, 'in a thousand years we may know this as well as we know things which appeared much more difficult to be known.' I have often since this conversation indulged myself in such reveries. If it were not liable to ridicule, I would say that an acquaintance with the language of beasts would be a most agreeable acquisition to man, as it would enlarge the circle of his social intercourse.

Paoli was very desirous that I should study the character of the Corsicans. 'Go among them,' said he, 'the more you talk with them, you will do me the greater pleasure. Forget the meanness of their apparel. Hear their sentiments. You will find honour and sense and abilities among these poor men.'

His heart grew big when he spoke of his countrymen. His own great qualities appeared to unusual advantage while he described the virtues of those for whose happiness his whole life was employed. 'If', said he, 'I should lead into the field an army of Corsicans against an army double their number, let me speak a few words to the Corsicans to remind them of the honour of their country and of their brave forefathers – I do not say that they would conquer, but I am sure that not a man of them would give way. The Corsicans', said he, 'have a steady resolution that would amaze you. I wish you could see one of them die. It is a proverb among the Genoese, "The Corsicans deserve the gallows, and they fear not to meet it." There is a real compliment to us in this saying.'

He told me that in Corsica criminals are put to death four and twenty hours after sentence is pronounced against them. 'This', said he, 'may not be over-catholic, but it is humane.'

He went on and gave me several instances of the Corsican spirit:

'A sergeant', said he, 'who fell in one of our desperate actions, when just a-dying, wrote to me thus: "I salute you. Take care of my aged father. In two hours I shall be with the rest who have bravely died for their country."

'A Corsican gentleman who had been taken prisoner by the Genoese was thrown into a dark dungeon, where he was chained to the ground. While he was in this dismal situation, the Genoese sent a message to him that if he would accept of a commission in their service, he might have it. "No," said he. "Were I to accept of your offer, it would be with a determined purpose to take the first opportunity of returning to the service of my country. But I will not accept of it. For I would not have my countrymen even suspect that I could be one moment unfaithful." And he remained in his dungeon.' Paoli went on: 'I defy Rome, Sparta or Thebes to show me thirty years of such patriotism as Corsica can boast. Though the affection between relations is exceedingly strong in the Corsicans, they will give up their nearest relations for the good of their country, and sacrifice such as have deserted to the Genoese.'

He gave me a noble instance of a Corsican's feeling and greatness of mind. 'A criminal', said he, 'was condemned to die. His nephew came to me with a lady of distinction, that she might solicit his pardon. The nephew's anxiety made him think that the lady did not speak with sufficient force and earnestness. He therefore advanced, and addressed himself to me: "Sir, is it proper for me to speak?" as if he felt that it was unlawful to make such an application. I bid him go on. "Sir," said he, with the deepest concern, "may I beg the life of my uncle? If it is granted, his relations will make a gift to the state of a thousand zechins. We will furnish fifty soldiers in pay during the siege of Furiani. We will agree that my uncle shall be banished, and will engage that he shall never return to the island." I knew the nephew to be a man of worth, and I answered him, "You are acquainted with the circumstances of this case. Such is my confidence in you, that if you will say that giving your uncle a pardon would be just, useful or honourable for Corsica, I promise you it shall be granted." He turned about, burst into tears and left me, saying, "I would not have the honour of our country sold for a thousand zechins." And his uncle suffered.'

After having said much in praise of the Corsicans, 'Come,' said he, 'you shall have a proof of what I tell you. There is a crowd in the next room waiting for admittance to me. I will call in the first I see, and you shall hear him.' He who chanced to present himself was a venerable old man. The General shook him by the hand and bid him good day, with an easy kindness that gave the aged peasant full encouragement to talk to his Excellency with freedom. Paoli bid him not mind me, but say on. The old man then told him that there had been an unlucky tumult in the village where he lived, and that two of his sons were killed. That looking upon this as a heavy misfortune, but without malice on the part of those who deprived him of his sons, he was willing to have allowed it to pass without enquiry. But his wife, anxious for revenge, had made an application to have them apprehended and punished. That he gave his Excellency this trouble to entreat that the greatest care might be taken, lest in the heat of enmity among his neighbours anybody should be punished as guilty of the blood of his sons who was really innocent of it. There was something so generous in this sentiment, while at the same time the old man seemed full of grief for the loss of his children, that it touched my heart in the most sensible manner. Paoli looked at me with complacency and a kind of amiable triumph on the behaviour of the old man, who had a flow of words and a vivacity of gesture which fully justified what Petrus Cyrnaeus hath said of the Corsican eloquence: 'Diceres omnes esse bonos causidicos.'[14]

I found Paoli had reason to wish that I should talk much with his countrymen, as it gave me a higher opinion both of him and of them. Thuanus has justly said, 'Sunt mobilia Corsorum ingenia.'[15] Yet after ten years, their attachment to Paoli is as strong as at the first. Nay, they have an enthusiastic admiration of him. 'This great man whom God hath sent to free our country,' was the manner in which they expressed themselves to me concerning him.

The peasants and soldiers were all frank, open, lively and bold, with a certain roughness of manner which agrees well with their character and is far from being displeasing. The General gave me an admirable instance of their plain and natural solid good sense. A young French marquis, very rich and very vain, came over to Corsica. He had a sovereign contempt for the barbarous inhabitants, and strutted about with prodigious airs of consequence. The Corsicans beheld him with a smile of ridicule and said, 'Let him alone, he is young.'

The Corsican peasants and soldiers are very fond of baiting cattle with the large mountain dogs. This keeps up a ferocity among them which totally extinguishes fear. I have seen a Corsican, in the very heat of a baiting, run in, drive off the dogs, seize the half-frantic animal by the horns, and lead it away. The common people did not seem much given to diversions. I observed some of them in the great hall of the house of Colonna where I was lodged amusing themselves with playing at a sort of draughts in a very curious manner. They drew upon the floor with chalk a sufficient number of squares, chalking one all over and leaving one open alternately; and instead of black men and white, they had bits of stone and bits of wood. It was an admirable burlesque on gaming.

The chief satisfaction of these islanders, when not engaged in war or in hunting, seemed to be that of lying at their ease in the open air, recounting tales of the bravery of their countrymen, and singing songs in honour of the Corsicans and against the Genoese. Even in the night they will continue this pastime in the open air, unless rain forces them to retire into their houses.

The *ambasciatore inglese*, as the good peasants and soldiers used to call me, became a great favourite among them. I got a Corsican dress made, in which I walked about with an air of true satisfaction. The General did me the honour to present me with his own pistols, made in the island, all of Corsican wood and iron and of excellent workmanship. I had every other accoutrement. I even got one of the shells which had often sounded the alarm to liberty. I preserve them all with great care.

The Corsican peasants and soldiers were quite free and easy with me. Numbers of them used to come and see me of a morning, and just go out and in as they pleased. I did everything in my power to make them fond of the British, and bid them hope for an alliance with us. They asked me a thousand questions about my country, all which I cheerfully answered as well as I could.

One day they would needs hear me play upon my German flute. To have told my honest natural visitants, 'Really, gentlemen, I play very ill,' and put on such airs as we do in our genteel companies, would have been highly ridiculous. I therefore immediately complied with their request. I gave them one or two Italian airs, and then some of our beautiful old Scots tunes: 'Gilderoy', 'The Lass of Patie's Mill', 'Corn rigs are bonny'. The pathetic simplicity and pastoral gaiety of the Scots music will always please those who have the genuine feelings of nature. The Corsicans were charmed with the specimens I gave them, though I may now say that they were very indifferently performed.

My good friends insisted also to have an English song from me. I endeavoured to please them in this too, and was very lucky in that which occurred to me. I sung them 'Hearts of oak are our ships, Hearts of oak are our men.' I translated it into Italian for them, and never did I see men so delighted with a song as the Corsicans were with the *Hearts of Oak*. 'Cuore di quercia,' cried they, 'bravo Inglese!' It was

quite a joyous riot. I fancied myself to be a recruiting sea officer. I
fancied all my chorus of Corsicans aboard the British fleet.

Paoli talked very highly on preserving the independency of Corsica.
'We may', said he, 'have foreign powers for our friends, but they must
be friends at arm's length. We may make an alliance, but we will not
submit ourselves to the dominion of the greatest nation in Europe.
This people who have done so much for liberty would be hewn in
pieces man by man rather than allow Corsica to be sunk into the
territories of another country. Some years ago, when a false rumour
was spread that I had a design to yield up Corsica to the Emperor,
a Corsican came to me and addressed me in great agitation: "What!
shall the blood of so many heroes, who have sacrificed their lives for
the freedom of Corsica, serve only to tinge the purple of a foreign
prince!"'

I mentioned to him the scheme of an alliance between Great Britain
and Corsica. Paoli with politeness and dignity waived the subject by
saying, 'The less assistance we have from allies, the greater our glory.'
He seemed hurt by our treatment of his country. He mentioned the
severe proclamation at the last peace, in which the brave islanders
were called the rebels of Corsica. He said with a conscious pride and
proper feeling, 'Rebels! I did not expect that from Great Britain.'

He, however, showed his great respect for the British nation, and
I could see he wished much to be in friendship with us. When I asked
him what I could possibly do in return for all his goodness to me, he
replied, 'Only undeceive your Court. Tell them what you have seen
here. They will be curious to ask you. A man come from Corsica will
be like a man come from the Antipodes.'

I expressed such hopes as a man of sensibility would in my situation
naturally form. He saw at least one Briton devoted to his cause. I
threw out many flattering ideas of future political events, imaged the
British and the Corsicans strictly united both in commerce and in
war, and described the blunt kindness and admiration with which the
hearty, generous common people of England would treat the brave
Corsicans.

The last day which I spent with Paoli appeared of inestimable value.
I thought him more than usually great and amiable when I was upon
the eve of parting from him. The night before my departure a little
incident happened which showed him in a most agreeable light. When

the servants were bringing in the dessert after supper, one of them chanced to let fall a plate of walnuts. Instead of flying into a passion at what the man could not help, Paoli said with a smile, 'No matter'; and, turning to me, 'It is a good sign for you, Sir. *Tempus est spargere nuces*. It is a matrimonial omen; you must go home to your own country and marry some fine woman whom you really like. I shall rejoice to hear of it.'

After leaving Corsica, Boswell spent the next three months travelling through France in a leisurely way, finally reaching Paris in January 1766. The next Journal entry is an unexpected and unhappy one.

1766

MONDAY 27 JANUARY. Heard mass at Théatins. Went to Ambassador's Chapel; old ideas of Church of England, in some measure. Sermon made you gloomy, or rather tired. At Wilkes's saw in *St James's Chronicle* Mother's death. Quite stunned; tried to dissipate [grief]. Dined Dutch Ambassador's; much of Corsica. At six, Mme Hecquet's as in fever.[16] Constance elegant.

TUESDAY 28 JANUARY. Yesterday morning sent to Foley; got letter from Father, written by David. Too true; Mother gone. Was quite stupefied. In all morning. Wept in bursts; prayed to her like most solemn Catholic to saint. Roused philosophy; sung Italian gently to soothe. But would not have hurt prejudices by doing so before others. Called on Principal Gordon, told him privately sad news. Had company with him who had said mass for requiem to old James. Lord Alford (Sir John Graham) genteel man. Curious feelings; was prudent, but with true philosophy sustained your distress; was decent. Had strong enthusiasm to comfort Father all his life.

Lord Auchinleck to Boswell

Edinburgh, 11 January 1766
My dear Son, – In my last I acquainted you that your dear mother was indisposed, and was to get a vomit that evening on which my

letter was wrote; I did not then apprehend her to be in any danger, but from that time forward she daily turned worse of a slow and obstinate fever, which at length put a period to her valuable life this morning half an hour after seven. This melancholy event you'll easily believe affects me deeply; I have lost my friend, my adviser and assistant in everything, and that has made me agree to use your brother's hand, which he out of compassion made offer of to me. My dear Jamie, had you seen and heard what we have been witnesses to these last three weeks, you would have agreed with us that many useful lessons were to be learnt. Your dear mother, who from the beginning of her illness had a fixed persuasion that she was to die of it, and in that view spoke to me seriously on different subjects and particularly in relation to you, for whom she had always a great affection, and who she hoped would return with proper dispositions – I say notwithstanding this her persuasion of approaching death, she was so far from showing any terror that she expressed a pleasure in the thoughts of it; and indeed nothing could be a greater proof of the reality and efficacy of true religion than what appeared in her conduct during the whole time of her indisposition; and notwithstanding the many medicines, blisterings and other operations she underwent, she never once complained; on the contrary, said that she thought she was likely to have an easy passage. This her conduct was not owing to insensibility, or to a disbelief or the least doubt of her immortality or of a future state, but to her most serious, constant and habituated attention to her duty both to God and to the world, and to a full persuasion in and through the merits of our blessed Redeemer of attaining endless bliss in the other world. Among her last words, a very little time before her death she audibly though with a faltering tongue said, 'I have fought the good fight of faith, I have finished my course, henceforth is prepared for me a crown of glory,' and when she had expressed a longing for death and was asked if she did not wish to recover to be a comfort to her family, she answered she wished to be with Christ, which is far better. She left us without any struggle or even a groan, and as it were fell asleep. She was one who all her life long was intent and diligent in doing her duty both to God and the world. You know her attachment to devotion and serious religion, and you know that she managed all my private affairs with the utmost accuracy, and was anxious to serve all her friends and acquaintances. I am now reduced to a destitute state; I have lost my friend, I have lost my adviser in all things which concerned both worlds. You have lost a most affectionate and kind mother, and will doubtless be affected deeply with this awful stroke as we and all your friends here are; and as, upon the back of this, diversions of any kind cannot have any relish with one of your sensibility, it will occur to you how much I need your assistance, this irreparable breach made upon me besides the having my old bodily trouble still hanging about me; and therefore it will be needless to tell you that I expect you home with all speed. Your brother remembers you with great affection. I am, my dear son, your affectionate father,

ALEX. BOSWEL.

P.S. The contents of this letter are not to be shown, being intended for yourself. Since writing this letter I have had the pleasure of yours from Marseilles and rejoice to hear of your arrival in France. Do not disquiet yourself about the money you have spent; if you turn out in the way I expect, I shall never grudge these expenses. You have got £100 credit on Paris. Farewell, my dear Jamie, may God bless and preserve you.

WEDNESDAY 29 JANUARY. Yesterday felt more the sad news. Recalled her kind, affectionate concern. Was deeply touched, but thinking of her being in heaven, was easy. Was pious and had manly hope. Had heard Mlle Le Vasseur was arrived, and had sent to her; went this morning to Hôtel de Luxembourg. She was with Mme de la Roche, *première dame de la Maréchale*. She was just as at Môtiers. Told her sad news. She told you her anxiety about journey, and said, 'Mon Dieu, Monsieur, if we could go together!' You said you came to propose it to her. She showed you Rousseau's letter from Paris, where he agrees to her coming, and gives directions to wash his new shirts, &c, adding, 'Do nothing hastily,' and another from London, saying, 'Resign yourself to suffering a great deal.' Made a long story of it. Quackery this. Went to Scots College, and Principal showed you, in little cabinet with British arms, many volumes of King James's own hand: royal letters, &c, &c, and then showed you cartulary of Glasgow, Queen Mary's letters and testament, her prayer book, &c, &c. You was truly pleased, and thrown into reverend humour which kept off grief. Wilkinson, a priest, dined. Then paid visits to Lord Alford, &c. Wilkes said Christian religion gave you nothing new but the resurrection of the body. WILKES. 'I care no more to be raised in the same body than in the same coat, waistcoat and breeches. Incarnation absurd.' STRANGE. 'Sir, if you admit one spirit in body, why not superior one?' Carlotti, Italian Marquis, once said to Wilkes, 'But my soul—.' WILKES. 'G–d damn your soul.'

We next see Boswell landing in Britain after an absence of two and a half years, accompanied by Thérèse Le Vasseur. The Journal for this period had been seriously cut by the time the papers reached Yale, but the following shows the truth of the story of their affair.

WEDNESDAY 12 FEBRUARY [*Dover*]. Yesterday morning had gone to bed very early, and had done it once: thirteen in all. Was really affectionate to her. At two set out in fly; breakfasted Rochester on beefsteaks. Mrs Morrice, a woman who had been married to a sergeant, and a bluff, true Englishman sat with you. Mademoiselle was much fatigued. Came to London about six, to Swan at Westminster Bridge. Was now so firm that London made no impression. You was good to her. Sent to Stewart, and then went to his house. You was quite easy. Macpherson was there. You was talked to much of Corsica, but said nothing but calm account of what you saw, and when they said, 'Who could send over this intelligence?' you said, 'You must ask Gazetteer.' Carried her to David Hume. Then went to Temple; embraced most cordially in old style. Wine and bread. Were too dissipated by innumerable ideas. Both cried, 'Hope shall not marry these women.'[17] You was for revolving all deaths. He said, 'No, it makes one callous.' Sat till four; went home. Up all night.

THURSDAY 13 FEBRUARY. Yesterday morning, after having read a daily all night, went and rung at Dempster's door, but he was not stirring. Then in post-chaise to Dr Pringle's. He embraced you cordially, saying, 'Glad to see you on several accounts.' Talked to you of letter to Lord Mountstuart. You was a little obstinate; found the Doctor very easy with you. Then went to Mlle Le Vasseur, with whom was Hume. You breakfasted, and then carried her out to Chiswick. She said Hume had told her you was 'mélancholique', which was in your family. You was too high. You was ready to kill any offender. You gave her word of honour you'd not mention *affaire* till after her death or that of the philosopher. Went to Rousseau; delivered her over. *Quanta oscula*,[18] &c! He seemed so oldish and weak you had no longer your enthusiasm for him. Told him all about Corsica, and he cried, 'Pardi! I am sorry not to have gone there.' He was incited by what he heard. He was to go to Wales. You asked if Scotland had not a claim to him. He said, 'I shall act like the kings; I shall put my body in one place, and my heart in another.'

Back to London. Immediately to Johnson; received you with open arms. You kneeled, and asked blessing. Miss Williams glad of your return. When she went out, he hugged you to him like a sack, and grumbled, 'I hope we shall pass many years of regard.' You for some minutes saw him not so immense as before, but it came back. Voltaire's Pope in chaise, and Dryden in coach.[19] JOHNSON. 'That is very well. But the truth is they ride both in coaches, only Dryden is always either galloping or stumbling; Pope goes on at an even trot.' You dined at the Cecil Street Coffee-house (Temple's place), and there you met George Redhead, a fat, jolly planter. You and Temple had fine chat. He was much easier than formerly. At eight you met at Mitre Mr Johnson. Told him how Baretti was corrupted and had said, 'As man dies like dog, let him lie like dog.' JOHNSON. 'Why, Sir, if he dies like dog, let him lie like dog.' BOSWELL. 'Baretti says, "I hate mankind, for I think myself one of the best of 'em, and I know how bad I am."' JOHNSON. 'Sir, he must be very singular in his opinion if he thinks himself one of the best of men, for none of Baretti's friends think him one of,' &c. He said no honest man could be a deist, for no man could be so after a fair examination of the proofs. BOSWELL. 'Hume?' JOHNSON. 'No, Sir, Hume owned to a clergyman in the bishopric of Durham that he had never read the New Testament with any attention.'

He said, 'Now you have five and twenty years, and you have employed 'em well.' BOSWELL. 'Oh, no! Do I know history, mathematics, law, &c? No.' JOHNSON. 'Why, Sir, though you may know no science so well as to be able to teach it, and no profession so well as to be able to follow it, yet your general mass of knowledge of books and men renders you very capable to study any science or follow any profession.' (This was enough.) I said Wilkes bid me not be a lawyer as I should be excelled by plodding blockheads. He said, 'Sir, in the formal and statutory practice of law a plodding blockhead may succeed, but in the equitable part of it a plodding blockhead can never succeed.' I said, 'I fear I shall not be a good advocate.' JOHNSON. 'Why, Sir, to be sure you will not be a good advocate at first, and, Sir, no man is a good advocate at first;

and perhaps in seven years you will not be so good a lawyer as your father, and perhaps never. But it is better to be a tolerable lawyer than no lawyer, and, Sir, you will always see multitudes below you.' You talked of attending great men. 'Sir, would you have done it?' JOHNSON. 'Sir, I was never near enough to them to court them, but I would have done it. You are never to do what you think wrong, and you are to calculate and not pay too dear for what you get. You must not give a shilling's worth of court for sixpence worth of good; but if you can get a shilling's worth of good for sixpence worth of court, you are a fool not to pay court.'

SATURDAY 22 FEBRUARY. Yesterday I called at Mr Bosville's at three o'clock, and freely took their family dinner. The Squire had bid me come in at any time, and Mrs Bosville said, 'We shall make no stranger of you, Sir.'²⁰ Miss was still quite reserved. You stayed all afternoon with the Squire and wrote from his house to Father. He showed you a humorous attack on *Joseph*, and showed you he was no orthodox. You supped and Miss opened you some oysters. You was just as you could wish to be.

SUNDAY 23 FEBRUARY. Yesterday at nine called at Mr Pitt's in Bond Street. Not up. BOSWELL. 'I'll call ten times.' Went back at eleven; shown into parlour, and but a very plain one. Another servant came: 'My master will be glad to see you, Sir.' Carried upstairs; entered room, a very decent one. A gentleman, Mr Dowdeswell, went away. Lord Shelburne and Lord Cardross were with him. He was tall man in black clothes, with white nightcap and foot all wrapped up in flannel and on gout-stool. He made a genteel reverence, and said, 'Mr Boswell, I came to town only yesterday, and have been engaged with the business of the House; otherwise, I should have sent to you and appointed a time when we might have met.' He talked of English gentlemen of good estates living independent in the country with great dignity. He said he was ashamed to say he had never read Rousseau, but would now read him. You told him Rousseau's great admiration of him, and how he'd never forget the gentleman who gave him a print of Mr Pitt. You told him Voltaire's saying of there being only a king and a half in Europe – King of Prussia and King of Sardinia. Mr Pitt was mightily pleased with it, but said, 'If it may be allowed to improve upon M. de Voltaire, I would give both to the King of Prussia, and say, "He is a king and a half," and let the other kings just be kings.' Lord Cardross showed away by being at his ease, leaning on knee and sticking switch into boot, saying, 'Mr Pitt. Eh?' He talked of materialism: (Good now! Metaphysics here!) You asked if it would not have been possible to have forced the Americans. Said he: 'Abstracting from the equity of the cause, it would not have been possible. They are all united.' Lord Shelburne showed a list of 280,000 acting militia that they could spare for war. Mr Pitt said, 'If severe measures were ever to be used, it must be done when they are divided; but let us use them with indulgence, and they'll always find it their interest to be with us.'

The lords went away. He then began in form: 'Mr Boswell, I am very happy to make your acquaintance. I had heard of you before. I had seen an account in the foreign papers of your being in Corsica.' (He had indeed asked some questions before the company.) 'Now, Sir, I will explain to you how I cannot properly receive communications from General de Paoli, for I am a Privy Councillor, and have taken an oath to hear nothing from any foreign power that may concern Great Britain without declaring it to the King and Council. Now, Sir, it is in your breast to judge whether what you have to say is of a nature fit to be told or not. I shall be very happy to hear your accounts of the island as a traveller. Some time hence things may turn about, and I may be at liberty to receive communications from Corsica, and then I shall be very happy to hear all you have to say. I am now just a private member of Parliament. I had once, Mr Boswell, something to do in the affairs of this nation. But when they had come to me in distress and in perplexity, "Think for us, act for us, venture for us!" and I had thought, acted and ventured – for 'em then to come and tell me, "Now you must think as we choose!" When I had rolled the stone to the top of the hill, then! My Lord Temple and I were the only two in the Council that stood firm. We waited to see if this would last, and, finding a change of measures, and that I could be of no farther use, I resigned; and ever since I have known no more of what has been doing in the Cabinet than the most remote man in the Kingdom. I know not what Genoa has been able to obtain by means of France. I—' BOSWELL. 'Sir, that the General – Paoli – felt severely: to be given into the bargain that poor Corsica should be considered as nothing.' PITT. 'Mr Boswell, I own it appears strange that an island of so great consequence to the navigation in the Mediterranean should be neglected. How are their harbours?' BOSWELL. 'One or two excellent, with some expense.' PITT.

'Sir, that is of great consequence to a fleet on some grand enterprise. We have no such place on Italy.' BOSWELL. 'Sir, General de Paoli said—' PITT. 'Sir, you'll remember my situation.' BOSWELL. 'Pray, Sir, may I ask you if you never received a letter from General de Paoli?' PITT. 'Never, Sir.' BOSWELL. 'Why then, Sir, after the Proclamation he wrote to you, and, as he has the highest admiration of your character, he was most sensibly hurt to be neglected by Mr Pitt.' PITT. 'Sir, I never received his letter. I suppose *those next the King* have taken care it should not be delivered. I could not have answered it – could not have been in correspondence with General de Paoli, but I should have taken care to let him know my regard for him. Sir, I should be sorry that in any corner of the world, however distant or however small, it should be suspected that I could ever be indifferent to the cause of liberty.'

Yesterday dined at Dempster's. Talked too much of Miss Bosville. Sandie Duncan, with honest Scots sagacity without sarcasm, said, 'What, is she so extremely pretty?' BOSWELL. 'Yes.' DUNCAN. 'Then we shall have no more of Paoli!' Stewart was there who wrote *The North Briton Extraordinary*. You paid him just compliments on it. You felt yourself even at Dempster's *almost* as well as you could wish, but found it prudent to be seldom with old dissipated company.

You met at Mitre Dr Goldsmith whom you had before called upon. You both went to Mr Johnson's, who was still bad and would not come out. 'Come then,' said Goldie, 'we will not go to the Mitre tonight, since we can't have the big man with us.' But we had sent for Davies, and I insisted on going. Goldsmith said, 'I think, Mr Johnson, you don't go near the theatres. You give yourself no more concern about a new play than if you had never had anything to do with the stage.' JOHNSON. 'Why, Sir, our tastes alter. The lad does not care for the child's rattle, and the old man does not care for the young man's whore.' GOLDSMITH. 'Nay, but, Sir, your Muse was not a whore.' JOHNSON. 'Sir, I don't think she was. But as we advance in the journey of life, we drop some of the things which have pleased us; whether it be that we are fatigued and don't choose to carry so many things any farther, or that we find other things which we like better.' BOSWELL. 'But, Sir, why don't you give us something in some other way?' GOLDSMITH. 'Ay, Sir, we have a claim upon you.' JOHNSON. 'No, Sir, I am not obliged to do any more. No man is obliged to do as much as he can do. A man is to have part of his life to himself. If a soldier has fought a good many campaigns, he is not to be blamed if he retires to ease and tranquillity. Sir, a physician who has long practised in a great city may be excused if he retires to a small town and takes less practice. Sir, the good I can do by my conversation bears the same proportion to the good I can do by my writings that the practice of a physician, retired to a small town, does to his practice in a great city.' BOSWELL. 'But I wonder, Sir, you have not more pleasure in writing than not.' JOHNSON. 'Sir, you *may* wonder.' In short, Goldsmith and I could make nothing against him.

He talked of making verses. He said, 'The great matter is to know when you have made good ones. I generally have 'em in my mind, perhaps fifty at a time, walking in my room; and then write 'em, and often from laziness wrote only the half lines. Sir, I have written a hundred lines a day. I remember I wrote a hundred lines of *The Vanity of Human Wishes* in a day. Doctor, I made one line t'other day, but I made out no more.' GOLDSMITH. 'Let us hear it, and we'll put a bad one to it.' JOHNSON. 'No, Sir, I have forgot it.'

We left him, and as we were going along Fleet Street, Goldsmith very gravely said, 'Don't you think that head's failed – wearing, eh?' O fine! BOSWELL. 'No, Sir, I think he is rather more impatient of contradiction than he was.' GOLDSMITH. 'Sir, no man is proof against continual adulation.'

Davies could not come to the Mitre, so Goldsmith carried me to his chambers in the King's Bench Walk, which he has furnished, and is quite magnificent. We talked of writing against authors from envy; I said if I wrote against anything it would be against his chambers. He gave me a repast and we were well. I touched him by the story of 'Johnson and Goldsmith and those blockheads', and upon his honour that he would not say anything of it, I told him 'twas Smith. 'Well,' said he, 'by telling me it was he, you have given me a plaster for the sore.' Such is human nature.

We talked of French and English. You said the English were like noble standard oaks, which could be alone and well. The French, slender shrubs, that are nothing but in a copsewood. Goldsmith said, 'I have passed the summer among the great,' and forsooth affected to talk lightly of this. You brought him down with Johnsonian principles and Johnsonian force.

Excerpt from Some of Boswell's Letters to the London Chronicle

THURSDAY 13 FEBRUARY. 'The gazettes of late have talked a great deal of a certain Mr Boswell, a Scots gentleman, who has been in Corsica. It was at first rumoured that he was a desperate adventurer, whose real name was M'Donald, and who had served during the last war in North America; but it has since appeared that he is a gentleman of fortune upon his travels, a friend of the celebrated John James Rousseau, who is an enthusiast for the Corsicans, and has been honoured with the title of their legislator. We do not give credit to the reports of Mr Boswell's having had instructions from his Court to treat with Signor de Paoli, but we are in great hopes that from what he has seen, he will be able to undeceive his countrymen with regard to the Corsican nation.'

SATURDAY 15 FEBRUARY. Yesterday James Boswell, Esquire, arrived in town from his travels.

4

'Dreaming of Delightful Nuptials':

Choosing the Lady of Auchinleck

In 1766 Boswell returned to Scotland and began his career as an advocate at the courts of Edinburgh. His first client in criminal practice, in that year, was John Reid, an agricultural labourer accused of sheep-stealing. For the next three years he made a fair success of this occupation; he brought out his Tour to Corsica *to general applause, and he made several trips to London, seeing Johnson, Garrick, Goldsmith and the rest and revelling in that brilliant society. The one missing link was a matrimonial one. Boswell was now 'In Search of a Wife', as the title of the corresponding Yale volume has it, and this chapter tells how he came to be married in 1769 and the various candidates that presented themselves to him. Principally these were: Zélide, still his faithful correspondent; Catherine Blair, a Scots heiress, whom he characterized as 'The Princess'; his beautiful cousin, Elizabeth Bosville, and a sixteen-year-old Dublin girl of rich background, Mary Anne Boyd ('Marianne'). In the interim he had a serious affair with Mrs Dodds, whom he met at Moffat, a kind of eighteenth-century health resort where people used to go and 'take the waters'. But the identity of the woman he did marry was to him unexpected and surprising; it is pleasant to look back on his never-failing love and respect for his new wife and be as sure as it is possible to be that he made the right choice.*

Boswell to Temple

Auchinleck House, 28 April 1766
My ever dear Temple, – Many a curious letter have you had from me in my different situations. A more extraordinary one than this you have never had. I write to you while the delirium is really existing. In

short, Sir, the gardener's daughter, who was named for my mother
and has for some time been in the family as a chambermaid, is so
very pretty that I am entirely captivated by her. Besides my principle
of never debauching an innocent girl, my regard for her father, a
worthy man of uncommon abilities, restrains me from forming the
least licentious thought against her. And therefore, in plain words, I
am mad enough to indulge imaginations of marrying her. Only think
of the proud Boswell, with all that you know of him, the fervent adorer
of a country girl of three and twenty. I rave about her. I was never
so much in love as I am now. My fancy is quite inflamed. It riots in
extravagance.

I know as well as you can tell me that a month's or perhaps ten
days' possession of this angelic creature would probably make her
appear to me insipid as does to you Celia 'who at Berwick deigns
to dwell'. I have a clear remembrance of my being tormented with
many such passions, all which went off in a little time, and yet,
Temple, I am still dreaming of delightful nuptials. She and I were
in a manner brought up together. As far back as I can remember,
we used to build houses and make gardens, wade in the river and
play upon the sunny banks. I cannot consider her as below me. For
these six or seven years past I have seen her little. Before I went
abroad she had begun to be timid and reserved, for Lord Eglinton
admired her extremely and wanted to seduce her. For my part I
saw nothing more about her than in many good-looking girls in the
neighbourhood. But since my return from my travels I have been quite
enchanted with her. She has a most amiable face, the prettiest foot and
ankle. She is perfectly well made, and has a lively, genteel air that is
irresistible.

I take every opportunity of being with her when she is putting on
fires or dressing a room. She appears more graceful with her besom
than ever shepherdess did with a crook. I pretend great earnestness
to have the library in good order and assist her to dust it. I cut
my gloves that she may mend them. I kiss her hand. I tell her
what a beauty I think her. She has an entire confidence in me
and has no fear of any bad design; and she has too much sense
to form an idea of having me for a husband. On the contrary,
she talks to me of not refusing a good offer if it is made to her.
Enchanting creature! must she be enjoyed by some schoolmaster or

farmer? Upon my honour, it cuts me to the heart. If she would not marry anybody else, I think I could let her alone. That we may not be too often seen together, she and I write notes to each other, which we lay under the cloth which covers my table. This little curious correspondence, which to her is an innocent amusement, makes my heart beat continually. She has a fine temper. She has read a great deal, for I always supplied her with books. In short, she is better than any lady I know.

What shall I do, Temple? Shall I lay my account with all its consequences and espouse her? Will not the exquisite languish of her eyes charm away repentance? Shall I not pass a life of true natural felicity with the woman I love and have a race of healthy and handsome children? Good heavens! what am I about? It would kill my father. Have I returned safe from London, from Italy and from France to throw myself away on a servant maid? You might apply to me what was said of St Paul when the viper fastened upon his hand after the shipwreck: 'Whom though he hath escaped the sea, yet vengeance suffereth not to live.'

I have got a lock of her hair which I dote upon. She allowed me to cut it off. If I should marry her, I would never suffer her to dress better than she does now. I think I could pass my whole life agreeably with her assistance. I am not fit for marriage in all the forms. A lady would not be compliant enough, and would oblige me to harass myself with an endless repetition of external ceremony and a most woeful maintaining of *proper conduct*. Whereas my dear girl would be grateful for my attachment, would be devoted to me in every respect, would live with me just as a mistress without the disgrace and remorse. After all my feverish joys and pains, I should enjoy calm and permanent bliss in her arms. Was there ever such madness?

My friend, give me your hand. Lead me away from what is probably a delusion that would make me give up with the world and sink into a mere animal. And yet is it not being singularly happy that after the gloom I have endured, the dreary speculations I have formed and the vast variety of all sorts of adventures that I have run through, my mind should not be a bit corrupted, and I should feel the elegant passion with all the pure simplicity and tender agitations of youth? Surely I have the genuine soul of love. When dusting the rooms with my charmer, am I not like Agamemnon amongst the Thracian girls? All this may do for a summer. But is it possible that I could imagine the dear delirium would last for life? I will rouse my philosophic spirit, and fly from this fascination. I am going to Moffat for a month. Absence will break the enchantment. I charge you in honour not to mention it. Write me how you are affected by this letter. My dear Temple, I am ever yours,

JAMES BOSWELL

Boswell to Temple

Moffat, 17 May 1766

My dearest Friend, – I have been a week here, and to prevent that rodomontade of which you have frequently accused me, let me tell you at once that my love for the handsome chambermaid is already like a dream that is past. I kept the extravagant epistle which was to inform you of it till I should see if absence would not free me from the delirium. I can now send you with a good grace what would certainly have alarmed you, but will now be truly amusing. Romantic as I am, it was so strange a scene in the play of my life that I myself was quite astonished at it. I give you my word of honour it was literally true. There are few people who could give credit to it. But you, who have traced me since ever I fairly entered upon the stage, will not doubt of it. It is a little humbling, to be sure. It was the effect of great force and great weakness of mind. I am certainly a most various composition. Pray recollect my letter from Rotterdam and compare it with the enclosed. They are both genuine effusions, both original pictures of the same man at different times.

As to Zélide, I am quite at my ease. I have had a letter from her father telling me that he took my proposal in very good part; at the same time he informed me that things were so far advanced between his daughter and M. le Marquis that the Marquis was actually applying to the Pope and the King of Sardinia for leave to marry a Protestant, and that therefore he and his daughter were bound in honour to fulfil their promises to him. As, however, the event of this application was uncertain, if I continued to be of the same mind after they were free of the Marquis, he would then mention my proposal to Mademoiselle and have the honour to be umpire between us. Nothing could be more genteel and friendly. I am glad I am off with Zélide. A *bel esprit* would never do at Auchinleck. My father and I have talked fully of her. He could not bear such a woman. You may remember you laughed very heartily at my finding fault with a *pretty* Dutchwoman. But my father judges extremely well when he finds fault with a *clever* Dutchwoman. 'I love', says he, 'one who has been accustomed to play in concert, be the music heavy or be it lively. For such a person will make harmony in any country. But one who has played in discord with those around her will hardly play in tune at all.' *Cum fueris Romae, Romano vivito more* is sound sense; and Otway says with much truth:

> Avoid
> The man that's singular . . .
> His spleen outweighs his brains.

Zélide, who must always *shine*, and Stockdale, who is *sublimated* and thinks you below him in *genius*, are weak beings, and would make one miserable to live with them. 'Tis true they can't help their levity. Very well. Neither could they help it were the one hump-backed and the other palsied. I am sorry for them. But I would not join my existence with theirs.

After all, Zélide may perhaps *take up*.

But this is a flight. Now, Temple, let me explain to you how I am already so free of the charming chambermaid. Absence alone was not enough. But I have found at Moffat a lady just in the situation of the one whom you formerly dallied with in Northumberland. But mine has no hope of ever being as yours now is, so that she is at full liberty, and therefore the king can do no wrong. I am quite devoted to her. I dare write no more, but when we meet – you shall hear of Elysium. Love reconciles me to the Scots accent, which from the mouth of a pretty woman is simply and sweetly melodious. It is indeed, and I could engage to make Temple himself swear so in a few months. I am all health, affection and gratitude.

I came to Moffat to wash off a few scurvy spots which the warmer climates of Europe had brought out on my skin. I drink the waters, and bathe regularly, and take a great deal of exercise, and have a fine flow of spirits. I am as happy as an unmarried man can be. The *felices ter et amplius*[1] enchants me as the mitre or the genteel chintz armchairs in a handsome parlour do you. This shall be my last irregular connection. I shall be attached to the generous woman for ever. I am plaguing you with romantic sallies, my Temple. Forgive me, and it shall be made up to you before I sleep.

Boswell to Temple

4 March 1767

In a former part of this letter I have talked a great deal of my sweet little mistress. I am, however, uneasy about her. Furnishing a house and maintaining her with a maid will cost me a great deal of money, and it is too like marriage, or too much a settled plan of licentiousness. But what can I do? I have already taken the house, and the lady has agreed to go into it at Whitsunday. I cannot in honour draw back. Besides, in no other way can I have her. But I have had more intelligence of her former intrigues. I am hurt to think of them. I cry, 'Damn her, lewd minx.' I am jealous. What shall I do?

Oh, my friend! were you but here; but, alas! that cannot be. Mamhead is not within a call. It ought to be so, for you should always be my pastor; and I might now and then be yours. Friend of my youth, explain to me how we suffer so severely from what no longer exists. How am I tormented because my charmer has formerly loved others! I am disgusted to think of it. My lively imagination often represents her former lovers in actual enjoyment of her. My desire fails, I am unfit for love. Besides, she is ill-bred, quite a rompish girl. She debases my dignity. She has no refinement. But she is very handsome, very lively and admirably formed for amorous dalliance. What is it to me that she has formerly loved? So have I. I am positive that since I first courted her at Moffat she has been constant to me. She is kind. She is generous. What shall I do? I wish I could get off, and yet how awkward would it be! And, after all, can I do better than keep a dear infidel for my hours of Paphian bliss? But, alas, since yesterday I am cooled. Think of your Berwick Celia and sympathize with me. One way or other, my mind will be settled before I can hear from you. This is a curious epistle to a clergyman. Admonish me, but forgive me.

Doctor Robertson will soon give the world his *Charles the Fifth*. Smith, I suppose, is in London. But I do not hear that his book on jurisprudence is in any forwardness. David Hume, you know, is gone back to be a minister of state, being appointed secretary to Mr Conway. I fancy he will hardly write any more. I was very hearty with him here this winter. Whenever you go to London, I will give you a letter of introduction to him. His quarrel with Rousseau is a literary tragicomedy. I wrote verses in the character of each of them. I also designed a ludicrous print. They have altered my idea and made a glister be applied to David. But you may have the substance of it from one of the London print-shops under the title of 'The Savage Man'. You must know Rousseau quarrelled with me too, and wrote me last summer a peevish letter with strong marks of frenzy in it. For he has never yet told me the cause of his offence. As you well observe, how different is our friendship!

I have got pretty well acquainted with Doctor Gregory. He was very desirous to know me. His book is ingenious and elegant, and he himself is one of the most amiable, pleasant men alive.

The session will be up this day sennight. I shall then set myself down to my Account of Corsica, and finish it in the vacation. I have got more materials for it. I had some time ago a letter of sixteen pages from General Paoli, and lately a letter of three pages from my Lord Chatham. David Hume told me sincerely he imagined my Account of Corsica would be a book that will stand, and he is obliging enough to transact the publication of it for me with Andrew Millar. All your old friends here are well, *in statu quo*, Jeel and all, and remember you kindly. Sinclair has never found his brother. I don't write often enough to Squire Bosville, but I shall give him a good letter tomorrow. His beauty, I am afraid, would be too fine for this northern air. Temple, will you allow me to marry a good Scots lass? Ha! ha! ha! What shall I tell you? Zélide has been in London this winter. I never hear from her. She is a strange creature. Sir John Pringle attended her as a physician. He wrote to my father, 'She has too much vivacity. She talks of your son without either resentment or attachment.' Her brothers and I correspond. But I am well rid of her. You say well that I find mistresses wherever I am. But I am a sad dupe, a perfect Don Quixote. To return to where it winces, might not I tell my little charmer that really I am an inconstant being, but I cannot help it? Or I may let my love gradually decay? Had she never loved before, I would have lost every drop of my blood rather than give her up. There's madness! There's delicacy! I have not had such a relief as this for I don't know how long. I have broke the trammels of business, and am roving unconfined with my worthy Temple.

What is to be thought of this life, my friend? Hear the story of my last three days. After tormenting myself with reflecting on my charmer's former loves and ruminating on parting with her, I went to her. I could not conceal my being distressed. I told her I was very unhappy, but I would not tell her why. She took this very seriously, and was so much affected that she went next morning and gave up our house. I went in the afternoon and secured the house, and then drank tea with her. She was much agitated. She said she was determined to go and board herself in the north of England, and that I used her very ill. I expostulated with her. I was sometimes resolved to let her go, and sometimes my heart was like to burst within me. I held her dear hand. Her eyes were full of passion. I took her in my arms. I told her what made me miserable. She was pleased to find it was nothing worse. She had imagined that I was suspicious of her fidelity, and she thought that very ungenerous in me, considering her behaviour. She said I should not mind her faults before I knew her, since her conduct was now most circumspect. We renewed our fondness. She owned she loved me more than she had ever done her husband. All was again well. She said she did not reproach me with my former follies, and we should be on an equal footing. My mind all at once felt a spring. I agreed with her. I embraced her with transport.

That very evening I gave a supper to two or three of my acquaintance, having before I left Scotland laid a guinea that I should not catch the venereal disorder for three years, which bet I had most certainly lost and now was paying. We drank a great deal, till I was so much intoxicated that instead of going home I went to a low house in one of the alleys in Edinburgh where I knew a common girl lodged, and like a brute as I was I lay all night with her. I had still so much reason left as not to 'dive into the bottom of the deep', but I gratified my coarse desires by tumbling about on the brink of destruction. Next morning I was like a man ordered for ignominious execution. But by noon I was worse, for I discovered that some infection had reached me. Was not this dreadful? I had an assignation in the evening with my charmer. How lucky was it that I knew my misfortune in time. I might have polluted her sweet body. Bless me! what a risk! But how could I tell her my shocking story? I took courage. I told how drunk I had been. I told the consequences. I lay down and kissed her feet. I said I was unworthy of any other favour. But I took myself.[2] I gloried that I had ever been firmly constant to her while I was myself. I hoped she would consider my being drunk as a fatal accident which I should never again fall into. I called her my friend in whom I had confidence, and entreated she would comfort me.

How like you the eloquence of a young barrister? It was truly the eloquence of love. She bid me rise; she took me by the hand. She said she forgave me. She kissed me. She gently upbraided me for entertaining any unfavourable ideas of her. She bid me take great care of myself and in time coming never drink upon any account. Own to me, Temple, that this was noble – and all the time her beauty enchanted me more than ever. May I not then be hers? In the meantime I must be shut up, and honest Thomas must be my guardian. He does excellently well. Pray what do you hear of Nicholls and Claxton? Make my compliments to them. There is a pretty book just now published, *An Essay on the History of Civil Society*, by the Moral Philosophy Professor here. Let me hear from you soon, and believe me, ever yours,

JAMES BOSWELL

Memorabilia, 1767

? MARCH. I am a singular man. I have the whim of an Englishman to make me think and act extravagantly, and yet I have the coolness and good sense of a Scotsman to make me sensible of it.

I have often found myself inclined to give praise in a great degree. The reason is that in giving praise one feels a pride similar to that of one giving money. When I deal out laudatory epithets I am like a great man bestowing his largesses. Our inclination to censure strongly is owing to the same imaginary dignity. We suppose ourselves men of power distributing punishments; such, indeed, are not often of much importance.

Lord Auchinleck used to pass his time in the country in continual attention to the improvement of his place, but would often busy himself with very small matters. He would, for instance, gather stones off the land for hours; nay, he would very gravely fill his pockets with them, and carry them to mend a broken part in some favourite part. His sons, though they had a high respect for him, could not but exercise their humour on such oddities in a great character. David said, 'He carries the stones in this manner upon the principle of utility, and no doubt he does some good to the road. But he would also do some good were he to fill his nails with sand, and sprinkle it upon the road. Why does he not always do good in some more important manner?'

I have seen contemptible beings exceedingly vain of being satirical. They do not consider how very little a dog is yet capable to bite. The veriest cur may scratch the heel of the most generous horse.

I have sometimes fallen into a strange, wild reverie, looking upon the human species as produced merely to exist a little here, and then be destroyed by the course of nature; so that all the diversities of character and of virtues have appeared as of little consequence. Methought I could use the words of him who was born blind, when Jesus was curing him, 'Methinks I see men as trees walking.'

I am a weaker man than can well be imagined. My brilliant qualities are like embroidery upon gauze.

Received 8 August, Temple to Boswell

Berwick, 7 August 1767

Dearest Boswell, – I just sit down to acquaint you that I was married yesterday. Do I repent? God knows; I'll tell you a twelvemonth hence. I own I can't yet perceive that it makes any difference. I awoke in the morning not at all surprised at myself. I got up, read, and eat and drank as usual. Indeed, I am apt to believe that almost all changes are much more in the idea than in the reality. The mind is a very complaisant and pliant gentleman, and easily suits himself to every situation. Thanks to your excellent father; I have in great measure adopted his idea.

But how can I talk so indifferently when you are so justly distressed? I feel with you most sincerely, both on your own account and that of the dear innocent exposed to such danger. Forgive me if I suspect

Mrs — herself, but I must suspect her; and, dearest Boswell, *guard*, *guard* against her artful openness and vulgarity. But you see the consequence of such connections, and how dare I call the punishment unjust? It is according to the order of nature and Providence, and you will ever find, my orthodox friend, that *faith* without *works* is nothing, that virtue is happiness and vice misery; henceforth, never have the audacity to refuse drinking David Hume in my company, and learn to reverence his name till you can imitate his example. I know I write confusedly and incorrectly, but consider my situation. My respects to your father, compliments to David, Wyvill and worthy Johnston. Most sincerely yours,

T.

In the summer of 1767 Boswell had begun courting 'the Princess' (Catherine Blair, a Scots heiress) but – as this letter to Temple shows – he was finding it a problematic relationship.

Boswell to Temple

Auchinleck, Sunday 8 November 1767
My dear Friend, – I wrote you from Adamton and told you how it was with the Princess and me. Next morning I told her that I had complained to you that she would not make up our last quarrel. But she did not appear in the least inclined to own herself in the wrong. I confess that between pride and love I was unable to speak to her but in a very awkward manner. I came home on Friday. Yesterday I was extremely uneasy. That I might give her a fair opportunity I sent her a letter, of which I enclose you a copy. Could the proud Boswell say more than you will see there? In the evening I got her answer. It was written with an art and an indifference astonishing from so young a lady. 'I have not yet found out that I was to blame. – If you have been uneasy upon my account, I am indeed sorry for it. I should be sorry to give any person uneasiness, far more one whose cousin and friend I shall always be.' She refused sending me the lock, 'because (in the eyes of the world) it is improper', and she says several very cool things upon that head. What think you of such a return to a letter full of warmth and admiration?

In short, Temple, she is cunning and sees my weakness. But I now see her; and though I cannot but suffer severely, I from this moment resolve to think no more of her. I send you the copy of a note which goes to her tomorrow morning. Wish me joy, my good friend, of having discovered the snake before it was too late. I should have been ruined had I made such a woman my wife. Luckily for me a neighbour who came to Auchinleck last night told me that he had heard three people at Ayr agree in abusing her as a d—ned jilt. What a risk have I run! However, as there is still a possibility that all this may be mistake and malice, I shall behave to her in a very respectable manner and shall never say a word against her but to you. After this, I shall be upon my guard against ever indulging the least fondness for a *Scots lass*. I am a soul of a more southern frame. I may perhaps be fortunate enough to find an Englishwoman who will be sensible of my merit, and will study to please my singular humour. By what you write of Mrs Temple I wish I had such a wife, though indeed your temper is so much better than mine that perhaps she and I would have quarrelled before this time, had we been married when you was.

Love is a perfect fever of the mind. I question if any man has been more tormented with it than myself. Even at this moment as I write, my heart is torn by vexing thoughts of this fine Princess of ours. But I may take comfort, since I have so often recovered. Think of the gardener's daughter. Think of Mrs D—. By the by, the latter shared in my late misfortune, but she is quite well again; and in a fortnight hence I expect a young friend, who if a male is to be George Keith, after my good Lord Marischal.

Boswell to Temple

Edinburgh, 24 December 1767
My dearest Friend, – In my last I told you that after I had resolved to give up with the Princess for ever, I resolved first to see her, and that when I did see her I was so lucky as to have a very agreeable interview, and was convinced by her that she was not to blame. This happened on a Thursday. That evening, her cousin and most intimate friend, the Duchess of Gordon, came to town. Next day I was at the concert

with them and afterwards supped at Lord Kames's. The Princess appeared distant and reserved. I could hardly believe that it was the same woman with whom I had been quite easy the day before. I was then uneasy.

Next evening I was at the play with them. It was *Othello*. I sat close behind the Princess, and at the most affecting scenes I pressed my hand upon her waist. She was in tears, and rather leaned to me. The jealous Moor described my very soul. I often spoke to her of the torment which she saw before her. Still I thought her distant, and still I was uneasy.

On Sunday the Duchess of Gordon went away. I met the Princess at church. She was distant as before. I passed the evening at her aunt's, where I met a cousin of my Princess, a young lady of Glasgow who had been with us at Adamton. She told me she had something to communicate, and she then said that my behaviour to the Princess was such that Mrs Blair and her daughter did not know how to behave to me. That it was not honourable to engage a young lady's affections while I kept myself free. In short, the good cousin persuaded me that the Princess had formed an attachment for me, and she assured me the Nabob had been refused.[3] On Monday forenoon I waited on Miss Blair; I found her alone, and she did not seem distant. I told her that I was most sincerely in love with her, and that I only dreaded those faults which I had acknowledged to her. I asked her seriously if she now believed me in earnest. She said she did. I then asked her to be candid and fair as I had been with her, and to tell me if she had any particular liking for me. What think you, Temple, was her answer? *No.* 'I really', said she, 'have no particular liking for you. I like many people as well as you.'

(Temple, you must have it in the genuine dialogue.) BOSWELL. 'Do you indeed? Well, I cannot help it. I am obliged to you for telling me so in time. I am sorry for it.' PRINCESS. 'I like Jeanie Maxwell (Duchess of Gordon) better than you.' BOSWELL. 'Very well. But do you like no man better than me?' PRINCESS. 'No.' BOSWELL. 'Is it possible that you may like me better than other men?' PRINCESS. 'I don't know what is possible.' (By this time I had risen and placed myself by her, and was in real agitation.) BOSWELL. 'I'll tell you what, my dear Miss Blair, I love you so much that I am very unhappy. If you cannot love me, I must if possible endeavour to forget you. What would you have me do?' PRINCESS. 'I really don't know what you should do.' BOSWELL. 'It is certainly possible that you *may* love me, and if you shall ever do so I shall be the happiest man in the world. Will you make a fair bargain with me? If you should happen to love me, will you own it?' PRINCESS. 'Yes.' BOSWELL. 'And if you should happen to love another, will you tell me immediately, and help me to make myself easy?' PRINCESS. 'Yes, I will.' BOSWELL. 'Well, you are very good' (often squeezing and kissing her fine hand, while she looked at me with those beautiful black eyes).

PRINCESS. 'I may tell you as a cousin what I would not tell to another man.' BOSWELL. 'You may indeed. You are very fond of Auchinleck; that is one good circumstance.' PRINCESS. 'I confess I am. I wish I liked you as well as I do Auchinleck.' BOSWELL. 'I have told you how fond I am of you. But unless you like me sincerely, I have too much spirit to ask you to live with me, as I know that you do not like me. If I could have you this moment for my wife I would not.' PRINCESS. 'I should not like to put myself in your offer, though.' BOSWELL. 'Remember, you are both my cousin and my mistress. You must make me suffer as little as possible. As it may happen that I may engage your affections, I should think myself a most dishonourable man if I were not now in earnest, and remember I depend upon your sincerity; and whatever happens you and I shall never again have any quarrel.' PRINCESS. 'Never.' BOSWELL. 'And I may come and see you as much as I please?' PRINCESS. 'Yes.'

My worthy friend, what sort of a scene was this? It was most curious. She said she would submit to her husband in most things. She said that to see one loving her would go far to make her love that person; but she could not talk anyhow positively, for she never had felt the uneasy anxiety of love. We were an hour and a half together, and seemed pleased all the time. I think she behaved with spirit and propriety. I admired her more than ever. She intended to go to her aunt's twelve miles from town next day. Her jaunt was put off for some days. Yesterday I saw her again. I was easy and cheerful, and just endeavoured to make myself agreeable.

Amidst all this love I have been wild as ever. I have catched another memorandum of vice, but a very slight one. Trust me in time coming. I give you my word in honour, Temple. I have nothing else to save me.

My black friend has brought me the finest little girl I ever saw. I have named it Sally. It is healthy and strong. I take the greatest care of the mother, but shall have her no more in keeping.

Boswell to Temple

Edinburgh, 8 February 1768

My dear Friend, – All is over between Miss Blair and me. I have delayed writing till I could give you some final account. About a fortnight after she went to the country a report went that she was going to be married to Sir Alexander Gilmour, Member of Parliament for the county of Midlothian, a young man about thirty who has £1,600 a year of estate, was formerly an officer in the Guards, and is now one of the Clerks of the Board of Green Cloth, £1,000 a year; in short, a noble match, though a man of expense and obliged to lead a London life. After the fair agreement between her and me which I gave you fully in my last, I had a title to know the truth. I wrote to her seriously, and told her that if she did not write me an answer I should believe the report to be true. After three days, I concluded from her silence that she was at last engaged. I endeavoured to laugh off my passion and I got Sir Alexander Gilmour to frank a letter to her, which I wrote in a pleasant strain and amused myself with the whim. Still, however, I was not absolutely certain, as her conduct has been so prudent all along.

At last she comes to town, and who comes too but my old rival, the Nabob. I got acquainted with Mr Fullarton, and he and I joked a good deal about our Heiress. Last night he proposed that he and I should go together and pay her a visit for the first time after her return from the country. Accordingly we went, and I give you my word, Temple, it was a curious scene. However, the Princess behaved exceedingly well, though with a reserve more than ordinary. When we left her, we both exclaimed, 'Upon my soul, a fine woman!' I began to like the Nabob much, so I said to him, 'I do believe, Mr Fullarton, you and I are in the same situation here. Is it possible to be upon honour and generous in an affair of this kind?' We agreed it was. Each then declared he was serious in his love for Miss Blair, and each protested he never before believed the other in earnest. We agreed to deal by one another in a fair and candid manner.

I carried him to sup at a lady's, a cousin of mine, where we stayed till half an hour past eleven. We then went to a tavern, and the good old claret was set before us. He told me that he had been most assiduous in attending Miss Blair, but she never gave him the least encouragement, and he declared he was convinced she loved me as much as a woman could love a man. With equal honesty I told him all that has passed between her and me, and your observation on the *wary mother*. 'What!' said he, 'did Temple say so? If he had lived twenty years in the country with them, he could not have said a better thing.' I then told him Dempster's humorous saying that all Miss Blair's connections were in an absolute confederacy to lay hold of every man who has a £1,000 a year, and how I called their system *a salmon fishing*. 'You have hit it,' said he. 'We're all kept in play: but I am positive you are the fish, and Sir Alexander is only a mock salmon to force you to jump more expeditiously at the bait.' We sat till two this morning. We gave our words as men of honour that we would be honest to each other, so that neither should suffer needlessly; and to satisfy ourselves of our real situation we gave our words that we should both ask her this morning, and I should go first. Could there be anything better than this? The Nabob talked to me with the warmth of the Indies, and professed the greatest pleasure on being acquainted with me.

Well, Temple, I went this morning, and she made tea to me alone. I then asked her seriously if she was to be married to Sir Alexander. She said it was odd to believe everything people said, and why did I put such a question &c? I said that she knew very well I was much in love with her, and that if I had any chance I would take a good deal of trouble to make myself agreeable to her. She said I need not take the trouble, and I must not be angry, for she thought it best to tell me honestly. 'What then,' said I, 'have I no chance?' 'No,' said she. I asked her to say so upon her word and upon honour. She fairly repeated the words. So, I think, Temple, I had enough.

She would not tell me whether she was engaged to the Knight. She said she would not satisfy an idle curiosity. But I own I had no doubt of it. What amazed me was that she and I were as easy and as good friends as ever. I told her, 'I have great animal spirits and bear it wonderfully well. But this is really hard. I am thrown upon the wide world again. I don't know what will become of me.'

Before dinner the Nabob and I met, and he told me that he went, and in the most serious and submissive manner begged to know if she was engaged. She would give him no satisfaction, and treated him with a degree of coldness that overpowered him quite, poor man.

Such is the history of the lovers of this cruel Princess, who certainly is a lucky woman to have had a sovereign sway over so many admirers.

Now that all is over, I see many faults in her which I did not see before. Do you not think she has not feeling enough, nor that ingenuous spirit which your friend requires? The Nabob and many other people are still of opinion that she has not made sure of Sir Sawney, and that all this may be finesse. But I cannot suspect so young a creature of so much artifice, and whatever may be in it I am honourably off; and you may wonder at it, but I assure you I am very easy and cheerful. I am, however, resolved to look out for a good wife, either here or in England. I intend to be in London in March. My address will be at Mr Dilly's, bookseller. But I expect to hear from you before I set out, which will not be till the 14 of March. I rejoice to hear that Mrs Temple is in a good way. My best wishes ever attend you and her. I am your most affectionate friend,

JAMES BOSWELL

11 February. I have allowed my letter to lie by till this day. The Heiress is a good Scots lass. But I must have an Englishwoman. My mind is now twice as enlarged as it has been for some months. You cannot say how fine a woman I may marry; perhaps a Howard or some other of the noblest in the kingdom.

After the collapse of his hopes for a brilliant marriage to Miss Blair, Boswell headed for London to see Johnson and the newly exiled Paoli. On the way he had a pleasing demonstration of the success of his new book.

SATURDAY 19 MARCH. We got to York at night and put up at Bluitt's Inn. We were dusty, bustling fellows, and no sooner was our baggage taken off than we posted to the theatre. We went into the back seat of one of the boxes, and indeed there was a pretty company. I loved to see so many genteel people in their own county town, in place of crowding to London. The play was *False Delicacy*, and the farce, *A Peep behind the Curtain*. Wilkinson, the mimic, played, and several of the performers did very well. We returned to our inn and had an excellent supper, the President encouraging the court to eat heartily.

I never saw a better inn. The waiters had all one livery: brown coats and scarlet vests. We had hitherto been raised very early, but we now resolved to take sufficient repose for a night. Upon my word, eating, drinking and sleeping are matters of great moment.

SUNDAY 20 MARCH. After a long sleep and a copious breakfast, we went and saw the cathedral. It is a prodigiously noble Gothic edifice. Small and Robertson stayed all the time of service. But I slipped away to a coffee-house where I fell into conversation with a Sir George (I believe, Armytage) about Corsica. He talked very warmly for them and seemed to know a good deal about them. I began to think he must have learnt his knowledge of me. So I asked him if the Corsicans had any seaports. 'Oh, yes, Sir,' said he, 'very good ones. Why, Boswell's *Account of Corsica* tells you all that.' 'Sir?' said I, 'what is that?' 'Why, Sir,' said he, 'a book just now published.' 'By an officer in that service, Sir?' said I. 'No,' said he. 'I have not the pleasure of being acquainted with the gentleman, but Mr Boswell is a gentleman who was abroad and who thought he would pay a visit to Corsica, and accordingly went thither and had many conversations with Paoli' (Pioli he pronounced it), 'and he has given its history and a full account of everything about the island, and has shown that Britain should make an alliance with Corsica.' 'But, Sir,' said I, 'can we believe what he says?' 'Yes, Sir,' said Sir George, 'the book is authentic and very accurate.' I was highly pleased.

MONDAY 21 MARCH. We came at night to Biggleswade, having travelled this day 105 miles. We had an admirable supper. After my former sufferings from bad health and low spirits, I exulted in my present vigour and cheerfulness.

TUESDAY 22 MARCH. I thought of marriage and was determined to have a good match, as I was become so agreeable and so happy a man. Miss Bosville my Yorkshire beauty, Mademoiselle de Zuylen my Utrecht *bel esprit* and friend, were both before me. Yet still I had no determined purpose. About two we arrived at London and put up at the Star and Garter in Bond Street. The streets and squares of the metropolis with all the hurry and variety struck me to a certain degree, but by no means as they had once done, and I contentedly felt myself an Edinburgh advocate. Our Lord President, who had made us live with economy upon the road, finding that of twenty-nine guineas set apart for our expenses there remained two, would needs conclude the session with a jovial repast. Accordingly, we had a cod with oyster and shrimp sauce, some other dishes, and three bottles of the best claret I ever drank. Prentice and Rowden, the two landlords, were called in to take a glass, and in short we were great men. Upon the whole, it was as good a journey as ever was made; and, as in all other scenes, though words do but imperfectly preserve the ideas, yet such notes as I write are sufficient to make the impressions revive, with many associated ones. What should there be in this house but a club every Tuesday called the Roman Club, consisting of gentlemen who were at Rome the same year I was; and who should be upstairs alone but my friend Consul Dick? I sent to him, and he came down immediately. We embraced and in a few words renewed our covenant of cordiality. I then got into a hackney-coach and drove to Mr Russel's, upholsterer, Half Moon Street, Piccadilly, where I had admirable lodgings. After unpacking my trunk, I sallied forth like a roaring lion after girls, blending philosophy and raking. I had a neat little lass *in armour*, at a tavern in the Strand. I then went to the Consul's and supped, and was quite hearty.

WEDNESDAY 23 MARCH. The Consul had provided me not only good lodgings, but a good servant. His name was Anthony Mudford, a Somersetshire lad who had served his time to a hairdresser. I gave him a guinea a week for everything. I called on Lord Mountstuart. But he was out of town. I waited on the Duke of Queensberry for ten minutes, as he had to dress to go to Court. He received me well.

I had this morning been at Tyburn seeing the execution of Mr Gibson, the attorney, for forgery, and of Benjamin Payne for highway robbery. It is a curious turn, but I never can resist seeing executions. The Abbé du Bos ingeniously shows that we have all a strong desire of having our passions moved, and the interesting scene of a man with death before his eyes cannot but move us greatly. One of weak nerves is overpowered by such spectacles. But by thinking and accustoming myself to them, I can see them quite firmly, though I feel compassion. I was on a scaffold close by. Payne was a poor young man of nineteen. He was pale as death, and half a corpse before the rope was put round his neck. Mr Gibson came in a coach with some of his friends, and I declare I cannot conceive a more perfect calmness and manly resolution than his behaviour. He was dressed in a full suit of black, wore his own hair cut round and a hat, was a man about fifty, and as he drove along it was impossible to perceive the least sign of dejection or gloom about him. He was helped up on the cart. The rope was put round his neck, and he stood with the most perfect composure, eat a sweet orange, and seemed rationally devout during prayers by Mr Moore, the ordinary of Newgate,4 who is really a good man and most earnest in the duties of his sad office, which I think a very important one. Stephen Roe, the last ordinary, was but a rough-spun blade. Never did I see death without some horror but in the case of Mr Gibson. It seemed a very easy matter. I always use to compare the conduct of malefactors with what I suppose my conduct might be. I believe I confounded the people about me by my many reflections. I affected being shocked that punishment might have an effect on their minds, though it had none upon my own. I never saw a man hanged but I thought I could behave better than he did, except Mr Gibson, who, I confess, exceeded all that I could ever hope to show of easy and steady resolution.

We went to Guildhall to see the poll for members. It was really grand. Harley (Lord Mayor), Beckford, Trecothick, Sir Richard Glyn, Mr Deputy Paterson and Mr Wilkes all stood upon the hustings, that is to say, a place raised by some steps at one end of the room. They had true London countenances. I cannot describe them. It was curious for me to look at Wilkes here and recollect my scenes with him at Rome, Naples and Paris. The confusion and the noise of the mob roaring 'Wilkes and Liberty' were prodigious. I met here Mr Herries and Sir William Forbes, and, after having had enough of the confusion, I went to them and drank a glass of claret. They showed me my Corsican gun and pistols. But the dog had broken loose and was running about town. Thomas, Mr Herries's servant, and Will, the butcher's man, and I went and patrolled an hour in the Borough, but did not see him. I returned by Dilly's and drank tea. Doctors Saunders and Smith were there. I found it to be a very hospitable house. In the Strand I enquired at the girls for a Miss Simson whom I had known formerly. One of them very obligingly went with me to a Miss Simson's. But she was not the same. However, they both seemed good-natured, and I sat and drank some port with them, and then tossed up which I should make my sultana. Luckily the lot fell on my obliging conductress. I however was *armed*.

THURSDAY 24 MARCH. I patrolled the great metropolis the whole morning. I dined at the worthy Consul's; a lady and a gentleman were there. We were easy enough. At night I still patrolled, I cannot tell where. But about ten I came to Sir John Pringle's. He received me with his usual grave, steady kindness. General Clerk was with him. The conversation turned on the wars of Venus.[5] The General assured me that oil was an infallible shield. Sir John nodded assent; I resolved to try it fairly. After the General went away I talked to Sir John of Mademoiselle de Zuylen. I had just received a letter from Mr Brown at Utrecht containing a very sensible proposal from her, that if I had any serious thoughts of her I should come to see her, and then we might judge whether we could live happily together or not. Sir John had opposed any such scheme. But I found him now better disposed to it, upon which I wrote to my father and begged permission to go to Utrecht.

FRIDAY 25 MARCH. I dined at my good kinsman Godfrey Bosville, Esquire's. Nobody was there, but just the family that I left. He received me with true kindness. Miss Bosville was now engaged to Sir Alexander Macdonald. Godfrey had drawn up a very full account of his family. It entertained me a good deal and put some comfortable ideas in my mind.[6] I then went to Covent Garden and in one of the courts called for a young lady whom I had seen when formerly in London. I did not find her, but I found Kitty Brookes, as pretty a lively lass as youth need see. The oil was called and I played my part well. I never saw a girl more expert at it. I gave her only four shillings, to try her generosity. She never made the least sign of discontent, but was quite gay and obliging. Just as I was going away I turned back and again we loved. Then was the time for her to ask something. Yet she made not the smallest advance. I fell on my knees and kissed her hand: 'My dear Kitty, you are a virtuous girl. I could marry you this moment.'

SATURDAY 26 MARCH. On my coming to London I had called on Mr Samuel Johnson, but found he was gone to Oxford and was living at New Inn Hall. I was very anxious to see again my revered friend. I had written him many letters and had received none from him of a long time. I had published my *Account of Corsica*, in which I had spoken very highly of him, yet he had taken no notice of it. I had heard he was displeased at my having put into my book a part of one of his letters to me. In short, I was quite in the dark concerning him. But, be it as it would, I was determined to find him out, and if possible be well with him as usual. I therefore set out early this morning in the Oxford fly. Anthony had an outside place. My travelling companions were an old, red-faced, fat gentlewoman who lived in the borough of Southwark, and whose husband dealt in a wholesale trade of brandy and wine. Dr Cockayne, a lecturer at one of the churches, lodged in her house, having his own maid-servant and a boy. But she would not board the Doctor. 'No, no. I knows him too well. Why, he's the greatest epicure, perpetually minding his belly. I tells him, "Why, Doctor, you do nothing else from morning to night. You sure have a false pocket." And so I roasts him. But he's a good-natured creature, and would have everyone to share with him. He gets up my daughter: "Come now, Miss, we'll have some tea and something very nice with it."' Besides this good woman, there was a clergyman, a stiff divine, a Fellow of a college in Oxford. He was very wise and laughed at the old lady. The fourth in the coach was a little tailor who has often tripped over to France and Flanders, and who therefore had a right to talk as a travelled man. All the road was roaring with 'Wilkes and Liberty', which, with 'No 45', was chalked on every coach and chaise. We breakfasted at Slough. We became very merry. We dined at Henley, and there we were as hearty as people could be. We had a good drive to Oxford, with always t'other joke on Dr Cockayne. We stopped at the gate of Magdalen College, of which our clergyman was a Fellow. He jumped out of the coach, and in a moment we saw what a great man he was; for he went into the barber's and got the key of his chambers, and two or three people followed him with his trunk, tea-things and I know not what all. The lady left us here too. The tailor and I put up at the Angel, where the coach inns; but we parted there.

I immediately had some coffee and then got a guide to show me New Inn Hall. Mr Johnson lived in the house of Mr Chambers, the head of that hall and Vinerian Professor at Oxford. I supposed the professor would be very formal, and I apprehended but an awkward reception. However, I rung and was shown into the parlour. In a little, down came Mr Chambers, a lively, easy, agreeable Newcastle man. I had sent up my name, 'Mr Boswell'. After receiving me very politely, 'Sir,' said he, 'you are Mr Boswell of Auchinleck?' 'Yes, Sir.' 'Mr Johnson wrote to you yesterday. He dined abroad, but I expect him in every minute.' 'Oho!' thought I, 'this is excellent.' I was quite relieved. Mr Chambers gave me tea, and by and by arrived the great man. He took me all in his arms and kissed me on both sides of the head, and was as cordial as ever I saw him. I told him all my perplexity on his account, and how I had come determined to fight him, or to do anything he pleased. 'What,' said he, 'did you come here on purpose?' 'Yes, indeed,' said I. This gave him high satisfaction. I told him how I was settled as a lawyer and how I had made two hundred pounds by the law this year. He grumbled and laughed and was wonderfully pleased. 'What, Bozzy? Two hundred pounds! A great deal.'

I had longed much to see him as my great preceptor, to state to him some difficulties as a moralist with regard to the profession of the law, as it appeared to me that in some respects it hurt the principles of honesty; and I asked him if it did not. 'Why, no, Sir,' said he, 'if you act properly. You are not to deceive your clients with false representations of your opinion. You are not to tell lies to a judge.' 'But', said I, 'what do you think of pleading a cause which you know to be bad?' 'Sir, you don't know it to be bad till the judge determines it. I have said that you are to state your facts fairly; so that your thinking, or what you call knowing, a cause to be bad must be from reasoning, must be from thinking your arguments weak and inconclusive. But, Sir, that is not enough. An argument which does not convince you yourself may convince the judge before whom you plead it; and if it does convince him, why, then, Sir, you are wrong and he is right. It is his business to judge, and you are not to be confident in your opinion, but to say all you can for your client and then hear the judge's opinion.' 'But, Sir,' said I, 'does not the putting on a warmth when you have no warmth, and appearing to be clearly of one opinion when you are in reality of another, does not such dissimulation hurt one's honesty? Is there not some danger that one may put on the same mask in common life, in the intercourse with one's friends?' 'Why, no, Sir. Everybody knows you are paid for putting on a warmth for your client, and it is properly no dissimulation. The moment you come from the bar you resume your usual behaviour. Sir, a man will no more carry the artifice of the bar into the common intercourse of society than a man who is paid for tumbling upon his hands will continue tumbling upon his hands when he ought to be walking on his feet.' Wonderful force and fancy. At once he satisfied me as to a thing which had often and often perplexed me. It was truly comfortable having him in his own old High Church Oxford, and I had besides many good ideas of the Vinerian Professor, the head of a hall, &c. These halls were originally additions to colleges where there was not sufficient room. In time some of them became unnecessary as the number of students decreased. There are no students in New Inn Hall. But it is kept up and gives the rank of Master to Mr Chambers.

I told Mr Johnson a story which I should have recorded before this time. The day before I left London, coming through Bloomsbury Square and being dressed in green and gold, I was actually taken for Wilkes by a Middlesex voter who came up to me. 'Sir, I beg pardon, is not your name Wilkes?' 'Yes, Sir.' 'I thought so. I saw you upon the hustings and I thought I knew you again. Sir, I'm your very good friend; I've got you five and twenty votes today.' I bowed and grinned and thanked him, and talked of liberty and general warrants and I don't know what all. I told him too, between ourselves, that the King had a very good opinion of me. I ventured to ask him how he could be sure that I was a right man and acted from public spirit. He was a little puzzled. So I helped him out. 'As to my private character, it would take a long time to explain it. But, Sir, if I were the devil, I have done good to the people of England, and they ought to support me.' 'Ay,' said he. I am vexed I did not make more of this curious incident. After carrying my voter half-way down Long Acre, I stopped and looked him gravely in the face. 'Sir, I must tell you a secret. I'm not Mr Wilkes, and what's more, I'm a Scotsman.' He stared not a little, and said, 'Sir, I beg pardon for having given you so much trouble.' 'No, Sir,' said I, 'you have been very good company to me.' I wonder he did not beat me. I said to Mr Johnson that I never before knew that I was so ugly a fellow. He was angry at me that I did not borrow money from the voter. Indeed, it would have made a fine scene at Brentford when he demanded payment of the real Wilkes, and called him a rogue for denying the debt.

Boswell to Temple

Edinburgh, 24 August 1768
I am exceedingly lucky in having escaped the insensible Miss Blair and the furious Zélide, for I have now seen the finest creature that ever was

formed: *la belle Irlandaise*. Figure to yourself, Temple, a young lady just sixteen, formed like a Grecian nymph with the sweetest countenance, full of sensibility, accomplished, with a Dublin education, always half the year in the north of Ireland, her father a counsellor-at-law with an estate of £1,000 a year and above £10,000 in ready money. Her mother a sensible, well-bred woman. She the darling of her parents, and no other child but her sister. She is cousin to some cousins of mine in this county. I was at their house while she and her father, mother and aunt were over upon a visit just last week. The Counsellor is as worthy a gentleman as ever I saw. Your friend was a favourite with all of them. From morning to night I admired the charming Mary Ann. Upon my honour, I never was so much in love. I never was before in a situation to which there was not some objection. But 'here every flower is united', and not a thorn to be found. But how shall I manage it? They were in a hurry, and are gone home to Ireland. They were sorry they could not come to see Auchinleck, of which they had heard a great deal. Mary Ann wished much to be in the grotto. It is a pity they did not come. This princely seat would have had some effect.

I received the kindest invitation to come and see them in Ireland, and I promised to be there in March. In the meantime both the father and the aunt write to me. What a fortunate fellow am I! What variety of adventures in all countries! I was allowed to walk a great deal with Miss. I repeated my fervent passion to her, again and again. She was pleased, and I could swear that her little heart beat. I carved the first letter of her name on a tree. I cut off a lock of her hair, *male pertinaci*.7 She promised not to forget me, nor to marry a lord before March. Her aunt said to me, 'Mr Boswell, I tell you seriously there will be no fear of this succeeding, but from your own inconstancy. Stay till March.' All the Scotch cousins too think I may be the happy man. Ah! my friend, I am now as I ought to be. No reserved, prudent, cautious conduct as with Miss Blair. No, all youthful, warm, natural; in short, all genuine love. Pray tell me what you think. I have a great confidence in your judgement. I mean not to ask what you think of my angelic girl. I am fixed beyond a possibility of doubt as to her. Believe me, she is like a part of my very soul. But will not the fond parents insist on having quality for their daughter, who is to have so large a fortune? Or do you think that the Baron of Auchinleck is great enough? Both father, mother and aunt assured me of my high character in Ireland, where my book is printed, the 'third' edition. That is no bad circumstance. I shall see in what style the Counsellor writes, and shall send some elegant present to my lovely mistress.

This is the most agreeable passion I ever felt. Sixteen, innocence and gaiety make me quite a Sicilian swain. Before I left London, I made a vow in St Paul's Church that I would not allow myself in licentious connections of any kind for six months. I am hitherto firm to my vow, and already feel myself a superior being. I have given up my criminal intercourse with Mrs —. In short, Maria has me without any rival. I do hope the period of my perfect felicity as far as this state of being can afford is now in view.

Boswell did indeed set out on his Dublin jaunt, in April of the following year. For company he took with him – despite his father's disapproval – his first cousin, Margaret ('Peggie') Montgomerie. She was a good and close friend of Boswell and they had always been on easy and humorous terms, even joking about the impossibility of their ever marrying. Peggie was two years older than Boswell, and was not of an affluent background.

TUESDAY 25 APRIL. Miss Montgomerie and I set out from Auchinleck. My father was so averse to my Irish expedition that she had not resolution to agree to accompany me. Dr Johnston took leave of me, and seemed most anxious for my safe return. My father walked out, and I did not take leave of him. It was a delightful day.

Boswell to Temple

Donaghadee, 3 May 1769

My dear Temple, – I am fairly landed in the kingdom of Ireland, and am tomorrow to proceed for Dublin to see my sweet Mary Ann. But, my worthy friend, to whom my heart is ever open and to whom I must apply for advice at all times, I must tell you that I am accompanied by my cousin Miss Montgomerie, whom I believe you saw at Edinburgh, and she perhaps may and perhaps ought to prevent my Hibernian nuptials. You must know that she and I have always been in the greatest intimacy. I have proved her on a thousand occasions, and found her sensible, agreeable and generous. When I was not in love with some one or other of my numerous flames, I have been in love with her; and during the intervals of all my passions Margaret has been constantly my mistress as well as my friend. Allow me to add that her person is to me the most desirable that I ever saw. Often have I thought of marrying her, and often told her so. But we talked of my wonderful inconstancy, were merry, and perhaps in two days after the most ardent professions to her I came and told her that I was desperately in love with another woman. Then she smiled, was my confidante, and in time I returned to herself. She is with all this, Temple, the most honest, undesigning creature that ever existed.

Well, Sir, being my cousin german, she accompanies me on my Irish expedition. I found her both by sea and land the best companion I ever saw. I am exceedingly in love with her. I highly value her. If ever a man had his full choice of a wife, I would have it in her. But the objections are she is two years older than I. She has only a thousand pounds. My father would be violent against my marrying her, as she would bring neither money nor interest. I, from a desire to aggrandize my family, think somewhat in the same manner. And all my gay projects of bringing home some blooming young lady and making an *éclat* with her brilliant fortune would be gone.

But, on the other hand, my cousin is of a fine, firm, lively temperament, and never can be old. She may have as many children as I wish, and from what she has already done as an aunt I am sure she would make a very good mother. Would not my children be more obliged to me for such a mother than for many thousands? Then, she has much to say with my father, who could not reasonably be enraged at having his niece for daughter-in-law. She would live in such a manner that at my death my family may be richer than if I married a fortune; and for the gay projects of fancy, is there any doubt that they are nothing when compared with real happiness? Many men seek to form friendships with the great, the embroidered, the titled. If they succeed, are they as happy as I am in the friendship of Temple? I fear that if I marry any other woman, my love for my cousin may often distract me. And what weighs much with me, Temple, is that amidst all this merriment and scheming, I really imagine that she truly loves me, that by my courting her so often she is so attached to me that she would silently suffer very severely if she saw me irrevocably fixed to another.

And yet my charming seraph, my Marianne, melts my heart. Her little bosom beats at the thoughts of seeing me – forgive my vanity – you know, strange as it may be, that women of all tempers and ages have been fond of me. Temple, you never failed me yet. What shall I do? This is the most delicate case of the many that I have laid before you. I must, however, tell you that my father is quite averse to Marianne, and declares he never will agree to it. But if *her* father gives me a round sum, I do not fear *mine*. But if I am certain that my cousin sincerely loves me, wishes to have me, and would be unhappy without me, what should I do? Should I be hard-hearted enough not to give happiness to *the woman I love, and the friend I can trust*? for such she literally is. And if I think of my own happiness, whether do you think that she or the seraph is most certain? And how shall I do not to hurt either of the two? Never did there live such a man as myself. I beseech you write to me without delay: Dublin is address enough for *Corsican Boswell*. Pray is not your wife about your own age? On the other hand, might I not by a couple of thousand pounds marry my cousin so as that both she and I may be more properly disposed of than if we went together?

My dear Temple, I know both your heart and your understanding. Be so kind as immediately to exert them both for me. I shall just amuse myself at Dublin in an easy, general style till your letter arrives. I think I could give up my *certain* felicity with my cousin, and take my chance of the brilliant Irish scheme. But when I throw into the scale the concern that I believe my amiable, worthy and desirable cousin has in it, what should preponderate? Let us ever be helpful to each other; and believe me to be, my dear Temple, your unalterable, affectionate friend,

JAMES BOSWELL

Boswell to Dempster

Edinburgh, 21 June 1769

I was received at Dublin with open arms by a numerous and creditable set of relations. But I give you my word, I found myself under no engagements. The young lady seemed the sweetest, loveliest little creature that ever was born. But so young, so childish, so much *yes* and *no*, that (between ourselves) I was ashamed of having raved so much about her. I candidly told my situation: that I had come quite contrary to my father's inclination. That was enough for the present, and a genteel distance was the proper conduct. At the same time I found myself like a foreign prince to them, so much did I take; and I was assured of her having for certain £500 a year. You know me, Dempster. I was often carried by *fancy*, like a man on the finest race-horse; and, at all events, I would have her. But my cousin hung on my *heart*. Her most desirable person, like a heathen goddess painted alfresco on the ceiling of a palace at Rome, was compared with the delicate little Miss. Her admirable sense and vivacity were compared with the reserved quietness of the Heiress. I was tossed by waves and drawn by horses. I resolved to fix nothing. My cousin gave me that advice herself, for I had assurance enough to consult her deliberately. My journey to Scotland with her, during which I was a little indisposed and had occasion to see a new proof of her affectionate attention, has inclined me to her more and more.

Here then I am, my friend, at no loss to determine whom I really love and value of all women I have ever seen, but at a great loss to determine whom I should marry. No man knows the scene of human life better than you do. At least, no man gives me such clear views of it. Therefore, pray assist me. And whatever is the drawing of your reason, pray let me have it agreeably coloured by your fancy. An advice from you to a friend is singularly excellent for two reasons. First, because it is always at least ingenious; and secondly, because you are not a bit angry though he does not follow it. I depend on you, my worthy Dempster, and am your ever affectionate friend,

J.B.

Vraye Foi.[8]

Boswell to Margaret Montgomerie

Edinburgh, 4 July 1769

You have very well observed that you cannot write as you would speak. I am just in the same situation. It is impossible for me to put upon paper the sentiments which I have felt since we parted; and yet if we were together, I am very sure I could make you fully understand them. I read your letters with such feelings as I never before experienced. I have imagined such when I have thought of my grandfather receiving a letter from Lady Betty. I do not imagine it possible for a man to value and love at the same time a woman more than I do *my lady*. You remember you said at Donaghadee that it would be wonderful if I stood Dublin. You know what happened, and I believe both you and I thought more highly of my heart than we did before. Indeed, you have often said you was of opinion I had no heart. Is it so, think you? And do you intend to assume the merit of giving me what I had not before? Or is it that fancy has so prevailed that my heart could never appear? Methinks I may compare my heart to a rock in the sea. While the tempest of passions blew and the waves of vain folly beat, it could not be perceived. But now that these begin to subside, it shows itself as firm as any rock that ever existed. Now that I have told you all my history relative to yourself during such a number of years, you need not wonder at my present situation.

I thank you, my dearest friend, for your calm advice. I will try to compose myself. But what I hinted to you shocked me so much that I declare I was thrown into the wildest melancholy, and resolved to go and at once break off all connection for ever, that I might no longer struggle with uncertainty and a kind of unnaturality, if I may use the word. You alone distracted my mind. But I believe I could settle that, provided I myself was unhappy, for then nothing can be said. I am more composed now, as from some late hints I imagine any scheme to be concerning some other person whom I do not know. Believe me, such a step in a family is terrible, and I fairly own to you that unless I had an absolute security against what might be done, I would renounce all relation. The worst is that a wild, ruinous scheme in some measure pleases my gloomy temper, and there is not a man alive to whom poverty and obscurity would be easier. I shall, however, make no rash vows, and when you come to town we shall have a long conversation on the subject. In the meantime, be quite easy as to *my lady*. I am now better than at any time. I walked a long time with Lord Monboddo today, and, without giving you any share in it, talked to him fully. He was clear, and made me admire the scheme.

Boswell to Margaret Montgomerie

Edinburgh, 20 July 1769

My dear Cousin, – I know I shall have a friendly and affectionate answer to the last letter which I wrote to you. But in the meantime,

I am going to write you a calm and determined epistle, in few words but of infinite importance to us both.

You never knew till we were in Ireland that I had at different periods of my life been deeply in love with you. That has, however, been the case; and had not vanity or some other artificial motive made me, from time to time, encourage my fancy in other schemes, the genuine inclinations of my heart would ever have been constant to my dear Peggie Montgomerie. As it was, you know how fond I have been of you, and how I have at different times convinced you that my love for you was truly sincere. While wavering in my resolutions, I was always determined that if your happiness depended upon having me, I would not hesitate a moment to make my best friend happy. And I accordingly begged in a late letter that you would tell me freely if that was the case.

I was at the assembly last night, and saw a variety of beauties. I was not inconstant to you for a moment. Indeed, after standing the trial you did in Ireland, there could be little fear. Any other person than you would be apt to disregard what I say in my present situation. But I think I may trust to the generosity of a *noble-minded woman*, as Dempster calls you. I therefore make you this proposal. You know my unhappy temper. You know all my faults. It is painful to repeat them. Will you, then, knowing me fully, accept of me for your husband as I now am – not the heir of Auchinleck, but one who has had his time of the world, and is henceforth to expect no more than £100 a year? With that and the interest of your £1,060, we can live in an agreeable retirement in any part of Europe that you please. But we are to bid adieu for ever to this country. All our happiness is to be our society with each other, and our hopes of a better world. I confess this scheme is so romantic that nothing but such love as you showed at Donaghadee could make you listen to it. Nor ought I to be surprised if a woman of your admirable sense and high character with all who know you should refuse to comply with it, should refuse to sacrifice every prudent consideration to me. But as I love you more than I can express, you will excuse me for making this proposal. I am ready upon these terms to marry you directly. And, upon my honour, I would not propose it now, were I not fully persuaded that I would share a kingdom with you if I had it. I also solemnly promise to do everything in my power to show my gratitude and make you happy.

Think seriously of this. Give me any positive answer you honestly can. But I insist on no mediocrity, no reasoning, no hesitation. Think fully, and one way or other tell me your resolution. I am much yours,

                                                                JAMES BOSWELL

Received 25 July, Margaret Montgomerie to Boswell

[*Enclosed in a wrapper endorsed by Boswell*] The most valuable letter of my valuable friend, which does honour to both her and me.
Vraye Foi.

                                        Lainshaw, Saturday 22 July 1769
I have thought fully as you desired, and in answer to your letter I accept of your terms, and shall do everything in my power to make myself worthy of you. J.B. with £100 a year is every bit as valuable to me as if possessed of the estate of Auchinleck. I only regret the want of wealth on your account, not being certain if you can be happy without a proper share of it. Free of ambition, I prefer real happiness to the splendid appearance of it. I wish you could meet me at Glasgow on Saturday. Could you not come that length in the fly and return on Monday? Let me know and I'll be there any day you will appoint.

My heart determines my choice. May the Almighty grant His blessing and protection, and we need not be afraid; His providence extends over all the earth, so that wherever you go I shall willingly accompany you and hope to be happy. Had you been, as you mention, in your former prosperity, I should perhaps have indulged myself in female prudence, &c, but I think this is not now the time for dissimulation. I am therefore ready to meet you when you please and to join my fate to yours. Is not this as full an answer as you could wish? Say nothing of the affair to your father, as you are sure he will never consent; and to disobey after consulting is worse than doing it without saying a word.

My heart is more at ease than it has been of a long time, though still I feel for what I'm afraid you suffer. Be assured, my dear Jamie, you have a friend that would sacrifice everything for you, who never had a wish for wealth till now, to bestow it on the man of her heart.

I wrote two letters, one on Friday and one on Tuesday. I hope the contents of neither have offended you. My anxiety about your happiness made me use every argument in my power to prevail on you to stay at home. In hopes of meeting with you soon, I shall only add that I most sincerely am, my dear Jamie, your faithful and affectionate

M.M.

The following Journal entries, as well as showing James Boswell getting ready for his marriage to Margaret Montgomerie, contain the start of a serious dispute between Boswell father and son about the inheritance of the estate at Auchinleck. To fully appreciate what happens the reader needs to know that Lord Auchinleck is considering marriage to a much younger woman.

SATURDAY 12 AUGUST. The session rose today. Lord Monboddo took leave of me, hoping to meet me next as a married man. My father was to have set out for Auchinleck today. But some business detained him. John went, and my father and I were easy and well. After dinner he talked of Margaret and me. Said we had both very good sense, but were thoughtless, and must become just different beings. I told him I was under a necessity to go to London for a little to clear my constitution. He acquiesced. The evening passed well.

SUNDAY 13 AUGUST. My illness was visibly decreasing, so I resolved to stay in and take care of it for a week or a fortnight, and be pretty well before I set out for London. My father and I had a warm dispute at night on male and female succession. I argued that a male alone could support a family, could represent his forefathers. That females, in a feudal light, were only vehicles for carrying down men to posterity, and that a man might as well entail his estate on his post-chaise, and put one into it who should bear his name, as entail it upon his daughter and make her husband take his name. I told him that the principle of family, of supporting the race of Thomas Boswell of Auchinleck, was what supported my mind, and that, were it not for that, I would not submit to the burthen of life here, but would go and pass my days in a warm climate, easy and gay. I bid him consider that he held the estate of Auchinleck, at least the old stamen of it, in prejudice of no less than four females. That excluding females might at a time hurt a fond father who had daughters and no sons. 'But what', said I, 'is a sorry individual to the preservation of a family? Is there any comparison? Besides, in that view, why will you make the son whom you see miserable on account of some woman who may appear nobody knows when?' I saw he was quite positive in the strange, delusive notion of *heirs whatsoever*, and I had the mortification to be sensible that my dissipated and profligate conduct had made him at all think of an entail, and made any arguments from me of little force. I, however, hoped to get him prevented from ruining his family. I was quite in a fever, for I declare that the family of Auchinleck is my only constant object in this world. I should say, *has been* so. For my dearest M. is now as firmly established. I determined to leave the country if he made the settlement which shocked me. I told him so, and I knew M. would not complain. Indeed I was too hot for a son to a father. But I could not help it. I was like an old Roman when his country was at stake.

I fell upon a most curious argument which diverted my own fancy so much that it was with difficulty I could preserve my gravity when uttering it. 'If', said I, 'you believe the Bible, you must allow male succession. Turn to the first chapter of Matthew: "Abraham begat Isaac, Isaac begat Jacob," &c. If you are not an infidel, if you do not renounce Christianity, you must be for males.' Worthy man! he had patience with me. I am quite firm in my opinion on this point. It will not do to say a grandson by a daughter is as near as a grandson by a son. It leads into a nice disquisition in natural philosophy. I say the *stamen* is derived from the *man*. The woman is only like the ground where a tree is planted. A grandson by a daughter has no connection with my original stock. A new race is begun by a father of another name. It is true a child partakes of the constitution of his mother, gets some of his mother's blood in his veins. But so does he as to his nurse, so does he as to the ox whose beef he eats. The most of the particles of the human frame are changed in a few years' rotation. The stamen only continues the same. Let females be well portioned. Let them enjoy liberally what is naturally intended for them: dowries as virgins, a share of what their husbands have while wives, jointures when widows. But for goodness' sake let us not make feudal lords, let us not make barons, of them. As well might we equip them with breeches, swords and gold-laced hats.

In every age some instances of folly have occurred to humble the pride of human nature. Of these, the idea of female succession is one of the most striking. A foolish fondness for daughters has introduced it, when fathers thought they could not do enough for them. Like the ancient Scottish clergy, who became so very fond of the Virgin Mary that, not satisfied with *Aves* and other acknowledgements, they gravely disputed in a synod at St Andrews whether they should not say *Pater Noster*, 'Our Father which art in heaven', to her. Spottiswood relates this as a most monstrous absurdity. To make a woman a feudal lord is much such another. If it be said that remote heirs male may be in the lowest ranks, surely remote heirs female may be so too. I love the late Earl of Cassillis, who, when settling his estate, being told by his man of business that he had called ali the heirs male, 'Then,' said he, 'give it to the devil.' This was the true spirit and dignity of the ancient peer.

Boswell is enjoying a last jaunt to London before his marriage (in fact he did not return for three years). Here, he is with Johnson, who has presumably just reached a point of weariness with his friend's constant praise of the Corsican rebels.

I know not from what spirit of contradiction he burst out into a violent declamation against the Corsicans, of whose heroism I talked in high terms. 'Sir,' said he, 'what is all this rout about the Corsicans? They have been at war with the Genoese for upwards of twenty years, and have never yet taken their fortified towns. They might have battered down the walls and reduced them to powder in twenty years. They might have pulled the walls in pieces, and cracked the stones with their teeth in twenty years.' It was in vain to argue with him upon the want of artillery: his powerful imagination was not to be resisted for the moment.

On the evening of the 10 October, I presented Dr Johnson to General Paoli. I had greatly wished that two men for whom I had the highest value should meet. They met with a manly ease, mutually conscious of their own abilities and of the abilities one of each other. The General spoke Italian and Dr Johnson English, and understood one another very well with a little aid of interpretation from me, in which I compared myself to an isthmus which joins two great continents. Upon Johnson's entering the room the General said, 'From what I have read of your works, Sir, and from what Mr Boswell has told me of you, I have long had you in great esteem and veneration.' The General talked of language being formed on the particular ideas and manners of a country, without knowing which we cannot know the language. We may know the direct signification of single words, but by these no beauty of expression, no sally of genius, no wit is conveyed to the mind. All this must be by allusion to other ideas. 'Sir,' said Johnson, 'You talk of language as if you had never done anything else but study it, instead of governing a nation.' The General said, 'Questo è un troppo gran complemento' (This is too great a compliment). Johnson answered, 'I should have thought so, Sir, if I had not heard you talk.' The General asked him what he thought of the spirit of infidelity which was so prevalent. JOHNSON. 'Sir, this gloom of infidelity, I hope, is only a transient cloud passing through the hemisphere which will soon be dissipated and the sun break forth with his usual splendour.' 'You think then', said the General, 'that they will change their principles like their clothes.' JOHNSON. 'Why, Sir, if they bestow no more thought on principles than on dress, it must be so.' The General said that 'a great part of the fashionable infidelity was owing to a desire of showing courage. Men who have no opportunities of showing it in real life take death and futurity as objects on which to display it.' JOHNSON. 'That is mighty foolish affectation. Fear is one of the passions of human nature, of which it is impossible to divest it. You remember that the Emperor Charles V, when he read upon the tombstone of a Spanish nobleman, "Here lies one who never knew fear," wittily said, "Then he has never snuffed a candle with his fingers."'

I was detained in town till it was too late on the 9th, so went out to him early in the morning of the 10th November. 'Now', said he, 'that you are going to marry, do not expect more from life than life will afford. You may often find yourself out of humour, and you may often think your wife not studious enough to please you, and yet you may have reason enough to consider yourself as upon the whole very happily married.'

Talking of marriage in general he observed, 'Our marriage service is too refined. It is calculated only for the best kind of marriages, whereas we should have a form for matches of convenience, of which there are many.' He agreed with me that there was no absolute necessity for having the marriage ceremony performed by a regular clergyman, for this was not commanded in Scripture.

I was volatile enough to repeat to him a little epigrammatic song of mine on matrimony, which Mr Garrick had a few days before procured to be set to music.

A Matrimonial Thought

In the blithe days of honeymoon,
With Kate's allurements smitten,
I loved her late, I loved her soon,
And called her dearest kitten.

But now my kitten's grown a cat,
And cross like other wives,
Oh! by my soul, my honest Mat,
I fear she has nine lives.

My illustrious friend said, 'Mighty well, Sir, but don't swear.' Upon which I altered, 'Oh! by my soul' to 'Alas, alas!'

He was good enough to accompany me to London, and see me into the post-chaise which was to carry me on my road to Scotland.

Boswell to Margaret Montgomerie

Edinburgh, Thursday 23 November 1769
My dear Peggie, – This is probably the last letter which I shall have an opportunity to write to *Miss Peggie Montgomerie*. Your kind favour (your last, too, as a young lady), which I received this morning, is another proof of your admirable heart and spirit. I went to your friend Lord Eglinton and delivered your polite message, which he received in the best manner. A favour is making for him, and he is to appear with it on Sunday. I cannot think of our coming to my father's house. It would be mixing gall with my honey. We shall concert what to do when we meet. I like your saying, 'Be you positive to take me with you.' Only think: *the day after tomorrow* we are to be *married*. Pray look back and recollect all our former scenes. I have some bitter oranges for the Captain. I am so earnestly invited to Bothwell Castle that I cannot refuse. So I shall be there tomorrow

night. Your gown comes with me. You can soon put it on. Let dinner be late. We shall both dress in white before it. I ever am your faithful and affectionate.

J.B.

This is written from worthy Grange's room.9 He offers you his best compliments.

Marriage Contract between James Boswell, Esq. and Miss Peggie Montgomerie, 1769

This is the marriage contract between James Boswell, Esquire, eldest son to the Right Honourable Alexander Boswell, Esquire, of Auchinleck, one of the Lords of Session and Justiciary in Scotland, and Miss Peggie Montgomerie, daughter to the late David Montgomerie of Lainshaw, Esquire.

The said parties do hereby agree that, in consideration of the sincerest mutual love and regard, they will, on or before the holy festival of Christmas next to come, be united to each other by marriage.

They solemnly engage to be faithful spouses, to bear with one another's faults, and to contribute as much as possible to each other's happiness in this world; hoping through the merits of their blessed Saviour, Jesus Christ, for eternal happiness in the world which is to come.

In faith of which, this paper, written by the said James Boswell, Esquire, is subscribed by him at London on the thirty-first day of October in the year of our Lord one thousand seven hundred and sixty-nine, before these witnesses: Pascal Paoli, General of the Corsicans, and Samuel Johnson, Doctor of Laws, and author of *The Rambler* and other works.

JAMES BOSWELL

*Io sottoscritto ho veduto, e sono stato presente quando il Signore Giacomo Boswell ha sottoscritto questo foglio.*10

PASQUALE DE PAOLI

SAM: JOHNSON, Witness

And by the said Miss Peggie Montgomerie at Lainshaw, on the twenty-fifth of November in the year of our Lord one thousand seven hundred and sixty-nine, before these witnesses: the Honourable Archibald Douglas of Douglas, Esquire, and the said James Boswell, Esquire.

MARGARET MONTGOMERIE

A. DOUGLAS, Witness

Announcement in the Scots Magazine

25 NOVEMBER. At Lainshaw, in the shire of Ayr, James Boswell, Esquire, of Auchinleck, advocate, to Miss Peggie Montgomerie, daughter of the late David Montgomerie of Lainshaw, Esquire.

'The Mournful Case of Poor Misfortunate and Unhappy John Reid'

The Court of Session, Edinburgh, 2 August 1774

JUSTICE-CLERK. John Reid, nothing remains to me now but to pronounce that judgement we the Court unanimously agreed should be pronounced. I am very sorry it is necessary. Your former trial should not have been mentioned, had it not been forced on [the] Court by your counsel, who has exerted all his talents and abilities in your defence. But the facts coming out in evidence put it out of his power to do you any service. I do not desire to revive the memory of what is past. God and your own conscience know [as to that]. But, Sir, you are now convicted by verdict of your country of the theft of nineteen sheep. You could not commit that without other crimes. But it can do you no harm to join with my brothers in giving you . . .

Sentence of Death against John Reid

The said Lords . . . decern and adjudge the said John Reid to be carried from the bar back to the Tolbooth of Edinburgh, therein to be detained until Wednesday the seventh day of September next, and upon that day to be taken forth of the said Tolbooth and carried to the common place of execution in the Grassmarket of Edinburgh, and then and there betwixt the hours of two and four o'clock in the afternoon of the said day to be hanged by the neck by the hands of the common executioner upon a gibbet until he be dead, and ordain all his moveable goods and gear to be escheat and inbrought to His Majesty's use, which is pronounced for doom.

THOMAS MILLER
ALEXANDER BOSWELL
HENRY HOME
JAMES FERGUSON
GEORGE BROWN
ROBERT BRUCE

This chapter, concerning the trial and execution of John Reid for stealing sheep, presents a grim picture after the light-hearted happiness of the last. Boswell's first defendant in criminal practice in 1766 was now under sentence of death, pending appeals for clemency, for an offence that carried the harshest possible penalty in those times and in that country. Spiritedly defended by Boswell, the judges in the Court of Session (including Boswell's father) had nonetheless condemned the prisoner, as recounted above, to death by hanging. The story that follows, of Boswell's petitions to those in high places, including, indirectly, to the monarch, and his reckless scheme (following theories then in vogue) of trying to resuscitate Reid after he had been hanged, gives the reader a stark reminder of the underside of eighteenth-century life and its harsh penal code. At the end we see Boswell, all his throws of the dice having come to nothing, shivering in his chair with the terror and disgust that scenes of public execution seemed always to arouse in him, brooding upon death and judgement and unable to be comforted even by those closest to him.

WEDNESDAY 10 AUGUST. In the forenoon I had visited John Reid, whom I found very composed. He persisted in averring that he got the sheep from Gardner. I really believed him after I had adjured him, as he should answer to GOD, to tell me the truth. I told him that I was of opinion that a petition to the King would have no effect, but that his wife had applied to me, and I should draw one which he should sign; but that he must not expect anything but death. He very calmly assured me he would expect nothing else. I wondered at my own firmness of mind while I talked with a man under sentence of death, without much emotion, but with solemnity and humanity. I desired John to write his life very fully, which he promised to do. I bid him say nothing as to the *facts* with which he was formerly charged. He had been acquitted by his country. That was enough. His acknowledging that he had been guilty might hurt some unhappy panel who was innocent by making a jury condemn on imperfect circumstantial evidence. It will be a curious thing if he gives a narrative of his life.

Boswell to the Earl of Pembroke

Edinburgh, 20 August 1774
My Lord, – Presuming on your Lordship's goodness, I trouble you with the enclosed petition to His Majesty from John Reid, an unfortunate man under sentence of death. I have also transmitted a copy to my Lord Suffolk, Secretary of State for the Northern Department.

John Reid was my first client in criminal business when he was tried in 1766. I have therefore a particular concern in his fate and wish much that he should not be hanged.

May I beg that your Lordship may make me certain that the petition reaches His Majesty. There is a prejudice against the man in this country. It would therefore be happy if a transportation pardon could be obtained for him at once, his crime at any rate not being atrocious. I have the honour to be with very great regard, my Lord, your most obliged and obedient humble servant,

JAMES BOSWELL

THURSDAY 25 AUGUST. I communicated to Crosbie a scheme which I had of making an experiment on John Reid, in case he was hanged, to try to recover him. I had mentioned it in secrecy to Charles Hay and Mr Wood the surgeon, who promised me assistance. Crosbie told me that he had lately had a long conversation on the subject with Dr Cullen, who thought it practicable. It was lucky that I spoke of it to Crosbie, for he was clear for trying it, and threw out many good hints as to what should be done. I resolved to wait on Dr Cullen and get his instructions. I was this forenoon at the burial of a daughter of the late Mr Sands, bookseller here. There is something usefully solemn in such a scene, and I make it a rule to attend every burial to which I am invited unless I have a sufficient excuse; as I expect that those who are invited to mine will pay that piece of decent attention.

I afterwards called at the prison, where I found Mr Todd, Lady Maxwell's chaplain, with John Reid. He seemed to be a weak, well-meaning young man. I again told John in his presence that there was hardly the least chance of a pardon and therefore that he ought to consider himself as a dying man. Yet I did now entertain a small additional glimpse of hope, because I saw in the newspapers that, a few days before, one Madan got a reprieve after he was at Tyburn, ready to be turned off, the man who really committed the robbery for which he was condemned having voluntarily appeared and owned it. I thought this incident might make the Ministry more ready to listen to John Reid's story that Gardner was the real thief. John was looking gloomy today. He told me he had some bad dreams which made him believe he was now to die.

I then called for McGraugh, who was put into the cage, he was so violent a prisoner. He was a true Teague. I asked him why he was confined. He could give but a very confused account; but he assured me that he had neither stolen victuals and drink nor taken them by force, but only called for them. I asked him if he had stolen anything. 'Only a paice (piece) of wood,' said he; 'but then, an't *plaise* your Honour, it was in the dark.' 'That will not make it better,' said I. Afterwards, however, I saw that this odd saying of his, like all the Irish sayings at which we laugh as bulls or absurdities, had a meaning. For he meant that as he had taken the wood in the dark, it could not be known he had done it; so that it could be no part of the charge against him and consequently was no justification of the sentence of the magistrates. I promised to do what I could for him. I also saw one Macpherson, a young goldsmith confined for debt, from whom I had a letter telling me that a young woman had come into prison and lent him her clothes, in which he made his escape but was taken again; and that the *innocent* girl was imprisoned. I told him that breaking prison was a crime; that the girl had been aiding in the escape of a prisoner and therefore was not innocent; but that she would not be long confined.

My wife and I drank tea at Dr Grant's. He was clear that a man who has hung ten minutes cannot be recovered; and he had dissected two. I was however resolved that the experiment should be tried. Dr Grant carried me up to a very good library which he has and showed me a number of anatomical preparations. The survey of skulls and other parts of the human body, and the reflection upon all of us being so frail and liable to so many painful diseases, made me dreary.

MONDAY 29 AUGUST. Keith Ralph, a young painter who had studied under Runciman, had drawn Mr Lawrie's picture very like. I had him with me this forenoon, and he agreed to paint John. He desired to see him today, to have an idea of his face, to see what kind of light was in the room where he lay, and to judge what should be the size of the picture. Accordingly I went with him. I had before this given a hint of my design to Richard Lock, the inner turnkey, a very sensible, good kind of man; and he had no objection. Accordingly we went up. Mr Ritchie, a kind of lay teacher who humanely attends all the people under sentence of death, was with John. I was acquainted with Mr Ritchie, as he had called on me about my client Agnes Adam. After standing a little and speaking a few words in a serious strain, I addressed myself to Ritchie in a kind of soft voice and mentioned my desire to have a remembrance of John Reid, by having a picture of him; that Mr Ritchie and I could sit by and talk to him, and that I imagined John would have no objection, as it would not disturb him. Ritchie said he supposed John would have none; that he was so much obliged to me, he would do much more at my request; and he would come and be present. Next morning between nine and ten was fixed. Mr Charles Hay, who waited in the street, went with me to Ralph's and saw some of his performances.

At four this afternoon Adam Bell was with me, along with Nimmo his landlord, consulting me to draw answers to a petition. I found myself much as in session time. Steuart Hall and Mr Wood the surgeon drank tea. Wood dispelled the dreary country ideas which Steuart Hall would have raised. I took a walk with him to Drumsheugh and round by the New Town, and talked of the scheme of recovering John Reid. He said he did not think it practicable. But that he should give all the assistance in his power to have the experiment fairly tried.

TUESDAY 30 AUGUST. At ten o'clock I was with John Reid. Before I got there, Ralph was begun with his chalk and honest Ritchie was exhorting him quietly. I was happy to see that this whim of mine gave no trouble to John. One of his legs was fixed to a large iron goad, but he could rise very easily; and he at any rate used to sit upon a form, so that he just kept his ordinary posture, and Ritchie and I conversed with him. He seemed to be quite composed, and said he had no hopes of life on account of the dreams which he had. That he dreamt he was riding on one white horse and leading another. 'That', said he, 'was too good a dream, and dreams are contrary.' He said he also dreamt a great deal of being on the seashore and of passing deep waters. 'However,' said he, 'I allwaye (always) get through them.' 'Well,' said I, 'John, I hope that shall not be contrary; but that you shall get through the great deep of death.' I called for a dram of whisky. I had not thought how I should drink to John till I had the glass in my hand, and I felt some embarrassment. I could not say, 'Your good health': and 'Here's to you' was too much in the style of hearty fellowship. I said, 'John, I wish you well,' or words pretty much the same, as 'Wishing you well' – or some such phrase. The painter and Mr Ritchie tasted the spirits. Richard the jailer makes it a rule never to taste them within the walls of the prison.

John seemed to be the better of a dram. He told me that the Reids of Muiravonside had been there, he believed, for three hundred years; that they had been butchers for many generations. He could trace himself, his father and grandfather in that business; that he never was worth £10 and never in much debt, so that he was always evens with the world. That in the year 1753 he enlisted in Sir Peter Halkett's regiment. But was taken up on an accusation of stealing two cows, for which he was tried at Glasgow and acquitted; after which, as his pay had run up to a considerable sum, the regiment let him alone, though he was several times taken up as a deserter at the instigation of ill-natured people; that he went up to London on foot and wrought there as a gardener for — till there was a hot press, and then he came to Leith in a brig commanded by John Beatson. That after this he enlisted in Colonel Perry's regiment, but that a writer or agent whom he knew in Glasgow got him off by taking a bill from him for £11, for which he granted John a discharge which they concealed, so that the apparent debt above £10 kept him from being forced away; that he was employed for several years as a driver of cattle to England, particularly under Mr Birtwhistle, the great English drover. That he was art and part in the theft of the sheep from the parish of Douglas, one of the articles in his trial in 1766. Graham, the man's herd, stole them and delivered them to him half a mile from the farm. That he did not steal the six score; that he married in 1759; that since his trial in 1766 he had led an honest, industrious life; that he received the sheep for which he was condemned from Gardner, and did not suspect them to be stolen. That his wife and children would be present at his death. I dissuaded him from this. He said his wife and he had lived comfortably fifteen years, and she said she would see him to the last and would *kep* him (i.e. receive his body when cut down); that his son, who was a boy of ten years of age, might forget it (meaning his execution) if he only heard of it, but that he would not readily forget it if he saw it. To hear a man talk of his own execution gave me a strange kind of feeling. He said he would be carried to his own burial-place at Muiravonside; that it was the second best in the kirkyard. There were symptoms of vanity in the long line of the Reids and the good burial-place; a proof that ideas of these kinds are natural and universal.

Ritchie and I sat awhile with him after the painter was gone, the first sitting being over. John said, 'Death is no terror to me at present. I know not what it may be.' Said Ritchie, 'You must either be infatuated, or you have, by grace, a reliance on the merits of Jesus Christ.' John said he trusted to the mercy of GOD in Christ; that he had been an unfortunate man, and insinuated that his fate was foreordained. Ritchie quoted the passage in James which I had quoted; but he seemed to be much hampered with Calvinistical notions about decrees, while he struggled to controvert John's wickedness being foreordained. Indeed the system of predestination includes all actions, bad as well as good. Ritchie pressed John much to make an authentic last speech. I told him that if he was guilty of the crime for which he was condemned, it was his duty to his country and the only reparation he could make, to acknowledge it, that his example might have a proper effect. He persisted in his denial, and did not seem willing to have any speech published. Ritchie said to me in his hearing that it was a perquisite for Richard, who had a great deal of trouble. I said we should get John to make a speech.

It was a very wet day. I grew dreary and wanted either Charles Hay or Grange to dine with me, but neither of them could come. I took a little bowl of warm punch by myself, except a glass which Veronica drank. Her sweet little society was a gentle relief, but I was too dismal to enjoy it much. I had a letter from my brother David which was a cordial. I drank tea with Grange, but was gloomy. I had by sympathy sucked the dismal ideas of John Reid's situation, and as spirits or strong substance of any kind, when transferred to another body of a more delicate nature, will have much more influence than on the body from which it is transferred, so I suffered much more than John did. Grange very sensibly observed that we should keep at a distance from dreary objects; that we should shun what hurts the mind as we shun what disagrees with the stomach and hurts the body – a very good maxim for preserving a *mens sana*. At night Mr Nairne called in and supped with us. He did me some good by his conversation.

WEDNESDAY 31 AUGUST. This was the second day of John Reid's sitting for his picture. Ralph the painter went through his part with perfect composure, hardly ever opening his mouth. He mentioned a Mr Cochrane of Barbachlaw. John said he was a strange man. He used to drink hard, till he *squeeled* like a *nowt*.[1] He would just play *bu*. Strange that a creature under sentence of death should tell such an anecdote and seem entertained. I spoke to him of his execution, thinking it humane to familiarize his mind to it. I asked him if he was here when Murdison died.[2] He said no, and on my saying, 'So you did not see him die,' told me that he had never seen an execution. 'No?' said I. 'I wonder you never had the curiosity.' He said he never had. That once, as he and some other drivers of cattle were coming from Yorkshire, they stopped at Penrith in Cumberland, where there was a man to be executed for murder next day; that some of his companions stayed to see it, but he and the rest did not. I then spoke of the way in England of having a cart and ours of having a ladder, and that it was said ours was the easiest way. 'I take it, John,' said I, 'I shall die a severer death than you.' 'I dinna (do not) think', said he, 'they can feel much; or that it can last ony (any) time; but there's nane (none) of them to tell how it is.' I mentioned Maggy Dickson, who had been hanged less than the usual time and was recovered, and said she felt no pain.[3] He told me he saw a Highlandman at Glasgow, a big strong man, who had escaped twice; first, the rope broke. 'And', said John, 'at that time it was thought they coudna (could not) hang them up again; and the second time, the gallows fell.' He said his wife was resolved that he should die in white; that it was the custom in his part of the country to dress the dead body in linen, and she thought it would cost no more to do it when he was alive. He this day again averred the truth of his story that he got the sheep from Gardner. He said to me that there was something he had done a great many years ago, before any of his trials, that had followed him all this time. That it was not a great thing either, nor yet a small thing, and he would let me know it. This was somehow curious and awful. Honest Ritchie, from time to time, threw out serious reflections, as thus: 'If any man sin, we have an advocate with the Father, even Christ the righteous. Christ is an advocate, indeed. Other advocates only plead for panels. But he takes upon him the offences of the panels and suffers in their stead.' Ritchie also gave a particular account of the behaviour of Pickworth,[4] and promised to give me a copy of a printed narrative of it which he wrote. I did not know before that Ritchie was an author.

I mentioned that it was remarkable that there was always fine weather on execution days, and I asked Ritchie what was the meaning of pigeons flying when people were executed. He said that he thought the notions which some people entertained of that signifying good to the persons executed were *fablish*. John then told of a woman who was executed, who told that morning to a minister after awaking from a sound sleep, 'If ye see some clear draps o' (drops of) rain faw (fall) on me after I'm custen owr (thrown over), I'm happy.' And John said the clear drops did fall. All this was most suitable conversation for John. I asked him if he had ever seen the hangman. He said no. I said I had seen him this forenoon going into the office of the prison. 'Ay,' said John, 'he'll be going about thinking there's something for him.' He seemed to think of him with much aversion and declared he would have no intercourse with him, one way or other; but he seemed somewhat reconciled when I told him that the hangman was a humane creature, and shed tears for unhappy people when they were to be executed. I inculcated upon John that he was now to have no hopes, since no answer had come to his application. He asked if there would not come an answer of some kind. I said not unless they were to grant something favourable, and that must have come before now had it been to come. He said he was thrown into a panic by hearing a horn blow in the street. I was desirous to have his picture done *while under sentence of death* and was therefore rather desirous that, in case a respite was to come, it should not arrive till he had sat his full time. It was finished today and was a striking likeness, a gloomy head. He asked if it would not be better to have had on his bonnet, and said he should have had on a better waistcoat. He asked too if his name would be upon it. I said it would be on the back of it. Said he: 'I thought it would have been on the fore (front) side of it.' There was vanity again. As the painter advanced in doing it, I felt as if he had been raising a spectre. It was a strange thought. Here is a man sitting for his picture who is to be hanged this day eight days. John himself seemed to wonder somewhat at the operation, and said, 'I'm sure you maun hae an unco (must have a strange) concern about this,' or words to that purpose. When it was finished and hung upon a nail to dry, it swung, which looked ominous, and made an impression on my fancy. I gave John a dram of whisky today again. When I got home I found several vermin upon me which I had attracted while in the jail. It was shocking. I changed all my clothes.

Received c. 31 August, Lord Erroll to Boswell

Slains Castle, 27 August 1774

Sir, – I have now lying before me yours of the tenth. I should be very willing to show any favour in my power to a client of yours, but in the present case I am certain no application from me would be of any avail. I never had a good opinion of Mr Clarke, although he was my tenant. And from your own account of Reid, I cannot find any reason for an indifferent person to apply in his favour. At the same time I cannot help applauding your doing so, as you are of opinion the jury condemned him on scrimp evidence, though I think a man being habit and repute of a bad character must always weigh with any jury. Lady Erroll joins me in best respects to you, and I am with very much esteem, Sir, your most obedient servant,

ERROLL

THURSDAY 1 SEPTEMBER. I breakfasted at Mr David Steuart's, Writer to the Signet, where was his father, Steuart Hall. At ten I called on Dr Cullen to talk with him of recovering John Reid. He was gone abroad. I found his son, my brother lawyer, and trusted him with the secret, and he engaged to get me a meeting with his father. It came on a heavy rain; so I sat a good while with Cullen in his study, and had very good ideas presented to my mind about books and criminal law, &c. Every man has some peculiar views which seem new to another. After taking a tolerable dose of law, Mr Hay and I went for a walk to Heriot's Garden, and then I dined with him. He had Dr Monro and several more company with him, and it was concerted that we should get information from the Anatomical Professor as to recovering a hanged person, which would be useful to Reid. Harry Erskine was there, and talked so much that it was long before we could get Dr Monro set upon the subject. He said in his opinion a man who is hanged suffers a great deal; that he is not at once stupefied by the shock, suffocation being a thing which must be gradual and cannot be forced on instantaneously; so that a man is suffocated by hanging in a rope just as by having his respiration stopped by having a pillow pressed on the face, in Othello's way, or by stopping the mouth and nostrils, which one may try; and he said that for some time after a man is thrown over, he is sensible and is conscious that he is *hanging*; but that in three minutes or so he is stupefied. He said that it was more difficult to recover a hanged person than a drowned, because hanging forces the blood up to the brain with more violence, there being a local compression at the neck; but that he thought the thing might be done by heat and rubbing to put the blood in motion, and by blowing air into the lungs; and he said the best way was to cut a hole in the throat, in the trachea, and introduce a pipe. I laid up all this for service in case it should be necessary. He told me that ten or twelve of his students had, unknown to him, tried to recover my clients Brown and Wilson, but had only blown with their own breaths into the mouths of the *subjects*, which was not sufficient. He said some people had applied to him for leave to put on fires and make preparations for recovering Lieutenant Ogilvy in his class.5 That he thought it would be very wrong in him to allow it, and told them he should have no objection if Lord Justice-Clerk gave his consent. That he spoke to Lord Justice-Clerk, who said that if such a thing was allowed, the College of Edinburgh should never again get a body from the Court of Justiciary. Indeed it would have been counteracting their sentence. He said he dissected Ogilvy publicly, and that there was no hurt on his head by the fall from the gibbet.

I sat long here today, thinking myself well employed in listening to Dr Monro, whom I seldom met. He asked me to sup with him next day with the Laird of MacLeod. I drank rather more than a bottle of Madeira. It was about ten when we parted. I made a good deal of impression on the company in favour of John Reid's innocence. As I considered him as now a gone man, I resolved to know the truth by being with him to the very last moment of his life, even to walk a step or two up the ladder and ask him *then*, just before his going off, what was the real matter of fact; for if he should deny *then*, I could not resist the conviction.

FRIDAY 2 SEPTEMBER. I lay till near ten. A little after I rose and was at breakfast and Mr Hay was come, while the tea-things were standing, I was called out to a man – and who was this but Richard Lock, who informed me that John Reid had got a respite for fourteen days; that Captain Fraser had been up with him and read it to him, and that he teared more now than he had ever seen him. I was put into great agitation. All my nerves started. I instantly dressed, and Mr Hay and I walked out, met Michael Nasmith, who had seen the respite in the Council Chamber, and he went thither with us, when Bailie Brown showed us it. Wright, the stationer, who was at the time —, cried out with a kind of unfeeling sneer, 'It will be lang (long) life and ill health'; and all the people in the Chamber seemed against poor John. We then went up to John, whom we found in a dreadful state. He was quite unhinged. His knees knocked against each other, he trembled so; and he cried bitterly. I spoke to him in a most earnest manner and told him, since the respite was only for fourteen days, the judges would be consulted and they would report against him. He must therefore consider that he had just fourteen days more allowed him to prepare for his awful change. He moaned and spoke of his being 'cut off after all, with a hale (whole) heart'. I said he must compose himself. He said he hoped he should, if it pleased GOD to continue him in his senses, as he had hitherto done. I said, 'You *would* make this application, though I told you I thought it would have no effect. If you suffer from it, it is owing to yourself.' It was striking to see a man who had been quite composed when he thought his execution certain become so weak and so much agitated by a respite. My wife put a construction on his conduct which seemed probable. She said it was plain he had all along been expecting a pardon and therefore was composed, but that now when he found that only a respite for fourteen days had come and that enquiry was to be made at the judges, he for the first time had the view of death. But if I can judge of human nature by close observation, I think he was before this time reconciled to his fate, and that the respite affected him by throwing him into a wretched state of incertainty. I gave him a shilling to get some spirits as a cordial. Messrs Hay and Nasmith went with me to the Justiciary Office, but we could learn nothing there but that John Davidson, the Crown Agent, had applied for an extract of the trial on Monday. The respite therefore must have been kept up some days.

I was quite agitated, partly by feeling for Reid, whom I had seen in so miserable a condition, partly by keenness for my own consequence, that I should not fail in what I had undertaken, but get a transportation pardon for my client, since a respite had come.

Michael Nasmith to John Wilson Jr, Writer in Glasgow[6]

Edinburgh, 6 September 1774

Dear Johnny, – You must know something more about poor John Reid's situation.

In 1766, when tried here for sheep-stealing, when the verdict of the jury was read finding him innocent, some of the judges took the liberty to give a different opinion, and the Lord Justice-Clerk in his speech in the Douglas Cause took some striking liberties with poor John's character. Upon these grounds, notwithstanding the verdict, all mankind were authorized by the Court to hold him guilty.

In last indictment habit and repute was libelled. Mr Boswell opposed this with great spirit. [The charge was] this: that eighteen were stolen, and that five of these were found in John's possession. John could not prove he purchased them, nor could he prove that he had not himself brought them home. Nor could he prove he was at home the night before they arrived. Of about twenty-five witnesses who were summoned for him, not one of them could say a word, and one of the Crown witnesses swore that he imagined (being Reid's next neighbour) that the sheep was brought home by John early before daylight in the morning, although John avers, and his wife too, that he was in his bed all that night, and that Russel, a lad employed by Gardner, brought them. The habit and repute bore everything before it. Five of the nineteen were found in his possession. Ergo the libel was found proved. Such a conclusion perchance may be right, but I defy mortal creature to say it is. Boswell was great. There never was a charge made with greater dignity and judgement. Had Corsica been at stake, he could not have stood forth with greater firmness, and at the same time with all that respect which was necessary, to show that the former trial could not influence in the present question. He implored the jury to disentangle themselves from all prejudices. The Lord Justice-Clerk complained loudly to the jury he and the Court had been arraigned. The verdict was returned finding the indictment proved.

A respite, I told you last night, has been obtained for fourteen days, but we now understand His Majesty wishes to have the Justiciary Court's report whether the poor man ought to die or live. You see where we are. We fear the Lord Justice-Clerk. The battle is betwixt Boswell and the Court. He is opposing all his interest. He is all humanity. Reid is his oldest client in the Justiciary Court. He wishes not to see him die where the proof is not conclusive, nor any man where the proof is no more than that five stolen sheep are found in his possession. A simple act of theft, and that only supported by presumption. Is it not hard?

Before the respite came, John's last speech was framed. It has been put into Mr Boswell's possession. Enclosed is a copy of that part of it respecting Gardner. It may be true. If it is, what a direful thing in this country of knowledge, and all the rest of it, for the poor man to be hung up!

WEDNESDAY 7 SEPTEMBER. Mr Nasmith called with a letter from Brown, the messenger who had taken up John Reid, addressed to John, and mentioning that, as they were upon the road, John asked him if he could apprehend anyone else and mentioned Gardner, who was accordingly apprehended. From this letter it appeared to me and Messrs Hay and Nasmith that John had been lying; for if he had got the sheep from Gardner without suspicion, would not he, when accused of stealing them, have instantly accused Gardner, loudly and keenly? No law was read today, we talked so long of John Reid. I determined to try again to know the truth.

I went up to John a little before two, with the messenger's letter in my hand. Seeing me have a paper, he gave an earnest look, I suppose in expectation that it was his pardon. But I at once accosted him as a dying man, upbraided him with having imposed on me, and said to him what I and Mr Nasmith had concluded from perusal of the letter. He calmly explained his conduct. 'Sir,' said he, 'Gardner had before this time come to my house and owned to me that he had stolen the sheep, and promised me great rewards if I would not discover him. Therefore, when I was taken up, I would not speak out against him, but wanted him to be apprehended, that he and I might concert what was to be done to keep ourselves safe. But he was but a very little time with me, and then was carried to Stirling.' I was not much convinced by this account of the matter. I had wrought myself into a passion against John for deceiving me, and spoke violently to him, not feeling for him at the time. I had chosen my time so as to be with him when two o'clock struck. 'John,' said I, 'you hear that clock strike. You hear that bell. If this does not move you, nothing will. That you are to consider as your last bell. You remember your sentence. On Wednesday the 7 of September. This is the day. Between the hours of two and four in the afternoon; this is that very time. After this day you are to look upon yourself as a dead man; as a man in a middle state between the two worlds. You are not in eternity, because you are still in the body; but you are not properly alive, because this is the day appointed for your death. You are to look on this fortnight as so much time allowed to you to repent of all your wickedness, and particularly of your lying to me in such a way as you have done. Think that this day fortnight by four o'clock you will be rendering an account to your Maker. I am afraid that you are encouraged by your wife to persist in obstinacy, not to disgrace her and your children. But that is a small consideration to a man going into eternity. I think it your duty to own your being guilty on this occasion if you be really so, which I cannot but think is the case. By doing so you will make all the atonement in your power to society. But at any rate I beseech you not to deny your guilt contrary to truth.' This was as vehement and solemn a harangue as could be made upon any occasion. The circumstance of the clock striking and the two o'clock bell ringing were finely adapted to touch the imagination. But John seemed to be very unfeeling today. He persisted in his tale. There was something approaching to the ludicrous when, in the middle of my speech to him about his not being properly alive, he said very gravely, 'Ay; I'm dead in law.' I was too violent with him. I said, 'With what face can you go into the other world?' And: 'If your ghost should come and tell me this, I would not believe it.' This last sentence made me frightened, as I have faith in apparitions, and had a kind of idea that perhaps his ghost might come to me and tell me that I had been unjust to him. I concluded with saying, 'You have paper, pen and ink there. Let me have a real account of everything.' He said he would. Richard Lock had come into the room before I was done speaking. I desired him to advise John to be candid.

John Wilson Jr to Michael Nasmith

Glasgow, 6 September 1774

Dear Sir, – This day I received yours of yesterday about the case of John Reid, who hath received His Majesty's respite of his capital punishment for fourteen days. I see Mr Boswell and you are still employed in the cause of humanity, nay, could our politicians see it, of good policy also – rescuing the lives of the lieges from destruction appointed too frequently by the barbarous laws of a civilized nation. Can any sober thinking person believe it that in a country which boasts so much of its knowledge and refinement, there should exist a law assigning death as the punishment of the crime of stealing eighteen sheep? *Ninety and nine* sheep, which once were less valued than one lost and recovered, are less valuable than the life of any of His Majesty's subjects. What pity it is that the sentiments of that excellent philosopher and politician the Marquis Beccaria have not hitherto been capable of opening the eyes of our legislators, who can suffer the laws on so slight occasions to murder the citizens with a formal pageantry. – I am truly sorry that I can add no information from Gardner, from whom you say Reid maintains he bought the sheep, he having above three weeks ago stayed a night only here in his passage to transportation. I am, dear Sir, your most obedient servant.

JOHN WILSON, JR

THE MOURNFUL CASE OF POOR MISFORTUNATE AND UNHAPPY JOHN REID, Now lying under sentence of death in the Tolbooth of Edinburgh, dated Wednesday night, the 7th of September 1774.

This is the very day on which I was doomed to die; and had it not been for the mercy of our most gracious Sovereign, whom GOD long bless and preserve, I should by this time have been a miserable spectacle, and my last speech crying dolefully through the streets of this city. O! listen then unto me, while I am yet in the land of the living, and think that it is my GHOST speaking unto you!

Much cry has been made against me by small and great. And how can a poor man like me withstand it? But before I go hence and be no more, I trust you will hear the words of truth, and peradventure your minds may be changed.

I am condemned because some of these sheep were found in my

flesh-house and I could not bring downright probation of him from whom I came by them. But I say now, as I told my lawyer, who said it unto the lords and will say unto the end, that William Gardner, and none else, was the man, and he is now a transported thief, though he was loose when I was seized and caused him for to be taen, that he might answer therefor and I not be the sufferer. John Brown the messenger in Linlithgow can attest this; and many an honest man has no witnesses present when he receives goods. But I see that my being tried two times before, though cleared by juries, many of whom, now alive, can bear testimony for me, has made me be thought guilty at all events.

I hope none of you shall by malicious report of enemies be brought to trial, since it is all one whatever is the fate thereof.

What will you say when Gardner's conscience smites him in America and he owns that I got the sheep honestly from him, and I am gone and cannot be recalled?

May all good Christians, then, charitably pray that as the King's heart is in the hand of the Lord, and he turneth it whithersoever he will, it may please him to save me from an ignominious death, which can do harm to no man.

WEDNESDAY 14 SEPTEMBER. Having gone out to the Justiciary Office in the morning, Mr Hay had called and missed me; so we had no law. I called at the bank for Maclaurin, and he and I took a walk in the Meadow. After dinner Ritchie called on me and said he was very desirous that John Reid should declare what he had committed long ago, which he thought had followed him. I promised to come to the prison, and accordingly went.

John was very sedate. He told Mr Ritchie and me that before his first trial, one night he drank hard and lay all night at the side of a sheep-fold; that when he awaked the devil put it into his head (or some such expression), and he drove off all the sheep in the fold (the '*hail hirsle*'); that before he was off the farm to which they belonged, he came to a water, and there he separated four of them, which he took home, killed, and sold; and he said it was alleged that he had taken five, but it never came to any trial. This was but a small matter. John said he would have it published. His owning this theft made me give more credit to his denial of that for which he was condemned, for why should he deny the one and confess the other? I told him that now I believed him, and I acknowledged that I had been too violent with him this day eight days. He seemed to be grateful to me; and said that few would have done so much for a brother, though a twin, as I had done for him. He said that he had always had something heavy about his mind since his last trial and never could be merry as formerly. He said that last night he had strange dreams. He saw a wonderful moon with many streamers. And he and a man who died some time ago, he imagined were walking together, and the man had a gun in his hand; that two eagles – two pretty speckled birds – lighted on a tree. (*I* had very near said that these signified Lord Cornwallis and Lord Pembroke, who were his friends; but I checked myself.) He called to the man to shoot, but he did not; and one of the eagles flew into the man's arms, who gave it to John, and he carried it. Ritchie very foolishly smiled, and said, 'Maybe, John, it may be a messenger of good news to you.' This might have given him hopes. 'No,' said I. 'Had it been a *dow* (dove), I should have thought it good; but an eagle is a bad bird.' 'Ay,' said John earnestly, 'a ravenous bird.' 'But', said Ritchie, 'it did not fly on John, but on the other man, who gave it to John.' 'Well,' said I, 'that is to say, the bad news will come to Captain Fraser, and he'll deliver it to John.'

I asked John if he ever saw anything in the iron room where he lay. He said no; but that he heard yesterday at nine in the morning a noise upon the form, as if something had fallen upon it with a *clash*. Ritchie and he seemed to consider this as some sort of warning. He said he had heard such a noise in the corner of the room a little before his respite came. And he said that the night before James Brown's pardon came, Brown was asleep, and he was awake, and heard like swine running from the door, round a part of the room, and *grumphling*. He seemed to be in a very composed frame. I said it was an awful thought that this day sennight at this time he would be in eternity. I said I hoped his repentance was sincere and his faith in Christ sincere, and that he would be saved through the merits of the Saviour, and perhaps he might this day eight days be looking down with pity on Mr Ritchie and me. I found that he had hardly written anything.

SATURDAY 17 SEPTEMBER. Mr Robert Boswell and I breakfasted at my uncle the Doctor's. Richard Lock came in the morning, after my return from the Doctor's, and told me, 'It is all over with John Reid. He dies on Wednesday. There's a letter come that no farther respite is to be granted.' I was struck with concern. Mr Hay came, and he and I walked a little on the Castle Hill and then called on Mr Nasmith. We agreed to dine together at Leith to relieve our vexation at the bad news. I first went up a little to John Reid. His wife was with him. He was not much affected with the bad news, as he had not been indulging hopes. I again exhorted him to tell nothing but truth.

TUESDAY 20 SEPTEMBER. Before breakfast I received a very good letter from Mr Nasmith dissuading me from the scheme of recovering John Reid, but he did not persuade me. Mr Hay came and he and I called on Mr Nasmith and took him with us to look for a place where the corpse might be deposited. We walked about the Grassmarket and Portsburgh, and saw some small houses to let. Mr Nasmith proposed that we might take one till Martinmas; but then it occurred that the landlord would make a noise if a hanged man was put into it. In short, we were in a dilemma. I thought of the Canongate Kilwinning Lodge, of which I was Master and could excuse myself to the brethren for taking liberty with it; but it was too far off. I did not think it right to trust a caddie,7 or any low man, with the secret. I asked John Robertson the chairman if he could find a house that would take in the corpse till the mob dispersed. He thought none would do it. Mr Nasmith went out of town. Mr Hay, after a short party at bowls, went with me and called for Mr Innes,8 Dr Monro's dissector. Mr Wood had not yet spoken to him; but he very readily agreed to give his help. He however could not help us to get a house. I called on Wood. Neither could he help us as to that article; and he began to doubt of the propriety of the scheme. I however remained firm to it, and Mr Hay stood by me. Mr Innes suggested one George Macfarlane, a stabler, where a puppet-show had been kept. Mr Hay and I went to the Grassmarket, where he lived. But first it occurred to me that there was one Andrew Bennet, a stabler, whom I had lately got out of prison. We went to him. He had no family but his wife, and they were both fools. They were prodigiously grateful to me, called me *his Grace*, Andrew having reproved his wife for calling me only *his Honour*. I told them that the friends of the poor man who was to be executed next day were anxious to lodge his body in some place till the mob should disperse, and, as he was a client of mine, I was desirous to assist them; so I hoped Andrew would let them have his stable for that purpose. He agreed to it, though his wife made some objection, and though he said he would rather let his *craig* (throat) be cut than allow it, unless to oblige me. I sounded them as to letting the body into their house; but Mrs Bennet screamed, and Andrew said very justly that nobody would come to it any more if that was done.9 It is amazing what difficulty I found in such a place as Edinburgh to get a place for my purpose. The stable here entered by a close next entry to the door of the house, and had no communication with the house; so that the operators must be obliged to take their stations in the stable some time before the execution was over. It was a small stable, and there was a smith's shop just at the door of it; so that we could not be private enough. However, I was glad to have secured any place.

When I came to the prison I found that John Reid's wife and children were with him. The door of the iron room was now left open and they were allowed to go and come as they pleased. He was very composed. His daughter Janet was a girl about fifteen, his eldest son Benjamin about ten, his youngest son Daniel between two and three. It was a striking scene to see John on the last night of his life surrounded by his family. His wife and two eldest children behaved very quietly. It was really curious to see the young child Daniel, who knew nothing of the melancholy situation of his father, jumping upon him with great fondness, laughing and calling to him with vivacity. The contrast was remarkable between the father in chains and in gloom and the child quite free and frolicsome. John took him on his knee with affection. He said to me that his daughter Jenny was the only one of his children whom he had named after any relation; and he went over all the names of the rest. They had almost all Old Testament names. They were seven in all. I again exhorted him to truth. One Miln in Leith Wynd, a kind of lay teacher,10 and Mr Ritchie were with him; and he was to have some good Christians to sit up with him all night.

Mr Hay went with me again to Mr Innes, who was satisfied with Bennet's stable and desired that there should be a blanket and a good quantity of warm salt prepared. We went again to Bennet's, and took a dram of whisky of his own distilling; and he and his wife promised to have the blanket and the salt in readiness, I having said that some surgeon had advised his friends to rub the body with warm salt to preserve it, as it was to be carried to the country. Bennet, though a fool, had smoked what was intended; for he said, 'Could they not cut him down living?' I said that would be wrong. I should have observed when I was with John this evening, it gave me some uneasiness to think that he was solemnly preparing for an awful eternity while at the same time I was to try to keep him back. He spoke himself very calmly of *the corpse*, by which he meant his own dead body; for I spoke to his wife before him about it: that I had secured a place for it, but I wished she could get a better place for it to be laid in till the mob dispersed. She said she would try Mrs Walker at the sign of the Bishop in the Grassmarket, who was very friendly to her. It was a comfort to me that neither John nor his wife had the least idea of any attempt to recover him.

Mr Hay and I met my worthy friend Grange in the Grassmarket tonight. He was much against the attempt. After supper Mr Wood called and told me that he had the proper apparatus ready; that he had also engaged Mr Aitkin, another surgeon, to attend, and that, if I insisted on it, he was willing to make the experiment, but that as a friend he could not but advise me against it; that it would be impossible to conceal it; the mob would press upon us, and continue looking in at the door. A great clamour would be made against me as defying the laws and as doing a ridiculous thing, and that a man in business must pay attention in prudence to the voice of mankind; that the chance of success was hardly anything, and this was to be put in the scale against a certainty of so many disagreeable consequences. But he suggested another thought which had great weight with me. 'This man', said he, 'has got over the bitterness of death; he is resigned to his fate. He will have got over the pain of death. He may curse you for bringing him back. He may tell you that you kept him from heaven.' I determined to give up the scheme. Wood got into a disagreeable kind of sceptical conversation about the soul being material, from all that we could observe. It is hard that our most valuable articles of belief are rather the effects of sentiment than of demonstration. I disliked Wood because he revived doubts in my mind which I could not at once dispel. Yet he had no bad meaning, but was honestly and in confidence expressing his own uneasiness. He said that the fear of death sometimes distressed him in the night. He seemed to have formed no principles upon the subject, but just had ideas, sometimes of one kind, sometimes of another, floating in his mind. He had a notion, which I have heard the Reverend Mr Wyvill support, that only some souls were designed for immortality. What a blessing it is to have steady religious sentiments.

Michael Nasmith to Boswell

Edinburgh, 20 September 1774

My dear Sir, – This is a matter of secrecy. We have properly speaking no person to advise with. The proposed attempt appears to be attended with so much humanity that the moment any of our friends may have it in confidence they may find themselves in the same situation we ourselves are. I have been therefore deliberating with myself how far the world may think we have acted a worthy part in having attempted to preserve his life.

The jury have returned an unanimous verdict finding him guilty. The Court of Justiciary have been unanimous in finding him worthy of death. Our Sovereign has given it as his opinion that the interests of society are at stake if he is suffered to escape. The voice of the whole people approves. In short, everything sacred in society seems to forbid the attempt.

Humanity and a strong belief of John's innocence have already impelled you to do much for him, but let us cast our eyes forward and see what effects the attempt may have upon the poor wretches who may hereafter be condemned to lose their lives. Death is already sufficiently terrible. I fear much that the proposed attempt, be the event what it will, may be attended with the worst consequences, consequences that neither of us would wish to be the authors of. In the awful approach of eternity the mind is disposed to grasp at every shadow. Few will hereafter come to suffer in this country to whose ears John's story may not have reached. If he is brought to life, they will hold it up as full evidence that they too may – and that there may be a Boswell at hand the moment they are cut down. If the experiment proves ineffectual, they will solace themselves with such thoughts as these: that he was old – that he had been desperately wicked – that though the experiment did not succeed upon him, the world is every day getting more knowledge, it may upon them – that heaven may have foreseen that they could not be otherways reclaimed than by suspending them in a rope and allowing them thereafter to return to life. To step out of this world in such a situation, without repentance, confession and resignation is a dismal thought.

To me the affair at present appears in these points of view and is not unworthy of the most cool deliberation. What do you think of talking to Mrs Boswell, who, if I am a right judge, possesses both judgement and humanity in abundance? I am, dear Sir, yours sincerely.

M. NASMITH

WEDNESDAY 21 SEPTEMBER. John Reid's wife called on me before breakfast and told me that Mrs Walker said she was welcome to the best room in her house for the corpse; but that afterwards her landlord had sent to her that she must quit his house if she allowed such a thing. I said that there would be no occasion for any place. The mob would not trouble the corpse; and it might be put directly on the cart that she expected was to come for it. After breakfast Mr Nasmith came, and was pleased to find that the scheme of recovery was given up. He and I went to Bennet's and told him there was no use for his stable. We walked backwards and forwards in the Grassmarket, looking at the gallows and talking of John Reid. Mr Nasmith said he imagined he would yet confess; for his wife had said this morning that he had something to tell me which he had as yet told to no mortal. We went to the prison about half an hour after twelve. He was now released from the iron about his leg. The Reverend Dr Webster and Mr Ritchie were with him. We waited in the hall along with his wife, who had white linen clothes with black ribbons in a bundle, ready to put on him before he should go out to execution. There was a deep settled grief in her countenance. She was resolved to attend him to the last; but Richard whispered me that the Magistrates had given orders that she should be detained in the prison till the execution was over. I dissuaded her from going and she agreed to take my advice; and then Richard told her the orders of the Magistrates. I said aloud I was glad to hear of it. The Reverend Dr Macqueen, who afterwards came in, told her it would be a tempting of Providence to go; that it might affect her so as to render her incapable to take care of her fatherless children; and Mr Ritchie said that the best thing she could do was to remain in the prison and pray for her husband. Dr Macqueen said to me he was so much impressed with the poor man's innocence that he had some difficulty whether he ought to attend the execution and authorize it by his presence. I said he certainly should attend, for it was *legal*; and, besides, supposing it ever so unjust, it was humane to attend an unhappy man in his last moments. 'But', said Dr Macqueen, 'I will not pray for him as a guilty man.' 'You would be very much in the wrong to do so,' said I, 'if you think him not guilty.' Dr Webster and I had no conversation as he passed through the hall except enquiring at each other how we did.

John's wife then went up to him for a little, having been told both by me and Mr Nasmith that she could not hope for the blessing of Providence on her and her children if by her advice John went out of the world with a lie in his mouth. I followed in a little, and found him in his usual dress, standing at the window. I told him I understood he had something to mention to me. He said he *would* mention it. He had since his trial in 1766 stolen a few sheep (I think five), of which he never was suspected. 'John,' said I, 'it gives me concern to find that even such a warning as you got then did not prevent you from stealing. I really imagine that if you had now got off you might again have been guilty, such influence has Satan over you.' He said he did not know but he might. Then I observed that his untimely death might be a mercy to him, as he had time for repentance. He seemed to admit that it might be so. He said that what he had now told me he had not mentioned even to his wife; and I might let it rest. I called up Mr Nasmith, with whom came Mr Ritchie. I said he might acknowledge this fact to them, which he did. I asked him, if I saw it proper to mention it as making his denial of the theft for which he was condemned more probable, I might be at liberty to do so? He said I might dispose of it as I thought proper. But he persisted in denying the theft for which he was condemned. He now began to put on his white dress, and we left him. Some time after, his wife came down and begged that we would go up to him, that he might not be alone. Dress has a wonderful impression on the fancy. I was not much affected when I saw him this morning in his usual dress. But now he was all in white, with a high nightcap on, and he appeared much taller, and upon the whole struck me with a kind of tremor. He was praying; but stopped when we came in. I bid him not be disturbed, but go on with his devotions. He did so, and prayed with decent fervency, while his wife, Mr Nasmith and I stood close around him. He prayed in particular, 'Grant, O Lord, through the merits of my Saviour, that this the day of my death may be the day of my birth unto life eternal.' Poor man, I felt now a kind of regard for him. He said calmly, 'I think I'll be in eternity in about an hour.' His wife said something from which he saw that she was not to attend him to his execution; and he said, 'So you're no (not) to be wi' me.' I satisfied him that it was right she should not go. I said, 'I suppose, John, you know that the executioner is down in the hall.' He said no. I told him that he was there and would tie his arms before he went out. 'Ay,' said his wife, 'to keep him from catching at the *tow* (rope).' 'Yes,' said I, 'that it may be easier for him.' John said he would submit to everything.

I once more conjured him to tell the truth. 'John,' said I, 'you must excuse me for still entertaining some doubt, as you know you have formerly deceived me in some particulars. I have done more for you in this world than ever was done for any man in your circumstances. I beseech you let me be of some use to you for the next world. Consider what a shocking thing it is to go out of the world with a lie in your mouth. How can you expect mercy, if you are in rebellion against the GOD of truth?' I thus pressed him; and while he stood in his dead clothes, on the very brink of the grave, with his knees knocking together, partly from the cold occasioned by his linen clothes, partly from an awful apprehension of death, he most solemnly averred that what he had told concerning the present alleged crime was the truth. Before this, I had at Mr Ritchie's desire read over his last speech to him, which was rather an irksome task as it was very long; and he said it was all right except some immaterial circumstance about his meeting Wilson with the six score of sheep. Vulgar minds, and indeed all minds, will be more struck with some unusual thought than with the most awful consideration which they have often heard. I tried John thus: 'We are all mortal. Our life is uncertain. I may perhaps die in a week hence. Now, John, consider how terrible it would be if I should come into the other world and find' (looking him steadfastly in the face) 'that you have been imposing on me.' He was roused by this, but still persisted. 'Then,' said I, 'John, I shall trouble you no more upon this head. I believe you. GOD forbid that I should not believe the word of a fellow man in your awful situation, when there is no strong evidence against it, as I should hope to be believed myself in the same situation. But remember, John, it is trusting to you that I believe. It is between GOD and your own conscience if you have told the truth; and you should not allow me to believe if it is not true.' He adhered. I asked him if he had anything more to tell. He said he had been guilty of one other act of sheep-stealing. I think he said of seven sheep; but I think he did not mention precisely when. As he shivered, his wife took off her green cloth cloak and threw it about his shoulders. It was curious to see such care taken to keep from a little cold one who was so soon to be violently put to death. He desired she might think no more of him, and let his children push their way in the world. 'The eldest boy', said he, 'is reading very well. Take care that he reads the word of GOD.' He desired her to keep a New Testament and a psalm-book which he had got in a present from Mr Ritchie and which he was to take with him to the scaffold. He was quite sensible and judicious. He had written a kind of circular letter to all his friends on whom he could depend, begging them to be kind to his family.

Two o'clock struck. I said, with a solemn tone, 'There's two o'clock.' In a little Richard came up. The sound of his feet on the stair struck me. He said calmly, 'Will you come awa now?' This was a striking period. John said yes, and readily prepared to go down. Mr Nasmith and I went down a little before him. A pretty, well-dressed young woman and her maid were in a small closet off the hall; and a number of prisoners formed a kind of audience, being placed as spectators in a sort of loft looking down to the hall. There was a dead silence, all waiting to see the dying man appear. The sound of his steps coming down the stair affected me like what one fancies to be the impression of a supernatural grave noise before any solemn event. When he stepped into the hall, it was quite the appearance of a ghost. The hangman, who was in a small room off the hall, then came forth. He took off his hat and made a low bow to the prisoner. John bowed his head towards him. They stood looking at each other with an awkward uneasy attention. I interfered, and said, 'John, you are to have no resentment against this poor man. He only does his duty.' 'I only do my duty,' repeated the hangman. 'I have no resentment against him,' said John. 'I desire to forgive all mankind.' 'Well, John,' said I, 'you are leaving the world with a very proper disposition: forgiving as you hope to be forgiven.' I forgot to mention that before he left the iron room Mr Ritchie said to him, 'Our merciful King was hindered from pardoning you by a representation against you; but you are going before the King of Heaven, who knows all things and whose mercy cannot be prevented by any representation.' The hangman advanced and *pinioned* him, as the phrase is; that is, tied his arms with a small cord. John stood quiet and undisturbed. I said, 'Richard, give him another glass of wine.' Captain Fraser, the gaoler, had sent him the night before a bottle of claret, part of which Richard had given him, warmed with sugar, early in the morning, two glasses of it in the forenoon, and now he gave him another. John drank to us. He then paused a little, then kissed his wife with a sad adieu, then Mr Ritchie kissed him. I then took him by the hand with both mine, saying, 'John, it is not yet too late. If you have any thing to acknowledge, do it at the last to the reverend gentlemen, Dr Macqueen and Dr Dick, to whom you are much obliged. Farewell, and I pray GOD may be merciful to you.' He seemed faint and deep in thought. The prison door then opened and he stepped away with the hangman behind him, and the door was instantly shut. His wife then cried, 'O Richard, let me up,' and got to the window and looked earnestly out till he was out of sight. Mr Nasmith and I went to a window more to the west, and saw him stalking forward in the gloomy procession. I then desired his wife to retire and pray that he might be supported in this his hour of trial. Captain Fraser gave her four shillings. It was very agreeable to see such humanity in the gaoler, and indeed the tenderness with which the last hours of a convict were soothed pleased me much.

The mob were gone from the prison door in a moment. Mr Nasmith and I walked through the Parliament Close, down the Back Stairs and up the Cowgate, both of us satisfied of John Reid's innocence, and Mr Nasmith observing the littleness of human justice, that could not reach a man for the crimes which he committed but punished him for what he did not commit.

We got to the place of execution about the time that the procession did. We would not go upon the scaffold nor be seen by John, lest it should be thought that we prevented him from confessing. It was a fine day. The sun shone bright. We stood close to the scaffold on the south side between two of the Town Guard. There were fewer people present than upon any such occasion that I ever saw. He behaved with great calmness and piety. Just as he was going to mount the ladder, he desired to see his wife and children; but was told they were taken care of. There was his sister and his daughter near to the gibbet, but they were removed. Dr Dick asked him if what he had said was the truth. He said it was. Just as he was going off, he made an attempt to speak. Somebody on the scaffold called, 'Pull up his cap.' The executioner did so. He then said, 'Take warning. Mine is an unjust sentence.' Then his cap was pulled down and he went off. He catched the ladder; but soon quitted his hold. To me it sounded as if he said, 'just sentence'; and the people were divided, some crying, 'He says his sentence is *just.*' Some: 'No. He says *unjust.*' Mr Laing, clerk to Mr Tait, one of the town clerks, put me out of doubt, by telling me he had asked the executioner, who said it was *unjust.* I was not at all shocked with this execution at the time. John died seemingly without much pain. He was effectually hanged, the rope having fixed upon his neck very firmly; and he was allowed to hang near three-quarters of an hour; so that any attempt to recover him would have been in vain. I comforted myself in thinking that by giving up the scheme I had avoided much anxiety and uneasiness.

We waited till he was cut down; and then walked to the Greyfriars Churchyard, in the office of which his corpse was deposited by porters whom Mr Nasmith and I paid, no cart having come for his body. A considerable mob gathered about the office. Mr Nasmith went to Hutchinson's to bespeak some dinner and write a note to the *Courant* that there would be a paragraph tonight giving an account of the execution; for we agreed that a recent account would make a strong impression. I walked seriously backwards and forwards a considerable time in the churchyard waiting for John Reid's wife coming, that I might resign the corpse to her charge. I at last wearied, and then went to the office of the prison. There I asked the executioner myself what had passed. He told me that John first spoke to him on the ladder and said he suffered wrongfully; and then called to the people that his sentence was unjust. John's sister came here, and returned me many thanks for what I had done for her brother. She was for burying him in the Greyfriars Churchyard, since no cart had come. 'No,' said I, 'the will of the dead shall be fulfilled. He was anxious to be laid in his own burying-place, and it shall be done.' I then desired Richard to see if he could get a cart to hire, and bid him bring John's wife to Hutchinson's. Mr Nasmith and I eat some cold beef and cold fowl and drank some port, and then I wrote a paragraph to be inserted in the newspapers. Mr Nasmith threw in a few words. I made two copies of it, and, both to the printer of the *Courant* and *Mercury,* subjoined my name to be kept as the authority. Richard brought John's wife and daughter. 'Well,' said I, 'Mrs Reid, I have the satisfaction to tell you that your husband behaved as well as we could wish.' 'And that is a great satisfaction,' said she. We made her eat a little and take a glass, but she was, though not violently or very tenderly affected, in a kind of dull grief. The girl did not seem moved. She eat heartily. I told Mrs Reid that I insisted that John should be buried at home; and as I found that as yet no carter would undertake to go but at an extravagant price, the corpse might lie till tomorrow night, and then perhaps a reasonable carter might be had. Mr Nasmith went to the *Courant* with the paragraph, and I to the *Mercury*. I sat till it was printed. It was liberal in Robertson, who was himself one of the jury, to admit it; and he corrected the press.

It was now about eight in the evening, and gloom came upon me. I went home and found my wife no comforter, as she thought I had carried my zeal for John too far, might hurt my own character and interest by it, and as she thought him guilty. I was so affrighted that I started every now and then and durst hardly rise from my chair at the fireside. I sent for Grange, but he was not at home. I however got Dr Webster, who came and supped, and he and I drank a bottle of claret. But still I was quite dismal.

Interlude:

'David Hume, Just A-Dying'

Boswell's habit of getting into the presence and the confidence of the famous paid off many times, but perhaps never as dramatically as in this compact piece of writing inflated from the notes he took while speaking to David Hume. Boswell caught the most famous sceptic philosopher of the age on the edge of death; to get his thoughts on the approaching end and set them down for posterity has been referred to as the 'journalistic scoop of the eighteenth century'.

An Account of My Last Interview with David Hume, Esq.

[Partly recorded in my Journal, partly enlarged
from my memory, 3 March 1777]

On Sunday forenoon the 7 of July 1776, being too late for church, I went to see Mr David Hume, who was returned from London and Bath, just a-dying. I found him alone, in a reclining posture in his drawing-room. He was lean, ghastly and quite of an earthy appearance. He was dressed in a suit of grey cloth with white metal buttons, and a kind of scratch wig.[1] He was quite different from the plump figure which he used to present. He had before him Dr Campbell's *Philosophy of Rhetoric*. He seemed to be placid and even cheerful. He said he was just approaching to his end. I think these were his words. I know not how I contrived to get the subject of immortality introduced. He said he never had entertained any belief in religion since he began to read Locke and Clarke. I asked him if he was not religious when he was young. He said he was, and he used to read *The Whole Duty of Man*; that he made an abstract from the catalogue of vices at the end of it, and examined himself by this, leaving out murder and theft and such vices as he had no chance of committing, having no inclination to commit them. This, he said, was strange work; for instance, to try if, notwithstanding his excelling his schoolfellows, he had no pride or vanity. He smiled in ridicule of this as absurd and contrary to fixed principles and necessary consequences, not adverting that religious discipline does not mean to extinguish, but to moderate, the passions; and certainly an excess of pride or vanity is dangerous and generally hurtful. He then said flatly that the morality of every religion was bad, and, I really thought, was not jocular when he said that when he heard a man was religious, he concluded he was a rascal, though he had known some instances of very good men being religious. This was just an extravagant reverse of the common remark as to infidels.

I had a strong curiosity to be satisfied if he persisted in disbelieving a future state even when he had death before his eyes. I was persuaded from what he now said, and from his manner of saying it, that he did persist. I asked him if it was not possible that there might be a future state. He answered it was possible that a piece of coal put upon the fire would not burn; and he added that it was a most unreasonable fancy that we should exist for ever. That immortality, if it were at all, must be general; that a great proportion of the human race has hardly any intellectual qualities; that a great proportion dies in infancy before being possessed of reason; yet all these must be immortal; that a porter who gets drunk by ten o'clock with gin must be immortal; that the trash of every age must be preserved, and that new universes must be created to contain such infinite numbers. This appeared to me an unphilosophical objection, and I said, 'Mr Hume, you know spirit does not take up space.'

I may illustrate what he last said by mentioning that in a former conversation with me on this subject he used pretty much the same mode of reasoning, and urged that Wilkes and his mob must be immortal. One night last May as I was coming up King Street, Westminster, I met Wilkes, who carried me into Parliament Street to see a curious procession pass: the funeral of a lamplighter attended by some hundreds of his fraternity with torches. Wilkes, who either is, or affects to be, an infidel, was rattling away, 'I think there's an end of that fellow. I think he won't rise again.' I very calmly said to him, 'You bring into my mind the strongest argument that ever

I heard against a future state'; and then told him David Hume's objection that Wilkes and his mob must be immortal. It seemed to make a proper impression, for he grinned abashment, as a Negro grows whiter when he blushes. But to return to my last interview with Mr Hume.

I asked him if the thought of annihilation never gave him any uneasiness. He said not the least; no more than the thought that he had not been, as Lucretius observes. 'Well,' said I, 'Mr Hume, I hope to triumph over you when I meet you in a future state; and remember you are not to pretend that you was joking with all this infidelity.' 'No, no,' said he. 'But I shall have been so long there before you come that it will be nothing new.' In this style of good humour and levity did I conduct the conversation. Perhaps it was wrong on so awful a subject. But as nobody was present, I thought it could have no bad effect. I however felt a degree of horror, mixed with a sort of wild, strange, hurrying recollection of my excellent mother's pious instructions, of Dr Johnson's noble lessons, and of my religious sentiments and affections during the course of my life. I was like a man in sudden danger eagerly seeking his defensive arms; and I could not but be assailed by momentary doubts while I had actually before me a man of such strong abilities and extensive enquiry dying in the persuasion of being annihilated. But I maintained my faith. I told him that I believed the Christian religion as I believed history. Said he: 'You do not believe it as you believe the Revolution.' 'Yes,' said I; 'but the difference is that I am not so much interested in the truth of the Revolution; otherwise I should have anxious doubts concerning it. A man who is in love has doubts of the affection of his mistress, without cause.' I mentioned Soame Jenyns's little book in defence of Christianity, which was just published but which I had not yet read. Mr Hume said, 'I am told there is nothing of his usual spirit in it.'

He had once said to me, on a forenoon while the sun was shining bright, that he did not wish to be immortal. This was a most wonderful thought.[2] The reason he gave was that he was very well in this state of being, and that the chances were very much against his being so well in another state; and he would rather not be more than be worse. I answered that it was reasonable to hope he would be better; that there would be a progressive improvement. I tried him at this interview with that topic, saying that a future state was surely a pleasing idea. He said no, for that it was always seen through a gloomy medium; there was always a Phlegethon or a hell. 'But', said I, 'would it not be agreeable to have hopes of seeing our friends again?' and I mentioned three men lately deceased, for whom I knew he had a high value: Ambassador Keith, Lord Alemoor and Baron Mure. He owned it would be agreeable, but added that none of them entertained such a notion. I believe he said, such a foolish, or such an absurd, notion; for he was indecently and impolitely positive in incredulity. 'Yes,' said I, 'Lord Alemoor was a believer.' David acknowledged that *he* had *some* belief.

I somehow or other brought Dr Johnson's name into our conversation. I had often heard him speak of that great man in a very illiberal manner. He said upon this occasion, 'Johnson should be pleased with my *History*.' Nettled by Hume's frequent attacks upon my revered friend in former conversations, I told him now that Dr Johnson did not allow him much credit; for he said, 'Sir, the fellow is a Tory by chance.' I am sorry that I mentioned this at such a time. I was off my guard; for the truth is that Mr Hume's pleasantry was such that there was no solemnity in the scene; and death for the time did not seem dismal. It surprised me to find him talking of different matters with a tranquillity of mind and a clearness of head which few men possess at any time. Two particulars I remember: Smith's *Wealth of Nations*, which he commended much, and Monboddo's *Origin of Language*, which he treated contemptuously. I said, 'If I were you, I should regret annihilation. Had I written such an admirable history, I should be sorry to leave it.' He said, 'I shall leave that history, of which you are pleased to speak so favourably, as perfect as I can.' He said, too, that all the great abilities with which men had ever been endowed were relative to this world. He said he became a greater friend to the Stuart family as he advanced in studying for his history; and he hoped he had vindicated the two first of them so effectually that they would never again be attacked.

Mr Lauder, his surgeon, came in for a little, and Mr Mure, the Baron's son, for another small interval. He was, as far as I could judge, quite easy with both. He said he had no pain, but was wasting away. I left him with impressions which disturbed me for some time.

ADDITIONS FROM MEMORY, 22 JANUARY 1778

Speaking of his singular notion that men of religion were generally bad men, he said, 'One of the men' (or 'The man' – I am not sure which) 'of the greatest honour that I ever knew is my Lord Marischal, who is a downright atheist. I remember I once hinted something as if I believed in the being of a God, and he would not speak to me for a week.' He said this with his usual grunting pleasantry, with that thick breath which fatness had rendered habitual to him, and that smile of simplicity which his good humour constantly produced.

When he spoke against Monboddo, I told him that Monboddo said to me that he believed the abusive criticism upon his book in the *Edinburgh Magazine and Review* was written by Mr Hume's direction. David seemed irritated, and said, 'Does the *scoundrel*' (I am sure either *that* or '*rascal*') 'say so?' He then told me that he had observed to one of the Faculty of Advocates that Monboddo was wrong in his observation that —————3 and gave as a proof the line in Milton. When the review came out, he found this very remark in it, and said to that advocate, 'Oho! I have discovered you' – reminding him of the circumstance.

It was amazing to find him so keen in such a state. I must add one other circumstance which is material, as it shows that he perhaps was not without some hope of a future state, and that his spirits were supported by a consciousness (or at least a notion) that his conduct had been virtuous. He said, 'If there were a future state, Mr Boswell, I think I could give as good an account of my life as most people.'

'I Was Elevated as if Brought into Another State of Being':

Boswell with Johnson

Throughout Boswell's middle years, from 1766 until Johnson's death in 1784, he spent a sizeable part of almost every year in England, mostly in London and much of the time in the company of his famous friend. The copious journals which he kept over this period not only provided the basis for some of the best parts of the Life *of Johnson, but are also among the most entertaining of Boswell's private papers that have come down to us. Records of his settled life as a lawyer in Edinburgh and on the estate of Auchinleck also exist, but it is when Boswell reaches London and the starry society there that his writing seems to enter another dimension. The journals we have included trace the story of the friendship between these two very different men, using mainly the unpublished diaries but also drawing upon the manuscript of the* Life *for a couple of brilliant scenes. The 1776 Journal in London, Lichfield, Ashbourne follows Boswell on his trip south (including a sad visit to his sick brother John), his triumphant arrival at the Thrales' house at Southwark, where Johnson is ensconced, and the subsequent jaunt they took to Johnson's native town and his place of education. As always it is the combination of Johnson's elevating conversation, faithfully recorded, with the little details of their days which is irresistible: Boswell tasting Staffordshire oatcakes for the first time, or the encounter with Johnson's down-at-heel ex-schoolfellow, Harry Jackson. Left out of the* Life, *of course, was Boswell's brooding upon his 'Oriental scheme' of having many women at once without guilt, upon which he seems to have harped so much that it provoked the only serious quarrel between him and Johnson. New, too, are the revelations about Boswell's behaviour on getting back to London after the sober and calm trip to the Midlands. His debauchery in the days that followed seems to have been all the more furious after the time in Johnson's company, spending evenings in quiet talk rather than drinking and whoring. Here also is the account, from the MS of the*

Life, *of the dinner at which Johnson was more or less reconciled to John Wilkes, a man of whom he strongly disapproved. The profligate MP (for such he had finally become) is not the only celebrated person Boswell draws into these pages: Oliver Goldsmith, the explorer James Cook, Adam Smith, all make their appearance, as does the then infamous Mrs Margaret Caroline Rudd (see p. 393), with whom Boswell was later to have a serious affair.*

After the 1777 Journal we have included a scene from the heyday of The Club, formed by Johnson and others in 1764 and to whose ranks Boswell, to his lasting pleasure and pride, was elected in 1773. Following that, the section Boswell marked 'Tacenda' ('to be hidden') shows him and two associates cross-examining Elizabeth Desmoulins, a member of Johnson's household, about the great man's sexual behaviour and his impulses while his wife Tetty was alive. It is a scene vividly drawn and one that, for obvious reasons, never made the published Life.

This section, devoted mainly to Boswell-with-Johnson, opens with a small selection from the original Journal of a tour to the Hebrides in 1773: the time when Boswell managed to lure Johnson to Scotland and kept the closest possible company with him, almost non-stop for ninety-four days: pure, undiluted Johnson, all to himself. In this sample, taken from the manuscript,* the pair visit an old Gaelic-speaking woman's hut on the shores of Loch Ness, have a disappointing time on the Isle of Skye as the guests of Sir Alexander MacDonald and his wife (Boswell's one-time marital candidate, his cousin Elizabeth Bosville) and have a terrifying adventure on a small boat among the Western Islands. In between, they find time to discuss the authenticity of Macpherson's Fingal *('Ossian') and remark on the decline of the ancient Scots laird and clan system as well as other diverse topics. Our Tour ends at Auchinleck, with Boswell trying to prevent a furious political and religious quarrel between his father and his companion.*

1773

TUESDAY 30 AUGUST. A little above Inverness, I fancy about three miles, we saw just by the road a very complete Druid's temple; at least we took it to be so. There was a double circle of stones, one of very large

---

* The only exception being the final episode, Johnson and Lord Auchinleck, which is taken from the printed *Tour.*

ones and one of smaller ones. Mr Johnson justly observed that to go and see one is only to see that it is nothing, for there is neither art nor power in it, and seeing one is as much as one would wish.

It was a delightful day. Loch Ness, and the road upon the side of it, between birch trees, with the hills above, pleased us much. The scene was as remote and agreeably wild as could be desired. It was full enough to occupy our minds for the time.

To see Mr Johnson in any new situation is an object of attention to me. As I saw him now for the first time ride along just like Lord Alemoor, I thought of *London, a Poem*, of the *Rambler*, of *The False Alarm*; and I cannot express the ideas which went across my imagination.

A good way up the Loch, I perceived a little hut with an oldish woman at the door of it. I knew it would be a scene for Mr Johnson. So I spoke of it. 'Let's go in,' said he. So we dismounted, and we and our guides went in. It was a wretched little hovel, of earth only, I think; and for a window had just a hole which was stopped with a piece of turf which could be taken out to let in light. In the middle of the room (or space which we entered) was a fire of peat, the smoke going out at a hole in the roof. She had a pot upon it with goat's flesh boiling. She had at one end, under the same roof but divided with a kind of partition made of wands, a pen or fold in which we saw a good many kids.

Mr Johnson asked me where she slept. I asked one of the guides, who asked her in Erse. She spoke with a kind of high tone. He told us she was afraid we wanted to go to bed to her. This coquetry, or whatever it may be called, of so wretched a like being was truly ludicrous. Mr Johnson and I afterwards made merry upon it. I said it was he who alarmed the poor woman's virtue. 'No, sir,' said he. 'She'll say, "There came a wicked young fellow, a wild young dog, who I believe would have ravished me had there not been with him a grave old gentleman who repressed him. But when he gets out of the sight of his tutor, I'll warrant you he'll spare no woman he meets, young or old."' 'No,' said I. 'She'll say, "There was a terrible ruffian who would have forced me, had it not been for a gentle, mild-looking youth, who, I take it, was an angel."'

Mr Johnson would not hurt her delicacy by insisting to 'see her bedchamber', like Archer in *The Beaux' Stratagem*. But I was of a more ardent curiosity, so I lighted a piece of paper and went into the place where the bed was. There was a little partition of wicker, rather more neatly done than the one for the fold, and close by the wall was a kind of bedstead of wood with heath upon it for a bed; and at the foot of it I saw some sort of blankets or covering rolled up in a heap. The woman's name was Fraser. So was her husband's. He was a man of eighty. Mr Fraser of Balnain allows him to live in this hut and to keep sixty goats for taking care of his wood. He was then in the wood. They had five children, the oldest only thirteen. Two were gone to Inverness to buy meal. The rest were looking after the goats. She had four stacks of barley, twenty-four sheaves in each. They had a few fowls. They will live all the spring without meal upon milk and curd, &c, alone. What they get for their goats, kids and hens maintains them. I did not observe how the children lay.

She asked us to sit down and take a dram. I saw one chair. She said she was as happy as any woman in Scotland. She could hardly speak any English, just detached words. Mr Johnson was pleased at seeing for the first time such a state of human life. She asked for snuff. It is her luxury. She uses a great deal. We had none, but gave her sixpence apiece. She then brought out her whisky bottle. I tasted it, and Joseph and our guides had some. So I gave her sixpence more. She sent us away with many prayers in Erse.

THURSDAY 2 SEPTEMBER [*Glenelg to Isle of Skye*]. A quarter before nine we got into a boat for Skye. It rained much when we set off, but cleared up as we advanced. One of the boatmen who spoke English said that a mile at land was two miles at sea. I then said to him that from Glenelg to Armadale in Skye, which was our sail this morning and is called twelve, was only six miles. But this he could not understand. 'Well,' said Mr Johnson, 'never talk to me of the native good sense of the Highlanders. Here is a fellow who calls one mile two, and yet cannot comprehend that twelve such miles make but six.' It was curious to think that now at last Mr Johnson and I had left the mainland of Scotland and were sailing to the Hebrides, one of which was close in our view; and I had besides a number of youthful ideas, that is to say, ideas which I have had from my youth about the Isle of Skye. We were shown the land of Moidart where Prince Charles first landed. That stirred my mind.

We reached the shore of Armadale before one. Sir Alexander came down and received us. He was in tartan clothes. My Lady stood at the top of the bank and made a kind of jumping for joy. They were then in a house built by a tenant at this place, which is in the district of Sleat. There was a house here for the family, which was burnt in Sir Donald's time. But there is really a good garden and a number of trees of age and size, mostly ash, and that too of a particular kind, the wood of which is very compact. There is a kind of recess here of land, as well as a kind of bay of the sea, more indeed the former. It is a pretty warm exposure. There is a little brook runs down from the hill through a tolerable bank of wood. I am a very imperfect topographer. The house is a very good tenant's house, having two storeys and garrets, but seemed very poor for a chief. Mr Johnson and I were to have had but one room. But I made the plan be altered; so one of the beds was taken out of his room and put into the next, in which I and the overseer of the farm were to lie; but happily Joseph was put in the overseer's place.

We had at dinner a little Aberdeenshire man, one Jeans, a naturalist, with his son, a dwarf with crooked legs. Jeans said he had been at Mr Johnson's in London with Ferguson the astronomer. Mr Johnson thought it strange how he found somebody in such distant places who knew him; that he should have thought he might hide himself in Skye. We had also Rorie Macdonald in Sandaig, an old brisk Highlander of sixty-eight, a near relation of Sir Alexander's, and his wife, a sister of Raasay's; Donald MacLeod, late of Canna, a very genteel man, and Donald Macdonald, son to Rorie, who was Lieutenant of Grenadiers in Montgomerie's Regiment (I took a liking to him from his first appearance), as also — Macqueen, son to Rorie's wife by the first marriage, who was going to America, and a Captain MacLeod from Sutherland.

We had an ill-dressed dinner, Sir Alexander not having a cook of any kind from Edinburgh. I alone drank port wine. No claret appeared. We had indeed mountain and Frontignac and Scotch porter. But except what I did myself, there was no hospitable convivial intercourse, no ringing of glasses. Nay, I observed that when Captain Macdonald and Mr Macqueen came in after we were sat down to dinner, Sir Alexander let them stand round the room and stuck his fork into a liver pudding, instead of getting room made for them. I took care to act as he ought to have done. There was no wheat-loaf, but only a kind of bannock or cake, raw in the heart, as it was so thick. Sir Alexander himself drank punch without souring and with little spirits in it, which he distributed to those men who were accustomed even in their own houses to much better. He gave it with a pewter dividing-spoon which had served the broth. At tea there were few cups and no tea-tongs nor a supernumerary tea-spoon, so we used our fingers.

I was quite hurt with the meanness and unsuitable appearance of everything. I meditated setting out the very next day. At night we had only Rorie and spouse and the naturalist and his son. When Mr Johnson and I retired for rest, he said it grieved him to see the chief of a great clan in such a state; that he was just as one in a lodging-house in London. However, he resolved that we should weather it out till Monday.

FRIDAY 3 SEPTEMBER. The day was very wet. Sir Alexander's piper plays below stairs both at breakfast and dinner, which is the only circumstance of a chief to be found about him. He had two chests of books, of which Mr Johnson and I ravenously seized some of the contents. It grew fair a little before dinner, and I took a little walk with Captain Macdonald, from whom I found that Sir Alexander was quite unpopular, and that all his deficiencies were well remarked. I made the Captain drink port wine today. Mrs Macdonald said that I fitted Sir Alexander in several suits better than anybody – a curious expression. I asked her how the old Laird of MacLeod came to be so much in debt. She said, 'You may as well read the *Spectator* as begin to tell all that'; and she said it was a pity that this young Laird should lose his *patronomic* estate when he was in no fault; meaning that he was labouring under a load of debt not contracted by himself.

When Sir Alexander was out of the room, I spoke of Sir James. The Highlanders fairly cried. Neither my Lady nor Mr Johnson were then present. I cried too, and we drank a bumper to his memory. It was really melancholy to see the manly, gallant and generous attachment of clanship going to ruin.

Sir Alexander composed today some Latin verses with which he presented Mr Johnson. After dinner the Knight and I met in Mr Johnson's room, where I was looking for pen and ink. I fell upon him with perhaps too great violence upon his behaviour to his people; on the meanness of his appearance here; upon my Lady's neither having a maid, nor being dressed better than one. In short, I gave him a volley. He was thrown into a violent passion; said he could not bear it; called in my Lady and complained to her, at the same time defending himself with considerable plausibility. Had he been a man of more mind, he and I must have had a quarrel for life. But I knew he would soon come to himself. We had moor-fowl for supper tonight, which comforted me.

Mr Johnson was vexed that he could get no distinct information about anything from any of the people here. He wished that a good comedian saw Rorie and his wife, to take from them a Highland scene.

SATURDAY 4 SEPTEMBER. Sir Alexander was in my room before I got up, with a bowl of buttermilk, of which I drank. Our quarrel was already evanished. I set Mr Johnson upon him this morning, who said that in seven years he would make this an independent island; that he'd roast oxen whole and hang out a flag as a signal to the Macdonalds to come and get beef and whisky. Poor Sir Alexander was always starting difficulties. 'Nay,' said Mr Johnson, 'if you're born to object, I have done with you.' He would have a magazine of arms. Sir Alexander said they would rust. Said Mr Johnson, 'Let there be men to keep them clean. Your ancestors did not use to let their arms rust.'

It was in vain to try to inspirit him. Mr Johnson said, 'Sir, we shall make nothing of him. He has no more ideas of a chief than an attorney who has twenty houses in a street and considers how much he can make of them. All is wrong. He has nothing to say to the people when they come about him.' My beauty of a cousin, too, did not escape. Indeed, I was quite disgusted with her nothingness and insipidity. Mr Johnson said, 'This woman would sink a ninety-gun ship. She is so dull – so heavy.'

SUNDAY 5 SEPTEMBER. Sir Alexander and Rorie and I walked to the parish church of Sleat. It is a poor one; not a loft in it. There are no church-bells in the island. I was told there were once some. What has become of them I could not learn. The minister was from home, so there was no sermon. We went into the church and saw Sir James's monument. It is a very pretty one. The inscription is rather too verbose. Mr Johnson said it should have been in Latin, as everything intended to be universal and permanent should be.

It was a beautiful day. My spirits were cheered by the mere effect of climate. I had felt a return of spleen during my stay in this mean mansion, and had it not been that I had Mr Johnson to contemplate, I should have been very sickly in mind. His firmness kept me steady. I looked at him as a man whose head is turning at sea looks at a rock or any fixed object. I wondered at his tranquillity. He however said, 'Sir, when a man retires into an island, he is to turn his thoughts entirely on another world. He has done with this.' And although Mr Johnson was calm, yet his genius did not shine as in companies where I have listened to him with admiration. It was enough if he was not weak.

Sir Alexander and I had another dispute tonight upon his method of proceeding, and he was again in a passion.

MONDAY 6 SEPTEMBER. I awaked a good deal uneasy from having drank too much. The morning too was very wet. So I was in bad plight. About noon it cleared, and I grew better. Sir Alexander supplied us with horses, and we set out, accompanied by Mr Donald MacLeod as our guide. The day was exceedingly agreeable. We rode for some time along Sleat, near the shore. The houses in general were made just of turf, covered with grass, and the country seemed well peopled. We came into Strath, and passed along a wild moorish tract of land till we came to the shore at Broadford. There we found good verdure and whin-rocks, or collections of stones like the ruins of the foundations of old buildings. We saw, too, three cairns of considerable size.

We came on a mile to Coirechatachan, a farm-house of Sir Alexander possessed by Mr Mackinnon, a jolly big man who received us with a kindly welcome. The house was of two storeys. We were carried into a low parlour, with a carpet on the floor, which we had not seen at Armadale. We had tea in good order, a *trea*, silver tea-pot, silver sugar-dish and tongs, silver tea-spoons enough. Our landlord's father had found a treasure of old silver coins, and of these he had made his plate. Mr Johnson was quite well here. Mrs Mackinnon was a decent well-behaved old gentlewoman in a black silk gown. At night we had of company Coirechatachan and his wife; Mrs Mackinnon, daughter to his wife and widow of his son; Mr Macpherson, minister of Sleat, and his wife, daughter of Coirechatachan; a niece of Coirechatachan's, Miss Mackinnon; Miss Macpherson, sister to the minister; and Dr Macdonald, a physician; as also young Mr Mackinnon, son to Coirechatachan. We had for supper a large dish of minced beef collops, a large dish of fricassee of fowl, I believe a dish called fried chicken or something like it, a dish of ham or tongue, some excellent haddocks, some herrings, a large bowl of rich milk, frothed, as good a bread-pudding as I ever tasted, full of raisins and lemon or orange peel, and sillabubs made with port wine and in sillabub glasses. There was a good table-cloth with napkins; china, silver spoons, porter if we chose it, and a large bowl of very good punch. It was really an agreeable meeting.

Old Coirechatachan had hospitality in his whole behaviour, as had his wife, who was what we call a ladylike woman. Mr Pennant was two nights here.[1] He and young Mackinnon went to the top of Ben Caillich, a very high mountain just by, on the top of which there is a cairn.

How superior was our reception here to that at Sir Alexander's! Mr Johnson got a good bedroom to himself. When I went upstairs, Mrs Mackinnon received me in an opposite bedroom with three beds in it, and with an air of hearty cordiality said, 'Come away and see if you can sleep among a heap of folks'; then kissed me on each side of the face, and bid me good-night. I had a good clean bed with red and white check curtains to myself. In a bed with blue worsted stuff curtains lay Donald MacLeod and Dr Macdonald; in a red one of the same kind, the minister and young Mackinnon.

TUESDAY 7 SEPTEMBER. Mr Johnson was much pleased; said we had a genteeler supper than ever we saw at Sir Alexander's. There were several good books here: Hector Boethius in Latin, Cave's *Lives of the Fathers*, Baker's *Chronicle*, Jeremy Collier's *Church History*, Mr Johnson's small Dictionary, several more books; a picture in oil colours, a mezzotinto of Mrs Brooks (by some strange chance in Skye), and a head of Prince Charles in Paris plaster. Also a print of Ranald Macdonald of Clanranald, with a Latin inscription about the Culloden cruelties.

It was a very wet, stormy day. So we were obliged to remain here, as it was impossible to cross the sea to Raasay. Mr Johnson called me to his bedside this morning, and to my astonishment he *took off* Lady Macdonald leaning forward with a hand on each cheek and her mouth open – quite insipidity on a monument grinning at sense and spirit. To see a beauty represented by Mr Johnson was excessively high. I told him it was a masterpiece and that he must have studied it much. 'Ay,' said he.

WEDNESDAY 22 SEPTEMBER [*at MacLeod's, at Ullinish*]. Talking of biography, he said he did not know any literary man's life in England well written. It should tell us his studies, his manner of life, the means by which he attained to excellence, his opinion of his own works, and such particulars. He said he had sent Derrick to Dryden's relations, and he believed Derrick had got all he should have got, but it was nothing. He said he had a kindness for Derrick, and was sorry he was dead.

His notion as to the poems given by Macpherson as the works of Ossian, was confirmed here. Mr Macqueen always evaded the point, saying that Mr Macpherson's pieces fell far short of what he knew in Erse, and were said to be Ossian's. Said Mr Johnson, 'I hope they do. I am not disputing that you may have poetry of great merit, but that Macpherson's is not a translation from ancient poetry. You do not believe it. I say before you, you do not believe it, though you are very willing that the world should believe it.' Mr Macqueen could not answer to this. Said Mr Johnson, 'I look upon Macpherson's *Fingal* to be as gross an imposition as ever the world was troubled with. Had it been really an ancient work, a true specimen how men thought at that time, it would have been a curiosity of the first rate. As a modern production, it is nothing.'

Mr Johnson said he could never get the meaning of an Erse song. They told him the chorus was generally unmeaning. 'I take it,' said he, 'they are like a song which I remember. It was composed in Queen Elizabeth's time on the Earl of Essex, and the burthen was

Radaratwo, radarati, radaratadara tandore.'

'But', said Mr Macqueen, 'there would be words to it which had meaning.' Said Mr Johnson, 'I recollect one stanza:

O then bespoke the prentices all,
Living in London both proper and tall,
For Essex's sake they would fight all.
Radaratwo, radarati, etc.'

When Mr Macqueen began again upon the beauty of Ossian's poetry, Mr Johnson cried, 'Ay, radaratwo, radarati.' Mr Rorie MacLeod, son to the sheriff, said he believed Macpherson's book to be a forgery; for that the Erse songs of Ossian which he had heard had no resemblance to Macpherson's English. Mr Macqueen is the most obstinate man I ever found. He has not firmness of mind sufficient to break. He is like a supple willow. No sooner is he pressed down than he rises again, just where he was. He always harped on this: 'Macpherson's translations are far inferior to Ossian's originals.' 'Yes,' said I, 'because they are not the same. They are inferior as a shilling is to a guinea, because they are not the same.' It was really disagreeable to see how Macqueen shuffled about the matter.

THURSDAY 23 SEPTEMBER. I took Ossian down to the parlour in the morning and tried a test proposed by Mr Rorie. Mr Macqueen had said he had some of him in the original. I made him read what he had, which was a passage on page 50, quarto edition, and Rorie looked on with me on the English, and said it was pretty like. But when Mr Macqueen read a description of Cuchullin's sword, with a verse translation by Sir James Foulis, Rorie said that was much liker than Macpherson's. Mr Macqueen repeated in Erse a description of one of the horses in Cuchullin's car. Rorie said Macpherson's English was nothing like it.

When Mr Johnson came down, I told him that Mr Macqueen had repeated a passage pretty like; and that he himself had required Macpherson's Ossian to be no liker than Pope's Homer. 'Well,' said he, 'this is just what I always said. He has found names, and stories, and phrases – nay passages in old songs – and with them has compounded his own compositions, and so made what he gives to the world as the translation of an ancient poem.' 'But', said I, 'it was wrong in him to pretend that there was a poem in six books.' JOHNSON. 'Yes, sir. At a time too when the Highlanders knew nothing of *books* and nothing of *six* – or perhaps were got the length of counting six. We have been told, by Condamine, of a nation that could count no more than four. I'd tell Monboddo that. It would help him. There's as much charity in helping a man downhill as in helping him uphill.' BOSWELL. 'I don't think there's as much charity.' JOHNSON. 'Yes sir, if his *tendency* be downwards. Till he's at the bottom, he flounders. Get him to it, and he's quiet. Swift tells that Stella had a trick, which she learnt from Addison, to encourage a very absurd man in absurdity, rather than strive to pull him out of it.'

Mr Macqueen evaded our questions about Ossian in so strange a manner that I said if Macpherson was capitally tried for forgery, two such witnesses would hang him; because the truth that comes from an unwilling witness makes the strongest impression, gives the fullest conviction. Mr Johnson said, 'I should like to see Mr Macqueen examined in one of our courts of justice about Ossian.' Said I, 'Were he to evade as he has done now, in one of our courts, he would be committed.' JOHNSON. 'I hope he would. Sir, he has told Blair a little more than he believes, which is published; and he sticks to it. Sir, he is so much at the head of things here that he has never been accustomed to be closely examined; and so he goes on quite smoothly.' BOSWELL. 'He has never had anybody to work him.' JOHNSON. 'No, sir. And a man is seldom disposed to work himself; though he ought to work himself, to be sure.' Mr Macqueen stood patiently by while all this passed.

On Skye, staying at Armadale, but this time without Lord and Lady MacDonald, who were on the mainland.

FRIDAY 1 OCTOBER. Mr Johnson was now in good humour at Armadale, and I was very much so.

SATURDAY 2 OCTOBER. I was quite as I could wish here. I had my former room, with Joseph to sleep in a bed by me; so that I had a home, while all but Mr Johnson were crowded into common rooms. I had now got the habit of taking a *scalck* or dram every morning. It really pleased me to take it. They are a very sober people, the Highlanders, though they have this practice. I always loved strong liquors. I was glad to be in a country where fashion justified tasting them. But I resolved to guard against continuing it after leaving the isles. It would become an article of happiness to me. I thought with satisfaction when I got up that it waited me, as one thinks of his breakfast; so much is a man formed by habit.

I told Mr Johnson this morning that Sir Alexander said to me once that he left Skye with the blessings of his people. Said Mr Johnson, 'You'll observe this was when he *left* it. It is only the back of him that they bless.' He said Sir Alexander should have come and lived among them, and made his house the court of Skye, had he and his Lady been fit for it. They should have had so many of the gentlemen's daughters to receive their education in the family, to learn pastry and such things from the housekeeper, and manners from my Lady. That was the way in the great families in Wales – at Lady Salusbury's, Mrs Thrale's grandmother's, and at Lady Philipps's. He designed the families by the ladies, as he spoke of what was properly their province. There were always six young ladies at Sir John Philipps's. When one was married, her place was filled up. There was a large school room where they learned needlework, &c. I observed that at the courts in Germany young people were educated. There is an academy for the pages. Mr Johnson said that manners were best learnt at these courts. 'You are admitted with great facility to the Prince's company, and yet must treat him with great respect. At a great court, you are at such a distance that you get no good.' I said, 'Very true. A man sees the court of Versailles, as if he saw it in a theatre.' He said the best book that ever was written upon good breeding grew up at the little court of Urbino – *Il Cortegiano* by Castiglione. He said I should read it, which I shall do. I am glad always to have his opinion of books. At Macpherson's, he read some of Whitby's Commentary, which he commended; said he had heard him called rather lax, but he did not perceive it. He had looked at a novel called *The Man of the World* at Raasay, but thought there was nothing in it. He said today while reading my Journal, 'This will be a great treasure to us some years hence.' He told me before that he was to copy part of it about Raasay, which he had not. I said I wished he would translate it. 'How?' said he. BOSWELL. 'Into good English.' JOHNSON. 'Sir, it is very good English.'

He said today that Sir Alexander exceeded *L'Avare* in a farce. I said he was quite a character for a play. Foote would take him finely. The best way to make him do it would be to bring Foote to be entertained at his house for a week, and then it would be *facit indignatio*. Said Mr Johnson, 'I wish he had him. I, who have eat his bread, will not give him him; but I should be glad he came honestly by him. Nay,' said he; 'they are both characters.' And then he took off my Lady: 'Thomson, some wine and water,' with her mouth full; adding, 'People are generally taught to empty their mouths of meat before they call for drink. She wants to be whipped in a nursery.'

He said he was angry at Thrale for sitting at General Oglethorpe's without speaking. He censured a man for degrading himself to nonentity. I observed that Goldsmith was on the other extreme, for he spoke at all ventures. 'Yes,' said he; 'Goldsmith, rather than not speak will talk of what he knows himself to be ignorant, which can only end in exposing him. I wonder if he feels that he exposes himself.' 'If', said I, 'he was with two tailors—' and was going on. Mr Johnson took it up

– 'Or with two founders, he'd fall a-talking on the method of making cannon, though both of them would soon see that he did not know what metal a cannon was made of.' We were very social and merry in his room this forenoon. We had again a good dinner, and in the evening a great dance. We made out five country squares without sitting down; and then we performed with much activity a dance which I suppose the emigration from Skye has occasioned. They call it 'America'. A brisk reel is played. The first couple begin, and each sets to one – then each to another – then as they set to the next couple, the second and third couples are setting; and so it goes on till all are set a-going, setting and wheeling round each other, while each is making the tour of all in the dance. It shows how emigration catches till all are set afloat. Mrs Mackinnon told me that last year when the ship sailed from Portree for America, the people on shore were almost distracted when they saw their relations go off; they lay down on the ground and tumbled, and tore the grass with their teeth. This year there was not a tear shed. The people on shore seemed to think that they would soon follow. This is a mortal sign.

I had written letters all forenoon. It was a very bad day, and at night there was a great deal of lightning. I was really fatigued with violent dancing. I do not like dancing. But I force myself to it, when it promotes social happiness, as in the country, where it is as much one of the means towards that end as dinner; so I danced a reel tonight to the music of the bagpipe, which I never did before. It made us beat the ground with prodigious force. I thought it was better that I should engage the people of Skye by taking a cheerful glass and dancing with them rather than play the abstract scholar. I looked on this tour to the Hebrides as a co-partnery between Mr Johnson and me. Each was to do all he could to promote its success; and I am certain that my gayer exertions were of much service to us. Mr Johnson's immense fund of knowledge and wit was a wonderful source of admiration and delight to them. But they had it only at times; and they required to have interstices agreeably filled up, and even little elucidations of his grand text. Besides, they observed that it was I who always 'set him a-going'. The fountain was locked up till I interfered. (I want a word here, as Macklin used to say when lecturing on oratory.) It was curious to hear them, when any dispute happened when Mr Johnson was out of the room, saying, 'Stay till Mr Johnson comes. Say that to *him*.' Had they been barbarians, he was an Orpheus to them. But I cannot give them that character with any justice.

I should mention that on Sunday last, Raasay sent his boat to Sconser for us, begging to have us again in his island, and if it was not convenient, he would come over and spend the evening with us. So Mr Donald MacLeod informed me.

Yesterday Mr Johnson said, 'I cannot but laugh to think of myself roving among the Hebrides at sixty. I wonder where I shall rove at fourscore.' This evening he disputed the truth of what is said as to the people of St Kilda catching cold whenever strangers come. He said, 'How can there be a physical effect without a physical cause?' He laughed and said that the arrival of a ship full of strangers would kill them; 'for', said he, 'if one stranger gives them one cold, two strangers must give them two colds; and so in proportion.' I wondered to hear him ridicule this, as he had praised Macaulay for putting it in his book. He said the evidence was not adequate to the improbability of the fact. That if a physician, rather disposed to be incredulous, should go to St Kilda and report the fact, he would begin to look about him. They said it was annually proved by MacLeod's steward. He turned jocular then and said, 'The steward always comes to seek something from them, and so they fall a-coughing. I suppose the people in Skye all take a cold when Sir Alexander comes.' They said Sir Alexander came only in summer. JOHNSON. 'That is out of tenderness to you. Bad weather and he, at the same time, would be too much.'

SUNDAY 3 OCTOBER. Mr Johnson told me there were two faults in my Journal: one was expatiating too much on the luxury of the little-house at Talisker. This fault, however, he mentioned as if he liked it – as if my expatiating had been congenial with his own feelings. The other fault was in my representation of the dispute about the Scottish clergy (*vid. supra*); 'for', said he, 'I did not say the man's hair could not be well dressed because he had not a clean shirt, but because he was bald.'

We did not get up till ten o'clock. Joseph said the wind was still against us. Mr Johnson said, 'A wind, or not a wind? that is the question,' for he can amuse himself at times with a little play of words, or rather of sentences. I remember when he turned his cup at Aberbrothock, he muttered, '*Claudite jam rivos, pueri.*' I added, '*Sat prata biberunt.*' I am most scrupulously exact in this Journal. Mr Johnson said it was a very exact picture of his life.

While we were chatting in the indolent style of men who were to stay here all day at least, we were suddenly roused with being told that the wind was fair, that a little fleet of herring vessels was passing by for Mull, and that Mr Simson's vessel was lying off the shore for us. Hugh Macdonald, the skipper, came to us, and we were hurried to get ready, which we soon did. I just wrote a few lines to my wife. I felt my heart light at the thoughts of getting away. Breakfast was got ready for us. Mr Johnson with composure and solemnity repeated the observation of Epictetus, that, 'As man has the voyage of death before him, whatever he does, he should always be ready at the Master's call; and an old man should never be far from the shore, lest he should not be able to be in readiness.' He had a horse, and I and the other gentlemen walked about an English mile to the shore, where the vessel was. Donald MacLeod, poor man, gave me a good bill upon Mr MacLeod of Ose for the deficient £8. Mr Johnson said he should never forget Skye, and returned thanks for all civilities. We were carried to the vessel in a small boat which she had, and we set sail very briskly about one o'clock. I was much pleased with the motion for many hours. Mr Johnson grew sick, and retired under cover, as it rained a good deal. I kept above, that I might have fresh air. I eat bread and cheese, and drank whisky and rum and brandy. The worthy Bailie had sent with us half a sheep and biscuits and apples and beer and brandy. There was a little room or den at the forecastle, with two beds and a fire in it. Dinner was dressed, and I was persuaded to go down. I eat boiled mutton and boiled salt herring, and drank beer and punch. I exulted in being a stout seaman, while Mr Johnson was quite in a state of annihilation. But I soon had a change; for after imagining that I could go with ease to America or the East Indies, I turned woefully sick, and was obliged to get above board, though it rained hard.

I regretted that we passed the island of Eigg, where there is a very large cave in which all the inhabitants were smoked to death by the MacLeods. They had murdered some MacLeods who were sailing near their coast. MacLeod and a number of the clan came to revenge the murder. The people of Eigg saw them coming, and all retired into this cave, which has a low and narrow entry, so that but one man can get in it at a time, but afterwards becomes spacious and lofty like a church. MacLeod and his people landed, and could not find a soul. They might perhaps have gone away. But one of the Eigg people, after waiting a long time in the cave, grew impatient and went out to see what was become of the enemy. Perceiving them not gone, he returned. There was a deep snow upon the ground, by which means he was tracked by the print of his feet. The MacLeods came to the mouth of the cave. Nothing could be done in the way of fighting, because but one man at a time could either go out or in, and would be killed directly. MacLeod called in to them that if they would give up the murderers, he would be satisfied. This they refused to do. Upon which he ordered a quantity of peats to be laid in the mouth of the cave and to be set on fire, and thus the people of Eigg, man, woman and child, were smoked to death. Young Coll told us he has been in the cave, and seen great quantities of bones in it; and he said one can still observe where families have died, as big bones and small, those of a man and wife and children, are found lying together.

Mr Simson was brisk in his hopes for a while, for the wind was for a while for us. He said if it continued so, he would land us at 'I' (i.e. Icolmkill) that night. But when the wind failed, it was resolved we should make for the Sound of Mull, and land in the harbour of Tobermory. We got up with the five herring vessels for a while. But four of them got before us, and one little wherry fell behind us. When we got in full view of the point of Ardnamurchan, the wind changed, and was full against our getting to the Sound. We were then obliged to tack, and get forward in that tedious manner. As we advanced, the storm grew greater, and the sea very rough. Coll then began to talk of making for Eigg or Canna or Coll. Macdonald, our skipper, said he would get us into the Sound. We struggled a good while for this. Then he said he would push forward till we were near the land of Mull, where we might cast anchor till the morning; for although before this there had been a good moon, and I had pretty distinctly seen not only the land of Mull, but up the Sound, and the country of Morvern as at one end of it, the night was now grown very dark. Our crew consisted of old Macdonald our skipper, a man with one eye and another sailor. Mr Simson himself, Coll and Hugh Macdonald his servant, all helped. Simson said he would willingly go for Coll if young Coll or his servant would undertake to pilot us to a harbour, but as the island is low land, it was dangerous to run upon it in the dark. Coll and his servant seemed a little dubious. The scheme of running for Canna seemed then to be embraced, but Canna was ten leagues off, all out of our way; and they were afraid to attempt the harbour of Eigg. All these different plans being in agitation, I was much frightened. The old skipper still tried to make for the land of Mull; but then it was considered that there was no place there where we could anchor in safety. Much time was lost in striving against the storm. At last it became so rough, and threatened to be so much worse, that Coll and his servant took more courage, and said they would undertake to hit one of the harbours in Coll. 'Then', said the skipper, 'let us run for it, in GOD's name,' and instantly we turned towards it. The little wherry which had fallen behind us had hard work. The master begged that, if we made for Coll, we should put out a light to him. Accordingly one of the sailors waved a glowing peat for some time. I had a short relief when I found we were to run for a harbour before the wind. But it was very short, for I soon heard that our sails were very bad, and were in danger of being torn in pieces, in which case we would be driven upon the rocky shore of Coll. It was very dark indeed, and there was a very heavy rain almost incessantly. The sparks of the peat-fire in the boat flew terribly about. I dreaded that the vessel might take fire. Then, as Coll was a sportsman, and had powder on board, I figured that we might be blown up. Simson and he both appeared a little frightened, which made me more so; and the perpetual talking, or rather shouting, which was carried on in Erse, alarmed me. A man is always suspicious of what is saying in an unknown tongue; and if fear be his passion at the time, he grows more afraid. The boat often lay so much to a side that I trembled lest she should be overset; and indeed they told me afterwards that they had run her sometimes to within an inch of the water, so anxious were they to make what haste they could before the night should be worse. I saw tonight what I never saw before, a prodigious sea with immense billows coming upon a vessel, so as that it seemed hardly possible to escape. There was something grandly horrible in the sight. I am glad I have seen it once. Amidst all these terrifying circumstances, I endeavoured to compose my mind. It was not easy to do it, for all the stories that I had heard of the dangerous sailing among the Hebrides, which is proverbial, or at least often mentioned, came full upon my recollection. It distressed me to think how much my dearest wife would suffer should I now be lost, and in what a destitute, or at least wretchedly dependent, state she would be left. I upbraided myself as not having a sufficient cause for putting myself in such danger. Piety afforded me a good deal of comfort. I prayed fervently to GOD, but I was confused, for I remember I used a strange expression: that if it should please him to preserve me, *I would behave myself ten times better.* Be the expression what it may, I shall never forget – at least I hope so – the good resolutions which I then formed. While I prayed, I was disturbed by the objections against a particular providence and against hoping that the petitions of an individual would have any influence with the Divinity; objections which have been often made, and which Dr Hawkesworth has lately revived in his preface to the *Voyages to the South Seas*; but Dr Ogden's excellent doctrine on the efficacy of intercession prevailed. I was really in very great fear this night.

It was half an hour after eleven before we set ourselves in the course for Coll. As I saw them all busy doing something, I asked Coll with much earnestness what I could do. He with a lucky readiness put into my hand a rope which was fixed to the top of one of the masts, and bid me hold it fast till he bid me pull. This could not be of the least service; but by employing me, he kept me out of their way, who were busy working the ship; and at the same time diverted my fear to a certain degree, by making me think I was occupied. There did I stand firm to my post while the wind and rain beat upon me, always expecting a call to pull my rope.

The man with one eye steered. Old Macdonald and Coll and his servant lay upon the forecastle looking sharp out for the harbour. It was necessary to carry much *cloth*, as they termed it, that is to say, much sail, in order to keep the vessel off the shore of Coll. This made terrible plunging in a rough sea. At last they spied the harbour of Lochiern, and Coll cried, 'Thank GOD, we're safe!' We run up till we were opposite to it, and then were wafted, I may say, though not gently, into it, where we cast anchor. The comfort which I felt may easily be imagined.

Mr Johnson had all this time been quiet and unconcerned. He had lain down on one of the beds, and having got free of sickness, was quite satisfied. Once during the doubtful consultations he asked whither we were going; and upon being told that it was not certain whether to Mull or Coll, he cried, 'Coll for my money.' I now went down, with Coll and Simson, beside him. He was lying in philosophic tranquillity, with a grey-hound of Coll's at his back keeping him warm. Coll is quite the *juvenis qui gaudet canibus*. He had when we left Talisker two greyhounds, two terriers, a pointer and a large Newfoundland water-dog. He lost one of his terriers by the road, but had five dogs still with him. I was miserably sick and very desirous to get to shore. When I was told that I could not get ashore that night, as the storm had now increased, I looked woefully, as Coll informed me. Shakespeare's phrase, which he puts into the Frenchman's mouth, of the English soldiers when starved: 'Piteous they will look, like drowned mice,' might have been applied to me.

TUESDAY 2 NOVEMBER [*on the way to Auchinleck*]. We were now in a country not only 'of saddles and bridles', but of post-chaises; and having ordered one from Kilmarnock, we got to Auchinleck before dinner.

My father was not quite a year and a half older than Dr Johnson, but his conscientious discharge of his laborious duty as a judge in Scotland (where the law proceedings are almost all in writing), a severe complaint which ended in his death, and the loss of my mother, a woman of almost unexampled piety and goodness, had before this time in some degree affected his spirits, and rendered him less disposed to exert his faculties; for he had originally a very strong mind and cheerful temper. He assured me he never had felt one moment of what is called low spirits, or uneasiness without a real cause. He had a great many good stories, which he told uncommonly well, and he was remarkable for 'humour, *incolumi gravitate*', as Lord Monboddo used to characterize it. His age, his office and his character had long given him an acknowledged claim to great attention, in whatever company he was; and he could ill brook any diminution of it. He was as sanguine a Whig and Presbyterian as Dr Johnson was a Tory and Church of England man; and as he had not much leisure to be informed of Dr Johnson's great merits by reading his works, he had a partial and unfavourable notion of him, founded on his supposed political tenets, which were so discordant to his own that, instead of speaking of him with that respect to which he was entitled, he used to call him 'a Jacobite fellow'. Knowing all this, I should not have ventured to bring them together, had not my father, out of kindness to me, desired me to invite Dr Johnson to his house.

I was very anxious that all should be well; and begged of my friend to avoid three topics, as to which they differed very widely: Whiggism, Presbyterianism and – Sir John Pringle. He said courteously, 'I shall certainly not talk on subjects which I am told are disagreeable to a gentleman under whose roof I am; especially, I shall not do so to *your father.'*

Our first day went off very smoothly. It rained, and we could not get out; but my father showed Dr Johnson his library, which, in curious editions of the Greek and Roman classics, is, I suppose, not excelled by any private collection in Great Britain. My father had studied at Leyden and been very intimate with the Gronovii and other learned men there. He was a sound scholar, and, in particular, had collated manuscripts and different editions of Anacreon, and others of the Greek lyric poets, with great care; so that my friend and he had much matter for conversation, without touching on the fatal topics of difference.

WEDNESDAY 3 NOVEMBER. [Johnson] this day, when we were by ourselves, observed, how common it was for people to talk from books; to retail the sentiments of others, and not their own; in short, to converse without any originality of thinking. He was pleased to say, 'You and I do not talk from books.'

THURSDAY 4 NOVEMBER. I was glad to have at length a very fine day, on which I could show Dr Johnson the Place of my family, which he has honoured with so much attention in his *Journey*. He is, however, mistaken in thinking that the Celtic name, *Auchinleck*, has no relation to the natural appearance of it. I believe every Celtic name of a place will be found very descriptive. *Auchinleck* does not signify a *stony field*, as he has said, but a *field of flagstones*; and this place has a number of rocks which abound in strata of that kind. The 'sullen dignity of the old castle', as he has forcibly expressed it, delighted him exceedingly. On one side of the rock on which its ruins stand runs the River Lugar, which is here of considerable breadth, and is bordered by other high rocks, shaded with wood. On the other side runs a brook, skirted in the same manner, but on a smaller scale. I cannot figure a more romantic scene.

I felt myself elated here, and expatiated to my illustrious mentor on the antiquity and honourable alliances of my family, and on the merits of its founder, Thomas Boswell, who was highly favoured by his sovereign, James IV of Scotland, and fell with him at the battle of Flodden Field; and in the glow of what, I am sensible, will, in a commercial age, be considered as genealogical enthusiasm, did not omit to mention what I was sure my friend would not think lightly of, my relation to the Royal Personage, whose liberality, on his accession to the throne, had given him comfort and independence. I have, in a former page, acknowledged my pride of ancient blood, in which I was encouraged by Dr Johnson; my readers therefore will not be surprised at my having indulged it on this occasion.

Not far from the old castle is a spot of consecrated earth, on which may be traced the foundations of an ancient chapel, dedicated to St Vincent, and where in old times 'was the place of graves' for the family. It grieves me to think that the remains of sanctity here, which were considerable, were dragged away and employed in building a part of the house of Auchinleck of the middle age, which was the family residence till my father erected that 'elegant modern mansion', of which Dr Johnson speaks so handsomely. Perhaps this chapel may one day be restored.

Dr Johnson was pleased when I showed him some venerable old trees under the shade of which my ancestors had walked. He exhorted me to plant assiduously, as my father had done to a great extent.

As I wandered with my revered friend in the groves of Auchinleck, I told him that if I survived him, it was my intention to erect a monument to him here, among scenes which, in my mind, were all classical; for in my youth I had appropriated to them many of the descriptions of the Roman poets. He could not bear to have death presented to him in any shape, for his constitutional melancholy made the king of terrors more frightful. He turned off the subject, saying, 'Sir, I hope to see your grandchildren!'

SATURDAY 6 NOVEMBER. I cannot be certain whether it was on this day or a former that Dr Johnson and my father came in collision. If I recollect right, the contest began while my father was showing him his collection of medals; and Oliver Cromwell's coin unfortunately introduced Charles the First, and Toryism. They became exceedingly warm and violent, and I was very much distressed by being present at such an altercation between two men, both of whom I reverenced; yet I durst not interfere. It would certainly be very unbecoming in me to exhibit my honoured father and my respected friend as intellectual gladiators, for the entertainment of the public; and therefore I suppress what would, I dare say, make an interesting scene in this dramatic sketch – this account of the transit of Johnson over the Caledonian Hemisphere.

Yet I think I may, without impropriety, mention one circumstance, as an instance of my father's address. Dr Johnson challenged him, as he did us all at Talisker, to point out any theological works of merit written by Presbyterian ministers in Scotland. My father, whose studies did not lie much in that way, owned to me afterwards that he was somewhat at a loss how to answer, but that luckily he recollected having read in catalogues the title of *Durham on the Galatians*; upon which he boldly said, 'Pray, sir, have you read Mr Durham's excellent commentary on the Galatians?' 'No, sir,' said Dr Johnson. By this lucky thought my father kept him at bay, and for some time enjoyed his triumph; but his antagonist soon made a retort, which I forbear to mention.

In the course of their altercation, Whiggism and Presbyterianism, Toryism and Episcopacy, were terribly buffeted. My worthy hereditary friend, Sir John Pringle, never having been mentioned, happily escaped without a bruise.

My father's opinion of Dr Johnson may be conjectured from the name he afterwards gave him, which was 'Ursa Major'. But it is not true, as has been reported, that it was in consequence of my saying that he was a *constellation* of genius and literature. It was a sly abrupt expression to one of his brethren on the bench of the Court of Session, in which Dr Johnson was then standing, but it was not said in his hearing.

MONDAY 8 NOVEMBER. Notwithstanding the altercation that had passed, my father, who had the dignified courtesy of an old baron, was very civil to Dr Johnson, and politely attended him to the post-chaise which was to convey us to Edinburgh.

Thus they parted. – They are now in another, and a higher, state of existence; and as they were both worthy Christian men, I trust they have met in happiness. But I must observe, in justice to my friend's political principles and my own, that they have met in a place where there is no room for Whiggism.

Boswell's Journals &c from 1776

Journal
in London, Lichfield, Ashbourne, &c

MONDAY 11 MARCH. [*Boswell is preparing for a spring jaunt to London. The duel which he is brooding on did not in the end take place.*] I got up a little after five. My dear wife gave me tea. Mr Lawrie was ready and serviceable, as was Joseph. But I was both gloomy and in pain. I took leave of my valuable spouse with an earnest embrace, and said, 'GOD grant we may meet in a better world!' I had still a duel in view. I went in a chair to the fly. We were four passengers. I need not be particular in describing them. One was a Captain Bidlington, a sea captain, something like Sir John Douglas, and a man of English humour and pleasantry. His manner was not violent, so did not offend me; but though I did not perceive it at the time, I dare say it insensibly did me good. I read some of Lord Monboddo's third volume on language. I was perpetually thinking of my challenge to Lord Advocate. I dreaded that my nerves might fail me; yet I was conscious of being determined. I travelled like a criminal, or rather a condemned man not a criminal, in a coach to the place of execution. I was ever and anon figuring Lord Advocate and me upon the field. I hoped that Sir John Pringle and Dr Johnson would invigorate my mind. I fancied that I might just think, think of a duel till I should overcome the fear of it by deadening my mind. That timorousness was a fault in my constitution; but that I had a noble principle of fortitude; and that I should have the advantage of Lord Advocate by being better prepared for it by the discipline of meditation. I slumbered a great deal in the coach. I read a little in the Bible which I got from Lord Mountstuart, and which I carry always with me. I got to bed before ten at Wooler. What misery does a man of sensibility suffer! I however fell asleep immediately.

TUESDAY 12 MARCH. (I am now writing on Monday the 18 at Messrs Dillys' in the Poultry, London. I have fallen sadly behind.) 'Sunshine broke in upon my mind' this day, as Dr Johnson said it would. I finished Lord Monboddo's third volume. His thoughts of the superiority of mind in the ancient Greeks and Romans revived me, and a duel seemed quite easy to me. I had a warm affection for my wife and children. But magnanimity elevated me above it when honour called. Bidlington was perpetually rhyming in an odd manner. For instance, when one said the tea brought for breakfast was *Congo*, he cried, 'Ah, I fear 'tis *wrongo*.'

We got to Newcastle to dinner. I sent for Dr Hall, physician, and Mr Leighton, surgeon. Hall came for a few minutes; told me that my poor brother John was not unhappy and that he thought it would be most desirable for the family that he should continue in his present state. Indeed it is better to be insensible than unhappy; better to have an obscurity of reason than as much light as to see one's self miserable. In passing, it occurs to me that much of human misery is for want of light enough. When there is a *lueur*, an imperfect light, we imagine we see hideous spectres. Full light shows us that there is nothing to fear; and fear is the great cause of our misery. How little is there of positive present evil. It is the imagination which torments us. This duel of mine, now, has alarmed and distressed me while in the dark. But, when I have an extensive view of it, I consider thus: If I am killed, the shock is momentary; and death comes as well at one time as another. My wife and children will be consoled in a short time. At any rate *I* shall not feel their uneasiness; but shall look on it as trifling, and expect them soon to join me in the world of spirits. If I am wounded, my spirits will be raised by a sense of honour and a sort of gallant vanity which a duel justly fought inspires. My greatest uneasiness was the fear of fear; an apprehension that my nerves, or whatever else it is, should yield to impressions of danger, though my *soul* was brave. I think there is a meaning here. I shall ask Dr Johnson. I must after this leave a margin in my journal for after remarks, either by myself or others.

I took a post-chaise and Wilson the landlord with me, and visited poor John. He looked better than when I saw him in May; but seemed to be quite in a stupor. I sat with him about ten minutes, I suppose, before he spoke a single word, though I said many different things to him, and shook him cordially by the hand. I thought of my duel at the time; and that it was well to have fought in a good cause before sinking into the state in which I saw my brother and which I feared might be my fate one day. I was going to leave him. He put forth his hand, seized mine and said, 'Take me with you.' I stopped awhile with him. I said, 'Do you know me?' He said, 'To be sure.' He had accepted of some sweet oranges from me. He said, 'Give me some money.' I gave him two shillings. He said, 'Give me some more.' I gave him another. Dr Hall had told me that it was not wrong to let him have a little to buy pepper-cake, a sort of gingerbread, or some such thing which pleased his taste. He said, 'How is your wife?' and he said, 'I am kept a prisoner here.' I covered my face for a little, and shed tears. There was something very striking to me in this scene. It shook my mind somewhat. But it was comfortable to see that he was not in pain of body or anguish of mind.

When I returned to Newcastle I had Leighton the surgeon to drink coffee with me. His quiet, common-sense, practical talk pleased me. But I was still ruminating (if one may say so of the future) on my duel, and thought myself a being whose life was near its shallows. It is strange how an immediate prospect of death affects one. I sat up writing to my wife, and this journal, till near twelve. The coach was to set out at two. I could not sleep.

WEDNESDAY 13 MARCH. Our journey went on very well, and we had a lady from Northallerton, I believe an old kept mistress, now a bawd. Her voice was melodious. Her manners gentle. Her looks the remains of comeliness. She had cards with a text of Scripture on one side and verses in a Methodist strain on the other, some of them very pretty; and we drew cards as people do *jokes* put up in sugar at a dessert. The coach broke down a mile from Doncaster. It was dragged along. I sat in it alone, read some of the Bible, and Collins's *Ode on the Poetical Character.* I was in good spirits, nay in high and fine flow of thought. My mind is a furnace. It melts and refines objects when there is a strong clear heat; but sometimes my furnace is smoky, and then the objects are blackened. We were to have lain at York; but the assizes being there, the inns (I am now writing on Tuesday the 19th at Oxford) were all full, so we took post-chaises, and went on to Tadcaster, where we had a comfortable supper and a good sleep. I was in the most perfect frame. I enjoyed the present, and was not afraid of death.

THURSDAY 14 MARCH. I was not quite so well; but was upon the whole manly. I was, however, like the thinking man in *The Rambler* who tried various ways of life, and served a campaign with *philosophical* courage. We drove on all night.

FRIDAY 15 MARCH. (I am now writing on Wednesday the 20th at Oxford.) The lady quitted the coach at Stilton. She was of that mixed character of licentiousness and enthusiasm[2] which we often find. I got upon the coach-box today from Stevenage to Hatfield. I was afraid I should fall; and I accustomed myself to overcome fear. The coachman was a stately fellow, as well dressed as a country squire, and quite a bishop in his line of life; for instead of driving one stage out and in, by which at an average two shillings a day may be got, he drove three, so that he got six shillings a day besides wages. There were two outside passengers, who sung and roared and swore as he did. My nerves were hurt at first; but considering it to have no offensive meaning whatever, and to be just the vocal expression of the beings, I was not fretted. They sang, 'And A-Hunting We Will Go', and I joined the chorus. I then sung 'Hearts of Oak', 'Gee Ho, Dobbin', 'The Roast Beef of Old England', and they chorused. We made a prodigious jovial noise going through Welwyn and other villages. What a contrast to the solemnity of Young's *Night Thoughts* written at Welwyn. I kept my duel in view all the while, and felt, I suppose, quite as a soldier or sailor does before an action. I had, however, only *passive courage*, as I have heard my father observe Prince Charles had. I set myself to *endure* whatever might come. But then I was advancing into danger. Captain Bidlington was enough to dissipate gloom, he was so lively and comical and entertaining with anecdotes of what he had seen in the course of a great deal of sailing both in King's ships and merchantmen. He had a smattering too of many kinds of knowledge.

The coach had been robbed by footpads in the morning near London; and last night at six another coach had been robbed. It was past six when we were at Highgate. The fear which I felt till we got upon the stones was uneasy. The coachman bid us keep a look-out. Some fellows wanted him to stop under pretence of wanting to be up on the outside; but he drove quickly on, and some of us looked out on each side. When we got to the — in St John Street, Smithfield, I was a little sorry to part with my fellow travellers; of so soft and warm a composition am I that I adhere a little to almost all with whom I come in contact, unless they have qualities which repel me.

I was desirous to see Dr Johnson, and state the subject of my challenge to Lord Advocate to him also; but I was so much fatigued with my journey that I durst not enter his house at so late an hour, knowing that it might be much later before I could get away. London struck me less now than ever. It was more a home. I was better used to it. I slept at Dilly's. I found here tonight a letter from my dear wife.

SATURDAY 16 MARCH. Had resolved to walk out early to breakfast with Dr Johnson, but time slips away fast in London while the mind is engaged with a variety of objects. I drank some tea with Messieurs Dilly, and got to the street about nine. I posted to Johnson's Court. But the great man had removed to Bolt Court, No. 7. I felt a foolish regret that he had left a court which bore his name; but it was better than foolish to be affected with some tenderness of regard for a place in

which I had seen him a great deal, from whence I had often issued a
better and a happier man than when I went in, and which had often
appeared to my imagination, while I trod its pavement in the solemn
darkness of the night, to be sacred to Wisdom and Piety. But he did
not dwell long enough in it, nor was there such an association between
him and it established, as to warrant a lasting value or veneration for
it, as for 'Marathon or Iona'.3 When I found his new house a much
better one, I was cheered. He had good rooms and a pretty little spot
of background. Frank, his Black, told me that he was at Mr Thrale's,
but that he would be home early in the forenoon. I said I should go
to him directly. I saw Mr Levett too, who assured me of his being
very well. Even Levett and Frank raised my spirits as concomitants
of the Great Man. I want a simile for this. I am sure many might be
found. Such as that a fine lady is cheered even by seeing the case, the
Great Mogul, of a pack of cards, or a drinker by hearing the sound
of a cork drawn. These are bad. My meaning is that objects, however
unimportant in themselves, please us by reviving the impression of
what was agreeable while they were present. Thus a happy lover
talks fondly of the groves and streams which he saw at the same
time with his mistress, though he would not care at all for them on
their own account. Dr Johnson's new house belonged to Mr Allen
the printer, who lived in Bolt Court. I met him as I was coming
out. 'Well, Mr Allen, you have now the Great Man' (or some such
phrase) 'for your *tacksman*.'4 We talked of his going to Italy. I said, 'I
wish him to see as much as possible that we may have the advantage
by reflection. His mind is at once a magnifying glass and a prism. It
enlarges and brightens, separates and colours objects.'

I took a boat at Blackfriars Bridge, and sailed to Southwark. Knocked
at Mr Thrale's door. Just as the servant opened it, Baretti appeared.
I coldly asked him how he did. Methought there was a shade of
murderous blood upon his pale face. I soon made a transition from this
disagreeable object to the parlour, where Mrs Thrale and Dr Johnson
were at breakfast. My reception here was truly flattering. At once I had
chocolade before me, and Dr Johnson was in full glow of conversation.
I was elevated as if brought into another state of being. Mrs Thrale
and I looked to each other while he talked (Baretti having soon left
the room), and our looks expressed our congenial admiration of him.
I said to her, 'This is *Hermippus redivivus*.5 I am quite restored by him,

by transfusion of mind.' Mr Thrale joined us, and cordially welcomed me. Dr Johnson said he had seen all the visibilities of Paris and around it; but that to have formed acquaintance with the people there would have required more time than he could stay. That he was just beginning to creep into acquaintance by means of Colonel Drumgold, a very high man, head of L'Ecole Militaire, a most complete character, for he had been first a professor of rhetoric and then became a soldier.

When I spoke with regret of the Laird of MacLeod's not acting as he should do to preserve the ancient family, and that it would be well if he were killed in America, Mrs Thrale said she did not understand this preference of the estate to its owner; of the land to the man who walks upon that land. 'Madam,' said Dr Johnson, 'it is not a preference of the land to its owner. It is the preference of a family to an individual. Here is an establishment in a country which is of importance for ages, not only to the chief but to his people, which extends upwards and downwards; that this should be destroyed by one idle fellow is a sad thing.'

He said entails were good, because it is good to preserve in a country serieses of men to whom the people are habituated to look up as to their heads. But he was for leaving a quantity of land in commerce, to excite industry and keep money in the country. 'For', said he, 'if no land were to be bought in a country, there would be no encouragement to get wealth, because a family could not be founded there. Or if it were got, it must be carried away to another country where land may be bought; and although the land in every country will remain the same, and produce as much when there is no money, yet all the happiness of civil life, which we know is produced by money being in a country, is lost.' 'Then,' said I, 'would it be for the advantage of a country that all its lands were sold at once?' 'Sir,' said he, 'so far as money produces good, it *would* be an advantage; for then that country would have as much money circulating in it as it is worth. But to be sure this would be counterbalanced by disadvantages attending a total change of proprietors.' (I believe this reflection occurred to me.)

I was for limiting the power of entailing thus: that there should be one-third, or perhaps one-half of the land of a country free for commerce. That the proportion allowed to be entailed should be parcelled out so as that no family could entail above a certain quantity. Let a family according to the abilities of its representatives be richer and poorer in different generations, or always rich if its heirs be always wise. But let its absolute permanency be moderate. In this way we should have a certainty of so many established roots; and as in the course of nature, there is in every age an extinction of so many families, there would be continual openings for men ambitious of perpetuity to plant a stock in the entailed ground. I would not have the very same land to be the entailed proportion, as probably it would not be so well improved. I mean that a man would have an opening in the allotted *quantity*. Indeed I would rather that an old family estate, when its proprietors fail, should go into the circle of commerce for a while, than be immediately transferred to a new family and again fixed. I would have the two races kept distinct. Dr Johnson said that mankind could better regulate entails when the evil of too much land being fixed by them was felt than we could do at present when it was not felt.

I mentioned Adam Smith's book just come out,[6] and as Sir John Pringle had the night before given his opinion that Smith, who had never been in trade, could not be expected to write well on that subject, any more than I upon physic, I started this to Dr Johnson. He thought that a man who had never traded himself might write well upon trade, and he said there was nothing that more required to be illustrated by philosophy. 'As to mere riches,' said he, 'that is to say, money, it is plain that one nation or one individual cannot get more of it but by making another poorer. But trade procures real riches: the reciprocation of the advantages of different countries. A merchant', said he, 'seldom thinks but of his own particular trade. To have a good book upon it, we must have extensive views. It is not necessary to practice to write well upon a subject.' I mentioned law. 'Why, Sir,' said he, 'in England, where so much money is to be got by the practice of the law, most of our writers upon it have been in practice; though Blackstone had not been much in practice when he published his *Commentaries*. Upon the Continent, the great writers on law have not all been in practice. Grotius indeed was. But Pufendorf was not; Burlamaqui was not.'

He told me that before going to Italy he was to take a jaunt to Oxford, Birmingham, Lichfield, his native town, and his old friend Dr Taylor's at Ashbourne in Derbyshire, and he asked me to go with him. I said I should be very happy to go; but I must first see if Douglas would pay me the compliment of gratitude of having me one of the counsel in his appeal. Dr Johnson said, 'He will not ask you. I speak upon general knowledge of human nature. Mankind are too unmindful of favours, or too inattentive, or too unwilling to part with their money, to act as he should do upon such an occasion. I wish he may, not merely for the few guineas that you may get, but for the credit which a man gets by being employed in his profession.'

I asked him if it was wrong in a lawyer to solicit employment. 'No, Sir,' said he. 'It is wrong to stir up lawsuits; but when once lawsuits are to go on, there is nothing wrong in a lawyer's endeavouring that he shall have the benefit, rather than another.' 'You would not solicit employment, Sir,' said I, 'if you were a lawyer.' 'No, Sir,' said he, 'but not because I should think it wrong, but because I should disdain it.' (I am now writing on Friday the 22nd at Henley in Warwickshire, while Dr Johnson is getting up to be ready to set out at seven in the morning. Let me see what may be done in such a space of time.) This was a good distinction, and a good rule to a man of my family and just pride. He said, however, 'Do not be wanting to yourself in using fair means. I would inject a little hint to him. Speak of his cause. Ask what hopes his lawyers give him, and let him have an opening.'

We talked of regulating the succession of an estate, while Mrs Thrale was by. He enlarged my view very much. 'Where', said he, 'a man gets the unlimited property of an estate, there is no obligation upon him in *justice* to leave it to one rather than to another. There is a motive of preference from *kindness*, and this kindness is generally entertained for the nearest relation. If I *owe* a particular man a sum of money, I am obliged to let that man have the next money I get, and cannot in justice let another have it. But if I owe money to no man, I may dispose of what I get as I please. There is not a *debitum justitiae* to my next heir. There is only a *debitum caritatis*.7 It is plain therefore that I have morally a choice according to my liking. If I have a brother in want, he has a claim from affection to my assistance. But I have also a friend in want, whom I like better. He has a preferable claim. The right of an heir-at-law is only this: that he is to have the succession in case no other person is appointed to it by the owner of an estate. He has only a preference to the King.' Thus far at Henley. A page is thus gained from idleness. (I am *now* writing on the same day at Birmingham while Dr Johnson is at the little house.) To have my mind enlarged from fetters of conscientious scrupulous justice was very cheering. At the same time my feudal *inclinations* for male succession remained warm.

SUNDAY 17 MARCH. I went to Langton's, who had a house in the same street [Harley Street]. I had seen Beauclerk's name upon a door in Hertford Street yesterday, he having removed from the Adelphi. He was in bed, and I left a card for him. Lady Rothes came to the door of Langton's house just as I was going to knock, so she ushered me in to the parlour, where I found Langton quite domestic with books and children. He lamented The Club's being overwhelmed with unsuitable members. Dr Johnson had said to me yesterday that Adam Smith was a most disagreeable fellow after he had drank some wine, which, he said, 'bubbled in his mouth'. He made a most excellent remark. 'Drinking', said he, 'does not improve conversation. It alters the mind so as that you are pleased with any conversation.' He is certainly right. Wine debases the intellect and blunts the taste. May it not, however, be doubted if there are not some men whose dull constitutions require being agitated by fermentation? Langton delicately cautioned me against my usual fault of repeating to people what is said of them, and then told me that he could perceive Beauclerk had lost his relish for Adam Smith's conversation, about which we had disputed last year. Beauclerk, it seems, was so ill that there was scarcely any hope of his recovery. The tranquillity of Langton's parlour was a good shade in London. Talking of literary men, I said there were many of them whose books we may like, but with whom one would no more wish to be personally acquainted than with a musician or a painter, merely from admiring their works. He agreed with me, and gave a striking instance of the mistaken desire of the society of *men* whose *performances* are excellent. 'When Johnson who rides three horses was at Oxford, Tom Warton did not go to see him ride.[8] He did not care for that. But he sat an evening with him. He got nothing for his pains. The fellow never opened his mouth.'

I then paid a visit to Mrs Stuart. She was dressing, but I bid the servant ask if she would see me for a few minutes. I was shown up to her bedchamber, where her maid was assisting her at her toilet. Mr Stuart came in. She said before him and her maid, 'Lord help me, I have been reading Hume's essay on natural religion, and it has almost made me an infidel.' I said, 'You shall not be an infidel as long as I live. Why do you read such books?' 'Oh,' said she, 'let truth have a fair examination.' I was sorry that she talked thus before her husband, who had not been taught religion or had forgot it, and her maid, who, I suppose, had it not firmly fixed. I resolved to have a serious conversation with her afterwards, and put good books into her hands. I had not arguments ready for her. I am not quite certain whether this incident happened on Sunday the 17 or Monday the 18. I then went to General Paoli's and dressed and had some most consolatory soup. I was quite at home there.

(I am now writing on the same day between one and two, to catch half an hour before dinner. I am fallen sadly behind in my journal. I should live no more than I can record, as one should not have more corn growing than one can get in. There is a waste of good if it be not preserved. And yet perhaps if it serve the purpose of immediate felicity, that is enough. The world would not hold pictures of all the pretty women who have lived in it and gladdened mankind; nor would it hold a register of all the agreeable conversations which have passed. But I mean only to record what is excellent; and let me rejoice when I can find abundance of that.)

TUESDAY 19 MARCH. (I am now writing in the Hon. Mrs Stuart's dressing-room, London, Monday evening April 1.) Between eight and nine in the morning I was at the Somerset Coffee-house, and there I found Dr Johnson waiting for the Oxford coach, and Mr Gwynn, the architect, attending him. I breakfasted comfortably, and then we three got into the coach, which, when it is desired, calls at the Somerset. The fourth passenger was Mr — of Merton College, a young gentleman of Gloucestershire. He very politely gave me his place that I might be drawn forward as Dr Johnson was.

In my journal of yesterday I strangely omitted to mention that between ten and eleven at night I called on Mr Garrick, found him sitting with Mrs Garrick and Miss More, the poetess,[9] and stayed with him till near twelve, drinking port and water and eating bread and a Hampton nonpareil.[10] He was quite easy and gay as usual. I said this morning in the coach that he would be relieved by his quitting the stage. Dr Johnson seemed to doubt it. 'Why,' said I, 'he will be Atlas with the burthen off his back.' 'But I know not', said Dr Johnson, 'if he will be so steady without his load.' He was clear that he should never play any more, but be quite the gentleman, and not partly the player; and that he should not any longer subject himself to be hissed or to be insolently treated by the performers whom he used to rule with a high hand, and who would gladly retaliate. I said I thought he should play once a year for the benefit of decayed actors, as it was given out he was to do. 'Sir,' said Dr Johnson, 'he'll be a decayed actor himself.'

(I am now writing at General Paoli's, London, Tuesday forenoon, April 2.) Dr Johnson found fault with ornamental architecture, because it consumes labour disproportionate to its utility. For the same reason he satirized statuary. 'Painting', said he, 'consumes labour not disproportionate to its effect, but a fellow will hack half a year at a block of marble to make something in stone that resembles a man.' This was a Gothic reflection, for certainly statuary is a noble art of imitation, and preserves the utmost expression of the human frame. Dr Johnson said the value of statuary was owing to its difficulty; 'For', said he, 'you would not value the finest cut head upon a carrot.' Here I take it he was not just; for although the difficulty may enter into the estimation of the value of a marble head, I take it the durability is the principal reason for a preference.

Gwynn was a rattling fellow, but the Doctor kept him in pure subjection, calling him 'Gwynnie'. I could discover too that the Doctor was his good friend in recommending him to employment at Oxford. It was a pleasant day. When we came to Oxford, we went immediately to University College to call on Mr Scott, one of the fellows, who had accompanied the Doctor from Newcastle to Edinburgh. With him we should have lodged, but he was gone into the country for some days; so we put up at the Angel Inn, and had the very parlour where Dr Johnson and Chambers and poor Frank Stewart supped with me in 1768.

Either this night or the one after he spoke to me of the melancholy to which I am subject, said that I had a very ticklish mind, and that I must divert distressing thoughts, and not combat with them. 'Remember always', said he, '—.' I said I sometimes tried to *think them down*. He said I was wrong. He bid me have a lamp burning in my bedchamber, and take a book and read and so compose myself to rest. This I supposed was his own method. But I told him I seldom waked in the night. When I do at home, my excellent spouse consoles me with easy, sensible talk. He said to have the management of one's mind was a great art, and that it might be attained in a considerable degree by experience and habitual exercise. His sage counsel I treasured up. He commended Burton's *Anatomy of Melancholy* and said there was great spirit and great power in what Burton said when he wrote from his own mind. I fancied tonight that I was prepared by my revered friend for conducting myself through any future gloom.

We had a double-bedded room, and were as companionable as during our journey to the Hebrides, while I felt that kind of consolatory respectful frame which Oxford has ever produced in me.

THURSDAY 21 MARCH [*on the road to Lichfield*]. We lay tonight at Henley, a Warwickshire village, a long range of very ordinary houses. The inn was good; we had each a bedroom.

FRIDAY 22 MARCH. After a sound sleep we got up well refreshed. Before we set out, Dr Johnson resumed the subject of my melancholy, and was displeased with my notion of *thinking down* that malady. He said, 'I have not been more shocked with anything that I have heard of a long time.' 'Sir,' said I, 'it was spirit and resolution.' 'Ay,' said he, 'but it was the spirit and resolution of a madman.' I said I had been in a mistake, for I imagined that he approved of that method. While we were in the chaise driving to Birmingham to breakfast, he said, 'When you have a place in the country, lay out twenty pounds a year upon a laboratory. It will be an amusement to you.' I said I had last summer taken a course of chemistry. 'Sir,' said he, 'take a course of chemistry, or a course of rope-dancing, or a course of anything to which you are inclined at the time. Contrive to have as many retreats for your mind as you can, as many things to which it can fly from itself.' There was a liberal philosophy in this advice which pleased me much. I *thought* of a course of concubinage, but was afraid to mention it.

I had read yesterday in the chaise *Reflections on the Study of Divinity* by Dr Bentham. Also a short Latin discourse on the same subject, and *De motibus Americanis*, both by the same professor. I was well satisfied with them. I had bought a Minellius Horace at Oxford, and having heard Beauclerk mention Dr Johnson's repeating '*Truditur dies die*', &c, one moonlight evening in London, soon after he got acquainted with him, holding by the rails, I got that ode in which the passage is by heart. By this time I had it not yet perfect. Amidst all this I had high happiness, and was warmly pious. Nothing disturbed me but a degree of unsettledness as to the consistency of concubinage, or rather occasional transient connections with loose women, and Christian morals. I was sensible that there was a great weight of interpretation against such licence. But as I did not see precisely a general doctrine for practice in that respect in the New Testament, and some Christians, even Luther, did not think it an indispensable duty to cohabit only with one woman, and my appetite that way was naturally strong and perhaps rendered stronger by encouragement, I could not decide against it. I *must* venture to consult Dr Johnson upon it. For he can, by his noble counsel, make my judgement clear and my resolution vigorous.

We put up at the Swan at Birmingham, breakfasted and dressed, and then walked out that I might see the town. We were first to call on Mr Hector, the surgeon, the Doctor's old schoolfellow. He told me I should see at Mr Hector's his sister, Mrs Carless, a clergyman's widow, 'the first woman', said he, 'with whom I was in love.' But he said his love for her dropped out of his head imperceptibly. He agreed with me that it was not true that a man never could be in love but once, and I think he also agreed with me that a man may be in love with several women at a time. He said Mrs Carless and he should always have a kindness one for another. When we came to Hector's door, a very stupid maid answered. She told us her master was out, and Mrs Carless too, and her master was in the country, but she could not tell when he was to return; in short she was a wretched receiver of his friends, and as Dr Johnson said, 'She would have behaved no better to people who might have wanted him hastily in the way of his profession.' He said, 'My name is Johnson; tell him I called. Will you remember the name?' She answered, 'I don't hear you, Sir,' or, 'I don't understand you, Sir.' 'Blockhead,' said he, 'I'll write.' I never heard *blockhead* applied to a woman before. However, he grew calm, and roared loud, '*Johnson*,' and then she catched it.

We then called at Mr Lloyd's, a Quaker. His wife told us he was not in the house, but asked us to dine, and the Doctor accepted the invitation. He said to me, 'After the uncertainty of all human things at Hector's, this invitation came very well.' We walked and looked at the town, and saw ranges of good new buildings.

These Quakers were opulent people and kept a good table. They told me that in the manufacture of gilt buttons two hundred ounces of gold were consumed weekly. Mr Hector and I went in a hackney-coach, which I remember was lined with red and white broad-striped check, which had a cleanly look, and saw Mr Boulton's manufactory about two miles from the town.[11] Boulton seemed to be a clever, fine fellow. I regretted that I did not know mechanics well enough to comprehend the description of a machine lately invented by him, which he took great pains to show me. 'I sell, Sir,' said he, 'what all the world desires to have – power.' And indeed his machine seemed to have prodigious force in raising water. We drank tea with him and Mrs Boulton. I was struck with the thought of a smith being a great man. Here I saw it. He had about seven hundred people at work. He was a sort of iron chieftain, and seemed to be fatherly to his tribe. A smith came to complain grievously of his landlord for seizing his goods. 'Your landlord is in the right, Smith,' said Boulton. 'But I'll tell you what: find you a friend or neighbour who will lay down one-half of your rent, and I'll lay down the other half, and you shall have your goods again.'

Mr Hector told me several anecdotes of Dr Johnson, which I have marked in a book of notes concerning the Doctor. I wished to be longer with him to get more, for Dr Johnson said I might pretty well depend on what he related. I had a gloom or a weariness at Boulton's which I could not cure while I was obliged to attend to the present object.

Mr Hector and I alighted at his house, where was Dr Johnson with his first love, Mrs Carless, who appeared to be an amiable woman, and had the remains of an agreeable countenance. Dr Johnson lamented to Hector the state of their schoolfellow, the Reverend Mr Charles Congreve, who now lived in London, quite as a valetudinarian, afraid to go into any house but his own, took a short airing every day in his post-chaise, had an old woman whom he called cousin who lived with him and jogged his elbow when his glass had stood too long empty, and encouraged him in drinking, in which he was very willing to be encouraged; not that he got drunk, for he was a very pious man, but was always muddy; that he confessed to one bottle of port every day and he probably drank more. That he was quite unsocial; his conversation was monosyllabical; and when Dr Johnson asked what a clock it was, this signal of his departure had so pleasing an effect on Congreve that he sprung up to look at his watch, like a greyhound bounding at a hare. When the Doctor took leave of Hector, he said, 'Don't grow like Congreve, nor let me grow like him when you are near me.'

When he again talked of Mrs Carless tonight, he seemed to have had his affection revived, for he said to this purpose: 'If I had married her, it might have been as happy for me.' 'I suppose', said I, 'there are fifty women with whom a man may be as happy as with any one in particular.' 'Ay, fifty thousand,' said he. I doubted if he was right. I have a strong imagination that I could not have been so happy in marriage with any other woman as with my dear wife. I cannot tell why, so as to give any rational explanation to others. I only know or fancy that there are qualities and *compositions of qualities* (to talk in musical metaphor) which in the course of our lives appear to me in her that please me more than what I have perceived in any other woman, and which I cannot separate from her identity.

I wished to have stayed at Birmingham tonight, but Dr Johnson would go forward to Lichfield. We set off I think about eight. The road was not very good, and the night not very clear, so this portion of our travelling was dull. We were long silent in the chaise. When we came within the focus of the Lichfield lamps, 'Now,' said he, 'we are getting out of a state of death.' His words were to that effect. We put up at the Three Crowns, none of the capital inns, but a good old-fashioned one kept by Mr Wilkins in [Bread-market Street], the very next house to Dr Johnson's, in which he was born and brought up. We had a little comfortable supper, I drank excellent Lichfield ale, which made me drowsy, and we had a tolerable two-bedded room.

SATURDAY 23 MARCH. At the inn Dr Johnson and I dined and had with us Mr [Harry] Jackson, an old schoolfellow of his, whom he treated with much kindness, though he seemed to be a low man, dull and untaught. He had coarse clothes, I think a greyish brown coat and black waistcoat, greasy leather breeches, a yellowish uncurled wig, and a countenance ruddy with drinking, as I supposed. It seems he had tried to be a cutler at Birmingham but had not succeeded, and now he lived poorly at home and was upon some scheme of dressing leather in a better way than usual, to his indistinct account of which Dr Johnson listened with patient indulgence, that he might advise him. He drank only ale. I never saw better than at Lichfield, brewed by our host, who had been a publican forty years. I drank here too for the first time oat ale, and saw oatcakes, soft like Yorkshire ones of wheat flour, at breakfast. It was pleasant to find *the food of horses* so much used in Dr Johnson's own town. He praised his town, said that they were the most sober, decent people of any town in England, the genteelest in proportion to their wealth, and spoke the purest English. I doubted a little as to this, for I thought they had provincial sounds, as *there* pronounced like *fear* or rather *feear*, instead of like *fair*. Also *once* pronounced *woonss*, instead of *wunss*; and I have heard Garrick imitate Dr Johnson in pronouncing, 'Who's for *poonch*?' (instead of punch).

There are no manufactures at Lichfield but two very strange ones for so inland a place, sail-cloth and streamers for ships, and these very limited; and saddle-cloths, which is a more suitable manufacture for the situation. I observed a good deal of sheepskins dressing. I said to Dr Johnson, 'You're an idle set of people.' 'Sir,' said he, 'we are a city of philosophers. We work with our heads, not with our hands. We make the boobies of Birmingham work for us.' I think that was his jocular expression.

There was here at present a company of players. Dr Johnson said forty years ago he had been in love with an actress here, Mrs Emmet, who acted Flora in *Hob in the Well*. Mr Stanton sent in his compliments and that he would be glad to wait on us. I liked this. He was a plain, decent man and thanked Dr Johnson for having got him moderate terms once at Ashbourne from Dr Taylor. Garrick was soon introduced. 'Garrick's conversation', said Dr Johnson, 'is gay and grotesque. It is a dish of all sorts, but all good things. There is no solid meat in it. There is a want of sentiment, not but that he has sentiment sometimes, and sentiment, too, very powerful and very pleasing; but it has not its full proportion in his conversation.'

We drank coffee and tea at Mr Peter Garrick's, where was a Miss Aston, an elderly maiden lady. I had seen in the forenoon with Mr Garrick in the house of Mr Newton, brother to the Bishop of Bristol, a fine portrait of Mr David Garrick by Dance, and some East Indian curiosities; and this afternoon I saw with Dr Johnson the museum of Mr Greene, an apothecary, a wonderful collection to be made by a man like him in a country town. He had his curiosities neatly arranged, with their names printed at his own little press, and he had at the top of the first flat of his staircase a board with the contributors marked in gold letters. He had also a printed catalogue, which I bought at the bookseller's. He was a bustling, good-humoured little man. He said Dr Johnson said he should as soon have thought of building a man of war as getting together such a museum. He drank a glass of wine with us at the inn in the evening.

I had yesterday talked of Dr Boswell's museum, and Dr Johnson asked why he quitted practice. I said because his whimsical change of religion had made people distrustful of him as a physician, which I thought unreasonable, as religion was unconnected with medical skill. Dr Johnson said it was not unreasonable, for when people see a man absurd in what they understand, they may conclude the same of him in what they do not understand. If a physician were to take to eating of horseflesh, nobody would employ him, though one may eat horseflesh and be a very skilful physician. He admitted that if a man were educated in an absurd religion, his continuing to profess it would not hurt him as a change to it would.

He this day, when we were at Peter Garrick's, as well as on the road to Oxford, attacked the French nation. Said that the great there lived very magnificently, but the rest miserably. That there was no happy middle station as in England. That the shops of Paris were mean, the meat in the markets such as would be sent to a gaol in England; and Mr Thrale had justly observed that the French cookery was forced upon them by necessity, for they could not eat their meat unless they added some taste to it. He said they were an indelicate people, would spit in any place, that at Madame de Boccage's the footman lifted sugar with his fingers and put [it] into his coffee. He was going to have put it aside, but hearing it was made on purpose for him, he e'en tasted Tom's fingers. She would make tea *à l'anglaise*. The spout of the pot did not pour freely. She bid the footman blow into it. He said France was worse than Scotland in everything but climate. Nature had done more for them, but they had done less for themselves than the Scotch had done.

This evening, I think, I talked to him of Dr Boswell's going to bawdy-houses and talking as if the Christian religion had not prescribed any fixed rule for intercourse between the sexes. He said, 'Sir, there is no trusting to that crazy piety.' I was humbled by this strong saying. After dinner I had visited his house. A beautiful, gentle, sweet maid showed it. In one of the garret rooms I kissed her, and she curtsied. I was charmed with her for the moment as with a rose or some pleasing object which makes a slight but very vivid impression.

MONDAY 25 MARCH. We breakfasted at Mrs Porter's. We had sent an express to Dr Taylor, who wrote in return that his chaise should come for us on Monday. While we were at breakfast, Dr Johnson received a letter which seemed to agitate him much. When he had read it, he said, 'One of the most dreadful things that has happened in my time.' The phrase, *my time*, like the word *age*, is usually understood to apply to something public or general. I figured something like an assassination of the King, like a Gunpowder Plot carried into execution, or like another Fire of London. When asked, 'What is it, Sir?' he answered, 'Mr Thrale has lost his only son.' This was to be sure a very great affliction to Mr and Mrs Thrale, and which their friends must consider as an event of sorrowful magnitude. But from the manner in which the intelligence of it was communicated, it appeared for the moment to be comparatively small. I was soon affected with sincere concern, and was curious to see how Dr Johnson would feel. He said, 'This is such a total —[12] to their family as if they were sold into captivity.' I said Mr Thrale had daughters to inherit his wealth. 'Daughters!' said he, 'he'll no more value his daughters than—' I was going to speak. 'Sir,' said he, 'don't you know how you yourself think? Sir, he wishes to propagate his name.' In short I saw masculine succession strong in the Doctor's mind. I said it was lucky he was not present. 'It is lucky for me,' said he. 'People in distress never think that you feel enough.' 'And', said I, 'they'll have the hope of seeing you, which will be a relief in the mean time, and when you get to them, the pain will be so far abated that they will be capable of being consoled by you, which in the first violence of it, I believe, would not be the case.' 'No, Sir,' said he, 'violent pain of mind, as of body, *must* be severely felt.' I said I had not much *feeling* of another's distress, as some people have or pretend to have, but I have this: that I would do all I could to relieve them. He said it was affectation to pretend to feel another's affliction as much as they themselves, as if one should pretend to feel equal pain with a friend while his leg is cutting off;[13] but I had expressed the true effect of concern. He said he would have gone to the extremity of the earth (I think these were his words) to have preserved this boy.

He was soon quite calm. The letter was from Mr Thrale's clerk, and bore, 'I need not say how much they wish to see you in London.' He said, 'We shall hasten back from Taylor's.'

FRIDAY 29 MARCH [*returning from Dr Taylor's, in Derbyshire, to London*]. I enjoyed the luxury of the approach to London in a post-chaise with Dr Samuel Johnson. 'Sir,' said I, 'you said one day at General Oglethorpe's that a man is never happy for the present but when he is drunk. Will you not add, or when driving quick in a post-chaise?' 'No, Sir,' said he, 'you are driving quick *from* something or *to* something.'

He talked of the melancholy to which I am subject, and said that some men, and very thinking men too, had not these vexing thoughts, but that most men had, in the degree in which they were capable of having them. He said that if I was in the country, and felt myself so distressed, I should force myself to take a book, and every time I did this I would find it the easier. He said, 'I should like to stay a summer at Auchinleck if it were yours.' He bid me divert melancholy by every means but drinking. I thought then of women, but no doubt he no more thought of my indulging in licentious copulation than of my stealing.

We alighted at Dilly's. He took a coach and hastened to Thrale's. I found two letters from my dear wife, one from worthy Grange, one from Temple, and one from Dempster, who was set out for Scotland. I was thus feasted. Bruce Boswell called on me, and I undertook to solicit interest to assist him in getting a ship. Charles Dilly was gone to the country. I dined with Edward; and Smith, the miniature painter from Scotland, who was going to the East Indies, was there. I drank as much as intoxicated me somewhat, and I hastened to the lady's with whom I had once been amorously connected and had lately twice renewed the connection. So wild was my mind now that I did not perceive the least doubt as to this casual intercourse, any more than any other gratification. She was not at home, which disappointed my desires. I called at my lodgings and to my agreeable surprise found the Douglas cases lying for me as one of the counsel. I was in a kind of brutal fever, went to the Park, and was relieved by dalliance. Suspicious that the cases might have been sent to me because it was known I was out of town, I called on Maconochie, and as he was not at home, left a note for him expressing what I had felt from an apprehension of neglect, all things considered, and my agreeable disappointment that I found myself one of the counsel. I supped at Mrs Stuart's. Her husband did not come home. Oswald and Aberdeen were there. I madly drank a bottle of claret by myself, none of them drinking with me, and this, meeting what I had taken at dinner, made me brutally feverish. So I sallied to the Park again, and again dallied. But, what was worse, as I was coming home to General Paoli's, I was picked up by a strumpet at the head of St James's Street, who went with me to the entry to the passage from Hay Hill by Lord Shelburne's, and in my drunken venturousness, I lay with her. Oh, what a sad apprehension then seized me! I got home between three and four, or a little earlier.

SATURDAY 30 MARCH. Awaked very ill with sickness and headache; wished to conceal my illness, or rather the cause of it. Got up at ten. The General discovered it, and genteelly reproved my drunkenness as a vice which hurts the character, and gives envious people an advantage over a man of parts. Poggi, an Italian painter, was taking a picture of him. We all breakfasted together this morning on tea. The General said no man was ever promoted to an office of trust, without merit or the appearance of merit. He said the Devonshire family had been hurt in this reign by the Court, which had occasioned much mischief. That the King would willingly cover the wound with a ribbon of any colour. I went and called on Spottiswoode, who told me that my being employed in the Douglas appeal was the suggestion of Douglas himself, who said it would be a shame if I were left out. This pleased me very much.

Jenny Taylor, the girl with whom I had lain last night, told me that she lived in Peter Street, Westminster. I was much afraid of having catched the venereal disorder, and went this forenoon to find her and examine her. But I could get no intelligence of her. Probably she lied as to her name and residence. Returning through the Park about three o'clock, I observed a pretty, fresh-looking girl, as I thought, standing with another. She told me her name was Nanny Smith, that she lived as a servant-maid with Mr Williams in New Bond Street, that she was out an errand. She agreed to go with me to the One Tun, Chelsea, a house of lewd entertainment in a garden, to which the other girl directed us, and there I enjoyed her. I dined at General Paoli's and drank coffee comfortably.

SUNDAY 31 MARCH. I dined at the Hon. James Stuart's. Nobody there but his sister, Lady Augusta, and Captain Corbet of the Horse Guards, her husband. A more fruitless afternoon of conversation (if *fruitless* may be used in this sense) I never passed. But we drank hard, and about ten o'clock I went away much in liquor. I went to Douglas's, thanked him for his attention, or rather, I believe, praised it as what was due to me. Lord and Lady Hope, Lady Louisa Hope and a Mr Randolph were there. I behaved pretty decently. But when I got into the street, the whoring rage came upon me. I thought I would devote a night to it. I was weary at the same time that I was tumultuous. I went to Charing Cross Bagnio with a wholesome-looking, bouncing wench, stripped, and went to bed with her. But after my desires were satiated by repeated indulgence, I could not rest; so I parted from her after she had honestly delivered to me my watch and ring and handkerchief, which I should not have missed I was so drunk. I took a hackney-coach and was set down in Berkeley Square, and went home cold and disturbed and dreary and vexed, with remorse rising like a black cloud without any distinct form; for in truth my moral principle as to chastity was absolutely eclipsed for a time. I was in the miserable state of those whom the Apostle represents as working all uncleanness with greediness. I thought of my valuable spouse with the highest regard and warmest affection, but had a confused notion that my corporeal connection with whores did not interfere with my love for her. Yet I considered that I might injure my health, which there could be no doubt was an injury to her. This is an exact state of my mind at the time. It shocks me to review it.

MONDAY 1 APRIL. Awaked very ill. Called on Captain James Erskine. Found him at his house in Pall Mall Court as last year. Sat awhile with him. 'When shall we dine together?' said he. I answered, 'I am engaged all this week.' 'This day sennight, then, at Le Telier's,' said he. I am pretty firm in my resolution not to dine at a tavern in London unless with Dr Johnson. But as Erskine is my relation, employed me last year as one of his counsel, and was at present I knew not in what circumstances, I could not refuse to meet him.

I went to Duck Lane, Westminster, and found my last night's harlot by the name of Nanny Cooms, and persuaded myself that she was not infected. But whom did I see in that blackguard lane but my pretended servant-maid, Nanny Smith, in a drummer's coat by way of a morning jacket! I was abashed and mortified at my simplicity. I asked Nanny Cooms and a girl who was with her about that jade Smith. They said she had lived in the house with them three months, and they could not answer for her, for the young man who lived with her, a corporal, was now in the hospital. This made me almost sick with fear. But Nanny Cooms had last night spoken to me of a pretty fair girl who was on call. I sent for her and enjoyed her, and - - - - - - - - a kind of licence I never had - - - -.¹⁴ I thought this should be the last act of this fit of debauchery.

TUESDAY 2 APRIL. I dined today at Sir John Pringle's, where was the celebrated circumnavigator Captain Cook and his wife, General Graeme, his lady and brother, Sir George Hume, a navy captain who had been at Mundell's School with me, but whom I had not seen for five-and-twenty years, and Lady Erskine, Sir Harry's widow, with her son Sir James, and a daughter. Cook, as Sir John had told me before, was a plain, sensible man with an uncommon attention to veracity. My metaphor was that he had a balance in his mind for truth as nice as scales for weighing a guinea. Sir John gave me an instance. It was supposed that Cook had said he had seen a nation of men like monkeys, and Lord Monboddo had been very happy with this. Sir John happened to tell Cook of this. 'No,' said he, 'I did not say they were like monkeys. I said their faces put me in mind of monkeys.' There was a distinction very fine but sufficiently perceptible.

I talked a good deal with him today, as he was very obliging and communicative. He seemed to have no desire to make people stare, and being a man of good steady moral principles, as I thought, did not try to make theories out of what he had seen to confound virtue and vice. He said Hawkesworth made in his book a general conclusion from a particular fact, and would take as a fact what they had only heard. He said it was not true that Mr Banks and he had revised all the book; and in what was revised Hawkesworth would make no alteration (I think he said this too). He said that a disregard of chastity in unmarried women was by no means general at Otaheite, and he said Hawkesworth's story of an *initiation* he had no reason to believe. 'Why, Sir,' said I, 'Hawkesworth has used your narrative as a London tavern keeper does wine. He has *brewed* it.' It was curious to see Cook, a grave steady man, and his wife, a decent plump Englishwoman, and think that he was preparing to sail round the world.¹⁵

I went from Sir John's to the Queen's Arms in St Paul's Churchyard, and supped at the monthly meeting of the partners of the *London Magazine*. I was quite the man of consequence, full of gaiety, and relished much the conversation of *the Trade*. Being apprehensive of venereal mischief, and desirous to hasten its appearance if it was lurking about me, I drank freely, but not to intoxication. Went home with Dilly comfortably to my room at his house.

WEDNESDAY 3 APRIL. I called on Dr Johnson; found him putting his books in order. He had gloves on, and was all dusty. He was quite in the character which Dr Boswell drew of him: 'A robust genius! born to grapple with whole libraries!' I gave him an account of Captain Cook, and told him I felt, while I was with the Captain, an inclination to make the voyage. 'Why, so one does,' said the Doctor, 'till one considers how very little one learns.' I said I was certain a great part of what we are told by the travellers to the South Sea Islands must be conjecture, because they cannot know language enough to understand so much as they tell. The Doctor was of that opinion. 'But', said I, 'one is carried away with the thing in general, a voyage round the world.' 'Yes,' said he, 'but one is to guard against taking a thing in general.'

He agreed that we should dine today at the Mitre after my return from the House of Lords, this being the day when counsel were to be heard on Duke Hamilton's petition for putting off the cause between Lord Selkirk and Douglas till his Grace should also bring forward his claim. I went to the Temple and got a decent tie-wig from Mr Tibbs, who let me have one last year. The hire is half a crown a time. I called on Mr Bigg, — of the Inner Temple, and got information when the commons were to begin for next term. I liked to think that I was of the society *Interioris Templi.*

I should have mentioned that Captain Cook told us that Omai,[16] whom he was to carry home, begged to have two things for himself: port wine, which he loved the best of any liquor, and gunpowder; but the Captain said he would not let him have the power of fire-arms, which he supposed he wished to have from some ambitious design. He said that for some time after Omai's return home he would be a man of great consequence, as having so many wonders to tell. That he would not foresee that when he had told all he had to tell, he would sink into his former state, and then, the Captain supposed, he would wish to go to England again ('Britannia', the Otaheite people say, as they cannot pronounce 'England'), but that the Captain would take care to leave the coast before Omai had time to be dissatisfied at home.

I introduced today the topic which is often ignorantly urged, that the universities of England are too rich; so that learning does not flourish as it would do if those who teach had smaller salaries and depended on their assiduity for a great part of their income. Dr Johnson said the very reverse was the case in the English universities. 'For', said he, 'they are not rich enough. Our fellowships are only sufficient to support a man during his studies to fit him for the world, and accordingly in general they are kept no longer than till an opportunity offers of getting away. Now and then, perhaps, there is a fellow who grows old in his college, but this is against his will, unless he be a man very indolent indeed. A hundred a year is reckoned a good fellowship, and that is no more than is necessary to keep a man decently as a scholar. We do not allow our fellows to marry, because we consider that state only as a nursery for the world. It is by being a tutor and having pupils that anything more than a livelihood is to be had. To be sure, a man who has enough without teaching will not probably teach, for we would all be idle if we could. In the same manner, a man who is to get nothing by teaching will let it alone. There was Gresham College intended as a place of instruction for London; as the professors were to read lectures gratis, they contrived to have no scholars; whereas, if they had been to be paid but sixpence a lecture, they would have been emulous to have a number of 'em. Everybody will agree that it should be the interest of those who teach to have scholars; and this is the case in our universities. That they are too rich is certainly not true, for they have nothing good enough to keep a man of eminent learning for his life. In the foreign universities, a professorship is a high thing. It is as much almost as a man can make of his learning; and therefore we find the most learned men in the universities abroad. It is not so with us. Our universities are impoverished of learning by the poverty of their provisions.' He said this to me during our last jaunt, and added that he wished there were 'half a dozen places of a thousand a year at Oxford to keep first-rate men of learning from quitting the University'. To be sure, literature then would have a dignity and splendour at Oxford, and there would be grander living sources of instruction.

I should have mentioned that when the Doctor said one was angry at a man for controverting an opinion which one believes and values, the Solicitor said, 'One rather pities him.' 'No, Sir,' said Johnson. 'To be sure when you wish a man to have that belief which you consider as an advantage, you wish well to him; but your primary consideration is your own quiet. If a madman were to come into this room with a stick in his hand, no doubt we should pity the state of his mind; but our primary consideration would be to take care of ourselves. We should knock him down first, and pity him afterwards.' He said too, 'A man will dispute with great good humour upon a subject in which he is not interested. I will dispute very calmly upon the probability of another man's son being hanged; but if a man pushes a dispute with me upon the probability that my own son shall be hanged, I shall certainly not be in good humour with him.' I added this illustration: 'If a man endeavours to convince me that my wife, whom I love very much, and in whom I have great confidence, is a disagreeable woman, and is even unfaithful to me, I shall be very angry; for he is putting me in fear of being unhappy.'

FRIDAY 5 APRIL. This being Good Friday, I intended as usual to breakfast with Dr Johnson, but in my way called on Sir John Pringle, found him in his drawing-room, and the sun beaming upon it. He talked of having visited officially last year some madhouses, and that when he asked the keepers if they gave the lunatics any medicine to try to do them good, they answered, 'You know, Sir, nothing will do them good.' 'It is true,' said he; 'and I wonder that this has not been used as an argument for the reality of demoniacs, for if madness were a bodily distemper, something might be done for it by medicine.' He said he had read Farmer on demoniacs but was not satisfied by him. Sir John seemed not to be quite clear in his belief upon this subject, but talked of it with a delicate gravity. He said there was no more occasion to believe the Evangelists to be inspired to have a belief in Christianity than to believe the Roman historians inspired to have a belief that Caesar reigned, and did what is recorded of him, and was killed in the way we read. He seemed to think Mahomet had a divine commission, for he converted a vast proportion of people to the belief of one GOD. I agreed with him, and said I believed both Mahomet and Confucius to be messengers of revelation. He was in an easy, communicative frame. My mind was unquiet with the thoughts of having acted immorally. Yet I was not quite clear. A man is not steady in his conviction of the truth of a principle which his warm passions are ever melting and the transgression of which gives him pain. I said to Sir John I did not see any positive precept as to the connection between the sexes. He insisted that the rule was explicit enough, but rather avoided an argument upon it.

As I was hastening up the Strand to breakfast at the Somerset Coffee-house, before going to St Clement's Church where Dr Johnson goes, I met Bruce Boswell, and took him to the Somerset with me, where over chocolade we talked a little of his affairs. I then went to St Clement's, and was so late that I would not go into the seat with Dr Johnson, but after service was over joined him at the door of the church, and walked home to his house with him. When we had sat some time, Mr Thrale called.

We had talked of the Romish Church. Dr Johnson said that in the barbarous ages priests and people were equally deceived, but afterwards there were gross corruptions by the clergy, such as indulgences to priests to have concubines, and the worship of images, though not inculcated yet knowingly permitted. I mentioned the licensed stews at Rome. That he strongly censured. 'Then, Sir,' said I, 'you would allow no fornication at all.' 'To be sure, Sir,' said he. 'I would punish it much more than is done, and so restrain it. In all countries there has been fornication, as in all countries theft; but there may be more or less of the one as well as of the other by the force of law. All men will naturally commit fornication, as all men will naturally steal.' I urged the common topic that whores were necessary to prevent the violent effects of lewdness, and prevent our wives and daughters from being ravished. But he was of opinion that severe laws, regularly enforced, would be sufficient, and would promote marriage. (By writing my journal so long after hearing him, my recollection of his conversation is very imperfect.)

Thrale bore the loss of his son with so manly a composure that it was not painful to be with him, which is much in a case of so great affliction. I introduced the intended tour of Italy which Mr and Mrs and Miss Thrale and Dr Johnson were to make, and on which they were to set out early in April. At Beauclerk's on Wednesday evening it was mentioned, and Beauclerk said that Baretti, who was to go with them, would keep them so long in the little towns of his own country[17] that they would not have time to see Rome. I repeated this today to put them on their guard. Dr Johnson was angry. Said he: 'We do not thank Mr Beauclerk for supposing that we are to be directed by Mr Baretti'; and he desired Thrale to go to Jackson (the 'all-knowing') and get from him a plan for seeing the most in the time that they had to travel.[18] 'We must, to be sure,' said he, 'see Rome, Naples, Florence and Venice, and as much more as we can.' Thrale appeared to me to have some difficulty about going, and I feared that he might lay aside the design if he was not hurried away. I therefore pressed their setting out speedily, for I was very desirous that Dr Johnson should see Italy and give us his grand remarks.

He said (I am not sure what day) that he did not see that he could make a book upon Italy, as so much had been said of it; but he added, 'I should be glad to get £200 or £500,' which was a proof that he supposed he *might* compose a valuable journal. Beauclerk said on Wednesday that Baretti could not go to several of the towns in Italy, as he should be hanged. 'Ay,' said I, 'the gallows is a roadpost for his direction at several places: *Turn from this.*' But I added what Dr Johnson told me: that it was not for crimes such as murder or robbery that he would be hanged, but for some political daring writings. Beauclerk and I had a dispute as to his killing a man in London.[19] I said I thought it murder. Beauclerk said he was not in the least to blame. That what he did was in self-defence, and what any of us might do. Adam Smith having just come in while we disputed, we asked his opinion. He said he thought it manslaughter, but a very brutal manslaughter.

Beauclerk had told me of a society called the New Club where people played to a desperate extent. JOHNSON. 'Depend upon it, Sir, this is mere talk. *Who* is ruined by gaming? You will not find six instances in an age. There is a strange rout made about this, whereas you have many more people ruined by adventurous trade, and yet we do not hear such an outcry about it.' THRALE. 'There may be few absolutely ruined, but very many are hurt in their circumstances.' JOHNSON. 'Yes, Sir, and so are there by other kinds of expense.' (I have heard him before upon the same subject. At Oxford he said he wished he had learnt to play at cards.)

I omitted to mention that I stated to Dr Johnson today this case: 'If I have a daughter who is debauched by a man, but nobody knows of it, should I keep her in my house?' He said I should. BOSWELL. 'But, Sir, am not I accessory to an imposition upon the world? And perhaps a worthy man may come and marry this strumpet unless I tell him her worthlessness.' JOHNSON. 'Sir, you are accessory to no imposition. Your daughter is in your house, and if a man courts her, he takes his chance. If indeed a friend, or indeed any other man, asks your advice if he should marry her, you should advise him against it without telling why, because your real opinion is then required. Or if you have other daughters who know of her wickedness, you ought not to keep her in your house. You are to consider this is the state of life. We are to judge of other people's characters as well as we can, and a man is not bound in honesty or honour to tell us the faults of his daughter or of himself. A man who has debauched his friend's daughter is not obliged to tell everybody, "Take care of me. Don't let me into your houses without suspicion. I once debauched a friend's daughter. I may debauch yours."'

After I had written to my wife, I went and paid a visit to a lady, who argued with me that marriage was certainly no more but a political institution, as we see it has subsisted in so many different forms in different parts of the world. 'Therefore,' said she, 'it is merely a mutual contract which if one party breaks, the other is free. Now,' said she, 'my husband I know has been unfaithful to me a thousand times. I should therefore have no scruple of conscience, I do declare, to have an intrigue, and I am restrained only by my pride, because I would not do what is thought dishonourable in this country, and would not put myself in the power of a gallant.' I argued that the chastity of women was of much more consequence than that of men, as the property and rights of families depend upon it. 'Surely,' said she, 'that is easily answered, for the objection is removed if a woman does not intrigue but when she is with child.' I really could not answer her. Yet I thought she was wrong, and I was uneasy, partly from my own weakness as a reasoner, partly from the pain which one feels on perceiving established principles sapped.

SUNDAY 7 APRIL. This being Easter day, I went through my usual forms. I breakfasted at the Chapter Coffee-house, then went to St Paul's, heard an excellent discourse by Mr Winstanley, and was solemnly devout. Mr Thrale sat by me. I received the Holy Sacrament, being a sincere Christian in faith, and hoping to be better in practice. Mrs and Miss Thrale were also here. I had written a few lines of condolence to Mrs Thrale on her son's death, when I arrived in town with Dr Johnson. She seemed in tender grief today, and said to me, 'What we have been now about is the true comfort.' I went to Dr Johnson's to my annual dinner. Mr Macbean, author of *Ancient Geography*, and who had been several years librarian to Archibald, Duke of Argyll, was there. He said he had been forty years from Scotland. 'Ay,' said Johnson, smiling, 'Boswell, what would you give to be forty years from Scotland?' I said I should not like to be so long absent from the seat of my ancestors. This gentleman, Mrs Williams and Mr Levett dined with us.

I repeated to Johnson the argument of a lady of my acquaintance, who maintained that her husband's having been guilty of numberless infidelities released her from her conjugal obligations, because they were reciprocal. JOHNSON. 'This is sad stuff, Sir. To the contract of marriage, besides the man and wife, there is a third party – society; and, if it be considered as a vow – GOD; and therefore it cannot be dissolved by their own consent alone. Laws are not made for particular cases, but for mankind in general. A woman may be unhappy with her husband, but she cannot be freed from him without the approbation of the civil and ecclesiastical power. A man may be unhappy because he is not so rich as another, but he is not to seize upon another's property at his own hand.'

THURSDAY 11 APRIL. Last day when I dined at Beauclerk's, Langton said to me, 'Shall we petition to have the young gentleman brought in?' (I am now writing on Saturday the 27 at Bath.) He meant Beauclerk's son, a child about two year old. Thinking this affectation in Langton, willing to check him and to indulge the spirit of contradiction, especially as I had heard Beauclerk satirize Langton's affectation of this sort and his plaguing people with his own children, I answered, 'I'll petition for no such thing. I don't like other people's children. I think it is pretty well if a man can bear his own.' Here I affected more roughness than I always possess, though in general it is certainly true that I do not like to have young children brought in, as I am disgusted with them, and dislike being in a manner forced to pay foolish compliments to their parents. Dr Johnson said last night at Thrale's that I was right. He maintained too that there were many people who had no concern about their children, who, from being engaged in business, or from their course of life in whatever way, seldom saw their children. 'I', said he, 'should not have had much fondness for a child of my own.' 'Nay,' said Mrs Thrale. 'At least,' said he, 'I never wished to have a child.'

He spoke last night of the *Spectator*; said that it was wonderful that there was such a proportion of bad papers in the half of the work which was not written by Addison. 'For', said he, 'there was all the world to write that half; yet not a half of that half is good.' He praised very highly, as one of the finest pieces in English, the paper on novelty.

'Yet', said he, 'one does not hear it talked of.' He said it was written by Grove, a dissenting *teacher*. He would not, I observed to myself, call him a *clergyman*; but he was candid enough to allow very great merit to his composition. Murphy said he remembered when there were several people alive in London who enjoyed a respectable reputation merely upon having written a paper in the *Spectator*. He remembered particularly Mr Ince, who used to come to Tom's Coffee-house. 'But', said the Doctor, 'you must consider how highly Steele speaks of Mr Ince.' Murphy said he did not know till lately that Lord Hardwicke had written the paper 'Philip Homebred'. Dr Johnson said it had no merit, it was quite vulgar, had nothing luminous.

On the road from Ashburnham[20] he said that it was commonly a weak man who married for love, and that it was a mistake to think that a woman (writing Sunday 28 April at Bath) who brings no fortune will be a better economist than one who does. 'No, Sir,' said he, 'such women are not used to the handling of money. It is new to them, and they take great delight in spending.'

He said that in France they had not the tavern life which is so agreeable in this country, where people meet all upon a footing, without any care or anxiety; for there is always some uneasy restraint when there is an entertainer and people entertained. The entertainer is anxious lest his guests should not be pleased; the guests are obliged to pay particular attention to *him*. There is a rivalship, too, in entertaining, which produces care. I have not his exact words, but his meaning.

I said at Lichfield that it was strange how well Scotsmen were known to one another, though born in very distant counties; that you do not find the gentlemen of two or three neighbouring counties in England known to one another. Dr Johnson at once explained this. 'Why,' said he (I am now writing Tuesday 30 April at Bath), 'You have Edinburgh, where the people from all your counties meet, and which is not so large but that they are all known. There is no such common place of collection in England except London, where from its great size and diffusion but a few can be known to each other.'

SATURDAY 13 APRIL. I had fixed a meeting with Dr Johnson this evening at the Crown and Anchor. He went home with Mrs Williams. I stayed and wrote a letter to my wife, and then went to the Crown and Anchor; found Nairne and in a little came Sir Joshua Reynolds, whom I had visited in the forenoon, and engaged to be with us. He gave me the genuine story of Johnson and Mudge. Mudge was a young lad about sixteen, grandson to the Mudge of whom Johnson has given a high character; he was waiting at Sir Joshua's before breakfast, eager to meet Dr Johnson, and he observed that he thought the Doctor had drawn his own character in — in *The Rambler*. When Dr Johnson came, Sir Joshua, who thought this a very pretty observation for a young man, repeated it to Dr Johnson, who answered, 'Does Mudge say so? Then Mudge lies.' I observed it could not possibly be a *lie*. Sir Joshua agreed that was clear; he besides was of opinion that the character was really Johnson's own. He said Johnson was like his macaw: very good humoured at times, but all at once without any reason that you can see, would grow angry and — you.

He said that he was once with him in Devonshire. The company, and Sir Joshua among the rest, had been out a-hunting; so at dinner Dr Johnson was left out of the conversation. Sir Joshua with a polite desire to bring him into it said, just by way of saying what occurred first, 'Well, Sir, I have been galloping over fields and jumping hedges and ditches today, and that is one thing I can do better than you.' Johnson angrily answered, 'Sir, when I have as mean a mind as you, I shall be vain of such things.' Sir Joshua said, 'It was a humbling thing that Johnson might say such things without people taking notice of them.'

Sir William Forbes and Langton came, and Dr Johnson arrived at last. There was an admirable dispute whether drinking improved conversation and benevolence. Sir Joshua maintained it did. 'No, Sir,' said Dr Johnson. 'Before dinner men meet with great inequality of understanding, and those who are conscious of their inferiority have the modesty not to talk. When they have drank wine, every man feels himself happy and loses that modesty, and grows impudent and vociferous. But he is not improved. He is only not sensible of his defects.' Sir Joshua said that the Doctor was talking of the effects of excess in wine, but that a moderate glass enlivened the mind by giving a proper circulation to the blood. 'I am', said he, 'in very good spirits when I get up in the morning. By dinner-time I am exhausted. Wine puts me in the same state as when I got up, and I am sure that moderate drinking makes people talk better.' 'No, Sir,' said Johnson, 'wine gives not light, gay, ideal hilarity, but tumultuous, noisy, clamorous merriment. I have heard none of those drunken –

nay, drunken is a coarse word – none of those *vinous* flights.' Sir Joshua said, 'Because you have sat by quite sober, and felt an envy of the happiness of those who were drinking.' 'Perhaps,' said Johnson, 'a contempt. And it is not necessary to be drunk one's self to relish the wit of drunkenness. Do we not judge of the drunken wit of Iago and Cassio, the most excellent in its kind, when we are quite sober? Wit is wit, by whatever means it is produced; and if good, will appear so at all times.' He admitted that the spirits are raised by drinking by the common participation of pleasure, but that cock-fighting or bear-baiting will raise the spirits of a company as drinking does, though surely they will not improve conversation. He also admitted that there were some sluggish men who were improved by drinking, as there are fruits which are not good till they are rotten. 'There are such men,' said he, 'but they are medlars.' But he candidly allowed that there might be a very few improved by drinking; but he maintained that he was right as to drinking in general and he observed that there is nothing which is not true of some man. Sir William Forbes said, 'Might not a man be like a bottle of beer which is improved by being set before the fire?' 'Nay,' said Johnson contemptuously, 'I cannot answer that. That is too much for me.' Worthy Sir William luckily did not mind this. Langton acquiesced in Dr Johnson's doctrine. Nairne either durst not speak or had nothing to say.

I said I knew wine did me harm; it inflamed me; did not improve my mind, but confused and irritated it; but that the experience of mankind had declared in favour of moderate drinking. Johnson said, 'I do not say it is wrong to produce this self-complacency by drinking. I only deny that it improves the mind. I scorned to take wine when I had company. I have drank many a bottle by myself; in the first place, because I had need of it to raise my spirits; in the second place, because I would have nobody to witness its effects upon me.'

THURSDAY 18 APRIL. Breakfasted Lord Eglinton's. General Paoli and I dined at the Mitre with Sir John Pringle and some more members of the Royal Society. I placed myself next to Captain Cook, and had a great deal of conversation with him; but I need not mark it, as his book will tell it all. Only I must observe that he candidly confessed to me that he and his companions who visited the South Sea Islands could not be certain of any information they got, or supposed they got, except as to objects falling under the observation of the senses; their knowledge of the language was so imperfect they required the aid of their senses, and anything which they learnt about religion, government or traditions might be quite erroneous. He gave me a distinct account of a New Zealander eating human flesh in his presence and in that of many more aboard, so that the fact of cannibals is now certainly known. We talked of having some men of enquiry left for three years at each of the islands of Otaheite, New Zealand and Nova Caledonia, so as to learn the language and (I am now writing on Wednesday the 22 of May at Edinburgh) bring home a full account of all that can be known of people in a state so different from ours. I felt a stirring in my mind to go upon such an undertaking, if encouraged by Government by having a handsome pension for life. We drank coffee at Brown's Coffee-house, and I felt myself as much at home and in as much tranquillity in London as I could wish to be.

I then went to the Royal Society and heard two pieces read. After Sir John Pringle had come down from the chair, I mentioned to him my inclination to go with Captain Cook. 'Take care,' said he, 'your old spirit' (or some such word) 'is reviving.' I should have mentioned that at the Mitre, as the company was rising from table, and Sir John making an apology for our not having had a very good dinner, I made a tolerable pun. 'I have had a feast,' said I (pointing to the Captain); 'I have had a good dinner, for I have had a good *Cook*.' I had some conversation with Dr Solander at dinner, and with Mr Banks at the Society.[21] The General, who I found was now a Fellow of the Royal Society, carried me in his coach, first home, where I wrote to my wife, and then he and I and Signor Gentili went to a rout at Mrs Bosville's, where I was completely easy. We stayed a very short while, and then went to a Subscription City Ball at Haberdashers' Hall, to which the General had tickets for himself and his two friends. There was a goodly company of city ladies and gentlemen, who seemed to be very courteous and cheerful. (I am now writing May 25 at Edinburgh.)

I met here with the Chief of the Mohawks, Theandenaigen,[22] grandson of him who visited England in Queen Anne's reign. (I am now writing on Thursday 30 May at Auchinleck, where I am calmly refreshing myself in the country, and where it is curious to recall the variety of ideas during my late travels by recording them.) I was told that an officer whom I saw here had conducted the Chief to England. I began a conversation with him, and found him very affable. He told me his name was Tice. And he did what should always be done when a name is mentioned for the first time: he spelt it – T i c e. The ear never almost catches a new name exactly, so it should be assisted by spelling. He was of English extraction, but had never been in Britain before. He had served in the last war, and during the present troubles in America had been at Fort St John with my cousin, Major Charles Preston, having with him this Mohawk Chief and a good many Indians. But he had left it in September. He spoke with high esteem of Preston, and I am not sure whether it was before or after knowing my connection with him that, upon my proposing to pay him a visit, he said he would be glad to see me any morning to drink tea with the Chief and him at the Swan with Two Necks in Lad Lane. They had put up at that inn on their arrival in London, and the Chief thought the people so civil that he would not leave the house to go into lodgings. I talked a little with the Chief tonight. He spoke English quite well. But I shall not put down any particulars concerning him here, as I am to draw up some account of him for the *London Magazine*. Came home with General Paoli in good time.

Soon after this, Boswell's journal of his London stay lapsed – perhaps he was too busy with social occasions to write it up properly – and to round off this typical account of one of his regular 'London jaunts' we here reprint, from the manuscript of the Life of Johnson, *the famous account of Johnson and his 'enemy', Wilkes, dining together, on 15 May 1776.*

Upon the much-expected Wednesday, I called on him about half an hour before dinner, as I often did when we were to dine out together, to see that he was ready in time and to accompany him. I found him battling with his books, as upon a former occasion, covered with dust and making no preparation for going abroad. 'How is this, Sir?' said I. 'Don't you recollect that you are to dine at Mr Dilly's?' JOHNSON. 'Sir, I did not think of going to Dilly's. It went out of my head. I have ordered dinner at home.' BOSWELL. 'But my dear Sir, you know you were engaged to Mr Dilly, and I told him so. He will expect you and will be much disappointed if you don't come.' JOHNSON. 'You must talk to Mrs Williams.'

Here was a sad dilemma. I feared that what I was so confident I had secured would yet be frustrated. He stood in some degree of awe of Mrs Williams and if she should be obstinate he would not stir. I ran downstairs to the blind lady's room and told her I was in great uneasiness, for Dr Johnson had engaged to me to dine this day at Mr Dilly's, but that he told me he had forgotten his engagement and had ordered dinner at home. 'Yes, Sir,' said she pretty peevishly, 'Dr Johnson is to dine at home.' 'Madam,' said I, 'his respect for you is such that I know he will not leave you unless you absolutely desire it. But as you have his company so often, I hope you will be good enough to forego it for a day, as Mr Dilly is a very worthy man, has often had agreeable parties at his house for Dr Johnson, and will be vexed if the Doctor neglects him today. And then, Madam, be pleased to consider my situation. I carried the message, and I assured Mr Dilly that Dr Johnson was to come; and, to be sure, he has made a dinner and invited a company and boasted of the honour he was assured he was to have. I shall be quite affronted if he does not go.'

She gradually softened to my entreaties, which were certainly as earnest as most entreaties to ladies upon any occasion, and was graciously pleased to empower me to tell Dr Johnson that, 'All things considered, she thought he should certainly go.' I flew back to him, still in dust and careless of what should be the event, indifferent in his choice – Dilly's or home – and the moment I had announced to him Mrs Williams's consent, he roared: 'Frank, a clean shirt,' and was very quickly dressed. When I had him fairly in the hackney-coach with me, I exulted as much as a fortune hunter who has an heiress in the post-chaise with him.

When we entered Mr Dilly's dining-room, he found himself in the midst of a company whom he did not know. I kept myself snug and silent, watching how he would conduct himself. I observed him whispering to Mr Dilly, 'Who is that gentleman, Sir?' 'Mr Arthur Lee.' 'Tut, tut, tut' (which was one of his habitual mutterings). Mr Arthur Lee was not only a Patriot, but an American and afterwards Minister from the United States at the Court of Madrid. 'And who is the gentleman in lace?' 'Mr Wilkes, Sir.' This information confounded him still more. He had some difficulty to restrain himself, and, taking up a book, sat down at a window and read, or at least kept his eyes upon it intensely for some time till he composed himself. His situation, I dare say, was awkward enough. But he no doubt recollected his having rated me for supposing that he could be at all disconcerted by any company, and he therefore tuned himself up to appear quite as an easy man of the world, who can adapt himself at once to the manners of those whom he may chance to meet.

The cheering sound of dinner being upon the table dissolved his reverie, and we all sat down in good humour. There were present besides Mr Wilkes and Mr Arthur Lee, who was an old companion of mine when he studied at Edinburgh, Mr (now Sir John) Miller, Dr Lettsom, the Quaker physician, and Mr Slater, the druggist. Mr Wilkes placed himself next to Dr Johnson, and behaved to him with so much attention and politeness that he gained upon him insensibly. No man eat more heartily than Johnson, or loved better what was nice and tasty. Mr Wilkes was at great pains in helping him with some fine veal. 'Pray give me leave, Sir – It is better here – A little of the brown – Some fat, Sir – A bit of the stuffing – Some gravy – Let me have the pleasure of giving you some butter – Allow me to recommend a squeeze of an orange – or the lemon perhaps may have more zest.' 'Sir, Sir, I am obliged to you, Sir,' cried Johnson, bowing and turning his head to him with a look for some time of 'surly virtue', but in a short time of complacency.

Foote being mentioned, Johnson said, 'He is not a good mimic.'[23] One of the company added, 'A merry andrew, a buffoon.' JOHNSON. 'Why yes, but he has wit too, and is not deficient in ideas or in fertility and variety of imagery, and not empty of reading; he has knowledge enough to fill up his part. One species of wit he has in an eminent degree: that of escape. You drive him into a corner with both hands; but he's gone, Sir, when you think you have got him – like an animal that jumps over your head. Then he has a great range for his wit. He never lets truth stand between him and a jest. And he is sometimes mighty coarse. The first time I was in company with Foote was at Fitzherbert's. Having no good opinion of the fellow, I was resolved against being entertained by him, and went on eating my dinner pretty sullenly, affecting not to mind him. But the dog was so very diverting that I was obliged to lay down my knife and fork, throw myself back upon my chair, and fairly laugh it out. No, Sir, he was irresistible. He upon one occasion had an extraordinary proof of the power of his talents. Amongst the many and various ways which he tried of getting money, he became a partner with a small-beer brewer, and he was to have a share of the profits for procuring customers amongst his numerous acquaintance. Fitzherbert was one who took his small beer; but it was so bad that the servants resolved not to drink it. They were at some loss how to notify their resolution, being afraid of offending their master, who they knew liked Foote much as a companion. At last they pitched upon a little black boy, who was rather a favourite, to be their deputy and deliver their remonstrance, and, having invested him with the whole authority of the kitchen, he was to speak to Fitzherbert in all their names upon a certain day that they would drink Foote's small beer no longer. On that day Foote happened to dine at Fitzherbert's, and this boy served at table. He was so delighted with Foote's stories and merriment and grimace that when he went downstairs, he told them, "This is the finest man I have ever seen. I will not deliver your message. I will drink his small beer."'

Somebody observed that Garrick could not have done this. WILKES. 'Garrick would have made the small beer still smaller. He is now leaving the stage, but he will play *Scrub*²⁴ all his life.' I knew that Johnson would let nobody attack Garrick but himself, as Garrick once said to me, and I had heard him praise his liberality, so to bring out his commendation of his celebrated pupil, I said loud: 'I have heard Garrick is liberal.' JOHNSON. 'Yes, Sir. I know that Garrick has given away more money than any man in England I know, and that not from ostentatious views. Garrick was very poor when he began life; so when he came to have money, he probably was very unskilful in giving away, and saved when he should not. But Garrick began to be liberal as soon as he could, and I am of opinion the reputation of avarice, which he has had, has been very lucky for him and prevented his having many enemies. You despise a man for avarice, but you don't hate him. Garrick might have been much better attacked for living with more splendour than is suitable to a player. If they had had the wit to have attacked him in that quarter they might have galled him more. But they have kept clamouring about his avarice, which has rescued him from much obloquy and much envy.

'When I was a young fellow I wanted to write the life of Dryden, and in order to get materials I applied to the only two persons then alive who had seen him. These were old Swinny and old Cibber. Swinny's information was no more than this, that at Will's Coffee-house Dryden had a particular chair for himself which was set by the fire in winter, and was then called his winter chair, and that it was carried out for him to the balcony in summer, and was then called his summer chair. Cibber could tell no more but that he remembered him a decent old man, arbiter of critical disputes at Will's. You are to consider that Cibber was then at a great distance from Dryden, had perhaps one leg only in the room and durst not draw in the other.' BOSWELL. 'Yet Cibber was a man of observation.' JOHNSON. 'I think not.' BOSWELL. 'You will allow his *Apology* to be well done.' JOHNSON. 'Very well done, to be sure, Sir. That book is a striking proof of the justice of Pope's remark,

> Each might his several province well command
> Would all but stoop to what they understand.'

BOSWELL. 'And his plays are good.' JOHNSON. 'Yes. But that was his trade, *l'esprit du corps*. He had lived always among players and play writers. I wondered that he had so little to say in conversation, for he had kept the best company and learnt all that can be got by the ear. He abused Pindar to me, and then showed me an ode of his own with this couplet,

> Perched on the eagle's soaring wing
> The lowly linnet loves to sing.

I told him that when the ancients made a simile, they always made it like something real.'

Mr Arthur Lee mentioned some Scotch who had taken possession of a barren part of America, and wondered why they should choose this. JOHNSON. 'Why, Sir, all barrenness is comparative. The *Scotch* would not know it to be barren.' BOSWELL. 'Come, come. He is pleasing the English. You have now been in Scotland, Sir, and say if you did not see meat and drink enough there.' JOHNSON. 'Why, meat and drink enough to give the inhabitants strength sufficient to run away from home.' All these quick and lively sallies were said quite sportively, quite in jest, and with a smile which showed that he meant only wit. Upon this topic he and Mr Wilkes could perfectly assimilate. Here was a bond of union between them, and I was conscious that as both had visited Caledonia, both were fully satisfied of the strange narrow ignorance of those who imagine that it is a land of famine. But they amused themselves with persevering in the old jokes. When I claimed a superiority in Scotland over England in one respect, that no man can be arrested there for a debt merely because another swears it against him; but there must first be the judgement of a court of law ascertaining its justice; and that summary arrestment of the person can take place only if his creditor should swear that he is about to fly from the country, or, as it is technically expressed, is *in meditatione fugae.* WILKES. 'That, I should think, may be safely sworn of all the Scotch nation.' JOHNSON (to Mr Wilkes). 'You must know, Sir, I lately took my friend Boswell to see genuine civilized life in an English provincial town. I turned him loose at Lichfield, my native city, that he might for once see real civility. For you know he lives among savages at home, and among rakes in London.' WILKES. 'Except when he is with grave, sober, decent people like you and me.' JOHNSON. 'And we ashamed of him.' WILKES. 'Boswell, you have kept a great deal of bad company.'

After dinner and at tea we had an accession of Mrs Knowles, the amiable accomplished Quaker, and of Mr Alderman Lee. Amidst some patriotic groans, somebody (I think the Alderman) said, 'Poor old England is lost.' JOHNSON. 'It is not so much to be lamented that old England is lost, as that the Scotch have found it.'

Mr Wilkes held a candle to show a fine print of a beautiful female figure which hung in the room, and pointed out the elegant contour of the bosom with the hand of a master. He afterwards waggishly insisted with me that all the time Johnson showed visible signs of a fervent admiration of the corresponding charms of the fair Quaker.

This imperfect record will serve to give a notion of this very curious interview, which was not only pleasing at the time, but had the agreeable and benignant effect of reconciling any differences and sweetening any acidity, which, in the various bustle of political contest, had been produced in the minds of two men, who, though widely different, had so many things in common – classical learning, political knowledge, modern literature, wit and humour and ready repartee – that it would have been much to be regretted if they had been forever at a distance from each other.

I attended Dr Johnson home, and had the satisfaction to hear him tell Mrs Williams how much he had been pleased with Mr Wilkes's company, and what an agreeable day he had passed.

Finally, we include from this year Boswell's unpublished account, originally written for his wife, of his first meeting with Margaret Caroline Rudd whom he had been trying to get to see for some time. For an introduction to this then notorious woman, we direct the reader first to her entry in our Who's Who (p. 393).

London, between 12 and 1 in
the morning of 23 April 1776

My dearest life,

Before I go to bed, and while the impressions of the extraordinary scene which I am going to mention are fresh and lively, I sit down to write to you. Many a time you heard me rave with a strange force of imagination about the celebrated Mrs Rudd – Margaret Caroline Rudd – and how I should certainly see her while I was in London. My curiosity did not go off, and I resolved to gratify it. I heard where she had taken lodgings in Westminster, and this forenoon I went and knocked at the door. A woman came. 'Does Mrs Rudd lodge here?' 'Yes, Sir.' 'Is she at home?' 'I'll call her maid.' The maid came and said she was not at home but would be at home in the evening, or I might find her any morning. Would I please leave my name? I said it was unnecessary to leave my name, but she would be so good as tell her mistress that a friend of Mr Macqueen's from Scotland had called and would call again. A quarter after nine in the evening I called again at her lodgings, No. 10 Queen Street. The maid said, 'She is just gone out, Sir, but will be home in half an hour. You will oblige me if you will walk up stairs. I told her that you called.' My answer was that I would call again in half an hour. I sauntered calmly to Westminster Bridge, and did not return till about ten. Still she was not come home, but I agreed to walk up stairs. I had a sort of palpitation at my heart when I knocked at the door. I was shown into a dining-room, decent enough, but how poor in comparison of her former magnificence! A couple of tallow candles gave me light. My fancy began to form fearful suppositions in this solitary situation. I thought the ghosts of the Perreaus might appear. I thought that there might be murderers or bullies in the house. But then the street was too public for that. Her books were a Court Calendar, Duncan's *Logic*, Watts' *Logic*, *Johnsoniana*, two copies of her *Genuine Letter to Lord Weymouth* and a defence of her around it, a letter to her from

Mrs Christian Hart, Pope's *Essay on Man* and his *Essay on Criticism* bound together, and *The Small Talker*, a very good novel against the practice of some men in gaining the affections of young ladies only for conquest, as they soon neglect them. I sat half an hour reading in the two last books.

Then I heard her coming up stairs. I was all impatience and trepidation, when there entered rather a little woman, delicately made, not at all a beauty, but with a very pleasing appearance and much younger than I imagined. In short, the first view of her surprised me somewhat, as it was not by any means such as to strike me with the awe either of dignity or of high elegance. She was dressed in black clothes, with a white cloak and hat. I begged pardon for intruding upon her, but I was a friend of Mr Macqueen's, and though I had no direct instructions from that family, she might believe that they would be glad to have accounts of her. She said she was much obliged to me for my civility. We sat down opposite to one another at a little distance, and I asked her how she was now. She said, 'As well as could be expected,' and immediately entered upon her unhappy story, which she told (I went to bed when I had written to the foot of the last page; I now continue my narrative, 24 April, between nine and ten in the morning) with wonderful ease and delicacy and an air of innocence quite amazing when one thought of what had been proved. She said the *Perr*eau family (as she called it) was a little commonwealth, it was so numerous and so spread over England and Ireland, and that all the connections endeavoured to throw the guilt upon *her*. I said it was shocking that the Perreaus had died denying as they did. 'Yes,' said she, 'it must shock everybody who has any tenderness of conscience. They should have died in silence.' She said she was to carry on a suit against Sir Thomas Frankland by which, if she got the full value of what he carried off belonging to her, she would recover £5,000 besides high damages.

She spoke with much earnestness of her anxiety to know whether her husband, Mr Rudd, was alive or not, and said she would go to Ireland to see if a man whom some would have to be he, and others an impostor, was he or not, though she thought that his long neglect of her set her free from him. But she would not think of marrying again after having been twice so unlucky; and indeed, unless it was a man of rank and fortune that could bear her up notwithstanding what

had happened to her, she should not think of marriage. She said she
loved reading, and that if she had not had resources in her own mind,
she must have been very unhappy. She said her confinement was very
severe upon her. She had formerly been consumptive two years. She
was almost blind when she came out again to the light, and her eyes,
I saw, were still weak. When I looked at her narrowly she seemed
to have some flushy heat on her cheeks, her nose contracted as she
breathed, and she spoke through her teeth. Yet there was upon the
whole – 'Celia altogether' – something so pleasing and insinuating
that I could believe her power to be what we have read. I said she
was reckoned quite a sorceress, possessed of enchantment. She smiled
and did not contradict me as to the past, but said she could enchant
nobody. I begged her pardon and, with exquisite flattery, said, 'My
dear Mrs Rudd, don't talk so. Everything you have said to me till
now has been truth and candour'; and I told her I was convinced she
could enchant, but I begged she would not enchant me too much,
not change me into any other creature, but allow me to continue
to be a man with some degree of reason. I was as cautious as if
I had been opposite to that snake which fascinates with its eyes.
Her language was choice and fluent and her voice melodious. The
peculiar characteristic of her enchantment seemed to be its delicate
imperceptible power. She perfectly concealed her design to charm.
There was no meretricious air, no direct attempt upon the heart. It
was like hearing the music of the spheres which poets feign, and which
produces its effect without the intervention of any instrument, so that
the very soul of harmony immediately affects our souls. She said she
had formerly deluded herself with hopes of enjoying happiness. She
now was satisfied with insensibility, not however in the extreme, but
comparatively speaking. 'You must not be insensible,' said I, and rose
and seized her silken hand, and afterwards, upon the argument being
renewed a little, kissed it. This was all experiment, and she showed
neither prudery nor effrontery, but the complaisance, or compliance
if you please, of a woman of fashion.

   She asked if Miss Macqueen was married; said she promised to be
a fine woman; said she liked Scotland and would perhaps visit it again,
and would go to the house of Mr Stewart of Physgill, to which she had
many invitations. She spoke of our New Town with commendation.
She said she had seen Mr Macqueen only once at his own house.

She seemed much displeased with Lord Galloway; said he was the most insincere man that could be, but very successful in making his way at a court. I said he was good-humoured and lively. She said that was partly natural, but a good deal mechanical. This was a very just remark and showed her knowledge of human nature. We talked then on forming a character by habit, and she said we might be anything we pleased. This is Dr Johnson's opinion. She said Lady Gower was a worthy, friendly woman and very sincere, which was not a little remarkable, as she had been so long a Court lady and excelled so much in that way; 'which', says she, 'is every morning having a plan – a part to play – for the day. Lady Gower', said she, 'is a good relation in every respect: a good wife, a good mother, and behaves exceedingly well to all Lord Gower's connections.' She praised Keith Stewart too, as sincere and friendly. I said nothing. She talked of Lady Galloway's building a house on her jointure lands, and never was at a loss for chit-chat.

I sometimes kept silence on purpose to observe how she would renew the conversation. She never let the pause be long, but with admirable politeness, when she found that I did not begin again to speak and might perhaps be embarrassed, said something quite easily, so as not to have the appearance of abruptness, to make me feel that I had stopped short, but rather of a continuation of our discourse, as if what she then said had grown out of what we had talked of before. Another thing which I remarked was that she did not aim at being witty. She did not dazzle with brilliance, but cheered one with a mild light. And what I thought also an uncommon excellence, she did not whine about her distress or affect to be plaintive, for she was sensible that the representation of unhappiness gives a certain degree of pain, and though pity is said to be akin to love, gaiety is a much more engaging relation. Seeing her eyes weak, I set the candles upon a table at some distance from her, but as she was then in such obscurity that I could hardly discern the pretty turns of her countenance as she talked, I soon brought back one of them to a table near her, saying that I must not deny myself altogether the pleasure of seeing her.

She said that during her confinement she was quite alone all the night. She would not have a maid in the same room with her, 'because', said she, 'there were hours when I did not wish to be at all disturbed, as I employed them in thought; and I hope I shall be the better for it.

I hope I am wiser.' When she talked of insensibility, I said she might as well be a nun. She said if it were not for her children she would retire to a convent. She liked France, but she would not be a nun. She would not shut herself up for life. She said people made many stories concerning her. It was said she lived with Lord Lyttelton. 'But,' said she, 'though one who has been a good deal at public places knows most people of distinction by sight, I really do not know Lord Lyttelton by sight, and he has contradicted the report. Besides, Lord Lyttelton is not a person with whom one would form a connection, as he is quite a profligate.' 'Nay, Madam,' said I, 'I heard today that you and Lord Loudoun were very well acquainted.' 'To be sure,' said she, 'if Lord Loudoun were to come into this room, I should know him; but as to any intimacy—' 'It is amazing', said I, 'with what confidence people will tell lies, but there is a vanity in being thought to know particularly about a lady so celebrated as you.' Said she: 'People are apt to form an idea of one whom they have never seen. A gentleman told me he had imagined that I was old and ugly.' 'Why,' said I, 'that was very extraordinary, though indeed it may have been owing to the reputation of your enchantment, as witches were said to be old and ugly. You are, however, much *younger* than I supposed.' 'But', said she, 'I am not a young woman. I am nine-and-twenty, and I do not think that young.'

She mentioned Cummyng, the herald-painter and Keeper of the Lyon Records, and said he and Sir John Dalrymple went to Scotland a month ago, but had business to transact for Government somewhere upon the road. Such absurd airs of consequence had been assumed, and I was silent upon that head. I spoke of her pedigree. She said, 'They would not allow me to be a gentlewoman and said my pedigree was forged – as if one would forge a pedigree when certainly one cannot raise money upon it.' The easy, unconcerned pleasantry with which she talked of forgery was wonderful.

While she again said something about her confinement and trial, she showed a pretty little foot, and I got up in a kind of lively sudden surprise and said, 'I cannot believe that you have gone through all this. Are you really Mrs Rudd?' She smiled and said, 'I *am* Mrs Rudd.' I said she must forget all the ill that had passed and be happy for the future, and I thought love would be the best remedy for her. She said very gently she did not think so. I run out in the commonplace style upon the happiness of love, but said she must now be very cautious in her choice. I said I hoped she would forgive the liberty I had taken in waiting upon her. I thought I might avail myself of being a friend of Mr Macqueen's, while I had a desire very natural to see a lady so distinguished for enchantment, and I should be much obliged to her if she would give me leave to call on her sometimes. She made me very welcome and said she was always at home. I returned her a thousand thanks.

During all this interview I was quite calm and possessed myself fully, snuffed the candles and stirred the fire as one does who is at home, sat easy upon my chair, and felt no confusion when her eyes and mine met. Indeed her eyes did not flash defiance but attracted with sweetness, and *there* was the reason of the difference of effect between her eyes and those of more insolent or less experienced charmers. She was not a robber but a thief. I wished her good night with a kiss which she received without affectation of any kind. I was *then* a little confused. Churchill satirizes Lord Lyttelton for being *curious in grief* in his *Monody* on the death of his first lady. I was here actually *curious in kissing.* I thought of Mrs Rudd's fame for enchantment and all her history. I concluded from every *circumstance* that she was now upon the town, though her conversation was so superior to that of common women. But I might be mistaken, for I never hinted at an intrigue. I wondered what she thought of me. I imagined I was very agreeable, and it pleased me much that she never asked my name or anything at all about me, which showed perfect good breeding. I would not for a good deal have missed this scene. We crowd to see those who excel in any art, and surely the highest excellence of art is the art of pleasing, the art of attracting admiration and fondness.

The story now leaps ahead, to 28 March 1781, to give us a glimpse of Boswell at The (Literary) Club. Among those present were Edmund Burke, Joseph Banks and the historian Edward Gibbon.

At our club on Tuesday Sir Joseph Banks, whom we call our Chancellor of the Exchequer, opened the budget; that is to say, he is our treasurer and gave us a state of our affairs. We buy our own wine and pay the master (or rather mistress, the man being dead) 1/6 for each bottle of claret we drink, and 1/- for each bottle of port. Taxes are levied annually for this wine. We had all the matter done today in parliamentary form. We had two guineas apiece to pay for the current year. But there was a question as to arrears. The first defaulter was Charles Fox: unanimously ordered that he should pay. Then *I* was read out. Upon which Mr Burke, who sat next me, said, 'By all means let him pay. If we can get anything out of Scotland, let us have it. We get a little land tax' (he had said before). 'But by the Customs and Excise we some years literally don't get a shilling. Besides,' said he, 'the Scotch were so violent for taxing their brethren in America that they should certainly be taxed themselves. The Club will consider of this. For I know no other reason why Mr Boswell should pay for last year when he was not in London.' It carried that I should not pay, because I held no place under Government, which Dunning, upon my telling him what had passed, said was the case with very few of my countrymen. Then Lord Charlemont was read out. 'Ah,' said Burke, 'the Irish *won't let* you tax them.' My Lord, who is one of the Volunteer officers, said he had come in his regimentals on purpose to defend himself. He was excused. So was the Dean of Ferns, being Irish. So was the Bishop of Killaloe, for he had formerly (when Dean of Derry) sent The Club a hogshead of claret to make up for his deficiency. It was hinted that the Dean of Ferns should do the same; and it was observed that the way to get a bishopric was to send a hogshead of claret to our club. Dr Johnson was excused because of his not drinking wine; and my account of his swallowing it greedily was considered by Burke as representing him rather under a kind of disease, a *rage*, as the French say; and that till he could drink as an honest fellow he was not to be reckoned among the taxed. Sir Robert Chambers was going to be excused. 'What!' said Burke, 'a man who is in the very centre of wealth, and absent to get money? No.' It was agreed he should be taxed. Somebody suggested that he might commute his arrears by sending a hogshead of wine. I moved that it should be a hogshead of Madeira that had been in the East Indies; and it being ordered that this should be intimated to him, it was afterwards suggested that a hogshead was not a Madeira measure, but a pipe. I moved that the word 'hogshead' be erased and instead thereof be inserted the word 'pipe'. Dr Adam Smith came last; and Burke and I were clear that a Commissioner of the Customs, who holds a lucrative place and was absent only because he is a tax-gatherer, should be taxed; which was ordered. Dr Johnson did not relish a repetition from me of this pleasantry. He said, 'I am glad I was not there.' Yet it was very well, I thought. Gibbon alone stickled for Smith, because he is a brother infidel. He is a disagreeable dog, this Gibbon. Mrs Thrale said, 'He squeaks like Punch. I imagine he'll squeak indeed before he dies, as he had a religious education.'[25] 'Yes,' said I ludicrously, 'he is an infidel puppet: *le marionet infidel.*'

There was not a bad *jeu d'esprit* of mine at The Club. Before dinner Banks called me 'Mr Crosbie'. Said I: 'He takes one Scotch lawyer for another. If it had been any other animals, he would have known the difference better.' This was a pleasant allusion to his skill as a naturalist, and took off the awkwardness of the mistake. We talked of Dr Johnson. I said that he could make himself very agreeable to a lady when he chose it. Sir Joshua agreed. Gibbon controverted. Dean Marlay said a lady might be vain when she could turn a wolf-dog into a lap-dog. Steevens told several anecdotes of Dr Johnson. But I will have them in writing from him, that they may be correctly recorded. Steevens has a very full mind and very animated powers of communication. He has the character of being very malignant. He will, it is said, write in the newspapers against people with whom he is living intimately. Said Dr Johnson: 'No, Sir, he is not malignant. He is mischievous. He only means to vex them.' But surely there is evil in this, though the distinction by the Doctor be well put. I said he was a man of good principles but bad practice; for he defends religion, yet he carried off a man's wife. The Doctor said I was right. I was quite happy the evening I spent at Mr Charles Boswell's, whom I had not seen since autumn 1769. His lady was very agreeable. I was glad they were married now. I had warmly recommended it. My spirits were gay and I indulged them; and seeing John Boswell, compared my then gaiety with my dreariness in Scotland. I *must* allow my temper an easy play.

Another leap forward, this time of two years, to April 1783. The following material, which Boswell marked 'Tacenda' ('to be hidden'), begins with Boswell, an acquaintance named Lowe, and Elizabeth Desmoulins – a member of Johnson's household – at the Doctor's home in London.

After dinner, when the Doctor had retired to take a nap, I believe, and Mrs Williams also was gone, Mrs Desmoulins, Lowe and I remained. Said Lowe: 'Now, Ma'am, let us be free. We are all married people.

Pray tell us, do you really think Dr Johnson ever offended in point of chastity? For my own part I do not believe he ever did. I believe he was chaste even with his wife, and that it was quite a Platonic connection' (grinning a smile with his *one* eye to me). MRS DESMOULINS. 'Ah, Sir, you are much mistaken. There never was a man who had stronger amorous inclinations than Dr Johnson. But he conquered them. Poor Logie, who was very intimate with him, knew this, and has talked to me of it. It has been said there was a criminal connection between him and Mrs Williams; and I remember a lady observed that no woman could behave so impudently if she did not know she had this awe over his head.' BOSWELL. 'But why an awe? What need he care?' MRS DESMOULINS. 'Sir, he would not like it. But I do not believe it.' BOSWELL. 'Nor I, indeed. I have heard people joke about it, and talk of Dr Johnson's seraglio, which included you as well as her, Madam. But nobody had a serious belief of anything for a moment.' LOWE. 'I do still think the Doctor never has had any inclination for women.' MRS DESMOULINS. 'But he has.' LOWE. 'I do not believe his marriage was consummated.' BOSWELL. 'Do you know, Ma'am, that there really was a connection between him and his wife? You understand me.' MRS DESMOULINS. 'Yes, yes, Sir. Nay, Garrick knew it was consummated, for he peeped through the keyhole, and behaved like a rascal, for he made the Doctor ridiculous all over the country by describing him running round the bed after she had lain down, and crying, "I'm coming, my Tetsie, I'm coming, my Tetsie! ph! ph!" (blowing in his manner).[26] She was near fifty when the Doctor married her, and he was only two-and-twenty, and I believe she never had any love for him but only to get money from him. They did not sleep together for many years. But that was her fault. She drank shockingly and said she was not well and could not bear a bedfellow. And I remember once when at Hampstead a young woman came on a visit. I lay in the room with Mrs Johnson in a small bed. She said, "It will not hold you both. So if you will promise not to tell Mr Johnson, you shall sleep with me. But if he should know this, he'd say, 'If you can bear a bedfellow, why not me as well as another?' " ' LOWE (waggishly). 'He has been so bad a bedfellow she could not bear him, and this has made her take to drinking. He has had no passion.' MRS DESMOULINS. 'Nay, Sir, I tell you no man had stronger, and nobody had an opportunity to know more about that than I had.' LOWE. 'I am sure, Madam, were I to indulge that passion, I should think you a very agreeable object.'

BOSWELL. 'You'll forgive me, Madam. But from what you have said, I beg leave to ask you if the Doctor ever made any attempt upon you?' MRS DESMOULINS (Lowe and I closing in upon her to listen). 'No, Sir, I have told you he commanded his passion. But when I was a young woman and lived with Mrs Johnson at Hampstead, he used to come out two or three days in a week, and when Dr Bathurst lived there, he'd go and stay with him till two or three in the morning. The maid went to bed, as she could not be kept up, and I used to sit up for him; and I have warmed his bed with a pan of coals and sat with him in his room many an hour in the night and had my head upon his pillow.' BOSWELL. 'What, when he was in bed, Madam?' MRS DESMOULINS. 'Yes, Sir. He'd desire me to go out of the room, and he'd go to bed; but to come back in a little while and talk to him – and I have come and sat on his bedside and laid my head on his pillow.' BOSWELL. 'And he showed strong signs of that passion?' MRS DESMOULINS. 'Yes, Sir. But I always respected him as a father.' BOSWELL. 'What would he do? Come now' (Lowe like to jump out of his skin), 'would he fondle you? Would he kiss you?' MRS DESMOULINS. 'Yes, Sir.' BOSWELL. 'And it was something different from a father's kiss?' MRS DESMOULINS. 'Yes, indeed.' LOWE (approaching his hand to her bosom). 'But would he? eh?' MRS DESMOULINS. 'Sir, he never did anything that was beyond the limits of decency.' LOWE. 'And could you say, Madam, upon your oath, that you were certain he was capable?' MRS DESMOULINS. 'Y-yes, Sir.' BOSWELL. 'But he conquered his violent inclination?' MRS DESMOULINS. 'Yes, Sir. He'd push me from him and cry, "Get you gone." Oh, one can see.' BOSWELL. 'So you saw the struggle and the conquest.' MRS DESMOULINS. 'I did.'

What a curious account. That he should bring himself to the very verge of what he thought a crime. Mr Burke, to whom I afterwards told it, thought there was nothing very curious – just common human nature. But it *was* certainly curious in so eminent a man. She said, 'I have many times considered how I should behave, supposing he should proceed to extremities – and as I told a lady who once put the question to me, I do own that such was my high respect for him, such the awe I felt of him, that I could not have had resolution to have resisted him.' BOSWELL. 'But you never felt any inclination for him as a woman does for a man?' MRS DESMOULINS. 'O no, Sir.' BOSWELL. 'I cannot imagine it of any woman. There is something in his figure so terribly disgusting.' MRS DESMOULINS. 'Yet, Sir, one cannot tell. His mind is such. Now Mrs Thrale has been exceedingly fond of him, and I am convinced now that he is in some way vexed about her. Either she has made a proposal to him which he has thought improper and has declined, or he, presuming on her great fondness, has made a proposal to her, which she has rejected. But I am convinced one or other is the case.' I mentioned the dispute between Sir Joshua Reynolds and me whether the Doctor would yield to the amorous solicitations of the Duchess of Devonshire. Mrs Desmoulins said he would not. He would instantly feel such a contempt and indignation that he would treat her with disdain. 'I believe, Madam,' said I, 'if the contempt and indignation rose at once, as I think it would do, he would spurn her from him. But if he at all hesitated – as the woman who deliberates is lost – it would be the same with him.' 'Yes, Sir,' said she, 'were he to deliberate, I allow he might yield.' She told us how he had spent hundreds of pounds in supporting Betty, her Scotch maid, afterwards with Mrs Williams, an abandoned, diseased creature; and when the workhouse was proposed, said, 'No – her feelings as delicate as yours.' Strange.

Our last year's extract in this chapter comes, again, from the manuscript of the Life. *It is the record of Boswell's last week when he had the company of Samuel Johnson (in June 1784), and his attempts to make Johnson's last months more comfortable.*

For some time I saw him frequently, but have preserved no memorandums till Tuesday 22nd June, when I dined with him at *The Literary Club*. There were present the Bishop of St Asaph, Lord Eliot, Lord Palmerston, Dr Fordyce and Mr Malone. He looked ill but had such a manly fortitude that he did not trouble the company with melancholy complaints. They all showed evident marks of kind concern about him with which he was much pleased, and he exerted himself to be as entertaining as his indisposition allowed him breath to be. Here I must again regret my neglect in recording.

The anxiety of his friends for preserving so valuable a life as long as human means might be supposed to have influence made them plan for him a retreat from the severity of a British winter to the mild climate of Italy. This scheme was at last brought to a very serious resolution at General Paoli's, where some of us had often talked of it. It was considered that he would be exceedingly helpless and dull were he to go alone, and therefore it was concerted that he should be accompanied by Mr Sastres the Italian master, who we were persuaded would wait on him with a very affectionate attention, and who very readily agreed to go. One essential matter however we understood was necessary to be previously settled, which was obtaining from the King such an addition to Johnson's pension as would be sufficient to put him in a situation to defray the expense in a manner becoming the first literary character of a great nation and, independent of all his other merits, the author of the *Dictionary of the English Language*. The person to whom I above all others thought I should apply to negotiate this business was Lord Thurlow, Lord High Chancellor of Great Britain, but I first consulted with Sir Joshua Reynolds, who perfectly agreed with me. I therefore, though personally very little known to his Lordship, wrote to him.

Here then was a ticket in the lottery of royal favour which I put into the wheel for him; and while the effect of it was to be progressively discovered I continued to see him without any difference in my behaviour, but exactly as if nothing of the sort had been done.

On Wednesday 23rd June, I visited him in the forenoon, after having witnessed the shocking sight of fifteen men executed before Newgate. I said to him that I was sure that human life was not machinery, that is to say, a chain of fatality planned and directed by the Supreme Being, as it had in it so much wickedness and misery, such instances of both as that by which my mind was now clouded. Were it machinery, it would be better than it is in these respects, though less noble, as not being a system of moral government. He agreed with me, and added, 'The smallpox can less be accounted for than an execution, upon the supposition of machinery; for we are sure it comes without a fault. But, Sir, as to the doctrine of Necessity, no man believes it. If a man should give me arguments that I do not see, though I could not answer them, should I believe that I do not see?' Talking of the religious discipline proper for unhappy convicts, he said, 'Sir, an ordinary clergyman will probably not impress their minds sufficiently. They should be attended by a Methodist preacher or a popish priest.'

On Friday 25 June I dined with him at General Paoli's, where he says in one of his letters to Mrs Thrale, 'I love to dine.' There were a variety of dishes much to his taste, of all which he seemed to me to eat so much that I was afraid he might be hurt by it; and I whispered to the General my fear and begged he might not encourage it. 'Alas!' said the General, 'see how very ill he looks; he can live but a very short time. Would you refuse any slight gratifications to a man under sentence of death? There is a human custom in Italy by which persons in that melancholy situation are indulged with having whatever they like to eat and drink, even with expensive elegancies.'

I showed him some verses on Lichfield which I had that day received from Miss Seward, and had the pleasure to hear him approve of them. He confirmed to me the truth of a high compliment which I had been told he had paid to that lady when she mentioned to him *The Colombiade*, an epic poem by Mme du Boccage: 'Madam, there is not in it any description equal to yours of the sea round the North Pole in your ode on the death of Captain Cook.'

I had some hopes that he would have accompanied me a part of the way to Scotland, that he might have had the benefit of air at a distance from London in a friend's house. But in this I was disappointed, for Dr Taylor, to whom I had written at his desire to know if his house, which he was repairing, would be in readiness, wrote to me that it would not; and a lady who used to express much regard for him, and to whom I therefore wrote of myself suggesting that his being under her roof might be much for the benefit of his health, fairly gave me to understand that she would not choose to have such a guest.

We this day dined at Sir Joshua Reynolds's with General Paoli, Lord Eliot, Dr Beattie, and some more company. Talking of Lord Chesterfield, JOHNSON. 'His manner was exquisitely elegant, and he had more knowledge than I expected.' BOSWELL. 'Did you find, Sir, his conversation to be superior?' JOHNSON. 'Sir, in the conversation I had with him, I had the best right to superiority, for it was upon philology and literature.' Lord Eliot, who had travelled along with Mr Stanhope, Lord Chesterfield's natural son, justly observed that it was strange that a man who showed he had so much affection for his son as Lord Chesterfield did by writing so many of those letters to him, almost all of them when he was Secretary of State, should endeavour to make his son a rascal. His Lordship told us that Foote had intended to bring on the stage a father who had thus tutored his son, and the son an honest man to everyone else, but practising his father's maxims upon him and cheating him. JOHNSON. 'I am much pleased with this design, but I think there was no necessity for making the son honest at all. No, he should be a consummate rogue; the contrast between honesty and knavery would be the stronger. It should be contrived so that the father should be the only sufferer by the son's villainy, and thus there would be poetical justice.'

An addition to our company came after we went up to the drawing-room. Dr Johnson seemed to rise in spirits as his audience increased. He said he was for Lord Orford's pictures and Sir Ashton Lever's museum being purchased by the public, because both the money and the pictures and curiosities would remain in Britain, whereas if they were sold abroad, the nation got indeed some money, but lost the pictures and curiosities, which it would be desirable we should have as models of taste and natural history. The only question was that as the nation was much in want of money, whether it would not be better to take a large price from a foreign state.

He this day said he should wish much to go to Italy, and that he dreaded next winter in England. I said nothing, but enjoyed a secret satisfaction in thinking that I had taken the most likely way to get him to Italy in a proper way.

On Monday 28 June I had the honour to receive from the Lord Chancellor the following letter.

The gist of this letter, which is printed in the Life, *was that the Lord Chancellor, Thurlow, was to use his influence to help Johnson get to Italy.*

This letter gave me an elevated satisfaction which has been seldom equalled in the course of the events of my life. I next day went and showed it to Sir Joshua Reynolds, who was exceedingly pleased with it, and in the warmth of his friendly joy said that he himself would undertake that Mr Sastres should have a pension of eighty pounds for his life. He thought that I should now communicate the negotiation to Dr Johnson, who might afterwards complain if the success with which it had now been honoured should be too long concealed from him. I intended to set out for Scotland next morning, but he cordially insisted that I should stay another day, that Johnson and I might dine with him, that we three might talk of his going to Italy and 'have it all out'. I hastened to Johnson and was told by him that he was rather better today. BOSWELL. 'I am really anxious about you, Sir, and particularly that you should go to Italy for the winter, which I believe is your own wish.' JOHNSON. 'It is, Sir.' BOSWELL. 'You have no objection but the money.' JOHNSON. 'Why no, Sir.' BOSWELL. 'Why then, Sir, suppose the King should give you the money? I have reason to think he will.' JOHNSON. 'Why should you think so?' BOSWELL. 'You are not to be angry with me.' JOHNSON. 'No.' BOSWELL. 'Why then I will tell you fairly what I have done. I have applied to the Lord Chancellor.' He listened with much attention while I communicated to him what had passed, then warmly called out, 'This is taking prodigious pains about a man.' 'O Sir,' said I, with most sincere affection, 'your friends would do everything.' He paused, grew more and more agitated, till tears started into his eyes, and he exclaimed with much emotion, 'GOD bless you all.' I was so affected that I also shed tears. After a little while he renewed his grateful benediction, 'GOD bless you all for JESUS CHRIST's sake.' We remained for some time unable to speak. He got up suddenly and quitted the room *attendri*.[27] He stayed out a short time till he had recovered his firmness, and I should suppose till he had offered up his solemn thanks at the throne of grace. We had a very little conversation, as I was in a hurry to be in the Court of Exchequer to hear the great cause of Sutton and Johnstone. I secured him for Sir Joshua Reynolds's next day.

On Wednesday 30 June he and I had the friendly confidential dinner with Sir Joshua Reynolds, nobody being present but ourselves. Both Sir Joshua and I were so sanguine in our expectations, knowing the very high esteem which the Sovereign had expressed for him, that we expatiated with confidence on the large provision which we were sure would be made for him, conjecturing whether it would be a donation at once or an augmentation of his pension, or both. He himself yielded so much to our enthusiasm as to suppose it not impossible that our hopes might in one way or other be realized. He declared that he would rather have his pension doubled than a grant of a thousand pounds, 'for,' said he, 'though probably I may not live to receive as much as a thousand pounds, a man would have the consciousness that he should be for the rest of his life in splendour.' Considering what a moderate proportion six hundred pounds a year bears to innumerable fortunes in this country, it is shocking to think that a man so truly great should think it splendour. As an instance of extraordinary generosity of friendship, he told us that Dr Brocklesby had offered him a hundred a year for his life. A tear started into his eye as he spoke this in a faltering tone. Dr Brocklesby told me that Johnson said he would accept of no such bounty but from the King.

We endeavoured to flatter his imagination with agreeable prospects of happiness in Italy. 'Nay,' said he, 'I must not expect that. Were I going to Italy to see fine pictures, like Sir Joshua, or to run after women, like Boswell, I might to be sure have pleasure in Italy. But when a man goes to Italy merely to feel how he breathes the air, he can enjoy very little.'

Talking of various enjoyments, I argued that a refinement of taste was a disadvantage, as they who had attained to it were seldomer pleased than such as had no nice discrimination and were therefore satisfied with almost everything that comes in their way. JOHNSON. 'Nay, Sir, be as perfect as you can in every way.'

Sir Joshua Reynolds's coach was to set us both down. When we came to the entry of Bolt Court, he asked me if I would not go in with him. I declined it from an apprehension that my spirits would sink. We bade adieu to each other affectionately in the carriage. When he had got down upon the foot-pavement, he called out, 'Fare you well!' and without looking back sprung away with a kind of pathetic briskness (if I may use that expression), which seemed to indicate a struggle to conceal uneasiness, and was to me a foreboding of our long, long separation. I remained one day longer in town to have the chance of talking over my negotiation with the Lord Chancellor, but the multiplicity of his important business did not allow of this. So I left the business in the hands of Sir Joshua Reynolds.

The Italian scheme ultimately came to nothing: officially no help was given, and Johnson declined the Chancellor's offer of a personal gift. We next see Boswell at home in Scotland, talking towards the end of 1784 to Henry Dundas – who later rose to the very top of Government in England – about his ambitions.

SUNDAY 12 DECEMBER. Mr Henry Dundas had appointed with me to breakfast with him this morning to have a confidential conversation. I considered that taking measures to establish myself in life was a work of necessity for myself and mercy for my family, and therefore might be done on Sunday. After breakfasting with his sister and daughters, we retired to his room, where we talked, I think more than an hour. The import of what he said was this: that when he approved of my going directly to settle in London and try the English bar, he took it for granted I had £1,000 or £1,200 a year to spend, so that I could maintain my family in London. But as I had now informed him I had not above £500 a year to spend, his opinion was different. That he would not give me a rash advice, but would think seriously, and talk with Mr Pitt, with the Attorney-General and with the Chancellor, and see whether I could get an office of some hundreds a year, or could be assured of immediate practice; either of which was indispensably necessary to make my settling in London rational. He said no man ever got good by pleading poverty; but I should give out that though a man of fortune, I had not a fortune that could afford a large expense. He said he could not find fault with my wishing to be in a wider sphere than in Scotland, for if an office of £10,000 a year should be created for him on condition of his being quiet here, he would not accept of it. (My imagination suggested this idea, and he eagerly adopted it.) He owned that the bar here was not what it has been; and he said he would not have me go to the bench for some time, at any rate, for that there would be an end of me (or some such phrase). He said I could then get no additional office; and I should first get something that I might carry to the bench with me. He gave me his hand and promised he would be in earnest to assist me; told me he had read my East India *Letter* at a Cabinet dinner; and if any office of some hundreds a year had then fallen, I should have had it. He told me he had a note of mine concerning my friend Johnston, and if an opportunity offered, would do for him. He also said he had been active to get my brother David an office, as he had pledged himself to my father. He told Lord Carmarthen, 'It was a deathbed promise and I must fulfil it.' I left him quite animated and full of manly hope, and saw no desponding objections. My wife thought all this might be artful, to keep me off from interfering with his numerous claimants of a seat on the bench. But I thought him sincere. We shall see. He promised to write me fully from London. I shall send him a memorial. I was in such agitation I could not settle. Wished to dine and drink wine with Sir W. Forbes. But having met Lord Lyle, walked with him to the Abbey and King's Park, and then dined at a tavern with him and his brother David, who was in hiding from a caption.[28] I was to give good advice. Drank rather too much. Not a well-spent Sunday.

FRIDAY 17 DECEMBER. (Writing 19.) This must be ever remembered as a melancholy day, for it brought me the dismal news of my great and good friend, Dr Samuel Johnson. His physician, Dr Brocklesby, favoured me with a very full letter dated on Monday the 13, the night of his death. I was stunned, and in a kind of amaze. I had company engaged to sup with us; and as it might have appeared vain affectation to forbid their coming, I received them and behaved with much ease, and said nothing of the dismal news but to worthy Sir William Forbes, just as he was going away. I did not shed tears. I was not tenderly affected. My feeling was just one large expanse of stupor. I knew that I should afterwards have sorer sensations.

SATURDAY 18 DECEMBER. (Writing 19.) I mentioned Dr Johnson's death to Mr George Wallace, Mr Nairne, Mr Maclaurin and Lord Hailes. He said, 'I wish everyone were as well prepared for the great change as he was.' I sat again some time with Sir William Forbes and talked of this sad event. My mind had for some days been unexpectedly vigorous, so that I could bear more than when relaxed by melancholy. My resolution was to honour his memory by doing as much as I could to fulfil his noble precepts of religion and morality. I prayed to GOD that now my much respected friend was gone, I might be a follower of him who I trusted was now by faith and patience inheriting the promises. But it gave me concern that I was conscious of a deadness of spiritual feeling, and indeed a cold indifference as to the awful subject of religion, having just a sort of superficial speculation that I might take my chance with a careless hope of mercy. This, I believe, is the state of most people, even of those who have had the ordinary religious education. I was desirous to be better. I went in the afternoon and paid a visit to old M. Dupont, whom I found wonderfully entire in mind, though quite feeble in body. He was reading the prophet Ezekiel in Arabic. I was humbled to think how little I applied to literature. I also visited Miss Scott, who had been ill of a fever. I had a message from her last night that she had been ill and that M. Dupont was very weak. So I went to wait on them. I was consoled to think that I continued the attention which my father showed to them. In the evening I read two accounts of Dr Johnson's death in the *Public Advertiser* and *London Chronicle*. And I had a letter from Mr Dilly mentioning it, and in the true spirit of *the trade* wanting to know if I could have an octavo volume of 400 pages of his conversations ready by February. I had had a letter from him lately suggesting that I might be the editor of all his works and write his life. I answered him that I had a large collection of materials for his life, but would write it deliberately. I was now uneasy to think that there would be considerable expectations from me of memoirs of my illustrious friend, but that habits of indolence and dejection of spirit would probably hinder me from laudable exertion. I wished I could write now as when I wrote my *Account of Corsica*. But I hoped I should do better than I at first apprehended.

SUNDAY 19 DECEMBER. (Writing the 28.) Was at the Old English Chapel in the forenoon and the New in the afternoon. Captain and Mrs Mingay drank tea with us. Dr Johnson's death filled me with a kind of amazement.

MONDAY 20 DECEMBER. (Writing 28.) I recollect nothing except making a motion in Exchequer for the first time. It was for the Laird of Logan. Also attended a meeting of the Faculty of Advocates.

TUESDAY 21 DECEMBER. (Writing 28.) I recollect nothing.

WEDNESDAY 22 DECEMBER. (Writing 28.) I recollect nothing.

THURSDAY 23 DECEMBER. (Writing 28.) My worthy friend Lord Rockville asked me to his family dinner with Lady Colville. I was in such sad spirits I could not go, but did not dine at all, and walked in the Greyfriars churchyard. The weather was severe.

FRIDAY 24 DECEMBER. (Writing 28.) The Court of Session rose for the Christmas vacation. I was quite dull.

SATURDAY 25 DECEMBER. (Writing 28.) The holy festival of Christmas could not dissipate the dreary clouds which hung upon my mind. It vexed me much that my old and confidential friend John Johnston of Grange, who had dined cordially with me every Christmas since ever I had a house, was not come to town. He had been ill, and the weather was rigid. But I was really angry that he had now failed to be with me. It seemed that this was an extraordinary year. Dr Johnson was gone. Grange was absent. My chief satisfaction was a kind of obstinate firmness which despair makes us feel. I went to Mr Wight's in the forenoon to consider a Submission to him and me by Craigengillan and his brother David concerning the extent of heirship movables, a question never decided by the Court of Session. I was sufficiently clear-headed. But my heart and imagination were dreary. I took my two daughters Veronica and Phemie to the New English Chapel. They were charmed with the evening service. I was cold and unhappy. Our three youngest children being in the country was a great want of pleasing variety.

TUESDAY 28 DECEMBER. (Writing 29.) Revised a long Memorial, altered it a little, and made several additions so as to form Answers for my friend Dempster to a Petition against him in the Court of Session by Watson of Turin. Went to drink tea with Mr George Wallace. But he had company at dinner. Drank tea with Mr James Donaldson, bookseller. Mr Mercer, wine-merchant, was there. I was somewhat cheered by conversation. Here I read Dr Johnson's will in an English newspaper. His death still made an impression of amazement upon my mind. I could not fully believe it.

7

'A Man Troubled in Mind':

The Last Ten Years

With the death of Johnson in 1784, a great light went out in Boswell's life. On the other hand, the ground was now cleared for his last and crowning achievement – his work as a biographer. It had been widely known for years that he was collecting material for a Life of Johnson, and those close to both of them knew that Johnson had given him permission for this, and supplied information. Immediately after Johnson's death the world turned expectant eyes on Boswell. Dilly, the publisher, wrote at once with an offer. Fearful of failure, and needing time to sift and arrange his mass of materials, Boswell part fended off, part whetted public appetite with his Journal of a Tour to the Hebrides with Dr Samuel Johnson, *which provided a specimen of the full-length, intimate portrait, showing the great man not only in his greatness but in his hours of ease and in the little things of his life – his casual remarks, what food and drink he enjoyed, his quirks and foibles. No biography written in this spirit had ever been given to the public before, in any country; some readers were offended at Boswell's flouting of the convention that the Life of a great man should be as large-scale and impersonal as his statue in a public square; most were pleased and interested, and have remained pleased and interested ever since. The way was clear for the great* Life, *but still it took over five years to write, years of anxiety and labour, often of misgiving and weariness. That Boswell carried it through was due to his own devotion to Johnson's memory and also to the steady help and encouragement he received from his good friend Edmund Malone, without whose help I personally do not believe the book would have come into the world.*

The extracts that follow concern the last decade of Boswell's life; they contain that one great achievement, which, fortunately, he lived to see complete and to know for certain that it had succeeded. For the rest, it was a sombre decade. Most things went wrong.

The curiously bifurcated nature of those last years – part soaring success, part crashing failure – has been discussed elsewhere in this book, especially in the Introduction (pp. xiv–xvii) and there is no need to restate it here. Partly Boswell's troubles were simply the result of his own temperament, but the story also has a villain, unmistakably James Lowther, Earl of Lonsdale, to whom he attached himself in the hope of being provided effortlessly with a seat in Parliament. Lonsdale, a power-broker who combined great wealth with total cynicism, could obviously have done this for him, but he preferred to keep him in a state of miserable subservience and suspense. In some of the most poignant pages of the Journal, we see Boswell having to swallow insult after insult, and brooding miserably (especially while snowed in at Lonsdale's bleak and remote country seat) not only on the personal humiliation to a laird and a man of ancient family, but also on the recognition, buried deeper in his own mind, that 'Corsica Boswell', the friend of liberty, was becoming associated with the borough-mongering of an insolent aristocrat who disdained everything that a man like Paoli had lived for. It was Boswell's final low point, and we can only be glad that he pulled himself up from it before death came to him, swiftly and not too unmercifully, in May 1795: the same month, and very nearly the same day of the month, as that great earth-shaking day of his life, thirty-three years earlier, when he had first met Samuel Johnson.

Boswell is buried at Auchinleck, but he did not die there. He died in a rented house in London; and London, once the irresistible candle-flame, the centre of light and power, had become in those last years a city of ghosts for him: not just those of his many friends who were dead, absent or alienated from him, but the ghost of the young scintillating Boswell of 1763, his many ambitions now in tatters.

THURSDAY 20 DECEMBER. Visited Malone in the morning. Then called at Mr Garforth's, where I heard Lord Lonsdale was still in town. Called to leave my card. But the servant said his Lordship would see me. So I waited, and by and by was shown in. He told me that he had considered my application for the Recordership of Carlisle. He had turned it in his mind upon his pillow; he had many applications – one from Lord Darlington. He did not wish entirely to deny them all. But as I wished for it as an opportunity for returning to the Northern Circuit, he had resolved that I should have it for some time and then I could resign it; and he talked as if he had appointed me to come that morning. When I appeared not to understand this, he said, 'Have you not had my note?' I told him no. Said he: 'I sent a note to you this forenoon desiring to see you. I own I have some notion of communications being made to people in a way that we cannot explain. For here you have come of yourself just at the time when I wished to see you. I am to set out tomorrow morning for Lowther, where I shall be only for a day, and then go to Whitehaven Castle, where I am to have a great deal of company, and if you will go with me, I will introduce you to them, which will be of advantage to you as returning to the Northern Circuit, and you shall go to Carlisle and be elected.'

I was agitated at finding now that Lowther really had resolved publicly to befriend me, but I was somewhat embarrassed. I told his Lordship that I was very much obliged to him; that I should be very happy to have the honour of attending his Lordship. But that I had several engagements, and Johnson's *Life* to finish. However, I would try, and I begged that his Lordship would allow me till the evening to consider of it. He did so. I ran home and talked with my wife, who was for my going. So was T.D., who thought *it could do no harm*. Messrs James and Cumberland Wilsons dined with us. At night I returned to Lord Lonsdale's and told his Lordship that I would wait on him. He kept Mr Garforth and me late, and then Mr Garforth and I walked through Berkeley Square cordially. He said this was a feather in my cap.

FRIDAY 21 DECEMBER. In a great hurry to be with Lord L. at nine *to a second*. Disturbed my family and was quite uneasy as I did not reach his door till twenty-five minutes after nine. Garforth smiled and said I would be time enough two hours after. Was shaved in the hall. Satterthwaite came. Mr John Lowther came about eleven knowing how it *might* be. I went to Partlet's Coffee-house in Shepherd's Market and had a pot of coffee and a muffin comfortably. Between twelve and one Colonel Lowther came and told me the coach was at the door. We talked of the Great Man. He said the way to get anything from him was not to ask it but rather to have somebody to oppose it, such as saying, 'What! would you bring Boswell into Parliament?' He seemed to think I might have a chance for Cockermouth in room of Senhouse, who hated being in. I objected that I should not choose to be a Member of Parliament without any will of my own but merely to utter Lord L.'s inclination. He said, 'He was very honourable to his Members and did not require this.' But Satterthwaite afterwards told me sagaciously that it was *understood* in all cases where a Member was brought in by any person that he should not go against him.

When I returned there was no appearance of his coming out of his room. The uncertain waiting was very unpleasant. Governor Penn came, and asked if that was the first set of horses, for he had known a set changed at the door, the first having waited very long. It was frost this morning. Penn said he knew him well, and when he was with him, he just eat, drank, and slept as it might happen, without any thought about the matter. 'It is a school', said he, 'to which people must be broke in.' I laughed and said, 'Harder than that of Pythagoras.' All the things were put into the coach. He ordered them all to be taken out again and, I suppose, packed in some other way. At length he came to us and first took Penn into another room, and then Garforth, who had been waiting since half past seven.

At last Satterthwaite was desired to go into the coach and to wait in it at the corner of Davies Street, to which it drove *down* Charles Street. Soon after, the Earl, accompanied by Mr John Lowther and Penn and me, walked *up* Davies Street and turned into Hill Street, and so got to the coach. What this round-about mode could mean was a mystery. But they told me he never went into the carriage at his own door, but had it waiting at some place out of sight. He and I sitting frontwards, and Satterthwaite and Mr John Lowther backwards, drove off. He felt himself hungry but did not stop till we came to Stevenage. There, in the kitchen, we had beefsteaks, a fowl with mushrooms, porter and four bottles of port. He and I this day sang several of the songs in *The Beggar's Opera*. We stopped at night at Buckden and had tea and white-wine whey.

SATURDAY 22 DECEMBER. Satterthwaite and I had colds, his the worst. We breakfasted at Stilton. Victor, his Norman servant, rode always on and had horses at the door each stage. He made the boys drive excessively hard. We dined at Grantham but poorly, there being what is called the squires' monthly dinner in the house, which took all their best things. Ale and two bottles of port. At night we stopped at Doncaster. We had sung less today. He felt himself ill in his stomach. Would take only tea and eggs, and Satterthwaite only an egg and white-wine whey, and Mr John Lowther only tea and a jelly. There was a comfortable supper put down and I eat some veal cutlet, a grey plover and a bit of another, and a tart, and had ale and gin and water. We had sung some more *Beggar's Opera* today, and he had talked a good deal of bawdy.

SUNDAY 23 DECEMBER. Excessively cold. A good deal of snow had fallen for two days. He had been very ill in the night and taken forty-four drops of laudanum. He was in my room before I was up, as I had disbelieved the maid's report, and indeed Satterthwaite had put me on my guard that, after the horses were put to and his company all up and ready, he sometimes would not come down for two hours. We had breakfast before setting out. Satterthwaite was worse. He did not seem to mind him but made him go and see his things put into the coach. Victor was exceedingly sick and seemingly unable to go on and hinted piteously to get into a carriage, but in vain. He was ordered to stop at Boroughbridge and have some dinner ready for us. When we got there (Mr John Lowther having gone out at Ferrybridge), Victor said he could go on. But He *of his own accord* desired he might be put into a warm bed and come in the stage-coach next day, and ordered a man from the inn to ride on and order horses and send one on from next stage. The landlord, Rushton, was a stupid, miserable-looking old man.

He damned and scolded about bad beef, &c, and was irritated that a bolt of the coach was broke and had to be mended, which took some time. Two shillings were charged. He would give only one; and because the Wetherby boys had not come in less than an hour and twenty minutes he gave them only sixpence apiece and nothing to the ostler, nor would he take back a guinea in the hire, which they said was light. His way was to call, 'Boys, I'm in a great hurry. Make haste or I'll give you nothing. I am not to waste my lungs calling to you. I have looked my watch. If I have to call to you again you shall have nothing. If I must waste my lungs I must save my cash.'

Only one bottle of port today, porter and ale. Then Gretabridge. Hard driving. Sad work for the last part of the road near to Lowther. Had asked me on road, 'What will you have?' I said, 'Only a little warm milk.' Satterthwaite said the same, but when L. was out of the room complained seriously to me of giving such a precedent, and said, 'When we had had a damned bad dinner, we should have had something good at night.' George Saul, whom we found here, had come from Lancaster and hardly eaten all day. He durst not say he would have anything till L. was out of room, and then said if he could have had but a piece of bread and cheese. I mentioned his wish and he had it. L. took warm milk. Dreadfully cold in the waste dining-room, and there was a railing of iron painted green to keep us off the hearth that it might be clean. In this whim He was obstinate. Bedroom cold, cold.

MONDAY 24 DECEMBER. Satterthwaite took care that each of us should have some tea and roll and butter in our rooms, but beware telling. Breakfast not till about one. I sat a long time with Satterthwaite in his room, where he had a good fire and bid me take care to have the same, as it was the most comfortable thing I would have here. He said there was a total want of all comforts. A man for instance might be days without having his shoes cleaned. Garforth sometimes wiped his with the carpet. He spoke strongly of the Earl's want of attention to make people happy about him, and told how a gentleman observed how great a man he might be if he were but commonly civil. 'Nay,' said another, 'if he were but commonly *un*civil.' He said no man of parts had ever submitted to go along with him. He said he did not wish to put those attached to him into good situations because that would make them independent. Yet, from his great fortune and influence he ought to have a Lord of the Treasury, a Lord of the Admiralty and a Commissioner both of Customs and Excise. Yet he said for himself he could not complain, for He had done very well for him. He said he talked freely to me as looking upon me now as attached to Him, and he would be glad to communicate with me.

All this struck a damp upon me, and I saw how fallaciously I had imagined that I might be raised by his interest, for I never would submit to be dependent. Satterthwaite said he thought all along that He would make me Recorder of Carlisle, for He had praised my conduct at the election and said I had gone as far for his interest as my character in my profession would allow. I now foresaw many difficulties in being Recorder, as he could not bear even decent attention to be paid to his opponents in the Corporation.

We were kept long hanging on for dinner even after it was on the table, and I believe sat down about seven. Tolerably well. Port, hermitage, frontignac, rather too much. In the forenoon He had a visit of Thomas Whelpdale, Colonel of the Westmorland Militia and High Sheriff of Cumberland, a rustic mortal. He was ordered to go to Whitehaven. After dinner L. read aloud, I think three acts of John Home's *Alonzo*.

TUESDAY 25 DECEMBER. Rose somewhat uneasy. Saul had been in the housekeeper's room and had tea. I went too. Found Mrs Elwood, a large, stately woman who gave me breakfast very civilly and talked of my Lord doing things just because other people did differently. It snowed heavily. But I have not for thirty years been absent from public worship on Christmas Day. So went briskly to Lowther Church. Very, very cold, and Dr Lowther very inanimate. Raised devotion as much as I could. Received the Holy Sacrament.

We were to have gone to Whitehaven today and much I wished to get away. But He, thinking roads would be better next day, sent off Satterthwaite and the cook in post-chaise that Satterthwaite might be at election of coroner next day. We had at dinner Mr Nicholson, Clerk of the Peace for Westmorland, a little, humpbacked man. I had read some in Boyd's *Justice of Peace*. A pretty good dinner. But he talked all himself, long, tedious accounts. After five bottles I improperly asked for another. He took none of the third part of it, and it was too heavy upon me. We had tea. I was drowsy and stole away to bed.

WEDNESDAY 26 DECEMBER. The day not looking well, He put off setting out, and sent a man with letters ordering roads to be cleared, and *resolved* to set out early next day. He talked to Saul and me in the forenoon, I believe three hours without intermission. We dined about six. His camp *butcher*[1] dressed for us ox-cheek broth, tripe and a bit of venison. Moderate drinking, but though I said I preferred not, he gave chiefly hermitage, which I disliked. Each day at breakfast he had honeycomb, which he took all to himself. I was quite dull and dispirited and gloomy, for we all sat in vile, timid restraint.

I paused and asked myself what I had to do with such a man. All the way down I had been uneasy and anxious at being away from my dear wife and children, and to look forward to a much longer absence overwhelmed me. I also felt how unworthy it was of the Laird of Auchinleck to hang on thus upon a savage. I thought I heard my worthy father say, 'James, I left you independent.' I wished to elope from him and was quite impatient to be gone, and I studiously meditated how I should decline the Recordership. It was dismal always when I went to bed. He slept a good deal after dinner, never minding his company, and we never had wine but from his own hand.

THURSDAY 27 DECEMBER. Tom Jarker, his gamekeeper, whom he had sent with orders to clear the roads, returned and reported that they would not be passable till Saturday. This quite sunk me. I now resolved to be off with the Recordership but knew not how to communicate it. The day was painfully cold. The dry logs, we were told, were all done, and we had some abominable green ones which he persevered in maintaining he would make burn, while Saul and I stood shivering. At last he left the room, when Saul got plenty of coals and mixing them with the green wood, made an excellent fire, which He was glad to see when he returned.

George Saul is a merchant in Lancaster. He was nine years in America. He is a large, stout man with a ruddy, good-humoured countenance and a black scratch-wig. Being in America has taught him the management of wood fires. He has for seven years been zealously attached to the interest of Lowther and has lived much with Lord Lonsdale, whom he respects and fears, yet sees his faults. There is a remarkable naïveté in his manner. He holds down his head and shakes it and winks when he talks of the Earl's opponents, calling them dogs who want to pull down the king if they could. When he looked at the cold, green wood which his Lordship had insisted should burn, he said, 'If this be your fifty thousand a year, my service to it.' The Earl inquired, and good dry logs were found in the servants' hall. We had them and the fire blazed, and we were warm at last.

Dinner was between six and seven, ox-cheek broth, tripe, plum pudding, which he said no man cook could make well, but the camp butcher did. We had Nicholson today at dinner. Only two bottles of wine, I forget which. But the grievous thing was that no man could ask for a glass when he wished for it but had it given to him just when the fancy struck L. The glasses were large, eight in a bottle.

While Lonsdale was drowsy after dinner, we sat in stupid silence, and I groaned inwardly. I could not help showing impatience at this treatment. I turned myself some time restlessly upon my chair and then went up to my room, where I meditated sullenly what I should do, sometimes thinking of setting out on foot for Clifton, a village two miles off through which the mail-coach comes, and from thence getting off for London this very night, sometimes of going to bed. The immediate pressure of uneasiness was terrible, and the dreary waste of the cold house, with nobody but Saul, a sycophantish fool, to talk to made me almost desperate. I fancy my mind was in a state very similar to that of those wretched mortals who kill themselves. I did not stay long but resumed resolution and went back to the dining-room, thinking to go off next morning in daylight. No notice appeared to have been taken of my absence, and I weathered out the night till about twelve, when I got to bed.

FRIDAY 28 DECEMBER. I had been very uneasy and hardly slept at all, but tossed and vexed myself during the night. It was galling to me to find that I was so miserably deceived in the notion which I had formed of the high honour and great advantage of being connected with Lowther. I viewed with wonder and regret my folly in putting myself at such an age as my forty-sixth year into a new state of life by becoming an English barrister. I saw that it was not a life of spirited exertion, as I had supposed, but of much labour for which I had ever been unfit, and of much petulant contest, which in some states of my changeful mind I could not bear. Being made Recorder of Carlisle *to bring me back to the Northern Circuit*, as I had put it in my application to L., I considered as again involving me in a tiresome, expensive, ineffectual struggle to get business which I had no probability of obtaining; whereas by cutting short at once after a fair trial of two years, I could return to Scotland and resume my place in the Court of Session as an advocate, and perhaps obtain a judge's place, and, if not, could certainly make my affairs easy by care and regular attention, and have my family in a much more creditable situation than I could afford for them in London. I looked upon this painful discovery of L.'s being the worst man in the world for a patron to be in effect a most beneficial event for me; and thus I reasoned. I resolved, however, not to fly off from him with a sudden violence but to accompany him and see his greatness at Whitehaven, which I had celebrated,[2] and then to tell him that I declined the Recordership, and to return to London without any appearance of disappointment. I saw in Him that vast wealth and influence do not produce proportionate happiness. I thought of a judicious saying of Commissioner Cochrane's that it was a misfortune to a family to become too rich, for then the representative went to London and became an alien.

I had a headache in the morning, and as I had no hope of being warm but in bed and wished to escape the dreary waiting for breakfast, I resolved to be ill and lie in bed all the forenoon. Now I meditated calmly on the infatuation of a gentleman of a large estate, fine Place and excellent house dooming himself to trouble and servile vexation.

I felt at my heart my absence from my dear wife and children; I upbraided myself for it, when there was no sufficient cause for it. Yet my *mistake* might excuse me. For Dempster had said to me on my getting acquainted with L. 'that one card played well is enough to raise you', and the Bishops of Killaloe and Dromore had both written to me concerning him as one who would bring me forward in England. But the thought that I had hurt the health probably both of my wife and children by bringing them to London, and the dismal apprehension that my wife might die and how I should then see how little of that rational, creditable happiness to which our situation in life entitled her she had enjoyed, but had without repining sacrificed it to my spirit of adventure – all these considerations made me deeply miserable.

Between ten and eleven I grew weary and rose. Saul had gone early to Penrith to see his mother-in-law and his daughter and was to return to dinner. I walked in a troubled frame between the dining-room and my bedroom and upon the gravel before the house till it was one o'clock, and still there was no appearance of L. or of breakfast. I *felt* the insolence so as to meditate writing to him in the keenest terms that he did not seem to know who I was. My impatience to be gone increased. The servants, a parcel of negligent wretches unless when the Lion roared and frightened them, were always solacing themselves in their hall and other places, so that none of them were to be seen, and consequently they did not observe when anyone went out or came in. I got my travelling-bag all packed, and taking it in my hand, I walked off.

When I came to the porter's lodge, the good civil old man with the Coomberland deealect looked rurally kind, and when I asked how far it was to Clifton and how far to Penrith, suggested, when he saw my bag, that I wanted to have some linen washed. The snow, which was lying deep, discouraged me somewhat; so I put my bag into his lodge, told him I was going to take the coach for London but I was afraid my Lord would not let me go; so charged him to say nothing, and perhaps I would take my bag in the evening.

I returned again for a little while to the house. But observing two men with carts going out at the gate, I went to them and was informed they were going to Clifton. So I put my bag into one of the carts and walked on before till I was out of sight of the house, and then got into another of them and sat upon a sack and drove along. Having had no breakfast, being very cold, and being sadly fretted, I was quite gloomy and could look upon nothing without disgust. A gleam of felicity came across my mind when I thought of being again with my wife, and I thought that nothing upon earth could make up to me for being absent from her, even for a week or two at a time. All my fondness for Miss Peggie Montgomerie, all her admirable conduct as a wife and mother were before me in a warm glow. But I feared that she would despise my impatience and flight, and that I should be made ridiculous on account of thus forfeiting my expectations from the Great Lowther, whom I had celebrated in lofty language. I was also not without apprehension that he might resent my abrupt departure as impertinent to him. But I thought I could write to him declining the Recordership in very smooth, respectful terms. And keep my own secret, never mentioning his intolerable behaviour.

The carts went towards Temple Sowerby, and I quitted them where they turned off from the Penrith road, and then walked on to Penrith carrying my bag, which was pretty heavy. I had seen no inn at Clifton which looked comfortable, so luckily did not stop there. At the end of Penrith I bought some paper at a shop and there left my bag, and then walked into the town uncertain what I should do. I got notice at the George Inn where Mr Saul was and, having found him, told him that I feared Lord L. might put off from day to day going to Whitehaven; that He had told me we were to be there on Tuesday, and I had come from London in that belief, as I was obliged to be back again on the 6th January, if I could, but certainly by the 8th or 10th; and that I now saw my time at Whitehaven would be so short it was not worth while to go, and I had better return directly; so I was come here to take the coach. I sounded him if he thought Lord L. would take it amiss if I went off. He was clear he would. So I being by this time somewhat better by exercise, resolved I would return and speak to him, and I could get off by the coach any day.

I went to the George and had a pot of coffee and muffin and toast, the first comfortable meal I had enjoyed for some days, and I insensibly felt myself restored. It struck me to compare my poor state at this house now with what it was when here last with my wife, &c.3 The cold and dark weather was gloomy, and for two days I had been troubled with one of my foreteeth being half broken off yet the root of the broken part not separated from the gum. It was a mouldering memento of my mortality.

I walked to Lowther with Saul and carried my bag all the way. I was fully tired and all in a sweat, so went to my room and changed myself from head to foot and felt stout. I was glad that I had avoided writing a letter to Lord L., for a strange one it must have been. I went down to the dining-room and sent a message to his Lordship that I begged leave to speak with him for a few minutes. He came instantly. I said to him in a flurry, but composing myself as well as I could, that I took the liberty to speak to him what I was going to have written, that I had lain awake all night thinking of the Recordership which his Lordship had been so good as to promise me, and that after much wavering it did appear to me that I ought not to accept of it. That his Lordship's having given me the preference had done me great honour; that I was conscious of this and had the honour as much as if I had been elected. (He very politely said it should be as I pleased and there was no appearance of his being displeased.) I said it was happy that the matter had not been communicated. 'No,' said He, 'it is entirely between you and me.'

I said I would presume to speak freely. The truth was I had been of a very good standing at the bar in Scotland. I had been flattered and persuaded that I might succeed in England, in a wider sphere. My ambition had led me to make the experiment. I found I had been deceived. Jack Lee and others who had encouraged me had told me that the difference of practice in the two countries was not great, that I had only to acquire a few elements and forms. But that I had found the difficulty very great at my time of life. That I had tried the Northern Circuit in vain, and had then gone the Home Circuit with as little success. That this of the Recordership was a *dernier ressort*, a forlorn hope, but that upon thinking it over and over again, I thought that my returning to the Northern Circuit and still having no business would make me appear in a much worse light; and that as one great motive of my wishing for the Recordership was to do what I could to promote his Lordship's interest, I thought my unfitness for the office was against that, for I should discredit his Lordship's recommendation. That there were many gentlemen who could be of much more use to him in that way, and that my being appointed, one newly come from the Scotch bar, might raise a clamour. I sincerely thanked him, was ashamed of my weakness, but thought I was now resolving for the best.

'Sir,' said he, 'you applied to me for this several times, and at last mentioned your returning to the Northern Circuit as a reason for your having it. I thought of it deliberately for some time. I never consult, neither the *officer* nor Garforth nor one of them. They may be partial or they may think themselves right. You applied to me several times. I gave no answer. I considered. I thought not only of myself and the Corporation but of you. It is said it is easier to get into a situation than to get well out. If a man does not get out well it is a reflection on the person who put him in. I considered your being Recorder of Carlisle. You could say to a Minister, "Here I am," and make it a step. I don't know your views. But you might go into Scotland or into some other situation. I may say without disparagement to you that there are many gentlemen on the Northern Circuit who know English law better than you. But what I should say to the Corporation: "Here is a man of great sense, of talents, who when a thing is properly prepared can judge of it with ability." And the business is all prepared by the Town Clerk. Besides, when the Recorder is consulted, other counsel are consulted at the same time.'

'Your Lordship is very kind. You put it in the most favourable light. I am now ambitious to have it. And as to the Circuit, there is no necessity for my beating the whole round. I may take more or less of it as I please. To be sure, you have many who go only to particular places. Why, Scott does not go all round. My Lord, I am very much obliged to you. Your Lordship has not only the power to give me the place but you have given me fortitude to take it. I am of an anxious temper.' 'You can think of it for four or five days or a week, and it shall be as you please. If you had had as much to do in life as I have had, you would not have that anxious temper.'

This conversation gave quite a new turn to my spirits. The Rev. Dr Lowther came, and our dinner was his supper, and he was very placid and, being a new being in our sphere of existence, gave relief. We had cow-heel soup, very good, as I now thought, cow-heel dressed with white sauce, and something else; a double bottle of a rich Spanish red wine and a bottle of port; and a pint of wine and a pineapple, which pleased my senses, and I felt myself wonderfully well. I told how I had got a good dish of coffee at Penrith. 'Why,' said Lord L., 'could not you have had it here?' 'I should be very glad to have it, my Lord,' said I. Upon which the bell was rung, and Payne the butler was directed to have it well made and, just as it bubbled, to have a little hartshorn put in. So minute! It was indeed very good. Saul, who said he liked coffee, told me he never had seen it here, and that the housekeeper told him she knew of none in the house except some of her own. The relief as to the Recordership, the novelty of Dr Lowther, the little comforts of the stomach, and the prospect of moving next day to Whitehaven Castle, which I was assured was warm, made me go to bed in tranquillity. Such is the human mind. Tell it not.

SATURDAY 29 DECEMBER. Rose well, and expected to get off about nine; but Lord L. *trifled* away the time, as Satterthwaite well expresses his way, till after eleven. Then He and I and Saul got into the old ship, as he calls the coach which brought us from London, and away we drove with four post-horses which He keeps, I know not how long at a time, at a guinea a day; but we soon had a couple more put to, and now, I think, for the first time in my life was I driven in a coach and six. I saw that Jarker's report was true, for the snow was high-piled up on each side where the road had been cut. We drove to Keswick, where we had six fresh horses. I could scarcely distinguish two of the lakes from the surrounding snow. But Saddleback and other mountains and the famed Skiddaw looked sublime. Lord L. now as upon the road from London kept both glasses up, so that the thick, heated air was disagreeable and gave me a headache. But he must have all his own way.

We went over the great steep of Whinlatter and so proceeded to Cockermouth, where I recollected having often thought of it before I saw it, or rather was at it, for it was too dark for me to see it. We then with four horses came to Whitehaven. Being again in a town and seeing lamps and shops was agreeable after the cold imprisonment at Lowther. The Castle, a large house originally built by old Sir James of Whitehaven, but new-faced in the Gothic style and augmented to three times the size by Lord L., stands at the upper end of the town. When we entered we found Whelpdale and Satterthwaite. Lord L. soon had me through the house, which he took great pleasure in showing. Its great extent, numerous and spacious rooms, and good furniture filled my mind. The kitchen was magnificent and the fire immense. I soon felt we were in a mild climate, and the large coal fires made me quite comfortable.

I expected that Lord L., Saul and I, and the two gentlemen whom we found here should have had a full social meal and plenty of wine.

But we three had only a small cod, a beefsteak and potatoes, and a bottle of port and a bottle of madeira, while they two sat by and were never offered a glass, though many hints were given and though Saul and I both offered a glass to them from our share. This was shocking. L. put it off by saying with an appearance of heartiness, 'There is little enough for ourselves, eh? And you would not have me go to the cellar again tonight.' Saul had resolution to say *he* would take the *trouble* of going, willingly. But nothing would do. I wondered at the patience of the two gentlemen. Lord L. harangued away and would not let me go to bed till about one in the morning. I went once away and he followed, diverting himself with my not being able to find my room. At last he accompanied me to it politely. It was an excellent one in all respects. I relished it.

SUNDAY 30 DECEMBER. When I went down in the morning, Whelpdale asked me if I had ever seen anything so *savage* as Lord L.'s behaviour to him and Satterthwaite last night, and said it was *lunacy*. Satterthwaite also spoke strongly, and said that all the time they had been here before us they had no dinner in the castle, but went and found it, till the day before, when they had some and one bottle of wine; and he said if such behaviour had happened before anybody but those who know his Lordship well, he would have left the room. Whelpdale said nobody submitted to keep company with him but needy people for the good of their families, or people who had some view of self-interest. He told me he never had a shilling from him, but he kept three of his sons at Eton School. He had paid £700 for Satterthwaite's company[4] and kept a son of his at Eton. And Saul had a view to the office of Collector of the Customs at Lancaster. I felt myself very awkward amidst such people. But I thought, 'What does the world *imagine* as to the *consequence* of living intimately with the Great Lowther, the powerful proprietor of £50,000 a year?' And in the world's estimation one wishes to exist high.

We had at breakfast Whelpdale's wife, a pretty, pleasing woman only thirty-four, though she has had eleven children. She is daughter of Green, the stage-doctor, who is still alive.[5] Whelpdale ran off with her to Gratney Green at sixteen. The Earl commissioned Saul to make the tea and had himself a pot of currant jelly, which he spread thick on his buttered toast but offered nobody a tasting of it. Mrs Whelpdale, Satterthwaite, Saul and I went to the old church, a very good one; and

Huddleston, the parson, officiated very well. The Rev. Mr Church sat awhile with us after the forenoon's service, but did not see the Earl. I felt much as at Edinburgh.

Near three we had a tolerable dinner, and the seven officers of the Cumberland Militia now here were with us. No hob or nobs.[6] The Earl distributed the wine, just four glasses each, about a pint. At four we rose and saw the militia parade behind the castle, a fine body of men. The Earl looked nobly in scarlet and showed me great attention, taking me with him along the ranks. We then had tea and a true, quiet Sunday evening. Then a little supper, eggs, roasted potatoes and slices of cold beef, and some port (a bottle among us). I mixed water with it. Went to bed a little after eleven.

MONDAY 31 DECEMBER. It was showery. After breakfast Lord L. took me into what he calls his evidence room, where all his papers are kept and he writes, and talked a long time of I do not remember what, and showed me the map of Cumberland. I asked when he thought my election might be. He answered, 'I cannot tell. I have sent for Jackson. I have not thought of it yet.' This was teasing to my impatience to be back to London. I was anxious to be with my family. I was uneasy to be absent when the Wartons came to town and there are many valuable literary meetings, and I was vexed that I had no settled time to go on with Johnson's *Life*, though I had the notes of the year 1778 with me. Time was wasted till past one, when He took me and Saul with him that I might see the harbour, for he would let nobody show it but himself, nor would he allow me to walk out and look about the town. The regular building of the streets and many good houses pleased me, but families living in cellars seemed very bad. Lord L. thinks so and is to build a great many more houses that it may be so no longer. He dragged me on so slowly along the quays in the thick rain that I was heartily wearied. I was surprised at the quantity of shipping, though we saw but a part. We dined tolerably and had tea and supper.

1788

TUESDAY 1 JANUARY. It was a very wet day. So we only went through the house. When he came into my room, which had once been his own,

'Here,' said he, 'is a room which may be celebrated. It may be said such and such things were written here.' When he chooses to pay a compliment nobody can do it more graciously. At dinner we had the militia officers and Captain Harris and Lieutenant Willox of the 40th Regiment. The Lieutenant was an Aberdeen man. The northern accent is so broad, and his superfetation of English was so thick, that I could not be quite sure he was Scotch, till he talked of the wind being in a particular *airt*,7 I suppose *àrd-point* in Erse.

Today, as on Sunday, we dined in a large room below. We had a coarse dinner. But madeira, of which I had four glasses. There were besides either three or four glasses of port. I took only one. The second was quite thick, for he never decants wine and, as he said himself the other night, the fire before which he always sets it brings off the crust. The other night he made Saul drink a thick glass which I declined. I let my thick one today stand before me, and when he observed I did not drink, I said, 'No more, my Lord.' I had no doubt he knew why, but said nothing. At last he said, 'Squire Denton will drink that glass.' I said, 'It is thick, my Lord.' So we all rose and away to tea. I wondered that the great Lowther, Lord Lieutenant, &c, &c, did not entertain the officers with more credit to his dignity. Such entertainment, and a total suppression of animal spirits by his talking all himself, fretted me, and I was sulky though I did not show it. Evening went on as last.

WEDNESDAY 2 JANUARY. A still wetter day. After breakfast Lord L. abused Burke as an unprincipled, wrong-headed fellow and would not allow that public speaking had any effect in Parliament. He was heated that I did not acquiesce and, to obviate my instancing Lord Chatham, said that I certainly did not know the history of this country. Even Smollett could have informed me. He then with a wonderful reach of memory gave the state of parties, and how Pitt had bowed to Lady Yarmouth, with whom he had often seen him, and had veered about against and for the German war and, in short, had all kinds of political intrigue, and so had got on.

Before dinner came Mr and Mrs Senhouse and a boy, their eldest son. This diversified the scene a little. In the evening came two young Mr Richardsons from Penrith, the eldest, who had been in India and had now succeeded to be squire, and the other Mr George, lieutenant in the 54th, who had not joined; and their sisters, Miss Mary and Miss Margaret, and Miss Lowther, sister of the Reverend Doctor, and Miss

Dun from Lowther, daughter of the surgeon-apothecary, and her aunt, Miss Adamson, and Captain Postlethwaite. To describe them all would take too much time. Let me only observe that it occurred to me one wonders what is the use of many insects in the universe; I now see that fops and fantastical misses may be of great use in dissipating melancholy. But it's fair to add that though they seemed as I have mentioned at first view, they proved on better acquaintance cheerful, pleasant people. No doubt they had not wit and such circumstances. We had a supper (slight enough) in the large, low room, and the Earl exerted himself wonderfully. I had today a packet of letters, from Bruce Campbell, James Bruce, Sir William Forbes, and Veronica that her mother's cough had been severe; but I hoped it was no worse than formerly.

THURSDAY 3 JANUARY. By nine o'clock we were at breakfast in the room where we had supped. Coffee, tea, chocolade – all pleasant. I forgot all anxiety and thought I could live for ever in this manner. The *Gazette* announcing Miller President, Macqueen Justice Clerk, and Maclaurin a Lord of Session. The *changes* produced an agitation not unpleasant, but I felt *somewhat* uneasy to think that had I steadily remained at the Scotch bar I might have had the judge's place. But I considered that I should not have relished it while under the strong delusion of hope at the English bar. Nay, yet I doubted if I should relish it. Then how much more enjoyment have I had than if I had been in Scotland! It was still rainy. My Lord took me and the two Richardsons to see his timber-yard, which is extensive, and a young bear sent to him from the Baltic. His slow progress and insensibility to rain fretted me. We went with him also and viewed Trinity Church and St James's Church.

At dinner, all was quite as it should be: two soups, fish, various dishes, a dessert as last night, hobbing nobbing. But no claret. The moderation in drinking, however, was commendable, and of great advantage to me. The conversation was quiet and decorous. I began to think that this was the best style, for though there was no vivid enjoyment, neither was there struggling – and then languor. Mr Peter Taylor, a merchant here, dined with us. At five we were at tea and coffee. Then the Earl and I and Saul and Taylor played whist till supper, between nine and ten. To bed between eleven and twelve.

FRIDAY 4 JANUARY. Every night almost during this jaunt, or whatever it may be called, I have dreamt a good deal, which is not my custom.

I must therefore be more agitated. A letter from my dear wife today, written so that I could perceive that what was contained in a letter from Veronica which I received yesterday, as to her being ill, had a more serious foundation than was expressed. But what could I do? To break off now, when I was confident my election must soon come on, would have been losing all my time and expense and sore labour, as *hanging on* most certainly is to me. I again reminded his Lordship how inconvenient it was to me to come down and that I *must* be in London again next week. He said, 'I am *thinking* of it.'

The weather was mild as in summer. He carried me and the Richardsons and Saul and viewed the harbour fully, and his great receptacle for coals, and the mode of loading the vessels with them by what is called a *hurry*, being a conduit of wood through which each wagon-load is tumbled from a great highth into the hold of a ship. The other night he took me under the arm while we walked in the house. He did the same today when we were out. I said, 'This is most comfortable living. I don't care how long it last, were I not obliged to be in London on business.' He seemed pleased and said, 'And I am sure I shall be the happier the longer you stay.' We had again dinner, coffee and tea, whist, and supper. It is a waste of time to be minute in writing what will afterwards be of no moment. I won at whist both last night and this. His play was only a shilling, and he and I betted a crown the rubber.

SATURDAY 5 JANUARY. Another fine day. He and I and the same gentlemen as yesterday went and viewed what is called the Northwall, a very good pier; also his great steam engine. The same course as yesterday, only I lost at whist part of what I had won, and after supper came Sir Michael and Lady Diana Fleming. I felt how a numerous company may be very happy at a house in the country. But then, to be sure, this is not intellectual and literary enjoyment. I speculated on what could be the intention of human beings thus created. 'Wait the great teacher Death,' says Pope. The detection of Lady Eglinton with the Duke of Hamilton made a fine agitation. *His* cold, ungrateful neglect of my valuable spouse, to whose brother he was under great obligations, and *her* being, I suppose, the insolent cause of it, made me rejoice at this event. I felt here a kind of calm seclusion from life, and, as I experienced that I could live in perfect moral practice, I trusted that I should henceforth assume a steadiness in that respect.

The half of my foretooth which was loose came out a day or two ago, but it did not affect me so much as I supposed it would have done.

I discovered much jealousy among the Great Man's minions. Postlethwaite said Satterthwaite liked to lead the life he did, and allowed him no merit for his patience. Satterthwaite said Whelpdale was a drunken, foolish body and so vulgar that it was a disgrace to have him appear as High Sheriff of Cumberland. Whelpdale said of Satterthwaite, 'I might have been in his place but would not, as it would ruin my constitution to keep such late hours. He has had no education and been little in company, but he is a very cunning man.' The truth is Whelpdale, though long in the army, is a coarse *Coomberland* squire with no knowledge or talents, creeping before Lord L. and abusing him behind his back. Satterthwaite as to the Earl is pretty much the same, but having served his time to an attorney is an understanding man in many things and has a certain depth of shrewd sense, and is also a well-bred man.

Satterthwaite told me today that by Lord L.'s directions he had written to Alderman Jackson at Carlisle to come directly, and he supposed that my election would be ordered as soon as he arrived. I had before said to Lord L. that I did not wish he should take the trouble of going, but I had again stated that I wished it much as a great honour. His Lordship said, 'We shall see.' Satterthwaite was of opinion I should express a great desire to have that honour but not to insist upon it, that there might not be a reason for delay. Such *management* must there be. His Lordship attends to the most minute article of his domestic economy.

SUNDAY 6 JANUARY. A very cold day. I received a letter from my brother David written by desire of Mr Devaynes, without my wife's knowledge, acquainting me that she was not at all well, and that though there was no immediate danger, I should return as soon as I conveniently could. The letter was prudently worded, but it alarmed me much. I mentioned it to Lord L., whose indifference as to my tranquillity was shocking. He said he had written for Jackson that he might settle as to my election, but if I were called away he would keep the place open and I might be elected in summer. I was in a miserable state of indecision. I was agitated even to trembling and quite impatient to be with her. Yet I was vexed to lose all my time and trouble and vexation for the difference of a day or two. Satterthwaite assured me

Jackson would come on Monday and advised me to wait. I told Lord L. I would.

I was at Trinity Church in the forenoon. Mr Church read the service very well, and a Mr Thomson from Ireland preached well on Christ's having come to destroy the works of the Devil. I was pleased to hear the influence of evil spirits asserted in these days of *narrow* thinking, as *unbelief* certainly is. Wild, hurried, distracted thoughts concerning my dear wife darted through my mind. We had dinner, tea and supper, and it was a dull evening. So necessary are cards to people in general.

MONDAY 7 JANUARY. Had tossed and dreamed a great deal. Lord Lonsdale carried me and Saul out to ride with him on the roads towards St Bees, from whence I had a full view of the town, of the bay, and also saw the Isle of Man and Scotland. He took us above a quarter of a mile into his Howgill colliery. To see the strata of coal and stone and the water conducted from where it issues and the methods by which air is circulated underground entertained me. But there was something horrid in the thought of being under the earth. He had at dinner today the trustees for the harbour, some creditable-looking, well-dressed merchants and ship captains: Mr Dixon, Captain Shamman, Mr Walker, &c, &c, Rev. Mr Church, Rev. Mr Huddleston; and in the evening came their ladies and daughters and Miss Fleming to tea and coffee in the great drawing-room, where were cards and at the same time in a saloon opening on the staircase, which made it cool, we had a ball. I roused all the animal spirits I could and danced several country dances. Lord Lonsdale danced with a wonderful complaisancy. We had, I think, for music two fiddles, a bass, a tabor and pipe, and two clarinets.

It was *impossible* not to have my mind somewhat shaken loose from its anxiety by all the circumstances of gay variety. I meditated with a kind of fluttering desperation not quite unpleasant upon human existence in general and my own in particular, wondering 'through what new scenes and changes must we pass', considering that sooner or later, if I did not die sooner than from my constitution I supposed, my dear wife must be removed from me into the next state of being, and trying in imagination how I could bear it, sometimes thinking to retire to a convent, sometimes to live private at Auchinleck, sometimes to hide myself in London, sometimes to be as much as possible in company.

But when I considered my duty to my children, particularly my three daughters, who would much require a father's protection, I thought to force myself to bear the troubles which I feel under a course of ordinary life and to weather it out at least till they should be able to take care of themselves. Sometimes ambitious stirrings to add wealth and consequence to my family by a second marriage, altogether free from that tender connection of hearts which I now experience. Thus was gloomy delay of the object for which I had left London forgotten for a while.

Between nine and ten we went to supper, handsomely served upon six tables in the great dining-room. Dividing us into separate *companies* had an admirable effect to produce ease and cheerfulness. His Lordship desired me to hand Mrs Dixon and sit by her at his table, which was the centre one next to the fireplace. She was sister to Mr Hamilton, surgeon here, and wife of Mr Dixon, merchant, to whom she had been married four or five years. She was a woman of manners more than common, had seen a good deal of the world, was refined yet not affected. I felt myself improved by talking with her. She had read my *Tour*, she told me, and was going to read it a second time. She admired the vivacity of Dr Johnson's ideas. Her husband had purchased an estate in Scotland, *Fairgirth*, near to Mr Maxwell of Munches's. They went to it every summer by sea, but she stipulated to return always by land. She talked with an elegance about everything. She was Mr Dixon's second wife and seemed to be pretty well advanced in years and somewhat paralytic, for her head shook. On my other hand sat a Miss Walker, one of two sisters, with hair black as ravens, without powder, a very pretty, pleasing girl. I took a fancy to the *Coomberland* pronunciation. There was a rural simplicity in it.

THURSDAY 10 JANUARY. Was to go to Carlisle. Lord L. proposed to give me a convoy on horseback, so I sent forward my chaise, and his Lordship, who most obligingly regretted my going away, and Messrs Satterthwaite and Saul rode with me so far, and then I rode on to —, where my chaise waited. I had a dull day alone after so much society, and being anxious about my wife. Got to Carlisle by ten. Had Alderman Jackson first with me, and heard how all was prepared. His shrewdness and address pleased me much. I had the mayor and him and Alderman Wherlings to sup with me, and could not but think within myself how wonderful it was that I was now so easy and even confidential in an English town.

FRIDAY 11 JANUARY. Rose remarkably well, and dressed as well as I could. Had a message to come to Joseph Porter's, where all Lord L.'s friends of the Corporation had breakfasted. I shook hands with them all and thanked them. They went to the Moot Hall and, after they had resolved, sent for me. I walked down and, being introduced, was told by the mayor of their intention to choose me Recorder if I would accept of the office. I said I should think myself much honoured. Only Mr Harrington (called 'Sword' Harrington) objected, and proposed Counsellor Clark. Four others would not hold up their hands for me. But there was so great a majority, I was declared duly elected. I then made a speech, thanking them and saying that my only uneasiness was that I should not be able to discharge the duties of the office as I wished to do. But it should be my sincere endeavour to do it to the best of my abilities. That I was sorry there were party dissensions among them, but with these I had nothing to do. My business was with the law and the solid prosperity of this ancient city. I then shook hands with all my electors. Sword Harrington walked off. I went up to Borriskill, one of the opposite party, and with a frank, good-humoured look said, '*Will* you give me your hand, Sir?' He was won; gave me his hand and said, 'I wish you joy, Sir.' I then (after having been sworn in, which I believe was before my shaking hands) asked my electors to go to the Bush with me and drink a glass of wine. The mayor, with me at his left hand (my *place*), walked up the street, followed by all my friends. I sent an invitation to the five of the opposite party, but they would not come. We did not sit down, but drank a few toasts in sherry: I their health, they mine; 'Prosperity to the Ancient City of Carlisle'; 'The King, the Earl of Lonsdale, and may His Majesty long have such an able supporter of the just rights of the Crown.' I was really elated, and could not but inwardly muse how extraordinary it was that I had obtained this promotion. Mine host, Howe, with wonderful gravity addressed me, 'Mr Recorder', as if I had been seven years in the office.

MONDAY 14 JANUARY. I set out in the heavy coach for Penrith between one and two, having secured a seat in the mail-coach, and at Buchanan's I had a comfortable supper and sleep, and was taken up about three in the morning by the mail-coach. I had a very good journey to London, and arrived at the General Post Office about eight o'clock on Monday morning. When I got to the door of my house, I was glad to find the knocker tied up, as this proved that my dear wife was not dead, as my anxious mind had frequently figured. Mrs Bruce informed me that she was a good deal better, but I soon saw from her appearance that she had been at the gates of death. She was, however, now so far recovered that I dismissed Sir George Baker, who visited her in the forenoon. I went to Mr Malone's in the evening, and was cordially social.

Margaret Boswell was safe on that occasion, but in the middle of the next year her consumption got worse. Boswell, in London, heard of this and began the long trip back to Scotland, where his wife was now living at Auchinleck. What followed was always a source of great guilt and grief to him.

Boswell to Temple

Auchinleck, 3 July 1789
My dear Temple, – Your letter upon my late most severe loss proves that you are now the same steady and warm-hearted friend that I have ever known you. O my friend! this is affliction indeed! My two boys and I posted from London to Auchinleck night and day, in sixty-four hours and one quarter, but alas! our haste was all in vain. The fatal stroke had taken place before we set out. It was very strange that we had no intelligence whatever upon the road, not even in our own parish, not till my second daughter came running out from our house and announced to us the dismal event in a burst of tears. O! my Temple! what distress, what tender painful regrets, what unavailing earnest wishes to have but one week, one day, in which I might again hear her admirable conversation and assure her of my fervent attachment notwithstanding all my irregularities. It was some relief to me to be told that she had after I was set out mentioned what I think I wrote to you, that she had pressed me to go up and show my zeal for Lord Lonsdale. But when on my return before the cause came on, I found that by my going away at that unlucky time I had not been with her to soothe her last moments, I cried bitterly and upbraided myself for leaving her, for she would not have left me. This reflection, my dear

friend, will I fear pursue me to my grave. She had suffered a great deal from her disease for some weeks before her death. But the actual scene of dying itself was not dreadful. She continued quite sensible till a few minutes before, when she began to doze calmly and expired without any struggle. When I saw her four days after, her countenance was not at all disfigured. But alas! to see my excellent wife, and the mother of my children, and that most sensible, lively woman, lying cold and pale and insensible was very shocking to me. I could not help doubting that it was a deception. I could hardly bring myself to agree that the body should be removed, for it was still a consolation to me to go and kneel by it and talk to my dear, dear Peggie. She was much respected by all who knew her, so that her funeral was remarkably well attended. There were nineteen carriages followed the hearse, and a large body of horsemen, and the tenants of all my lands. It is not customary in Scotland for a husband to attend his wife's funeral. But I resolved if I possibly could to do her the last honours myself, and I *was* able to go through with it very decently. I privately read the funeral service over her coffin in the presence of my sons and was relieved by that ceremony a good deal. On the Sunday after, Mr Dun delivered almost verbatim a few sentences which I sent him as a character of her. I imagined that I should not be able to stay here after the sad misfortune. But I find that I cling to it with a melancholy pleasure.

Honest David is perpetually pressing my confining my family to Scotland. But alas, my dear friend, should I or could I now be satisfied with narrow provinciality, which was formerly so irksome and must now be much more so? I have agreed that my second daughter shall pass the winter at Edinburgh, as she has desired it, in order to finish her education. But were my daughters to be *Edinburgh-mannered girls*, I could have no satisfaction in their company. Veronica wishes to be boarded this winter with a lady in London. Little Betsy, who is just nine year old, goes tomorrow to a quiet boarding-school at Ayr, our county town, till I settle where to place her for a year or two. I am thinking of a convent in France, or rather in Flanders, where she can be well educated a certain length very cheap, and then I would finish her at one of the great English boarding-schools. Yet if I can find a good and cheap English one I may probably not send her abroad. Can you and Mrs Temple advise me? My eldest son I am resolved shall go to Eton this winter. I am to have only chambers in the Temple after

Christmas. I may perhaps come to you in autumn if Malone goes to Ireland, so that the revising of Johnson's *Life* cannot proceed till winter. I am much obliged to you for your prayer. I *experience* that piety affords the only true comfort. My kindest love to you and yours. I am forcing myself to be as busy as I can and think of going the Northern Circuit. Ever most affectionately yours,

J.B.

Pray write often, though but a few lines.

1790

Boswell is in London, still trying to use Lonsdale to further his career but with less and less hope of success.

SUNDAY 13 JUNE. My heart was sore for my son James, who complained of being very unhappy at Westminster School. Poor little fellow, on the Sunday when I first walked down with him to introduce him, he said to me, 'Is it not hard that what should be the most agreeable part of life is made the most unhappy by being at school, and that to learn only the dead languages?' I could not *argue* against this, but insisted on that kind of education having formed the greatest men in this nation. He was much cast down as we walked, but when we got to Prince's Street, he said, 'I find myself more composed.' Last Sunday, which was the day on which he actually entered to the boarding-house, I was very anxious. I made him kneel with me in the forenoon, and I prayed aloud for him, that as he was now about to enter on a new situation in life, GOD would be pleased to bless him and preserve him from the temptations to which he would be exposed. This day Veronica and he and I went to evening service about four o'clock: prayers and sermon in our parish church of Marylebone. My spirits were sadly depressed. I dined tête-à-tête with Malone and revised forty-six pages of my *Life of Johnson*.

MONDAY 14 JUNE. The Parliament being dissolved, the hurry and agitation hurt my weak nerves. I breakfasted with honest Baldwin, my printer, and concerted that in case I should be called away for some weeks, my compositor, Plymsell, an intelligent and accurate man, should have other employment that he might leave, and resume my book on my return. I went to Dilly's and was so ill that I could scarcely articulate. His kindly expressions consoled me somewhat. I resolved that as I had no chance for success in Ayrshire, not to go to the election but write to my friends that I declined to stand. My servant James found me here, Lord Lonsdale having sent twice for me and having desired that I should be inquired for wherever I might be supposed to be. I was sorry that I had been found, for Colonel Lowther had told me that when he suggested my coming in for Carlisle, the Earl disapproved and said, 'He would get drunk and make a foolish speech.' This, if fairly reported, was an absolute proof that his Lordship had no confidence in me, and indeed his not employing me in Westminster Hall[8] might show this. I could not bear the thoughts of being engaged by him in some of his political jobs.

I came home and found Temple and his daughter returned. I was against going to Lord Lonsdale's and saw him now in such a light that I declared I would not accept of one of his seats in Parliament. However, Temple urged me to go to him, which I did, and found him at dinner though it was but about three o'clock; indeed dinner was almost over, and he had drunk a good deal of wine. He said he had not seen me for a long time. I said that I supposed he would be very busy, and was unwilling to intrude. He told me that the King's Bench had nearly been moved against me because, the mayor being at the same time one of the senior aldermen, there were at present but three Justices of Carlisle, and by his Lordship's own absence and mine the order of poor's rates could not be made, and a complaint was to have been made against the Recorder for not being there. Therefore it was necessary for me to go down directly, and the Recorder must also be present at the election. He talked meanly of this being all I had to do for my £20 salary. This sudden requisition vexed me not a little. I mentioned my worthy old friend having come all the way from Cornwall chiefly to see me, and endeavoured to evade the shock; but I found him determined, and was obliged to engage to go with him to Lancaster in my way next day at twelve. Penn, whom he had set up at Lancaster and said he would spend £50,000 rather than not have a seat there for him, was ready to set out, accompanied by Colonel Lowther. Both of them talked to me, as it were, in half hints, that I must not hang back *now*.

I hastened home and lamented to Temple my unfortunate situation.

He was friendly and soothing. I had eat and drunk a little at Lord Lonsdale's. I was heated. I rashly went three times in the course of this day to a stranger. I was feverish. My brother T.D. and his wife dined with us. Both Temple and he thought that I should write to Lord Lonsdale resigning the Recordership. I accordingly had a letter sketched. But I went to Malone, who insisted that as I had asked the office, I should go down, resolutely discharge the duty, see whether it was meant to bring me into Parliament or not, and if not, to resign some time afterwards and withdraw from so disagreeable a connection. I came home and on many accounts was in a wretched state.

TUESDAY 15 JUNE. Had rested very ill; hot, feverish, tossing. My dear friend Temple was quite uneasy to see the state in which I was. It hurt me particularly that my dismal hypochondria had returned at the time when he had kindly come to see me after a seven years' separation. I was so troubled in thought that I absolutely groaned. About half past eleven I went to Lord Lonsdale's. He was not stirring. I came home and wrote a letter of earnest expostulation against being obliged to quit London at this moment, declaring at the same time that if really necessary, I would go.

Boswell to Lonsdale

Queen Anne Street West, 15 June 1790
My Lord, – I am persuaded your Lordship would not intentionally distress me, which my quitting town at this moment would do very much on account of circumstances in my private affairs with which it would be improper to trouble your Lordship.

I should at any rate be very unwilling now to go so near my own county as Carlisle because I have resolved to withdraw myself as a candidate upon finding that I should only discover9 my weakness; and it would, I fear, have an awkward appearance to be almost in the neighbourhood and not go to the election. The real truth is that my views now are such that my want of success is no disappointment to me, but I would avoid any disagreeable circumstances.

If it be really necessary that the Recorder should be present at the election at Carlisle, I shall certainly be there at the time of which I can have due notice, for while I hold that place I shall be faithful to its duties. But I earnestly request that your Lordship may not ask me to go down sooner. I have the honour to be with great respect, my Lord, your Lordship's most obedient, humble servant.

I sent this, and said I would call directly. I did so and found him alone and stated to him all my unwillingness. He talked of the importance of preventing complaints, and said that I must go unless I resigned the office of Recorder so that another might be appointed. I jumped inwardly at this, but calmly said, 'I rather would resign.' Finding this, he began to mutter that reflections would be thrown out, &c, &c, &c. 'My Lord,' said I, 'your Lordship shall have no reflections on my account. I'll go directly, do the business handsomely, and then resign with a good grace.' I was happy to think that I had announced my resignation before the subject of my not being brought into Parliament had been in question.

I should have mentioned that I called this forenoon on Sir Michael Le Fleming, who told me that he had pressed on the Earl my being elected for Carlisle, and urged that having a man who was known might even have *some* influence on the minds of a Committee; but that his Lordship had resolved to set up two blackguards. Sir Michael said that in short Lord Lonsdale liked my company much and wished to have me go with him, and being not perfectly decided in his own mind, might wish to have me ready as a stopgap if it should so strike him. I told Sir Michael warmly that this was quite unsuitable to me, that I was as proud as Lucifer, and that I would have no connection with Lord Lonsdale farther than paying my respects to him as an independent gentleman. I dined with some satisfaction with my guests and daughter. After dinner Temple and I sauntered in Wimpole Street, and he advised me to return to the Scotch bar, as he saw no prospect of my getting any *advantage* by being in London. I could not bear the thoughts of sinking so, and said I would try one other winter and attend Westminster Hall and apply to the Lord Chancellor. In short I was quite dislocated.

The Earl had told me that, if he could, he intended to set out at four or five in the morning. Knowing how uncertain he was, and dreading the torment of waiting, I settled with him that he should send and let me know when he was ready. In the evening Temple and I had a little cold negus as in old times, after our daughters had gone upstairs. I revived somewhat. I went to bed with the stillness of a desperate man, ready to be called at four, at the same time supposing that perhaps the Earl might not go till next evening.

WEDNESDAY 16 JUNE. I stayed at home all day in a strange state of mind, to be ready at a call. My dear friend Temple did all in his power to console me. Malone, upon a message from me, came, and we settled that my *Life of Johnson* should go on at press a certain way[10] during my absence. About eleven at night came a note from Lord Lonsdale summoning me to breakfast with him next morning at half past eight, and then proceed to the north. This was now a distressing knell. I considered that the time was when I should have been elated by such a message. But now all ambitious hopes were gone.

THURSDAY 17 JUNE. Rose in very bad spirits. A little conversation with my dear friend Temple, and parted cordially. At nine, L.'s. No appearance. Waited almost two hours. Went home. All gone out. Returned. He at breakfast. Irritated at my going. Jackson with him. Before whom and Robinson his servant (when I represented how hard it was on me to go), he was in a fury, and said, 'You have some sinister motive.' 'How can your Lordship say so?' 'Because I know the man to whom I speak. I suppose you want to have a large fee.' 'Did your Lordship ever see anything in my conduct to make you think so?' 'You asked the Recordership of me. I did not wish you should be Recorder. But you were so earnest, I granted it. And now when duty is required, you would give it up. What have you done for your salary? I will advise the Corporation not to accept your resignation till you have attended the Midsummer Sessions as well as the election. I suppose you think we are fond of your company. You are mistaken. We don't care for it. *I* should have heard of no difficulties. It is your own concern. I suppose you thought I was to bring you into Parliament. I never had any such intention. It would do you harm to be in Parliament.' This was a full discovery. I had leave of absence for an hour; went to Malone, and told him. He advised me to go in apparent good humour and get away as soon as I could. It vexed me that I was dragged away from the printing of my *Life of Johnson*, and that perhaps Malone might be gone to Ireland before I could get back to London.

At L.'s again. Time was trifled away till the afternoon, I am not sure what hour. L. took me under the arm, and we walked by Grosvenor Square to Oxford Street, near Hanover Square, to get into his coach.

As we walked, the bringing into Parliament was resumed, and he showed his poor opinion of me, saying I would get drunk and make a foolish speech. I talked too freely of my liberal and independent views, and of their inconsistency with being brought in by him unless special terms were granted. He was provoked. In the coach the same subject was unfortunately resumed, and I expressed myself, I do not recollect exactly how, but so as to raise his passion almost to madness, so that he used shocking words to me, saying, 'Take it as you will. I am ready to give you satisfaction.' 'My Lord,' said I, 'you have said enough.' I was in a stunned state of mind, but calm and determined. He went on with insult: 'You have kept low company all your life. What are *you*, Sir?' 'A gentleman, my Lord, a man of honour; and I hope to show myself such.' He brutally said, 'You will be settled when you have a bullet in your belly.' Jackson sat silent.

When we came to Barnet and entered the inn, I told him he had treated me very ill and very unjustly. He said, 'I will give you satisfaction *now*. I have pistols here.' 'If you please, my Lord; and I will be obliged to you for pistols.' 'What, Sir, against myself? Certainly not.' I went out and inquired if there was any regiment quartered there, thinking that I might get one of the officers to lend me pistols and be my second. There was none. I returned to him and said I would go back to London and find a friend, and let his Lordship know when we could meet. We had a cold dinner, during which he said it would seem strange to me when the friend I should bring would say that his words to me were warranted; that I was the aggressor, and ought to ask pardon; that I had attacked his honour. Looking on him really as a madman, and wishing upon principle never to have a duel if I could avoid it with credit, I protested that I had no such intention as he supposed; and then in order to give him an opportunity to have the matter adjusted, I asked his pardon for using expressions which his Lordship had imagined attacked his honour, but which I solemnly declared were not so meant by me. He then said he would not have used such words to me if he had not thought that my expressions were meant as he had supposed. Then we drank a glass of wine.

Captain Payne joined us and sat some time. After he was gone, and I was walking before the door of the inn, L. sent for me, and when I came, held out his hand and gave it me, saying, 'Boswell, forget all that is past.' Jackson said to me that the affair had been very well settled, and not a syllable about it should ever transpire. He said L. was interested in not mentioning it. After this we travelled on socially enough, but I was inwardly mortified to think that I had deceived myself so woefully as to my hopes from the Great Lowther, and that I was now obliged to submit to what was very disagreeable to me without any reward or hope of any good, but merely to get out of the scrape into which I had brought myself.

TUESDAY 22 JUNE. I lay till twelve, merely to get time over. Sir James Johnstone and I drank our coffee together. I read a little in Terence. I had many wavering schemes: to go into the mayor's house; to go to Newcastle and be under Mr Leighton's care; to go to Mr Senhouse's; to go to Springkell. My having no servant with me and being in bad health made it awkward for me to go to any gentleman's house. The mayor and I took a short saunter. Walking was painful to me. He dined with me at my inn. I had drunk very little wine since I left London, so that I was low; but that was better than being heated. I drank tea with the Rev. Mr Carlyle in his study, and had really a glimpse of satisfaction. He was translating an Arabian history, and his books and literary conversation relieved me somewhat. I came again to my inn, dejected and insignificant, and having lain till twelve, went to bed again at eight. I shrunk from the thought of having to waste time here for about three weeks. I recollected my valuable wife with most affectionate regret, and felt how helpless I was when deprived of her. I endeavoured to cherish the hope of meeting her in a better world. I thought how unlike I now was to the father of five children: a son at Eton, a son at Westminster, &c, &c.

THURSDAY 24 JUNE. Had slept unsound, dreaming a great deal, in particular that Veronica approached me suddenly, saying, 'Now my mother's disease is come at last – a consumption'; and she looked ill, and when I took her hand, there was a clammy sweat upon it. I awaked much affected. I began to think, to recollect my worthy, rational, steady father. What was I doing here at Carlisle? In what a scattered state was the Family of Auchinleck? I was very sad. Scarcely had I any hope. I had yesterday received a letter from my brother David communicating from Lady Auchinleck Euphemia's uneasiness at staying longer at the Edinburgh boarding-school. I resolved to relieve her. I rose a little after eight. Walked out at the Scotch Gate weary and uneasy. Came to Jollie's shop. Tried various books; could fix to none except the 'Life' of Dr Leechman by Wodrow; not well done, and the group of Glasgow College ideas made me dreary as in my youth. Called on Hodgson, surgeon-apothecary, once my landlord at the assizes. Breakfasted with him, his wife and a widow who boarded with them. Felt myself a man troubled in mind. Wished to lodge at his house. But it was now full. Went to the mayor's and settled to have a room at his house at night. Felt an alarm as to my local complaint, as if inflammatory and tending to mortification. Wrote letters to Lady Auchinleck, Euphemia, Mr Robert Boswell and Mr Alexander of Ballamyle. Said to Lady Auchinleck that I was unhappy here, but it was but a variation of uneasiness; that I could be of no service to my daughters, but I feared the contrary; prayed GOD to bless my children and make them happier than their father. I was much relieved by writing with great kindness to Euphemia. I dined at the Bush on a roast chicken and drank about a pint of port, and felt a certain degree of animation and some glimmering of hope that I might still have some enjoyment in life. I read some in Terence with satisfaction.[11] I went to the coffee-house and drunk coffee and read newspapers for a long time. Then went to the mayor's, Mr Wherlings the postmaster's, where I had settled that I would lodge. I sat an hour or two very dully with him and his daughter, and then took possession of a good room, well furnished.

FRIDAY 25 JUNE. Had enjoyed a good night's rest and dreamed none. When I rose, was alarmed with the pain of my local complaint, which I had mentioned to Knubley yesterday, and this morning mentioned to my barber, that I might inquire who were the best surgeons here. Resolved however to wait some time before calling one, as I hoped to cure myself. It was a rainy day. I did not stir out, but finished reading the *Andria* of Terence, and read Mountfort's comedy of *Greenwich Park*. Wondered at its gross licentiousness being allowed on the stage. Was weakly dejected and could hardly think it possible that I could ever be able to do any good. Was as low as I had ever been in the country. But felt that the mind will acquiesce wonderfully in any situation. Resolved that I never again would allow my spirits to exult. Yet had an unwillingness to think that I should have no more enjoyment in life. Notwithstanding the reconciliation and shaking hands with L., had a certain uneasiness as if I had not been spirited enough with him, and felt a strange regret that I had not had the *éclat* of being in the field against the Great Lowther. But the *serious* apprehension that I might have been cut off by *violence* from my young family, and my *magnum opus*, the *Life of Johnson*, left unfinished, weighed on the other side. I breakfasted, dined, and drank tea with my landlord and his daughter, both good-humoured and obliging. Took only two glasses of wine. I eagerly counted the hours.

SATURDAY 26 JUNE. Had not rested very well. Had dreamed disagreeable Edinburgh dreams. It was still rainy weather. I read a great part of Waller's poems, which I had never read before but very imperfectly. Did not think so very highly of them as I supposed I should. But this was probably owing to my unhappy state of mind. I read a part of Terence's *Eunuchus*. It had strangely happened that I had never read more than one, or at most two, of his plays. I resolved to read them all. I borrowed a Delphin edition from a bookseller's and made a study of Terence, whose mode of writing I found difficult to me. I read some in old volumes of magazines, which gave me dull and dreary impressions of the nothingness of human affairs. I weathered out the day stupidly and uneasily. No company but the mayor and his daughter. Drank two glasses of wine. My complaint was no better. The precept for election came today. It was a *degree* of consolation that it *must* begin in eight days. I wrote to Mr Earle for advice, and I wrote a very earnest letter to Governor Penn, stating my wretchedness and entreating that if he could prudently venture it, he would intercede with the Earl to let me go, as everything might now be done without me. I was sensible that I *deserved* that part of my unhappiness occasioned by my complaint, for *what* can be more culpable at my time of life, and in my situation as the head of a family, than the wild conduct of a licentious youth? I was now incapacitated from taking the relief which exercise and society might perhaps have afforded. I had a poor, selfish comfort in a good bed. I was a despicable being.

Boswell to Penn

Carlisle, 26 June 1790

My dear Sir, – I cannot express to you how very miserable I am. In the first place, some time before I left London I was afflicted with a return of the bad spirits to which I am subject, which have continued in a sad degree and been much increased by the mortifying discovery made to me by Lord Lonsdale – not that his Lordship was not to bring me into Parliament, for you and everyone who ever mentioned that subject to me can attest that I declared I did not expect it – but that he had formed such an opinion of my character as I am conscious I do not deserve, so that an ambitious hope which I had cherished of being connected with and patronized by one of the greatest men in this country is utterly blasted.

I have not stirred out for two days. To confess the truth, I am ill, painfully ill, as I deserve to be, and dare not, nor will not trust to any practitioner here. I am therefore following the method of Mr Earle but, as you may imagine, am very anxious to be with him. When you consider the complication of evils to which I am now subjected without having a soul with whom I can communicate, I am sure you will feel for me. Let Lord Lonsdale think of me as he pleases, there is not a man alive who would with more zeal have laboured to assist in establishing his real consequence, or one who is more gratefully sensible of any favour done to him. All *that* is now out of the question. But surely his Lordship would not wish to afflict one who never intentionally offended him. For GOD's sake, then, my dear Sir, if you can possibly do it without my incurring his Lordship's displeasure, be so good as to represent to him my unhappy state more or less as you may think prudent, and asking his pardon for my weakness, entreat of him to let me have his permission to leave Carlisle.

I have applied to you in my distress, conscious that were you to apply to me in a like situation, I should be earnest to assist you. I depend on your not mentioning a word of what I write except to the Earl himself if you think you may venture, and that you will burn this unhappy scrawl when you have read it. At any rate, I trust that you will by Monday's post let me have the consolation of hearing from you. I am, dear Sir, yours most sincerely.

P.S. You cannot imagine how it vexes me to be forced to write thus. But I suffer severely. Pray forgive me.

SUNDAY 27 JUNE. Awaked miserably relaxed.[12] It was a wet day. Went to St Cuthbert's Church and heard Rev. Mr Carlyle preach very well, but was devoured by hypochondria. Had a long rational letter from Veronica. Saw how bad a father I was. Had a letter from Sir John

Scott, in a friendly manner recommending a quiet resignation and not to contend with L. Dined as dully as I had ever done at Glasgow or anywhere. Went to the Cathedral at four. All was dull and dead within me. I was convinced that true religion is the gift of GOD's grace. A weary evening. Read today some more of Waller, part of Miln the dissenting teacher's lectures on the Creation, the Deluge, &c, of which he could tell nothing. Was sick of his speculations. Read some of the *Spectator* and had a faint relish of it. But I was quite depressed. Of what avail were all the happy days I had ever enjoyed with *the Gang*, &c?[13] Was it *possible*, I thought, that I could ever again enjoy such? Dr Warren some months ago told me that a change of spirits would come, and cautioned me against imagining that I never could be well again. But alas! as I then told him, that very thought is the worst part of the disease. I could not conceive at present how mankind in any situation could for a moment be deluded into a feeling of happiness, or even of quiet. I was *sure* that if I were at *Edinburgh* all the despicable dejection of my early years would return. I dreaded that in a moment of desperation I might go thither. But I trusted that I should have as much firmness as to keep myself between London and Auchinleck.

WEDNESDAY 30 JUNE. With difficulty could I get up at nine. I had suffered great pain in the night from my complaint, and been sadly apprehensive of its growing very bad. I experienced a very singular thing: the recollection of one dream in the course of a following one. I had first dreamed that I was accompanying my dear M.M. through a wood. I had then another dream which I do not remember; but in the midst of it I was thus struck: 'Stay, I am forgetting a former dream' (for I was conscious that I was then dreaming), and by degrees I recalled it. During these wretched nights I have had variety of dreams; one of last night was that I visited Mr Langton at Oxford, and saw his numerous family.

Boswell to Malone

Carlisle, 30 June 1790

My dear Malone, – I do not think it is in the power of words to convey to you how miserable I have been since I left you. You have had distress of mind. But your active spirit never failed within you.

I have heard you say that you never sat listless by the fire. I have during these wretched days sat so, hours and hours. Everything that ever vexed me has returned. I feel myself a poor, forlorn being, with no permanent vigour of mind, no friend that can enable me to advance myself in life. A fortune sadly encumbered – children whom I can with difficulty support and of whom I am at a loss how to dispose with advantage and propriety – such is the general prospect. And *for immediate* feelings, added to *ennui* and self-upbraiding, I am again unfortunate enough to have *one* sore of a certain nature contracted, I think, Monday forthnight, which *alone* gives me more pain and alarm than *several* which I had lately.

How shocking is it to think that I was dragged away from my friend Temple, who came from Cornwall almost on purpose to see me and saw me so little – and was forced to interrupt my *Life of Dr Johnson*, the most important, perhaps *now* the only concern of any consequence that I ever shall have in this world. And what galls me and irritates me with impatience is the thought that I lose those hours which you could now have given me for revising my manuscript and that perhaps you may be gone before I get back to town. Even the fear of not being in London when at last your Shakspeare comes out is shocking. My dear friend! for GOD's sake if you possibly can, let me have some consolation. The melancholy to which I am subject I know cannot be helped. But I beseech you try to alleviate such of my sufferings as can admit of soothing.

1791

Boswell still in London, still working on the Life, *and still very 'hyp'd'*.

MONDAY 21 FEBRUARY. During this dismal mist of mind, I one day sat a part of the morning with Mrs Fitzgerald. I several times sat a little while with my brother T.D., whose good sense and orderly activity consoled yet mortified me. Courtenay was truly friendly and showed me much kindness. He now lodged within a few doors of me. I was very ill today. The embarrassed state of my affairs overwhelmed my spirits. Yet here was Courtenay with a wife and seven children, and not a shilling. But the blasting of all my ambitious hopes was galling.

I however still had glimpses of hope. I abhorred my new house, from my having been dismal ever since I came into it. My two daughters who were with me seemed in so ill-governed a state, and with so little prospect of being in a better, and they both, but especially the second, had so little respect for me (as indeed how could they for a sickly-minded wretch?) that I was irritated by their behaviour and wished earnestly to have them stationed somewhere with propriety at a distance from me. I was at home all day.

TUESDAY 22 FEBRUARY. Though resolved against entertaining for a long time, I had fixed to give Courtenay some hodgepodge[14] today. I had a note from him that he would be kept late in the House of Commons, so I should not wait. His son and T.D. dined with us about half past six. Mrs Sharp, a maiden lady, great-granddaughter of the Archbishop of St Andrews, drank tea with us. After she and the two others were gone, Courtenay came about ten and had his hodgepodge and bit of roast beef, and obligingly assisted me in *lightening* my animadversions on Mrs Piozzi in my *Life of Johnson* – for my own credit. His manly mind conveyed to me some sympathic force.

WEDNESDAY 23 FEBRUARY. Not at all well. At home till the evening, when Courtenay sent for me to come and sit with him and not mope by myself, when my daughters and his son were at Signor Corri's. I went, but for a time was quite ineffective and could hardly speak. I became somewhat easier, and drank a little mountain. I contemplated his firmness with wonder. He insisted that my daughters should eat oysters with him, and accordingly his son brought them to us about eleven, and I felt myself a little cheered. He had suggested that I should ask the Chancellor to make me a Commissioner of Bankrupts, and was for my trying Westminster Hall resolutely; and, on my mentioning it, thought Hamilton might introduce me to the Chief Baron, Eyre. So here were schemes.

THURSDAY 24 FEBRUARY. The day was fine. I felt a respite. An invitation came to dine next day at Mr Dance's.[15] I dined at home. Little James was with us, it being a whole holiday. He went in the evening. I became suddenly so well that I wished to go into company and be gay. But restrained myself and laboured at *Life*.

FRIDAY 25 FEBRUARY. Not quite so well. But a letter which I had, I think yesterday, from my dear and valuable friend Temple animated me by suggesting that my friends would at last do something for me; advising me to cultivate them, and let *hope travel on*. I dined at Mr Dance's with his brother the City architect, Sir Joshua Reynolds and Miss Palmer, Serjeant Rooke and his lady and a young lady, her relation, Hon. Mrs Boscawen, Laundress to the Queen, and Mr Drew the attorney. It was a curious scene to me to behold Dance, whom I had known at Rome in 1765 by no means in a great situation, now married to a lady of a jointure of £10,000 a year (Mrs Dummer), a genteel, well-bred, agreeable woman, with all the magnificence of wealth. I looked back also to my old friend his brother, Love the player, and I now for the first time met George the architect, of whom I had heard Love often speak. It was not pleasing to find that Sir Joshua had all this time known that I was in sad spirits, and never once called or sent to inquire about me. We must take our friends as they are. 'Courtenay has a *heart*.' I enjoyed the good things and the *English conversation* of today a great deal better than I expected to do. In the evening played whist and lost 15/–.

SATURDAY 26 FEBRUARY. There had fallen a great quantity of snow, and the weather was windy and very cold. I was engaged to dine at Mr Dilly's with Mr Cumberland[16] and Dr Mayo. I hesitated whether I should go. But thought Cumberland's conversation might do me good. So boldly marched. The other guests were Mr Graham, husband of Mrs Macaulay, and the Rev. Mr Alison from Barbados. I had told Cumberland before dinner of my bad spirits. He said, thank GOD he himself had not that complaint; but he had seen his wife suffer a great deal from it, and he had observed the best remedy was change of place. We had a warm room, a good dinner and good wines, and I grew wonderfully easy. Mr Sharp joined us after dinner. He was acquainted with Cowper, the poet, his account of whom was frightful, for with a great deal of genius and even pleasantry, he has at bottom a deep religious melancholy, to divert the shocking thoughts of which he is now translating Homer. He has been woefully deranged – in a strait waistcoat – and now is sometimes so ill that they take away his shoe-buckles, that he may have nothing within his reach with which he can hurt himself. It seems he apprehends himself to be in a state of *reprobation*, being impressed with the most dismal doctrines of Calvinism. I was quite shocked to hear of such a state of mind. My own was good by comparison. Sharp gave me hopes of a great sale for my *Life of Johnson*. He said there were so many people in both the universities, &c, &c, who expected to see themselves, or those whom they knew, in it that they would be eager to have it. We played whist; I won. We supped, and I felt my gloom much lightened.

Cumberland carried me in a hackney-coach as far as Charles Street, St James's, where he lodged. I talked to him of the sad loss which I had suffered by the death of my excellent wife. He said if he should have that misfortune, he would request some amiable woman to marry him and comfort him. And now, though he had denied it before dinner, perhaps from want of recollection, I found that he was subject to mental affliction; for he told me that sometimes when he awaked in the night, his thoughts were terrible, and his relief was to wake Mrs Cumberland and be soothed by a soft female voice speaking tenderly to him. I mentioned the dangers of not finding a woman attached to one as a second wife, and of the discord which such a connection often produced in a family. Nevertheless I allowed myself to imagine I might possibly form a fortunate union.

SUNDAY 27 FEBRUARY. Do not recollect how the forenoon was passed. Dined at home. Went with my daughters and little James to St George's Church in the afternoon. At Lady Lucan's in the evening. Talked with Lady Lonsdale a good deal and with Dr Burney. Was in indifferent spirits. Dr Warren felt my hand cold, and said, 'You have not taken a bottle of wine today.' I went with him in his chariot to be carried to the first stand of hackney-coaches, as it was a wet night. Missing them in a long drive, I had time for a good long conversation with him. He told me that some people had a power of inspiring cheerfulness instantaneously; that when I was myself, I was one of those, and that for some time he had missed the effect which I used to have upon him; that I *must* drink more wine, for having been used to it, I required it, especially when low. When my spirits were better, I might take less. I said it was humiliating that man should be dependent on such material circumstances. 'Sir,' said he, 'such is his nature. Man is naturally a timid animal. The savages skulk and venture into danger by a kind of force. They must rouse themselves by noises, or by the use of something which intoxicates, and the great Ruler of the World has contrived that something of that nature is everywhere to be found. In this town we see people with all the advantages of rank and fortune who yet are uneasy, and must have recourse to wine, and that pretty liberally.' I went with him as far as George Street, Westminster, where he went to his brother the Bishop's, and proposed that I should sit in the carriage till he came out; but as he was to be some time there, I came out and walked home in the rain, the hardship of which I felt brace me.

TUESDAY 15 MARCH. Dined at Mr Osborn's, an elegant repast in quite a different style from yesterday; the company: Sir Joseph Banks, Mr Agar, Sir W. Musgrave, General Rainsford, &c, &c, &c. My daughters (it being Veronica's birthday) had this evening, for the first time, a *small party*. I came home soon on purpose to be at it; but I should have been ready to receive the company, and felt an awkwardness at going into the room. There were about thirty ladies and gentlemen – Mrs Bosville and the Colonel, Sir Joshua Reynolds, Chevalier Freire the Portuguese Minister, and M. Allo the Spanish Secretary, who played on his guitar – and Veronica played and sung. There was a whist-table. Major Green stayed and had some wine and water.

WEDNESDAY 16 MARCH. I should have mentioned a curious dream some nights ago. I thought I was in company with Mr John Wesley, who said, 'You will not see me standing with the rest of you at the Last Day.' 'How so, Sir?' said I. 'Because', said he, 'I am to be received into the immediate presence of GOD.' 'Have you, Sir,' said I, 'had that revealed to you?' He answered, 'I have.' This day I felt myself restless, so walked about a good deal and at four called on Wilkes with intention to dine with him, and was accordingly asked. We had Miss Wilkes, the Rev. Mr Beloe and the Rev. Mr Stockdale, who was now a water-drinker and talked of it with a vain ostentation. Though wild in his manner, he had a good deal of literature, and his reminding me of my dear friend Temple pleased me. Wilkes was, as he never fails to be, very pleasant. I drank liberally, and first went to the Essex Head Club and then to Admiral Lloyd's *late party* at the Somerset.[17]

Boswell to Temple

6 April 1791

My *Life of Johnson* is at last drawing to a close. I am correcting the last sheet and have only to write an advertisement, to make out a note of errata and to correct a second sheet of contents, one being done.

I really hope to publish it on the twenty-fifth current. My old and most intimate friend may be sure that a copy will be sent to him. I am at present in such bad spirits, that I have every fear concerning it – that I may get no profit, nay, may lose – that the public may be disappointed and think that I have done it poorly – that I may make many enemies and even have quarrels. Yet perhaps the very reverse of all this may happen.

When my book is launched, I shall, if I am alive and in tolerable health and spirits, have some furniture put into my chambers in the Temple, and force myself to sit there some hours every day, and to attend regularly in Westminster Hall. The chambers cost me £20 yearly, and I may reckon furniture and a lad to wait there occasionally £20 more. I doubt whether I shall get fees equal to the expense.

Boswell's Life of Johnson *was indeed launched, on 16 May of that year, and was, as has been related earlier, an astounding hit. As he had prophesied, Boswell himself had little success as a London lawyer, and spent the last four years of his life swinging between depression and occasional elation. Our last excerpts are from a sequence of letters between James and his sixteen-year-old son, James Jr.*

James Boswell Jr to Boswell

18 October 1794

Am sorry to find you writing about 'your dull and depressed spirits'. Pray, Sir, do not suffer yourself to be melancholy. Think not on your having missed preferment in London or any of these kind of things, the unreasonableness of which you yourself upon reflection must be sensible of if you consider that your manner of living has never been that of a man of business and that, in short, you have been entirely different in every respect from those who have been (in that line) more successful – they who have obtained places and pensions &c have not the fame of having been the biographer of Johnson or the conscious exultation of a man of genius. They have not enjoyed your happy and convivial hours. They have not been known to Johnson, Voltaire, Rousseau, and Garrick, Goldsmith, &c, &c. They have not visited the patriots of Corsica. In short, would you rather than have enjoyed so many advantages have been a rich, though dull, plodding lawyer? You cannot expect to be both at the same time. Every situation in life has its advantages and disadvantages. Let me then have in your next letter a declaration that you are now in excellent spirits.

Boswell to James Boswell Jr

27 October 1794

My dear James, – Last night I had the pleasure to receive a most sensible and animating letter from you concerning my depression of spirits and complaining of want of success in life; and truly, I must acknowledge that 'thou reasonest well'. For I am at all times satisfied that the circumstances in my lot which you enumerate are to me more valuable than any place or pension which I could have had without them. But unluckily I have all my life indulged fond hopes of raising myself, and of consequence my family, by obtaining some preferment which would be both honourable and profitable. In the common estimation of mankind a Lord of Session's place would have realized that hope. In mine, however, whose views were enlarged by being so much in England, any provincial appointment has long appeared beneath me. The manners of Edinburgh, too, disgusted me and, in short, London has for these thirty years and upwards been the object of my wish as my scene of exertion. Much enjoyment have I had there, but as yet every ambitious aim has been disappointed. My constitutional melancholy is ever lurking about me, and perhaps I should impute to this the chief part of my unhappiness. The country does not at all suit me. I have no relish of its amusements or occupations. My temper is gloomy and irritable, and I am continually fretted by hearing of trespasses upon my woods and lands, and tenants falling behind in their rents. Add to this that my circumstances are so straitened that I am in a wretched state of uneasiness how to get my family supported, and at the same time pay the annuities and interest of debts which must be annually cleared. The expense of living here is much greater to me than in London. The wine and corn and hay consumed cost me half as much every week or more than all that is laid out in town; and then there must here be every day a dinner sufficient for a company, as we cannot be sure of being alone. I do not think I have had two comfortable days, putting together all the hours which should be reckoned so, since the 1st of July when I arrived here. Entertaining company is a weary labour to me, and when I pay visits I seem to myself to be fighting battles, yet I dread returning to London with your sisters, who distressed me so much there.

James Boswell Jr to Boswell

10 November 1794

I have now two letters of yours to answer. In that of the 27th of October you say, 'I am at all times satisfied that the circumstances in my lot which you enumerate are to me more valuable than any place or pension I could have had *without them.*' By which you seem to mean that you wished for preferment with them. Look round the world; observe them who are rising at the bar, in the state or any occupation. Do they live in that manner? Very differently indeed! Hard at work, surrounded with papers, poring over Coke upon Littleton, &c, without one moment to themselves, hardly. When you see Warren rising from the middle of his dinner to go (perhaps out of town) to a patient, Mansfield (as his son informs me he very frequently was obliged to do) going to bed with his papers by his bedside, do you envy him his money? I dare to say you do not. Such is the life that must be led by those who acquire money.

You complain of your constitutional melancholy. That, to be sure, together with other vexatious circumstances, sometimes harasses you. But who so merry and gay as you in company, though at times gloomy at home? Why may it not be so their happiness may be as much put on as yours is? I have since your absence been pretty frequently at my uncle's and I know that he (for one) is very far from being happy. With such a share of felicity as you have now, and have had, I see no reason why you should be discontented. Read Clarendon, or if you find that he is tedious lay him down and take up some other book. Or rather, what I would advise you to do is something in the way of an author – any little pamphlet or anything to keep you going. Write a play. What's become of *The Pawnbroker* and *The Improver*,[18] &c, &c. Don't give way to your melancholy but drive it off; there are a thousand ways.

Boswell to James Boswell Jr

21 November 1794

My dear James, – Before me lies your admirable letter of the 10th, in which you write *de consolatione* like a true philosopher, who has observed human life and made just reflections. I will try to avoid repining. Yet at the same time I cannot be contented merely with literary fame and social enjoyments. I must still hope for some creditable employment, and perhaps I may yet attain it.

The last complete letter we have from Boswell's hand, written the day he went down with his brief fatal illness, shows him making an exit from active life with his head held high. The members of the Literary Club, who had naturally taken on the business of supplying an inscription for Johnson's grave in Westminster Abbey, had asked Samuel Parr, a classical scholar, to provide the actual wording. Parr, a touchy man, had insisted that whatever he provided should be accepted in advance, sight unseen, and should go on to the monument without discussion. Boswell, concerned for Johnson's reputation and anxious to see things done properly, states his views in a letter at once firm, clear and reasonable.

Boswell to Malone

Great Portland Street, 13 April 1795

Dear Sir, – Whatever respect you and I and all who take a concern in erecting a monument to Dr Johnson may have for the learning and abilities of Dr Parr, I am clear that we could not be justified in adopting implicitly without so much as having seen it, the inscription which that gentleman has written. We are answerable to the memory of our illustrious friend, to the present age, and to posterity. Let me add: we are answerable to another tribunal, without whose approbation of the epitaph the monument cannot be admitted into St Paul's Church: I mean the Dean and Chapter of that Cathedral.

When Sir Joshua Reynolds asked Dr Parr to furnish an epitaph, I cannot suppose that he meant to preclude even himself from all consideration, and all power of objection; far less that he could entertain a notion that the other gentlemen with whom he had not conferred on the subject, would be so tied up. He certainly understood that this epitaph, as in all similar cases, was to be subject to revision. He had before him the example of Dr Johnson himself, who was requested to write Dr Goldsmith's epitaph; and how did that great man conduct himself? You will find in my octavo edition of his *Life*, volume 2, page 448, a letter from him to Sir Joshua in which he says, 'I send you the poor dear Doctor's epitaph. Read it first yourself; and if you then think it right, show it to The Club. I am, you know, willing to be corrected.'

I trust that when Dr Parr reconsiders his unusual proposition, he will be satisfied that, without any offence to him, it must receive a negative. I am with much regard, dear Sir, your faithful, humble servant,

JAMES BOSWELL

Boswell's last letter, which he signed and of which wrote the first few words.

Boswell to Temple

8 May 1795

My dear Temple, – I would fain write to you with my own hand but really cannot.

Alas! my friend, what a state is this. My son James is to write for me what remains of this letter and I am to dictate. The pain, which continued for so many weeks, was very severe indeed, and when it went off, I thought myself quite well, but I soon felt a conviction that I was by no means as I should be, being so excessively weak as my miserable attempt to write to you afforded a full proof. All, then, that can be said is that I must wait with patience.

But O my friend, how strange is it that at this very time of my illness you and Miss Temple should have been in such a dangerous state! Much reason for thankfulness is there that it has not been worse with you. Pray write or make somebody write frequently. I feel myself a good deal stronger today notwithstanding the scrawl.

God bless you, my dear Temple! I ever am your old and most affectionate friend, here and I trust hereafter,

JAMES BOSWELL

James Boswell Jr to Temple, enclosed with the preceding letter

Reverend Sir, – You will find by the foregoing, the whole of which was dictated to me by my father, that he is ignorant of the dangerous situation in which he was, and I am sorry to say still continues to be. Yesterday and today he has been somewhat better, and we trust that the nourishment which he is now able to take, and his strong constitution, will support him through. I remain with respect,

JAMES BOSWELL JR

James Boswell Jr to Temple

16 May 1795

My father received your letter yesterday, which I read to him as he was unable to do it himself. He continues much in the same state as he was when I wrote last: he is very weak but it is to be hoped that by taking a sufficient quantity of nourishment he will recover strength and health.

James Boswell Jr to Temple

18 May 1795

I am sorry to inform you that since I wrote last my father is considerably worse; he is weaker, and almost all the nourishment he takes comes off his stomach again. He had expressed a very earnest desire to be lifted out of bed, and Mr Earle, the surgeon, thought it might be done with safety. But his strength was not equal to it and he fainted away. Since that he has been in a very bad way indeed and there are now, I fear, little or no hopes of his recovery.

T.D. Boswell to Temple

19 May 1795

I have now the painful task of informing you that my dear brother expired this morning at two o'clock; we have both lost a kind, affectionate friend, and I shall never have such another. He has suffered a great deal during his illness, which has lasted five weeks, but not much in his last moments; may God Almighty have mercy upon his soul and receive him into His heavenly kingdom. He is to be buried at Auchinleck, for which place his sons will set out in two or three days; they and his two eldest daughters have behaved in the most affectionate, exemplary manner during his confinement.

Notes

Chapter 1: 'I Could Not Contain My Ardour'

1. *who was forfeited*: whose estate was made forfeit to the Crown after the 1745–6 Jacobite Rising.
2. *genius*: individual guiding spirit, able to steer the mind in a particular direction.
3. *negus*: hot sweetened wine.
4. *Digges*: West Digges, a well-known Scots actor and a man Boswell looked up to and even tried to imitate.
5. *brought the Canongate*: brought back memories of the Edinburgh theatre, which was in that street.
6. *Dodsley*: the bookseller who had brought out Boswell's poem 'The Cub at Newmarket' some time before.
7. *Downing Street*: this was before that street became the one where the Prime Minister resides. Boswell's lodgings no longer exist.
8. *complacency*: i.e. she was 'complaisant', gentle and accommodating.
9. *black young fellow*: black meaning dark-skinned or -complexioned. Others including Rousseau and J.B.'s lover Mrs Dodds are called 'black' in this sense.
10. *the half of his star*: indicating that the Duke of Kingston was a Knight of the Garter.
11. *the Revolution*: of 1688.
12. *praeses*: an official at a Scottish election.
13. *joint sixpenny cut*: a 'cut' or dig at Malloch, the playwright they seem to have despised, in a sixpenny pamphlet produced jointly by all three.
14. *Smith*: Adam Smith, the economist and philosopher.
15. See Who's Who.
16. *Wilkes*: John Wilkes (see Who's Who) was in court that day, on charges relating to his attack on King and Government in the *North Briton*, No. 45.

17. Captain Macheath was a character in Gay's popular *The Beggar's Opera*.
18. *Colley Cibber*: well-known actor and playwright.
19. *Life Guard*: i.e. two soldiers of the Royal Household.
20. *Court-end*: the West End of London, as we would say now. Also the fashionable side of town then, in part since that was where the Court was to be found.

Chapter 2: 'A Crowd of Great Thoughts'

1. *break off*: start off, begin.
2. *your jeu d'esprit*: an untraced work.
3. Σωτὴρ Κόσμου: Saviour of the World.
4. *Kate Macaulay*: Mrs Catherine Macaulay, 1731–91, historian and controversialist, of Whig principles very different from those of J.B. and S.J.
5. *Cairnie*: J.B. had been sending regular maintenance money to Peggy Doig, mother of his son Charles, through Cairnie, an Edinburgh doctor.
6. *loss*: lack, shortcoming.
7. *Reysesac*: portmanteau, trunk.
8. *O dear Saint-Preux*: the hero of Rousseau's *La Nouvelle Héloïse*.
9. *album is album*: Rousseau's pun turns on the Latin for white, or blank (French *blanc*).
10. *About six I set out*: following this visit to Rousseau Boswell spent some hours writing the 'Sketch of My Early Life' which we have reprinted as the prologue to this volume.
11. *your lady*: Boswell's married lover; see Prologue, p. 5.
12. *figmagairies*: whims, idiosyncrasies.
13. Voltaire was in fact seventy, having been born in 1694.
14. *Et penitus toto divisos orbe Britannos*: 'And the Britons, completely cut off from all the rest of the world'. From Virgil's *Eclogues*.
15. *the Pretender*: the old Pretender, James Stuart, whom Boswell saw later in Rome and who died in 1766.
16. *potius optandum quam probandum*: 'matter of faith rather than of demonstration'.

Chapter 3: 'A Gentleman of Fortune upon His Travels'

1. *cicisbays*: a *cicisbeo* was an escort for a married woman, accompanying her to evening functions and occasions such as the opera.
2. *religiosus et semper contentus*: religious and always content.

3. *siccitas animi*: dryness of the soul.
4. *Lord Talbot's duel*: in 1762 Wilkes had offended Earl Talbot in one of his satirical articles, but neither really wanted to injure the other in combat and they were soon reconciled.
5. *If I died . . . murder*: Wilkes means that Boswell, a Scot and a Royalist, would be suspected of killing his populist friend.
6. William Flexney published Charles Churchill's poems.
7. *Ebbene . . . galantuomo*: 'Good enough, I trust myself with you as a man of honour.'
8. *Ero totalmente . . . una bestia*: 'I was completely innocent. When I was put in bed with my husband, I found things [*roba*] around me, and thought it was an animal.' Here, as throughout, we are indebted to Professor Pottle for translations of the original Italian, which in this case is grammatically rather ambiguous and the overall meaning confused.
9. *Julie*: the heroine of *La Nouvelle Héloïse*.
10. *Voi siete . . . fate il male*: 'You yourself are precisely that Rousseau. Just like him. You talk a great deal about virtue, and yet you do wrong.' NB the next sentence, 'I was . . . sentiment', was struck out by Boswell before he sent the letter to Rousseau.
11. *never . . . play*: i.e. at cards, for money.
12. *Ah . . . momenti*: 'Ah, I shall lament these moments.'
13. *noctes . . . Deum; Vincet . . . cupido*: 'the nights and banquets of the gods'; 'The love of country will prevail, and the overwhelming desire for praise.'
14. *Diceres . . . causidicos*: 'You would say they are all good pleaders.' Boswell's own footnote.
15. *Sunt . . . ingenia*: 'The dispositions of the Corsicans are changeable.' Boswell.
16. *Mme Hecquet's*: a brothel, the Hôtel Montigny, where J.B. had met Mlle Constance the previous day.
17. *Hope . . . these women*: refers to Zélide and Ann Stow, in fact Temple's later bride.
18. *Quanta oscula*: such kissing.
19. *Voltaire's . . . coach*: See p. 124.
20. *Miss Bosville*: Elizabeth Bosville, J.B.'s cousin, one of his prospective marriage partners, and later the wife of Sir Alexander MacDonald (see Who's Who, and Chapter 6).

Chapter 4: 'Dreaming of Delightful Nuptials'

1. *felices . . . amplius*: 'Thrice happy and more (are they who are united in passionate love)' – Horace.

2. *I took myself*: restrained, checked himself.
3. *the Nabob*: a man who had made good in India, in this case one Mr Fullarton.
4. *the ordinary*: the chaplain of Newgate.
5. *the wars of Venus*: they are obviously discussing methods of preventing or curing venereal disease (probably gonorrhoea).
6. *in my mind*: the reader may be interested to know that the following episode was a victim of the cuts made before the manuscripts were sold to Isham (see Introduction, pp. xxii–xxiv).
7. *male pertinaci*: ill-defended.
8. *Vraye Foi*: 'true faith', the Boswell family motto.
9. *worthy Grange*: John Johnston, of Grange.
10. *Io . . . foglio*: 'I, the undersigned, was present and saw James Boswell, Esquire, subscribe this document.'

Chapter 5: 'The Mournful Case of Poor Misfortunate and Unhappy John Reid'

1. *nowt*: Scots and Northern English: beast of the cattle variety (cf. 'neat').
   bu: bull.
2. *Murdison*: a sheep-stealer recently hanged.
3. *Maggy Dixon*: hanged in Edinburgh, but was discovered to be alive in her coffin.
4. *Pickworth*: hanged in 1721.
5. *Ogilvy*: helped his mistress to poison her husband, his own brother, in 1765.
6. *Writer*: a minor lawyer, John Johnston, for example, was a 'writer'.
7. *caddie*: (Scots), young fellow, boy (cf. cadet), hence errand-boy, porter, messenger, odd-job man.
8. *Mr Innes*: author of a textbook on dissection.
9. The house was probably a tavern.
10. *lay teacher*: Nonconformist minister. J.B. follows Johnson's example in reserving the term 'clergyman' for a man ordained in the Church of England.

Interlude: 'David Hume, Just A-Dying'

1. *scratch wig*: one which covers only part of the head.
2. *wonderful*: i.e. astonishing, giving rise to wonderment.
3. J.B. never filled in this gap.

Chapter 6: 'I Was Elevated as if Brought into Another State of Being'

1. *[Thomas] Pennant*: (1726–98), traveller and naturalist; his books include *A Tour in Scotland*, 1771.
2. *enthusiasm*: i.e. religious enthusiasm, demonstrative piety.
3. *Marathon or Iona*: the reference is to a famous passage in Johnson's *Journey to the Western Islands* (section, 'Inch Kenneth').
4. *tacksman*: a laird's chief tenant or agent.
5. *Hermippus Redivivus*: a medical treatise recommending that ageing men should inhale the breath of young women.
6. *Adam Smith's book* was *The Wealth of Nations*.
7. *debitum justitiae, debitum caritatis*: obligation of justice, obligation of charity (legal terms).
8. *Tom Warton*: (1728–90) scholar, Professor of Poetry at Oxford.
9. *[Hannah] More*: (1745–1833) playwright, novelist, immensely successful writer of religious tracts.
10. *Hampton nonpareil*: a kind of apple.
11. *[Matthew] Boulton*: (1728–1809), pioneer with James Watt in the building of steam engines.
12. Boswell never supplied the missing word.
13. *his leg is cutting off*: we would say 'is being cut off', but that particular grammatical compound had not yet been developed in the English language.
14. The gaps were a result of amateur censorship (see Introduction).
15. *sail round the world*: this, beginning in July 1776, was Captain Cook's last voyage, in which he was killed on Kealakekua Beach.
16. *Omai*: a native of Tahiti, who came to England with Cook and became a familiar figure in the London of the 1770s. He returned home on Cook's last voyage and died soon afterwards.
17. *his own country*: his own province or district.
18. *Jackson*: Richard Jackson, politician and lawyer, celebrated for his fund of general knowledge.
19. *killing a man in London*: Giuseppe Baretti was physically attacked one evening in 1775 by a woman, evidently a streetwalker, beat her off, then found himself in conflict with three men who were lounging nearby. In the scuffle he took out a small pocket knife and struck at one of them, who later died from the wound. Baretti was detained and charged with murder, but was acquitted and set free at his trial, which Johnson and other friends attended as character witnesses.
20. *Ashburnham*: Ashbourne, Derbyshire, where Dr Taylor received Johnson and Boswell the previous month.
21. *[Sir Joseph] Banks*: (1743–1820), immensely distinguished scientist,

President of the Royal Society, accompanied Cook on his voyage round the world, 1768–71.

22. *Theandenaigen*: a Mohawk, also known as Joseph Brant; educated at a church school in Connecticut; prominent in Indian affairs, much employed as an emissary of the British Government to the Indian nations.

23. *[Samuel] Foote*: (1720–77), actor and playwright, successful in comedy parts, particularly famous for taking off other actors on the stage; man about town, irrepressible droll.

24. *Scrub*: a downtrodden servant in Farquhar's comedy *The Beaux' Stratagem*.

25. Mrs Thrale meant that Gibbon would have a deathbed religious conversion for fear of damnation. 'Infidel' means 'atheist'.

26. This refers to a time in 1736 when the newly married Johnson was, briefly, a schoolmaster, and two of his pupils were the Garrick brothers David and Peter.

27. *attendri*: 'quite melted in tenderness' (from the *Life*).

28. *caption*: arrest.

Chapter 7: 'A Man Troubled in Mind'

1. *his camp butcher*: the butcher Lonsdale took with him when he went to camp with the Northumberland Militia, of which he was Colonel.

2. *I had celebrated*: in his pamphlet, *Letter to the People of Scotland*, 1785.

3. *when here last with my wife*: when they passed through Penrith on their way to make a new home in London in 1786.

4. *paid £700*: that is, to buy him a commission; Satterthwaite was a captain.

5. *Green*: an entertainer who 'healed' patients on the stage.

6. *hobs or nobs*: convivial drinking of toasts, merry-making.

7. *airt*: direction.

8. i.e. the law courts in Westminster Hall.

9. *discover*: reveal.

10. *a certain way*: to a certain extent.

11. J.B. is a true eighteenth-century literate; when he needs cheering up, he reads a Latin writer of comedies – in the original, naturally.

12. *relaxed*: this word, as always in J.B., means jaded, listless.

13. *the Gang*: his London friends.

14. *hodgepodge*: a stew of mutton and vegetables.

15. *Dance*: a portrait-painter.

16. *Cumberland*: a successful playwright.

17. *the Somerset*: a coffee-house in the Strand.

18. *The Pawnbroker, The Improver*: perhaps J.B. told his son he intended to write works (plays?) so entitled; but no trace of them has survived.

Who's Who

BARETTI, GIUSEPPE, 1719–89, Italian man of letters who, despite spending some thirty years (in three separate sojourns) in England, also managed to maintain a continuous presence in Italian literature, notably in his sharply critical periodical, *La Frusta Letteraria* ('The Literary Scourge', 1763–5). In England he did important work in making Italian life and language better known, published a long string of books including an Italian dictionary (1760) and a very successful travel book, *Journey from London to Genoa* (1770). He was a member of Johnson's circle and lived for a while in the Thrale household, teaching their children. He and J.B. detested one another.

BOSWELL, ALEXANDER, 1707–82, J.B.'s father, Laird of Auchinleck from 1759 until his death in 1782. A judge, feudal laird and classical scholar; Whig by politics, Presbyterian Church. After the death of his wife Euphemia in 1766, he married his young cousin at the same time as James's wedding in 1769, leading to a dispute between father and son over the succession to Auchinleck which manifested itself as a dispute about female–male lines and priorities in the feudal system. A disciplinarian; stern but fair towards his children; disapproved of many of Boswell's activities, including his flirtation with Catholicism and his choice of a bride. In many respects his views were diametrically opposed to those of Samuel Johnson.

BURKE, EDMUND, 1729–97, statesman, orator, author on political subjects. Started the *Annual Register* (which still continues), 1759; MP 1765; first speech, 1766, on American question. Whig in that he was critical of Tory policy, but never in inner council of Whigs. Concerned over extortionate attitude of British officials in India, led attack on the Governor-General, Warren Hastings (1732–1818), resulting in Hastings's downfall though acquitted. Supported Wilberforce against slave trade. Was sympathetic towards American independence, but not towards French democracy; violent attack in *Reflections on the French Revolution*, 1790, and thereafter advocated war against France.

DEMPSTER, GEORGE, 1732–1818, a Scots lawyer turned English MP, and a good and continuing friend of Boswell's, though not as close to him as Temple or John Johnston.

ERSKINE, ANDREW, the Hon., d. 1793, in 1762 a lieutenant in the Army, and a close companion of Boswell's in the early London journals. Suffered from Boswell-like depression and, desperate about debts, later committed suicide.

GARRICK, DAVID, 1717–79, the most celebrated actor of his day, particularly famous in Shakespearean roles. Member of The Club; lifelong friend of Johnson, since as a native of Lichfield he had been one of the pupils at the 'academy' S.J. set up, and ran for a time till it folded in 1737, when the pair set off for London to seek their fortune. Responsible for many innovations in staging at Drury Lane Theatre, of which for many years he was co-manager. The first director since Jacobean times to put on Shakespeare's plays in their original texts, without modernization.

GOLDSMITH, OLIVER, 1730–74, poet, playwright, journalist, prolific miscellaneous writer. Some immensely successful works, notably the comedy *She Stoops to Conquer*, 1773, but often poor and in debt. Johnson once rescued him from the clutches of his creditors, who had him besieged in his lodgings, by taking the manuscript of *The Vicar of Wakefield* and selling it to a publisher; it appeared to acclaim in 1762. Member of The Club.

HUME, DAVID, 1711–76, historian, empirical philosopher, master of pellucid exposition (*Essays Moral and Political*, 1771; *Essays Concerning Human Understanding*, 1748; *Suicide and Immortality*, 1777). Affiliation with French thinkers; briefly *Chargé d'Affaires* at French Court,

1765; in Scotland, in constant disfavour through sceptical tinge of his opinions, held with unwavering firmness, e.g. no belief in personal immortality.

JOHNSON, SAMUEL, 1709–84, poet, scholar, biographer, writer on issues of ethics and conduct. Works include *The Rambler* (essays, 1750–2), *A Dictionary of the English Language* (1755), *Journey to the Western Islands of Scotland* (1775), *Lives of the English Poets* (1783); subject of Boswell's famous biography (1791).

JOHNSTON, JOHN, of Grange, d. 1786, a lifelong friend of Boswell. A former schoolfellow in Edinburgh, Johnston was to remain an undistinguished minor lawyer as well as Laird of Grange in Dumfriesshire.

KEITH, GEORGE, ninth EARL MARISCHAL, 1693?–1778, Scottish aristocrat and sworn Jacobite (later disillusioned). Employed by the King of Prussia in 1754 as Governor of the territory of Môtiers in the Val Travers near Neuchâtel in Switzerland, which at that time was under Prussian control. When J.-J. Rousseau, fearing persecution from the authorities, left France in 1762 and settled in Môtiers for three years, Lord Marischal gave him kindly protection.

LOWTHER, JAMES, first EARL OF LONSDALE, 1736–1802, a powerful and unscrupulous man, coal-owner and political fixer with immense influence in the north of England (the family seat and Whitehaven Castle were near Carlisle). Adopted Boswell in 1787 and involved him in plots to return tame MPs to Parliament. Accused of borough-mongering and corruption, he drove Boswell to distraction with his changeability and harsh treatment. See Introduction and Chapter 7 headlink.

MACDONALD, SIR ALEXANDER, 1745–95, Baronet of Sleat, the seat of the MacDonald clan on Skye, and brother to James, who was Boswell's brilliant young Oxford-educated friend in London in 1762 before his early death four years later. Sir Alexander quarrelled furiously with J.B. during the tour to the Hebrides, when J.B. accused him of penny-pinching, lack of hospitality and letting down the old ideas of how a Scots laird should behave. He repeated these attacks on MacDonald in his account of the tour (1785) and was challenged to a duel by MacDonald's son. The combat never took place, although the prospect was enough to upset J.B. seriously for a while.

MACPHERSON, JAMES, 1736–96, published highly coloured epics in incantatory prose dealing with the exploits of the Gaelic hero Finn MacCumhail (whom he called 'Fingal') and alleged them to be translations from the work of the legendary poet, Finn's son Oisin (whom he called 'Ossian'). They were loosely based on actual Highland legends, but, though immensely popular throughout Europe, were never accepted by informed people as authentic translations.

MALONE, EDMUND, 1741–1812, Dubliner; settled permanently in England and spent his life in literary scholarship. Member of Johnson's circle, the Literary Club. Published pioneering research on the chronology of Shakespeare's plays, 1788; edited Shakespeare, 1790. Gave Boswell crucial help and encouragement in writing *Life of Johnson*.

MONBODDO, JAMES BURNETT, LORD, 1714–99, Scottish judge (like Lord Auchinleck, his title was a legal honorific); published a three-part work (*On the Origin and Progress of Language*, 1773–6) that argued for an evolutionary view of human origins.

PAOLI, PASQUALE, 1725–1807, Corsican patriot; soldier, scholar, political philosopher; leader, mentor and inspirer of his people in their pilgrimage towards independence. When Corsica was conquered by the French in 1769 he escaped in an English ship, settled in England and lived there till 1789, a member of the circle of Johnson and his friends.

PITFOUR, JAMES FERGUSSON, LORD, Episcopalian and reputed Jacobite, one of the great lawyers at the Scots bar. He was long passed over because of his politics, but was finally raised to the bench in 1764.

PITT, WILLIAM ('the Younger'), 1759–1806, statesman; Prime Minister slightly acquainted with J.B., who described him in a letter to Temple as 'an insolent fellow'. J.B. approached him with hopes of an Anglo-Corsican alliance or entente, without any success.

PRINGLE, DR JOHN, 1707–1782, friend of Lord Auchinleck, and given to advising the young James Boswell and taking him under his wing. Pringle was the Queen's personal physician, and later, as Sir John, was President of the Royal Society.

REYNOLDS, SIR JOSHUA, 1723–92, portrait-painter, first President of the Royal Academy; one of Johnson's closest friends, to whom J.B. dedicated the *Life*. His masterly paintings are our chief source for the personal appearance of Johnson, Boswell, Henry Thrale, Baretti, Burney, and so on.

ROUSSEAU, JEAN-JACQUES, 1712–78, born in Geneva, son of a feckless father who neglected his education while reading to him many tales of the marvellous which developed his imagination. He ran away from home and, in the course of a wandering life, became a passionate self-taught musicologist (at one time he hoped to make a living from a new system of notation he had invented) and an even more passionate student of human nature. His ideas penetrated all Europe in such works as the novels *La Nouvelle Héloïse* and *Emile* and in his (ostensibly) entirely frank *Confessions*. The established political and social order in France was already under attack by men of letters and intellectuals generally, as typified by Montesquieu, Voltaire, Diderot, and in general the contributors to the *Encyclopédie* (1751–72), that grand attempt to systematize and rationalize all human knowledge; but whereas the Encyclopédistes were rationalistic, atheist and scientific, Rousseau admitted the part played by the heart as against the head, asserting the original innocence of mankind till corrupted by false institutions, believing in a personal God and the immortality of the soul. His affinities (for all his rebelliousness and the laxity, by orthodox standards, of his moral conduct) were with the religious mystics rather than with the hard-headed, evidence-weighing Encyclopédistes.

RUDD, MRS MARGARET CAROLINE, d. 1799. Boswell first met this lady in 1776, when she was one of the most talked-about people in London. Briefly, she had been charged with helping her associates, Robert and Daniel Perreau, in the forgery of large numbers of bonds or promissory notes so as to obtain money to cover Daniel's financial speculations. Large sums of money were involved, and when the first forgeries came to light, the two brothers tried to save themselves by blaming Mrs Rudd, who, they said, had duped them all along, telling them that the bonds were a gift from William Adair – in whose name the bonds were signed. The signatures were in fact forgeries by Mrs Rudd herself, but the Perreaus were as guilty as she: in retaliation she turned King's Evidence, offering herself as a prosecution witness and claiming that she had been forced into forging the notes by physical threats. Daniel and Robert were sentenced to death; but unfortunately for Mrs Rudd, her claim to immunity from prosecution was not upheld and twelve judges decided that she too must stand trial. After six months in jail, she appeared at the Old Bailey at the end of 1775, and was found not guilty: public sympathy was with her, and she ably conducted her own defence, dressed in mourning and cleverly emphasizing her fragility and powerlessness. Her acquittal was popular in the country, and it also doomed the Perreaus, whose guilt was re-emphasized by her own innocence in the eyes of the law: they were hanged in January 1776. Boswell met her a few months afterwards. (In fact, they later had a quite serious affair.) Her earlier life – she was born in 1745 – has also a certain aura of romance and adventure about it: she had had a successful career as a blackmailer, using false names and extracting money from wealthy men, before becoming the mother of three children to Daniel Perreau, a speculator of rich tastes but no solid finances, in 1770.

SHERIDAN, THOMAS, 1719–88, 'old Mr Sheridan', father of Richard Brinsley Sheridan the playwright; actor and writer; taught elocution in Edinburgh and London.

TEMPLE, WILLIAM JOHNSON, 1739–96, another schoolfellow of Boswell's and his most faithful friend and confidant. Abandoned a legal career to become a clergyman, with a living in Devon, subsequently Cornwall. Disapproved of much of Boswell's behaviour, especially in the last years in London. (See p. xxi–xxii for more on Temple.)

THRALE, HENRY, 1728–81, brewer (chief rival to Whitbread), MP for Southwark. Owner of a large, comfortable house at Streatham (then in the country), where his wife Hester (1741–1821) dispensed hospitality and agreeable conversation to a brilliant circle centred on Johnson, who had his own room in the house for twenty years.

VOLTAIRE, FRANÇOIS-MARIE AROUET, 1694–1778, who wrote under the name Voltaire (a rough anagram of Arouet; deeply admired French epic poet and tragic dramatist, exquisite writer of witty light verse, philosopher, social critic, ironist, ceaseless fighter for liberty against authoritarian government, whose weight he felt early, writing his first successful tragedy *Oedipe* during an eleven-month imprisonment in the Bastille for writing a political lampoon. Lived for a time in England, whose tradition of civil liberty he admired; later in Prussia, at the court of Frederick II; finally, wary of the French authorities, he settled in Switzerland, ultimately reaching the compromise of a splendid mansion (with sixty servants and horses – his immense literary output having made him rich) at Ferney, on French soil but close to the Swiss border, where Boswell visited him.

WILKES, JOHN, 1727–97, rebellious and highly conspicuous politician, thorn in the side of the government, idol of the London populace; 1762, joined with the satirical poet Charles Churchill in a periodical the *North Briton*; arrested and imprisoned for libelling King George III in the 45th number (see p. 85), but discharged on claiming parliamentary privilege (he sat for Aylesbury); J.B. met him during one of several sojourns on the continent when absence was prudent. Three times elected MP for Middlesex, three times rejected because Parliament had expelled him for libel; finally took his seat unopposed. Lord Mayor of London 1774.

DE ZUYLEN, BELLE ('Zélide'), 1740–1805, Dutchwoman of wit and charm, briefly pursued by Boswell in Holland; after rejecting him and other suitors, married a worthy but dull Swiss, M. de Charrière, and wrote a series of novels in French. Her life was enlivened by blameless but intense friendships with men of letters, notably Benjamin Constant and Albert von Chamisso.

Index

Italicised entries are found in the Who's Who, pages and roman numerals in the introduction. The initials JB and SJ refer to James Boswell and Samuel Johnson.